Steve Ryfle *and* **Ed Godziszewski**

Forewords by John Carpenter *and* Megumi Odaka

Afterword by Shogo Tomiyama

GODZILLA THE FIRST 70 YEARS

THE OFFICIAL ILLUSTRATED HISTORY OF THE JAPANESE PRODUCTIONS

ABRAMS, NEW YORK

CONTENTS

FOREWORD

BY JOHN CARPENTER

I consider myself to be one of the original, hardcore fans of Gojira, known in the West as Godzilla. I saw *Godzilla, King of the Monsters!,* the Americanized version of the original film, sometime in 1956. Raymond Burr's character, reporter Steve Martin, narrated the movie and described Godzilla's every action as the monster turned Tokyo into a city of rubble and fire, but those of us in the audience really didn't need his help. Every moment in this dark, black-and-white Japanese masterpiece was a mind-blowing ride for a seven-year-old monster-crazy kid growing up in Bowling Green, Kentucky.

At the same time, the film also filled me with a sense of dread. There was something about the overall tone—an underlying sadness, a sense of grief and horror. Back in those days, everybody was thinking about atomic war. We knew it would be the end of the world. Mainstream Hollywood movies didn't deal with it—the subject was too scary. They thought audiences would reject it. Why talk about the end of the world? But it was reality. And so, it was up to science-fiction and monster movies to help us face that fear. *Them!* (1954) was one of the first of this kind, with the atomic tests in New Mexico turning ants into giant man-eating monsters. But that first Godzilla film was something different. It came from Japan, the only nation to suffer atomic bombs dropped on two of its cities, and the movie gave expression to these emotions so powerfully that audiences in America and around the world could understand. This sense of dread and horror, which was there from the beginning, is one of the reasons Godzilla has had such longevity, I believe.

As a young boy in the theater on that day, I was cowering. Godzilla was formidable and scary. But I was also fascinated by the special effects, which were so interesting and creative. Eiji Tsuburaya practically invented the giant monster genre; he had to create new methods in order to make the movie. Originally, most big monsters were created with stop-motion animation, or by putting a fin on the back of real lizards.

Tsuburaya created a Godzilla suit and a miniature model city. It was groundbreaking at the time; he used a lot of techniques people hadn't thought of. With Tsuburaya creating the special effects and Ishiro Honda directing, the original films from Toho came to our local theaters in the fifties and sixties—not just *Godzilla*, but also *Rodan, The Mysterians, Mothra, King Kong vs. Godzilla, Godzilla vs. the Thing*, and more. They were different from the American science-fiction films of the time, and they let our imaginations run wild in a world of giant, incredible creatures. Movie critics never gave these movies any respect. They didn't get it, but those of us sitting in the balcony did.

Anywhere I am, Godzilla is always with me because I can spontaneously start humming Akira Ifukube's incredible music to myself. Ifukube's Godzilla theme is one of the great all-time pieces of film music, incredibly complex yet based on deceptively simple phrases that become embedded in your consciousness. It's hard to imagine Godzilla without Ifukube's music, which gives the monster such incredible power and scariness.

Godzilla is everything. He's an all-purpose monster. He takes care of business. He's fought everybody from King Kong to King Ghidorah. Personally, I prefer Godzilla to be scary and up to no good, but he's evolved over time. He became silly in the 1970s, but that was OK, it suited the era. Now Godzilla is a Hollywood star, and the monsters are created with computers. There's really good work being done, but personally, I am nostalgic for the look and feel of the original films, the ones I grew up with and raised my son on.

Godzilla is the longest-running movie franchise in the world. Today, Godzilla is respected the world around, but the truth is that these movies were appreciated in silence for many years. It wasn't cool to be a fan of Godzilla. Well, I was not cool—but that was fine with me.

You now hold in your hands a comprehensive history of Japan's King of the Monsters, authoritatively written by two genre historians. This is, of course, a well-deserved tribute to a cinematic monster of unparalleled influence.

In 2024, *Godzilla Minus One* received an Academy Award for Best Visual Effects. Finally, in my lifetime, the big guy is getting the respect and admiration and ovations he is due. I'm a happy man.

RIGHT: A young couple aboard a party boat is terrified when the monster surfaces in Tokyo Bay in *Godzilla*.

FOREWORD

BY MEGUMI ODAKA

—

I never planned on becoming an actor. I grew up near the sea in Shonan, Kamakura, Japan. My uncle Yuji Odaka was a film actor who appeared in movies with famous Japanese actors such as Yujiro Ishihara. My aunt Mayumi Shimizu was also a well-known actress. She appeared on the popular television series *Kita no Kuni Kara* (*From the North Country*, 1981–82). It was my aunt who learned about the second Toho Cinderella Audition in 1987 and recommended I try it. I was fourteen years old and in the second year of middle school when I won the Grand Prix in that contest and subsequently joined Toho.

I had no previous acting experience. When I was cast in my first film, *Princess from the Moon* (1987), I was given the role of a poor blind girl named Akeno. My aunt and uncle gave me acting lessons. I was still attending school, but every Sunday I would visit their house, and they taught me about film, about how to work with director Kon Ichikawa, and how to act with Toshiro Mifune.

There was no audition for *Godzilla vs. Biollante*. I was simply informed by someone at Toho that I had gotten the role, and I was to play a psychic named Miki Saegusa. I was now in my second year of high school, but I had never seen a Godzilla movie; most of the early films were made before I was born. I thought I should learn more about Godzilla, so I saw the one featuring Yasuko Sawaguchi-san [*The Return of Godzilla*]. When I learned that *Godzilla vs. Biollante* would be released during the New Year holiday season, I felt excitement and pressure. It was a big deal.

When I first met director Kazuki Omori, he handed me a VHS tape of *Firestarter* (1984). He said, "Watch this movie. This is what a psychic girl is like." I imagined such a child would have a sense of calm concentration, and that I should portray my character that way. Filming at Toho's Big Pool when Biollante's tentacle vine came out of Lake Ashi, the Biollante prop came crashing down in front of us on the pier. Of the four cast members, I was the only one who jumped in surprise. The staff members laughed, saying, "You're playing a fearless character but you're the most scared." How could everyone seem just fine while I was terrified? There was a gap between my character and my real self. For the scene at the Kansai International Airport heliport in which Miki Saegusa tries to read Godzilla's mind, director Omori told me not to move too much. He emphasized having a focused and concentrated mindset, not being distracted, and acting with conviction. I worried that my awkwardness showed through. I simply focused on trying to get my role right. From Sawaguchi-san, I learned to just concentrate on the task given to you. Watching my senior actors do that had a strong influence on me. Being a naturally nervous person, playing a calm character was a challenge.

Miki was a very Asian kind of psychic. I watched a lot of movies to understand different interpretations of psychic people. Miki's version of a psychic was akin to a priestess who can communicate with God, or in this case, Godzilla. Throughout the six Godzilla movies that I appeared in, I always struggled to portray this character. I received a lot of advice, so Miki was a character created by many people, not just me.

Not long after *Godzilla vs. Biollante* was released, I learned I would appear in the next Godzilla film as well. I was surprised and grateful. I used to say I liked *Godzilla vs. King Ghidorah* best because of its entertainment value, but now I would say *Godzilla vs. Mothra*. My preference has changed as I've gotten older and had more experiences. I always felt that Mothra itself was very feminine. *Godzilla vs. Mothra* had a cool Indiana Jones–like vibe, and I was really moved by the Cosmos' singing. It made me feel a connection to the universe and to the stars.

While filming *Godzilla vs. Mechagodzilla II*, I became very close to actress Ryoko Sano, who played the lead female role. I could sense her deep affection and compassion for Baby Godzilla. She had a strong maternal instinct; I had never met anyone like her before. When I saw her embracing Baby, while it's not a living creature, it really touched my heart. There was a sense of affection and emotional connection. In a sense, it always felt like Godzilla was supported by something very maternal, like Mother Earth, in a profound way. Sometimes, when I considered the themes underlying Godzilla movies, especially in *Godzilla vs. Mothra*, I felt that message strongly. The role of women isn't just about action or fighting— though those things are cool and I like them—there's a fundamental, maternal feeling that flows through these movies, which I think is very Japanese.

When director Okawara shouted, "Ready! Start! Go!" it was so loud that it made the air vibrate. The staff would immediately focus and work intensely; it was like he was conducting an orchestra. Each Godzilla film felt different, much like different pieces of classical music. Okawara's style was very masculine, but his work also reminded me that women characters were equally important.

For *Godzilla vs. SpaceGodzilla*, I worked with director Kensho Yamashita. The location was Okinawa and Amami Oshima. We had a really sad theme song at the end of that movie. During filming, my mood was sad despite the beautiful locations. Miki was worried that humanity's only way of dealing with Godzilla was to fight. That was the source of my feelings; I was really into my character. [Costar] Jun Hashizume had been at the studio since when I was fourteen years old; he was like a big brother to me, so I was comfortable showing emotion in that situation. But the story of the film was about something ephemeral, with a melancholy feeling in the air. Still, in our cast, we had Yosuke Saito, who always managed to make us laugh, and Akira Emoto-san was also there, so there was definitely time for us to unwind.

In *Godzilla vs. Destoroyah*, Miki becomes very close to Godzilla Junior and witnesses its death in an emotional scene. I was still young, and I hadn't yet experienced the death of anyone close, so I tried to imagine how I would feel if my pet had died. Rewatching that scene later on, I felt really sad. As I acted in special effects–driven films, I began to feel emotions toward the characters. In every single movie, I would ask the director for help. My feelings and my acting were evolving at that time, but I couldn't judge my own performances, so I had to rely on the audience's reaction. The mood that was created on set or on location by the entire crew also helped me. Over the course of six Godzilla films, building a relationship with Godzilla and Godzilla Junior also motivated me and helped me.

Recently we lost both Kenpachiro Satsuma, who played Godzilla in all of the Heisei series films, and director Omori. Just remembering Satsuma-san's farewell party makes me emotional. I loved his portrayal of Godzilla. It felt like Godzilla was alive; the special effects staff were all working to bring Godzilla to life. When Godzilla would return to the sea, with the filming crew surrounding him, it wasn't exactly sad, but I felt wistful. Everyone on set was just trying to make sure Godzilla survived, Mr. Satsuma most of all. During breaks, he would talk to me, and we'd have tea together. He was very kind. We were comrades working on the film. He felt like a Japanese father figure to me, in a way. I also really miss speaking with Omori.

I hope that when people watch Godzilla, not just the Heisei films but the entire series, they can appreciate the feelings and intentions that were in our hearts. Especially after personal experiences that have made me more reflective, it would mean a lot to me if people would look at Godzilla films as a way to see and appreciate different eras and milestones in their own lives. Godzilla is something that can't be completely defined in words—it means something different to each one of us. For that reason, being part of six Godzilla films was truly an honor.

INTRODUCTION

On March 10, 2024, at the 96th Academy Awards, *Godzilla Minus One* received the Oscar for Best Visual Effects. What might have seemed impossible for the entirety of Godzilla's history was now reality. Long ignored or scorned by critics and the Hollywood establishment, Japan's King of the Monsters was now recognized and embraced by its peers in the film industry with the highest of all honors in a ceremony broadcast live around the globe.

Perhaps this reversal of fortune should come as no surprise. Godzilla may have toiled away on the fringes of cinema for decades, but—paradoxically, perhaps—no other fictional entertainment icon has occupied the world's attention in such a far-reaching and enduring way. Whether feared as a harbinger of doom or cheered as a hero, Godzilla has survived, thrived, and destroyed on the international stage for seventy years and counting, starring in the longest-running film franchise in history while earning a prominent and permanent place in popular culture worldwide.

The legend is well known. Godzilla emerged from the ashes of World War II to terrorize Japan and the world in a time of postwar anxiety and peril. With booming footfalls and an unmistakable, deafening roar, Toho, arguably the most famous Japanese motion picture company, unleashed a simple-yet-powerful metaphor for the dangers of the atomic age. Military power was no match for the seemingly unstoppable creature, a tragic figure born of man's misuse of scientific knowledge and the power it bestows. *Godzilla* issued a plea to end the nuclear arms race before it's too late; the monster itself would come to symbolize both a defining moment and place in history—August 6, 1945, at Hiroshima—and the perpetual precipice upon which humanity had placed itself.

Since then, Godzilla has outlasted at least thirty Japanese prime ministers and a dozen American presidents; innumerable Hollywood stars have come and gone. It has survived despite that, from the beginning, critical response to the original *Godzilla* and its sequels was largely negative both in Japan, where kaiju ("strange beast" or "monster") films were routinely dismissed as children's entertainment, and in the West, where they were often haphazardly dubbed into foreign languages and subjected to reediting, greatly diminishing the filmmakers' achievements and making a laughingstock of the genre.

There have been peaks and valleys, to be sure, yet Godzilla's unparalleled longevity in the fickle world of entertainment is a singularly remarkable feat. The monster has prevailed by remaining familiar and true to its origins even as it has evolved with the changing times, growing from a uniquely Japanese figure with an overseas cult following into a gargantuan global franchise. Godzilla's career is rooted in

LEFT: The military uses napalm to coax Godzilla toward the artificial lightning towers in *Mothra vs. Godzilla.* ■ **OPPOSITE:** Godzilla stalks the countryside near Mount Fuji in *King Kong vs. Godzilla.*

"THE FIRST *GODZILLA*, WHICH I SAW AS A KID, HAD SUCH DRAMA IN IT, AND IT HAD SUCH A SENSE OF TRAGEDY. AND IN THE MIDDLE OF ALL OF THIS, THERE WAS A MONSTER THAT I FELL IN LOVE WITH. I LOVE THAT CREATURE. I LOVE GODZILLA."

—Guillermo del Toro, filmmaker

TOP LEFT: The Millennium series: *Godzilla: Tokyo SOS.* ■ TOP RIGHT: The Heisei era: *Godzilla vs. Destoroyah.*

the early films produced from 1954 to 1975 and associated with the Showa era (1926–89). This fifteen-film cycle began during the golden age of postwar Japanese cinema, a time when masters such as Akira Kurosawa, Yasujiro Ozu, and Kenji Mizoguchi directed some of their finest works and, simultaneously, Japan's commercial cinema—of which the Godzilla series and other *tokusatsu* (special effects) films were a vital part—became a dominant form of popular entertainment. The Showa films are characterized by the work of directors that include Ishiro Honda and Jun Fukuda and the special effects artistry of Eiji Tsuburaya; the stories are bound by a loose-fitting continuity that sometimes deviates into the future (e.g., *Invasion of Astro-Monster, Destroy All Monsters*) or the imagination (*All Monsters Attack*).

Following a nine-year hiatus, Toho hit the reset button with *The Return of Godzilla*, a serious-minded sequel to the original film made thirty years earlier and disregarding everything in between. Six more movies followed, interconnected through the presence of Miki Saegusa, a young woman with a psychic connection to the monster. This cycle, commonly associated with the Heisei era (1989–2019), pitted a territorial, aggressive Godzilla against updated versions of familiar foes such as Rodan, Mothra, and Mechagodzilla, until the radiation that once spawned Godzilla triggered a climactic, fatal meltdown.

A third cycle, the Millennium series, comprised six films from 1999 to 2004 and would offer a final bow for the traditional special effects pioneered by Tsuburaya a half-century earlier. In Hollywood, meanwhile, Godzilla's digital transformation has vastly expanded the monster's worldwide reach and box-office fortunes, and Toho's internationally successful entries *Shin Godzilla* and *Godzilla Minus One* have put forward important new interpretations of the monster from some of Japan's most vital present-day filmmakers.

Godzilla has consistently held up a mirror to the changing world, offering a cautionary tale about not only nuclear war, but also capitalist greed, environmental desecration, exploitation of indigenous peoples, the Cold War, nationalism, US–Japan relations, and more. And through it all, Godzilla has always entertained, connecting with people across generations, nationalities, and cultures. From Japan to Joplin, Missouri, audiences thrill to the creature's titanic battles with foes ranging from King Ghidorah to Mechagodzilla. Today those battles are brought to life on-screen with digital photorealism, but they are built upon a long legacy of Japanese imagination and craftsmanship, a breathtaking world of giant monsters originally created with the classic combination of men in suits and miniature models.

Godzilla: The First 70 Years is a narrative and visual history focusing specifically on the feature films and anime produced in Japan, from the original *Godzilla* in 1954 to the Oscars triumph of *Godzilla Minus One* in 2024, chronicling the triumphs, challenges, and meaning of seven decades of city-trashing, kaiju-smashing mayhem from Toho Studios. It is a tribute to Godzilla's creators and costars—the filmmakers, special effects wizards, cast members, and stunt actors inside the monster suits—and an appreciation of the artistry involved in bringing Godzilla to cinematic life, then and now.

Notes on the text: For familiarity and ease of reading, Japanese names are presented in the Western manner, with the subject's given name followed by their surname (e.g., "Eiji Tsuburaya" rather than "Tsuburaya Eiji"). Macrons (diacritical marks) are not used in the text. Japanese and foreign words are presented in italics unless they are widely accepted in English and/or in Western culture, such as ramen, sushi, manga, anime, and kaiju.

Summaries and analyses of films produced by the Toho Motion Picture Company are based on their original, Japanese-language release versions except where noted. Films are referenced by their official English-language title at the time of this book's publication; this may be different from the title or titles under which any given film was previously released.

Godzilla is widely assumed to be male. However, third-person gendered pronouns are uncommon in the Japanese language, therefore Godzilla is referred to either by name or the equivalent of "it" in Japan; the authors adhere to this practice when discussing the Godzilla films produced and/or distributed by Toho.

ONE

BEAST OF BURDEN: 1954 TO 1975

(*GOJIRA*)
RELEASED: NOVEMBER 3, 1954 (JAPAN)

GODZILLA

This is a special news bulletin. Godzilla continues to advance toward the Tokyo-Yokohama coast. The security barrier is charged with high-voltage electricity. Please exercise extreme caution."

Searchlights scan the bay for any sign of the threat. Tanks roll through evacuated streets. A battery of field cannons is positioned along the shoreline. Giant electrical towers have been erected along miles of waterfront between Tokyo and Yokohama to keep the invader out, not unlike the barbed wire obstacles once placed on island beaches against a land incursion. Godzilla slowly emerges from the sea and approaches the barricade with caution. A switch is thrown and the towers are charged with fifty thousand volts, to no avail. Godzilla claws at the electrical cables, unharmed. The cannons roar and soldiers fire machine guns from fortified positions, all without effect. Entangled in the power lines, Godzilla summons the full force of its power, exhaling heat rays that instantly melt the towers to white-hot metal. The monster advances into the city, igniting entire blocks into a fast-spreading inferno. Fire engines crash in hurried attempts to respond. People are incinerated in the streets or trampled underfoot; buildings are knocked over and crushed like toys. A mother and two children, resigned to the inevitable, await their fate as Godzilla approaches. Tanks hurl artillery shells at the giant, and retaliation is swift and deadly. Jet fighters open fire, coaxing the monster back into the sea. Civilians cheer the pilots on—spirits are lifted, but it is a hollow victory. Tokyo is in ruins, and Godzilla still lives . . .

"WHAT SURPRISED ME THE MOST WHEN I SAW *GODZILLA* AGAIN AFTER SEVERAL YEARS WAS THAT THIS WAS MORE OF A WAR MOVIE THAN A MONSTER MOVIE. THE 'WAR' IN IT WAS NOT THE FUTURE ANTIHUMAN WAR TYPICAL OF SCIENCE-FICTION MOVIES, BUT A HUMAN WAR THAT REMINDS US OF THE RECENT PAST. IT'S NOT WAR AS A FANTASY, IT'S WAR AS A MEMORY OF REALITY."

—Saburo Kawamoto, film critic

FATEFUL ORIGINS

"Memories of war," wrote historian Yoshikuni Igarashi, "were still ubiquitous in postwar [Japanese] society. However, increasingly removed from the scene of destruction, the memories were transformed into amorphous destructive forces. Monstrous forms that defy human comprehension were burdened with the mission to represent memories of war loss."

From the beginning, the legacy of war has been Godzilla's burden. Forged in the flames of Hiroshima and Nagasaki, and cursed with the wrath of a vengeful spirit, Godzilla appeared in 1954 in an origin story that was equal parts disaster drama, science fiction, and myth. In a deep crevice beneath the Pacific Ocean, a prehistoric animal from a time when Earth was ruled by giants survives undetected until a hydrogen bomb test disturbs its eons-long sleep and dislodges the beast from its underwater habitat. Scarred and enraged by the devastating blast, the monster instinctively lashes out at humankind with a fury equivalent to the bomb that baptized it, unleashing destruction and death surpassing even that which Japan had experienced roughly a decade earlier. As if on war footing, the nation steels itself: evacuations are enforced, a massive security perimeter is quickly constructed, and military forces assemble, yet the creature is invulnerable. Images of Godzilla's destruction recall the bombings of Hiroshima and Nagasaki, or the Doolittle Raid; the magnitude of damage and death is indeed beyond comprehension. Godzilla's motivation is at once unfathomable and self-evident. No explanation is asked or offered for its rage.

As with much of postwar Japanese cinema and art, the endless shadow of World War II memories would be cast—sometimes invisibly, often clearly—over the first Godzilla movie and every sequel thereafter, for although the monster was created to entertain, its arrival was foreshadowed by history-changing events. At the time of Godzilla's birth, Japan was just nine years removed from the twin atomic bombings that killed nearly three hundred thousand in August 1945; even less time had passed since the war's end, and the nation endured sweeping, disruptive changes under the US-led Allied occupation. Between 1945 to 1952, the military was disbanded, a vast Asia-Pacific empire was dissolved, the government was transformed from a monarchy into a parliamentary democracy, and the education and economic systems were remade. Poverty, food shortages, job scarcity, civil unrest, and general uncertainty characterized life during this period of transition. The 1950s brought new peace and prosperity as factories supplied the US with provisions for the Korean War; cities once reduced to rubble arose anew. The Mutual Security Treaty enabled Japan, with its new pacifist constitution, to focus on economic growth. But this revival began against the bleak international backdrop of the Cold War and an escalating arms race. Even as it forged a peaceful path for itself, Japan was trapped between America and the Soviet Union and their doomsday weapons tests in the South Pacific and Central Asia.

Godzilla's appearance was presaged by a nightmarish event that crystallized Japan's fears of another Hiroshima. On March 1, 1954, the US detonated the 15-megaton Castle Bravo hydrogen bomb at Bikini Atoll in the Marshall Islands, the most powerful thermonuclear weapon ever tested by the Pentagon. The blast showered a small Japanese commercial fishing vessel, the *Lucky Dragon No. 5*, with radioactive fallout, contaminating the tuna catch, sickening the crew, and causing the eventual death of one crew member from acute radiation poisoning. The fateful story of the little boat shocked the Japanese public and exploded into an international crisis, straining Japan-US relations. Citizens boycotted tuna and organized a widespread antinuclear and pacifist movement; by August 1955, over thirty million people would sign petitions demanding nuclear testing be banned.

As these dramatic events unfolded in the spring of 1954, a producer with Toho Studios was confronting a crisis of his own. Tomoyuki Tanaka had overseen early works by Akira Kurosawa and other major directors, but his latest project, *In the Shadow of Honor*, an adventure drama to be shot on location in Indonesia, was in disarray. The story concerned an Imperial Army soldier joining the Indonesian postwar struggle for independence. This was to be a major production, starring Ryo Ikebe as the soldier and

Yoshiko "Shirley" Yamaguchi as his half-Indonesian love interest. They were two of Japan's most popular actors; it would be Toho's first-ever color feature, and the international story was intended to open markets for Japanese films in Southeast Asia. However, in late March, just before shooting was to begin, the Indonesian side suddenly canceled the project (reportedly due to an ongoing disagreement between the countries over WWII colonial war reparations, which would not be resolved until 1958), and Tanaka now felt tremendous pressure to create a replacement of equal commercial prospects lest he lose face with his boss, Iwao Mori, Toho's powerful chief of production.

"I was up against a deadline when I first thought of *Godzilla*, and I made it all up at the last minute," Tanaka later recalled. Flying back home from Jakarta, "I was sweating the whole way. I wanted to do [a] story where the ocean played an important role in the film. Around that time, there was a major uproar over nuclear testing. So I thought, *What if there was this big monster near Bikini which was awakened by the shock of hydrogen bomb testing? And what if that monster invades Japan?"* Tanaka tapped into these real-life postwar anxieties with a story about a rampaging dinosaur revived by an atomic blast, loosely inspired by Eugène Lourié's *The Beast from 20,000 Fathoms*, which Warner Bros. had released to great success in the US just a few months earlier. *The Beast* had followed in the wake of RKO's 1952 reissue of *King Kong*; both releases had cost their respective companies very little and earned a relative fortune. Thus, with monsters making big profits and nuclear fears making headlines, Tanaka's proposal—under the working title *The Giant Monster from 20,000 Miles Beneath the Sea*—was savvy and relevant. Its timing was also advantageous. In 1951, Toho founder and president Ichizo Kobayashi had launched a three-year plan to reestablish the company as one of Japan's leading studios. The occupation years had seen a contraction in the film industry and a slowdown in production overall; Toho in particular was nearly shuttered in the late 1940s by massive labor strikes. Now, however, domestic movies were resurgent, and audiences were returning. Kobayashi's plan would culminate in 1954 with three of Japan's most ambitious and expensive productions to date: Akira Kurosawa's *Seven Samurai*, Hiroshi Inagaki's *Musashi Miyamoto*, and *Godzilla*.

OF DREAMS AND NIGHTMARES

In a sense, the story behind *Godzilla* began in 1937, when Kobayashi—railroad executive, real estate tycoon, founder of the legendary Takarazuka Grand Theater's female dance revue, and movie mogul—merged his Photo Chemical Laboratories (PCL) studio with two other companies to form Toho. One of those companies, J.O. Studio, employed Eiji Tsuburaya, who was among Japan's most inventive cinematographers and its leading practitioner of special effects. Tsuburaya was a proven innovator with a lifelong love of aviation and model airplanes. He had joined the fledgling movie industry in 1919, at just eighteen, and developed into one of the country's top camera operators within a decade. Tsuburaya experimented with new methods such as slow motion, double-exposure, screen process, optical printing, and screen projection, and devised his own shooting crane. In the late 1930s, Tsuburaya established Toho's special effects division, and his work flourished in a series of government-backed war dramas, for which he simulated large-scale military conflicts using models, pyrotechnics, and detailed miniature sets; his propensity for visual spectacle helped make Toho's *The War at Sea from Hawaii to Malaya* (1942) the most profitable Japanese feature to date and winner of *Kinema Junpo*'s Best Picture award. Tsuburaya's importance to "national policy" productions was such that he was put in charge of a factory that created miniatures for educational films made for the Imperial Navy's Special Attack Units to train aviators on weapons systems. Tsuburaya achieved high status at the studio as his works made Toho the unchallenged leader in effects pictures. However, like others who worked on wartime pictures, he was expelled from the movie industry during the occupation years.

"INSPIRED BY THE HUGE SUCCESS OF *KING KONG,* I THOUGHT, SOMEDAY I'LL MAKE A FILM THAT THRILLS THE AUDIENCE LIKE THAT. TWENTY YEARS LATER, I FINALLY GOT MY CHANCE WITH GODZILLA. YET THE CHALLENGE WAS DAUNTING. SINCE IT WAS THE FIRST (GIANT MONSTER) FILM IN JAPANESE CINEMA HISTORY, BOTH THE MOVIE STUDIO AND WE, THE CREATORS, WERE TENSE. WE HAD NEVER DONE THIS BEFORE, SO THERE WERE MANY MOMENTS OF DOUBT, FAILURE, AND ACCIDENTS."

—Eiji Tsuburaya, special effects director

In the late forties and early fifties, Hollywood films such as *Mighty Joe Young*, *Destination Moon*, and *When Worlds Collide* won Academy Awards for special effects, and studio chief Mori was now determined to reclaim Toho's position as Japan's leader in the field. When Tanaka approached his superior with his monster-on-the-loose proposal, Mori was intrigued by its possibilities; he sent the anxious producer to confer with Tsuburaya, who had since resumed working for Toho (as a contractor rather than an employee—a status that would later enable him to form his own production company) after the occupation and was slowly laying the groundwork for establishment of a new special effects department. A monster movie was an opportunity to deploy Tsuburaya's talents in potentially new and bigger ways, but no film of this kind, on such a scale, had ever been attempted in Japan. Could Tsuburaya pull it off?

Tsuburaya was also intrigued. In 1933, at age thirty-two, he had seen *King Kong* for the first time. It changed his life. "That's when I decided to dedicate my career to special effects," Tsuburaya later recalled. "I obtained a print of the film for research and analyzed *Kong*'s effects frame by frame." Tsuburaya had dreamed of making his own monster movie ever since; he even unsuccessfully pitched a story about a gigantic octopus attacking Japan. Now, in his early fifties, Tsuburaya was offered a chance to fulfill that dream. He had no clue how he might achieve this unprecedented task, but he readily accepted the challenge. Based on Tsuburaya's word, Mori greenlit the production under a cryptic working title: *G Project*.

G Project was certainly an outlier. Few prior Japanese films might be considered science fiction, much less a monster movie. It was a risky gamble, and directors were not lining up for the job. Tanaka intended to tap Senkichi Taniguchi, the top studio hand attached to the aborted *In the Shadow of Honor*, but Taniguchi demurred. Instead, the project was put in the hands of Ishiro Honda, a rising director of mostly downbeat postwar dramas. Honda had recently collaborated with Tsuburaya on a major hit, the effects-heavy war docudrama *Eagle of the Pacific* (1953), about the triumph and tragedy of Admiral Isoroku Yamamoto. Honda had entered Japan's young film industry in the early 1930s as an assistant director and ascended through the studio system, learning to make films alongside fellow trainee and lifelong friend Akira Kurosawa. Honda understood, on a personal level, the producer's intention to tie the monster to the nuclear threat. Like many of his generation, he had survived the war only to be forever traumatized by it. In 1936, Honda was drafted into the Imperial Army and made to put his film career on hold, serving three tours of duty as a foot soldier in China. Near the war's end, Honda was held as a prisoner of war; during his repatriation, he had observed the scorched ruins of Hiroshima, an experience that would haunt him. The son of a Buddhist priest, Honda was a quiet, nominally cheerful man and a skilled craftsman with a humanist streak. His earliest films were documentaries, a background that would contribute greatly to *Godzilla*'s realistic feel. For the director, Godzilla was not an allegorical representation of the bomb but a physical manifestation of it. "Most of the visual images I got were from my war experience," he commented. "After the war, all of Japan, [including] Tokyo, was left in ashes. . . . If Godzilla had been a dinosaur or [an] animal, it would have been killed by just one cannonball. But if it were equal to an atomic bomb, we wouldn't know what to do. So I took the characteristics of an atomic bomb and applied them to Godzilla."

As in Hollywood, Japanese studios often employed writers of literature and commercial fiction to pen scenarios. To expand his rough idea into a treatment, Tanaka looked to Shigeru Kayama, a popular author of speculative adventure tales often involving strange creatures. "If someone chooses me, that means it's not an ordinary story that they are looking for," Kayama would recall. "But when I first heard the concept, that a monster comes back to life because of the hydrogen bomb and goes on a rampage, I felt

FAR LEFT: Attracted by the flashbulbs of the photographers, Godzilla attacks the TV tower. In this scene, Godzilla is performed by a hand puppet that is also used in other close-ups throughout the film. ■ **LEFT:** In between takes, special effects director Eiji Tsuburaya (*far left*) gives instructions to Godzilla actor Haruo Nakajima (*inside the suit*) while crew members touch up the costume.

a little uneasy." The writer worried the subject matter was too sensitive. "One wrong move and it could easily turn into a joke." But he welcomed the opportunity to protest nuclear weapons and the fear they cast over the world.

Kayama created the plot, characters, themes, and structure that would lay the foundation of the film and, by extension, the Godzilla franchise. His original treatment apparently borrowed ideas from one of his previous short stories, "Jira Monster," published in 1952, about a giant reptile that walks on its hind legs, repels bullets, and terrorizes a primitive people; there were also similarities to *The Beast from 20,000 Fathoms*, *King Kong*, and the 1925 silent-film version of *The Lost World*. Kayama's creature behaved like a hungry wild animal, attacking a ship transporting safari animals from Africa; this and other details would evolve as the story was expanded into a screenplay, cowritten by director Honda and screenwriter Takeo Murata. Honda and Murata enclosed the sailor Ogata (played by Akira Takarada), scientist Serizawa (Akihiko Hirata), and ingenue Emiko (Momoko Kochi) in a love triangle, which would prove pivotal to the human drama. Kayama had written the paleontologist, Dr. Kyohei Yamane (Takashi Shimura), as an eccentric man clad in a cape and sunglasses; in the screenplay, he became a symbol of rational science, intent on studying Godzilla's ability to withstand the hydrogen bomb. Godzilla morphed from Kayama's hungry predator into a merciless, unstoppable force. The screenplay also tactfully handled thorny issues: The US is certainly responsible for the H-bomb test that begets Godzilla, yet America is unmentioned; Japan defends itself without support from the roughly two hundred and fifty thousand US troops controversially stationed there in 1954; and the chilling first scene, with a fiery blast destroying a ship, is eerily evocative of the *Lucky Dragon* tragedy. Everything is played straight; there is one brief moment of gallows humor, but here the writers slyly insert overt references to the disasters of 1945 and 1954:

```
                     WOMAN ON TRAIN
     Atomic tuna, radioactive fallout, and now this Godzilla to top it off!
                  What if it shows up in Tokyo Bay?

                          MAN
             It'll probably go straight for you first.

                         WOMAN
     I barely escaped the atomic bomb in Nagasaki—and now this!
```

Excitement grew as copies of the *G Project* script, with "Classified" stamped in red on the cover, circulated among the production team. The Motion Picture Code of Ethics Committee approved the screenplay and included a requirement that the country's newly christened military, the Japan Self-Defense Forces (JSDF), be portrayed "with the utmost care and respect." (This small stipulation would have a lasting influence. In accordance with constitutional limitations, the JSDF attacks Godzilla only after it enters Japanese territory; in this and many subsequent films, the troops defend Japan valiantly, but monsters are, most often, vanquished not by military might.)

On July 5, 1954, Toho Studios officially announced that preproduction had begun on an unprecedented project titled *Gojira* (later transposed as "Godzilla" for the English-speaking world). Filming would begin in early August and be split among three teams. The A group included the actors and crew, shooting the dramatic scenes under the supervision of Honda. The B group would shoot the special effects sequences under Tsuburaya's watch, and the C group, a subdivision of Tsuburaya's team, would handle composite photography to combine live-action and effects footage in certain scenes. This novel approach, with two directors working in parallel, would become standard procedure in Japan's eventual special effects boom. The studio revealed few details about the production, and the image of the monster remained top secret.

"Around that time, rumors were spreading among the other film studios," remembered writer Kayama. "'It seems Toho is up to something strange. They're planning something incredible and massive.'" As the first of its type, *Godzilla* was a significant gamble for Toho, with a budget of approximately ¥60 million, triple that of the average Japanese feature; prints and advertising would push this to about ¥100 million (about $275,000). Tanaka, Tsuburaya, and Honda were determined to prove any skeptics wrong; they would depict a giant monster attack with the seriousness of a documentary. "The critics had no respect for science-fiction films, so we said, 'Let's play this completely straight,'" recalled assistant director Koji Kajita. "At first, everyone was anxious, [but] once we began filming, we started to feel the potential."

SMALL WONDERS

Tsuburaya soon concluded that the stop-motion animation method employed by Willis O'Brien in 1933's *King Kong* was impractical for *Godzilla*, if not impossible. Instead, he would simulate a giant monster by utilizing miniature sets—like those he'd built for war films a decade earlier—to upsize an actor in a costume; the creature's design, construction of the monster suit, and the task of acting in it would all pose significant challenges. (See the "Creating Godzilla" and "Inside Godzilla" sections.) To help lead the multifaceted creative teams assembled for the production, Tsuburaya turned to trusted colleagues and industry pros. Akira Watanabe, who had created a realistic miniature of Pearl Harbor for *The War at Sea from Hawaii to Malaya*, headed the SFX art department; Kuichiro Kishida, a veteran lighting technician for Kurosawa and other major directors, supervised the moody lighting of Godzilla's attacks. The studio had no cameramen with significant experience and skills shooting special effects, so Tsuburaya assigned Sadamasa Arikawa, a young apprentice who joined Tsuburaya during his occupation exile period, as chief effects cinematographer. Arikawa would function as something akin to Tsuburaya's lieutenant for much of the crew.

The special effects crew was a rank-and-file group of freelancers and part-time staffers, many of whom were excited to be working on a film for the first time. When the *G Project* script was completed, crew members eagerly scanned it to learn how much of the film was their responsibility. "I was shocked. . . . The number of scenes marked 'SFX' in the script was like no film made before," remembered Arikawa. Still, only the upper echelon of the effects team was identified in the staff list attached to the screenplay. Young team members protested their plight—many were pulling all-nighters; some would eat and sleep at Toho or nearby for two months straight to complete the film on time. Their work was largely of the get-your-hands-dirty variety, and others treated them with disregard. "Every director had their own group at the time, and Tsuburaya's group had a much lower status than any other in the studio," recalled Shinji Hiruma, a model maker who assisted the SFX team. Eizo Kaimai, a member of the monster suit–making team, concurred: "In the studio cafeteria, they would write 'Tsuburaya family' on our lunch tickets. Were we like yakuza, or what? They treated us like that." But Arikawa urged them to use the chip on their collective shoulder as motivation. "We will make this film a success and let the world know we should be treated the same as everyone else," he recalled thinking. "We'll show them." With a shooting schedule of just seventy-one days, a budget that was extremely tight, and a high-pressure atmosphere, everyone working under Tsuburaya would be severely tested.

MAP OF DESTRUCTION

Godzilla razes famous prewar landmarks during its Tokyo attacks. In its first assault, the creature comes ashore at eastern Tokyo Bay and demolishes Shinagawa Station, a major rail hub. In its second, thirteen-minute-long foray, the monster heads for the world-famous Ginza shopping district, torches the Matsuzakaya department store, and tears down the Hattori Clock Tower. It crosses the Sukiya Bridge (which, coincidentally, was demolished not long after the film's release) and smacks Toho's cake-shaped Nippon Gekijo (Nichigeki) theater. It smashes through the National Diet Building and finally tears up the Kachidoki Bridge, a drawbridge at the mouth of the Sumida River. (This route would have taken Godzilla past the Imperial Palace, which does not appear in the film and apparently survived unscathed.)

Tsuburaya demanded the miniature sets be rendered in realistic detail, and he could be difficult to please. Blueprints for actual locations were not available, so the special effects art staff created their own drawings. "[They] checked everything in Ginza, including the height of electric poles and the sizes of advertising billboards, walking around with 5-foot [2.5-m] sticks to take measurements," recalled Arikawa. At that time, Ginza consisted mostly of wooden structures just one or two stories tall. The Buildings Standards Law, enacted after the 1923 Great Kanto Earthquake due to seismic concerns, limited Tokyo structures to 102 feet (31 m); at 164 feet (50 m) tall, Godzilla would tower over the city. Toho's carpentry staff built the Ginza miniature set, but Tsuburaya rejected their first version and ordered the entire thing rebuilt. All told, the team spent almost thirty days to successfully re-create Ginza, where Godzilla wreaks some of its most memorable havoc.

Before launching the ambitious production, Tsuburaya had gathered his team for a meeting. "Remember, we are going to make this together," he told them. "It's not going to be me as the director doing it all and everyone just following behind." Tsuburaya was a quiet leader who entrusted his staff with tremendous responsibility, but he was very much in command on the set and did not tolerate careless mistakes. While

TOP: The intricately detailed miniature Matsuzakaya department store is set ablaze. ■ **ABOVE:** Because the first Godzilla suit was too heavy and inflexible to be used for filming, it was cut in half. Here, Haruo Nakajima wears the bottom half like pants (with suspenders) for close-ups of Godzilla's feet destroying buildings.

"THE JAPANESE GODZILLA FAR SURPASSES THE HOLLYWOOD-MADE 'HYDROGEN BOMB FILMS' OF THE SAME ERA IN INTENSITY AND IMPACT. WHILE THE AMERICAN FILMS REMAIN COMPETENT HORROR MOVIES AT BEST, THE JAPANESE GODZILLA TRANSCENDS ITS COUNTERPARTS, REACHING A LEVEL OF HORROR THAT SIGNIFICANTLY SURPASSES WHAT AMERICAN FILMS OF THE TIME ENVISIONED."

—Shunya Yoshimi, sociologist

TOP RIGHT: Godzilla comes ashore and is about to encounter the electrified high-tension towers erected around the city as a defense barrier. ▪ **RIGHT:** Against the pitch-black Tokyo night, Godzilla appears as a specter of destruction and death. Cameraman Sadamasa Arikawa said, "Special effects can show a monster stepping on people, but actually creating a sense of fear is much more complex. It's not the same as the type of fear you get from a scary ghost story." ▪ **BOTTOM LEFT:** The team of "Godzilla handlers" prepares the monster suit as suit actor Haruo Nakajima (*left front*) and special effects director Eiji Tsuburaya (*left rear, with hat and glasses*) wait. ▪ **BOTTOM RIGHT:** Smashing through the miniature set of the National Diet Building, Japan's house of parliament. The Diet Building was built 1/33 scale rather than the typical 1/25 scale so that Godzilla would appear to stand over it, rather than the other way around.

GORILLA + WHALE = GODZILLA. OR DOES IT?

THE MYSTERIOUS ORIGINS OF THE MONSTER'S NAME

How did Godzilla get its iconic, one-of-a-kind name? A definitive answer remains elusive. It may have been derived from "Jira Monster," the title of a short story about a giant prehistoric cryptid previously published by scenario writer Shigeru Kayama. Or it could have been influenced by an idea for a film about a giant *kujira* (whale), which Eiji Tsuburaya and screenwriter Takeo Murata reportedly proposed some time before *Godzilla*. However, the most well-known story, often told by the late producer Tomoyuki Tanaka, is that the name is a compound of *gorira* (gorilla) and *kujira*. "Gojira," Tanaka explained, was the nickname of a man (sometimes—but not always—described as big and burly; sometimes remembered as an actor, a stagehand, or a publicity man) employed at Toho when the film went into production.

> **Tomoyuki Tanaka:** *The inspiration came from someone with a very imposing appearance. . . . They were nicknamed "Gojira." [A colleague of mine] suggested, "Why not use a name like this?" I thought such a strange title would never be suitable for a film. Over time and through discussions, we generated about twenty or thirty different titles, but none seemed satisfactory. . . . Then I met a newspaper reporter at a café. He said, "Hmm, that's an interesting name for a monster." At first, our executives and even the studio staff didn't take it seriously, but we gradually realized that it was the perfect title. It seemed like a fitting name for the protagonist of the film.*

Tanaka's story has plot holes, however. The identity of Gojira (the man) remained unknown for decades, even after his nickname had become internationally famous. In the early 2000s, a Japanese TV program posthumously identified a Toho employee as the person in question, although the studio has not confirmed the man's identity. Many doubt the veracity of the story.

> **Haruo Nakajima:** *There was a newsletter circulating in the studio that said they were looking for a name for the monster, and they were asking the employees to submit names. I'm not sure if they ended up using one of the names that were submitted. [Asked if he believes whether the Toho man identified on TV was the real "Gojira"] I have no idea. That guy came out of the blue.*

> **Tadashi Matsushita (former member, Toho literature department):** *Some say there was a person in Toho who was nicknamed Gojira. [But] I remember using the name Gojira repeatedly without knowing this fact.*

A conflicting memory, however, comes from a former member of the Toho publicity department.

> **Fumi Saito:** *Everything about the production [was] a secret. We couldn't promote it with the title Gojira. We couldn't promote it as G Project—we didn't even know what that meant. We wanted to create a buzz around the title, but we couldn't reveal scenes or snapshots from the actual production. It was quite the task to promote it while maintaining secrecy. I've promoted films by [Akira] Kurosawa and others, but this was the most difficult; we were apologizing left and right in our promotional materials. Even the real man behind the nickname Gojira complained to us.*

Did the man called Gojira really exist? Or is the story merely a legend? "I expect the name was thought up after very careful discussions between Mr. Tanaka, Mr. Tsuburaya, and my husband," said Kimi Honda, wife of Ishiro Honda. As for the mystery man, she added, "The backstage boys at Toho loved to joke around with tall stories, but I don't believe that one." And what is the most likely explanation, if unconfirmed? Kayama's diaries show that the writer had already named the monster Gojira as he began to write the film's story, long before any talk of burly men, gorillas, and whales would surface.

Mystery also surrounds how "Gojira" became known overseas as "Godzilla." The English-language spelling is a phonetic translation of the three monosyllabic katakana characters (*Go-Dzi-La*) that spell the monster's name in Japanese; it was most likely coined by a staffer within Toho's international division prior to the sale of the film to American buyers in 1956 (the title is spelled this way in the contract documents); however, no individual has ever claimed credit for it.

OPPOSITE, CLOCKWISE FROM TOP LEFT: Godzilla attacks the Hattori Clock Tower in Ginza, a finely detailed miniature model. The moody lighting enhances Godzilla's silhouette and reveals the depth of the miniature set. ▪ Godzilla is about to destroy the cake-shaped Nippon Gekijo (Nichigeki) theater, a popular movie house. This scene includes a quick insert shot of an animated model of Godzilla's tail striking the building. ▪ Overturning the Kachidoki Bridge, the final act of destruction in Godzilla's long rampage across Tokyo.

LEFT: Godzilla emerges from Tokyo Bay. ▪ **ABOVE, TOP TO BOTTOM:** Distraught that the authorities would rather destroy Godzilla than study it, Dr. Yamane (Takashi Shimura) retreats to his study. ▪ Reporter Hagiwara (Sachio Sakai, *right*) visits Dr. Serizawa's (Akihiko Hirata) home to question the scientist about rumors that he may have a way to combat Godzilla. ▪ Emiko (Momoko Kochi), Dr. Yamane (Shimura), and reporter Hagiwara (Sakai) examine the wreckage on Odo Island after the typhoon.

crew members regarded the "Old Man" (*Oyaji*) as a mentor, they feared his wrath. "Tsuburaya spoke to us in a relatively gentle manner during meetings," said Godzilla suit actor Haruo Nakajima, "but when it came time to shoot, he was a professional who made no compromises at all."

Arikawa recalled a near-disaster while filming the memorable moment when Godzilla causes a train derailment at Shinagawa Station. The shot involved many moving parts: six miniature train cars would be manually pushed into the frame as monster actor Nakajima brought Godzilla's foot down, pyrotechnics detonating at the moment of impact. Arikawa had one chance—a blown take, and the entire setup would have to be rebuilt. The camera was positioned at ground level; Arikawa lay flat, with his jaw on the floor, looking through the viewfinder, battling discomfort as he checked the lighting and other details. Tsuburaya yelled "Action!" and the scene went as planned until Arikawa thought he caught a glimpse of a light stand in the corner of the frame. "I thought I would be fired for sure," he remembered. When it was time to watch the rushes the next day, he wanted to hide. As the lights went down in the screening room, the young man was sweating. The train passed through the frame; the camera panned and followed. Suddenly, Godzilla's foot smashed the locomotive. Sparks flew and train cars flipped over. Arikawa braced for Tsuburaya's scolding, but the light stand never appeared. *Oh my God*, he thought. *My job is saved*.

THE LEGEND BEGINS

Mysterious shipping disasters plague Japanese coastal waters. Authorities are baffled; there are few survivors, and they describe the sea catching fire before they sank. In a tiny fishing village on Odo Island, the fisherman Masaji washes ashore on a raft, suffering skin burns and nearly dead, but when he says a monster attacked his boat, no one believes him. The island's waters are suddenly devoid of fish, and an elder believes these strange occurrences must be the work of Godzilla, a legendary sea beast that could only be pacified by human sacrifice. Others mock the man's warning, but late one night an eerie typhoon strikes the island, thunderclaps shaking the earth like giant footfalls. Masaji, awakened by the tremors, is frightened by something horrifying in the night; a powerful, unseen force flattens his home and tramples the village. The government dispatches a scientific investigative team to the island, led by paleontologist Dr. Kyohei Yamane. While Yamane is surveying a huge, radioactive footprint, the din of giant footsteps is heard again, and suddenly a giant animal appears over a ridgeline and roars mightily. Yamane deduces the creature is a prehistoric marine reptile, reawakened by H-bomb tests at Bikini Atoll. While all of this is transpiring, a key subplot unfolds: Yamane's twentyish daughter, Emiko, and her sailor boyfriend, Ogata, secretly want to marry, but first she must terminate her arranged betrothal to Dr. Serizawa, a reclusive research scientist. Emiko never breaks the news to her fiancé, however, because Serizawa has something more urgent to discuss. In his basement lab, he shows Emiko an experiment, the sight of which (off camera) terrifies her; Serizawa makes Emiko promise never to tell a soul. Godzilla is sighted in Tokyo Bay, and the military responds by dropping depth charges, ignoring Yamane's plea to preserve the creature for study. Angered by the bombs, Godzilla storms ashore after nightfall, trashing a rail depot and the harbor area. To protect the city from further damage, the authorities quickly erect a high-voltage perimeter, but Godzilla destroys it and lays waste to Tokyo. As casualties mount, a distraught Emiko reveals Serizawa's secret: He has accidentally created a deadly chemical compound, the Oxygen Destroyer, capable of killing Godzilla. Serizawa refuses to share his discovery, fearing it would ignite a new, more dangerous arms race. He agonizes over his predicament—to introduce a new weapon of mass destruction, or allow the human carnage to continue? Ultimately, he relents, destroying his research papers to ensure the Oxygen Destroyer can never be re-created.

BOTTOM LEFT: Odo Island fisherman Masaji (Ren Yamamoto) washes ashore after his boat is sunk by Godzilla. Mayor Inada (Keiji Sakakida, *left*) and Masaji's little brother, Shinkichi (Toyoaki Suzuki, *right*), attempt to revive him. Later, after Masaji is killed by Godzilla, orphaned Shinkichi becomes a ward of the Yamane family in Tokyo. ▪ **BOTTOM RIGHT:** Villagers wear *tengu* (devil) masks and perform the ceremonial dance of Odo Island, all that remains of a long-held tradition of rituals to appease the malevolent god-monster, known in local folklore as Gojira.

> **"EXTRAS WERE GATHERED FROM PLACES LIKE SHOWA WOMEN'S UNIVERSITY IN SANGENJAYA. THEY HAD BARRACKS WHERE PEOPLE (WHO) REPATRIATED FROM OVERSEAS AFTER THE WAR LIVED. WE'D BRING BUSES, GATHER A LOT OF ELDERLY PEOPLE, PAY THEM DAILY WAGES, AND HAVE THEM ACT. BUT NOBODY KNEW HOW BIG GODZILLA WAS SUPPOSED TO BE, SO DIRECTING THEM TO RUN AWAY WAS TRICKY. SOMETIMES THEY WOULD LAUGH WHILE RUNNING."**
>
> — Kenji Tokoro, assistant director

RIGHT: Shigeru Kayama's story portrayed Godzilla as a hungry predator feeding on animals. This scene of Godzilla eating a cow was filmed but left out of the final cut. Godzilla eats its meals off-screen; the Odo Island mayor tells of twelve cows and eight pigs lost in the monster's attack. ■ **BOTTOM LEFT:** Reaching the top of the mountain on Odo Island, Dr. Yamane (Takashi Shimura, *center*) points to the ridgeline where he believes he has seen a gigantic creature. ■ **BOTTOM RIGHT:** As the panicking villagers flee down the hillside, Ogata (Akira Takarada) comes to the aid of a terrified Emiko (Momoko Kochi).

THE SOUND OF THUNDER

COMPOSER AKIRA IFUKUBE AND THE MONSTROUS MUSIC OF *GODZILLA*

Akira Ifukube was approached to score *Godzilla* in June 1954. Toho's music director, Keikichi Kakeshita, personally delivered the screenplay to Ifukube's home and, upon reviewing it, the composer felt great excitement over the subject matter. Ifukube, who grew up in the densely forested and mountainous environment of Hokkaido, Japan's northernmost island, interpreted Godzilla as the natural world's revenge on modern civilization, an idea he reveled in. Ifukube was especially enthused that Godzilla was a giant reptile because, as a boy, he enjoyed catching snakes and keeping them as pets.

Contrary to popular legend, Ifukube did not write and record the *Godzilla* score in only one week without seeing any footage of the film. Rather, the composer labored over the music for several months, starting in June 1954 until the recording session in late October of that year. Ifukube had also been permitted by Eiji Tsuburaya to view some of the preliminary effects footage, which allowed the composer to quite effectively translate his personal impressions of Godzilla's terrible majesty into music.

The famous, rhythmically propulsive music of *Godzilla*'s opening titles is characterized by an obsessively repetitive motif comprising the notes C-B-A, the incessant recurrence of which is an example of the composer's trademark use of ostinato, or the repetition of a melodic or rhythmic figure. Ifukube learned the ostinato technique as a child from hearing Japanese folk music as well as the music of the Ainu, the indigenous people of northern Japan. Although the melody built around the C-B-A motif is well-known today as the theme for Godzilla itself, the composer originally intended it to represent the military's struggle against the monster.

For the scenes in which Godzilla assaults Tokyo, Ifukube wrote a simple but ominous theme that evokes the beast's great size. Using snarling brass and low-pitched instruments such as a contrabassoon, the music accompanying Godzilla's attacks is distinguished by its series of rising notes, starting on C♯, which highlights the monster's towering height. The steady rhythm of this music is punctuated by thunderously dissonant tone clusters from the piano, which are executed by crashing down on the instrument's lowest-pitched white and black keys with both forearms. The effect reminds the audience of Godzilla's weighty, shattering footfalls as it advances relentlessly across the city.

Some of *Godzilla*'s most memorable music is its most mournful. In the "Prayer for Peace," which is sung by a choir of young schoolgirls during a television broadcast and ultimately convinces Dr. Serizawa to deploy his Oxygen Destroyer against Godzilla, Ifukube uses the Phrygian mode, an ancient musical scale that is used frequently in many of the world's folk music traditions as well as in medieval European church music. This endows the "Prayer" with a striking sense of religious solemnity. The Phrygian mode is used again in the music that accompanies the deaths of both Godzilla and Dr. Serizawa after the activation of the Oxygen Destroyer at the bottom of Tokyo Bay. Consequently, Ifukube's score at the conclusion of *Godzilla* conveys both grandeur and gravitas, and due to its archaic sound, the film's climax takes on the atmosphere of something out of an epic Greek tragedy.

—Erik Homenick

FAR LEFT: Junior high and high school students at Toho Gakuen School of Music in Setagaya portray the girls choir that performs composer Akira Ifukube's "Prayer for Peace" in a televised vigil. The actual vocals heard on the film soundtrack were recorded by a twenty-person professional vocal group. ■ LEFT: Ifukube at his home in Tokyo, 1996.

BOTTOM LEFT: Dr. Yamane (Takashi Shimura) reveals his findings to members of the National Diet. Legislators fight over whether to disclose Godzilla's ties to H-bomb tests or maintain secrecy for fear of widespread panic and straining diplomatic ties, mirroring similar arguments over the *Lucky Dragon* incident. ■ **BOTTOM RIGHT:** Tension in the Yamane household as Ogata (Akira Takarada, *right*) discusses what is to be done about Godzilla with Dr. Yamane (Shimura, standing). Emiko (Momoko Kochi) and Shinkichi (Toyoaki Suzuki, *left*) listen in.

A LIVING GOD

Godzilla generates dread and terror by gradually revealing the monster's physical form and the mystery of its origins. More than a Western-style monster, Godzilla—like all kaiju that would later follow—is an extension of Japan's complex tradition of spirit-gods rooted in ancient legends and religious practices. At first, Godzilla is invisible—like a supernatural being—striking ships from beneath the sea and then descending upon Odo Island while cloaked in the eye of a typhoon. The first actual sighting is a classic moment in horror cinema, as Godzilla peers above the mountain, revealing its awesome size and fearsome visage. But by the time the heroes reach the summit, the creature has again vanished into the sea, leaving behind only footprints. When it makes landfall at the rail yard, Godzilla is a ghostlike silhouette against the Tokyo night sky. Not until the final, extended rampage is Godzilla's fearsome power fully unleashed, equivalent to another in Japan's long history of natural disasters, or the slow-moving shockwave of a massive explosion. Mythical and rational explanations for the monster's existence are provided by the Odo Island wise man (Kokuten Kodo) and Dr. Yamane. Neither story is truer than the other, and the scientist names the monster after the islanders' folk legend.

Godzilla realized Tsuburaya's dream, yet whereas *King Kong* is an epic American fantasy-adventure, *Godzilla* is grounded in the tragic experiences of the Japanese during and after the war, and the interaction between Tsuburaya's visuals and Honda's sober, unsentimental direction draws clear parallels. People frantically evacuate, carrying belongings on their backs, or hide in subway tunnels as if fleeing an air raid. The morning after Godzilla's attack, nothing remains standing; the streets are buried under rubble, and a thick smoke layer hangs above, a blanket of gloom. Disaster shelters overflow with victims. A doctor tests a child for radiation, and the Geiger counter goes berserk. A girl wails as her mother succumbs to terrible burns. The black-and-white cinematography of Masao Tamai—renowned for shooting Mikio Naruse's 1950s drama masterpieces—accentuates the impact of these images with noir-like, high-contrast light and shadow throughout.

The story takes place over roughly a week in late summer, and Honda's cast sweats visibly under the oppressive heat and impending doom. The ensemble of characters faces intertwined moral, ethical, and personal dilemmas. Shimura, star of Kurosawa's *Ikiru* and *Seven Samurai*, and one of cinema's finest actors, lends great gravitas as Yamane, who sees Godzilla as not an evil menace but a holocaust survivor. His pleas

"BEFORE THE THEATRICAL RELEASE, WE HAD A SCREENING IN THE SAME AUDITORIUM (WHERE THE CHOIR SCENE WAS FILMED). WHEN I WAS IN ELEMENTARY SCHOOL, I HAD EXPERIENCED AN AIR RAID IN HACHIOJI, AND THE SCENE WHERE GINZA WAS DESTROYED LOOKED JUST LIKE THE BURNED-OUT FIELDS AFTER THE AIR RAID. IT WAS QUITE SHOCKING."

—Yasue Suzuki, former Toho Gakuen School of Music student, member of "Prayer for Peace" choir

SAYONARA, GODZILLA

After production of *Godzilla* wrapped, Toho gave the monster a mock burial at sea. The film's lead actors, Akira Takarada (Ogata) and Momoko Kochi (Emiko), joined by the (empty) Godzilla suit, rode through the streets of Tokyo in the back of a truck, waving to a bemused public along their route.

Arriving at the docks of the Sumida River, they boarded a boat. Takarada put on a Hawaiian shirt and Kochi changed into a hula dancer outfit. With a group of children looking on, Takarada played the ukulele and serenaded Godzilla with the Hawaiian folk song "Aloha Oe" ("Farewell to Thee") as Kochi placed a lei around the monster's neck and performed a hula dance. Once the ship set sail, the stars changed back into their street clothes. With Godzilla positioned at the bow of the boat, a Shinto priest performed ceremonial funeral rites for Godzilla, and the boat set sail for Tokyo Bay. There, Godzilla was hoisted over the side on a winch by both Takarada and Kochi. Pausing the ceremony for a moment, Takarada donned a diving suit to accompany Godzilla as the monster was lowered into the water while Kochi tossed in a bouquet of flowers, calling out, "Sayonara, Godzilla!" Godzilla finally descended into the water to its final resting place, never to be seen again.

Or so it was reported at the time. The event was actually an elaborate publicity stunt, staged to generate press coverage. A photo essay of the event was published in the February 1955 issue of *Heibon* magazine. Based these photos, many have assumed the original Godzilla suit was lost forever. In reality, it was retrieved from the water and returned to the studio for storage. But what eventually happened to the original Godzilla suit after that is a mystery. It did not appear in *Godzilla Raids Again* or any subsequent Toho productions, and no known photographs of the suit have ever surfaced afterward.

 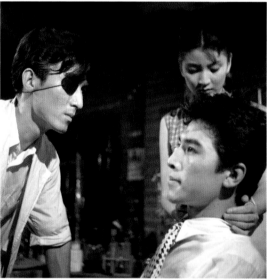

FAR LEFT: Dr. Serizawa (Akihiko Hirata) entrusts Emiko (Momoko Kochi) with his dangerous secret: the discovery of a chemical compound that instantly liquefies all living matter in water—the Oxygen Destroyer. ■ LEFT: The confrontation between Dr. Serizawa (*left*) and Ogata (*right*) over the use of the Oxygen Destroyer against Godzilla. Serizawa wins the fight, but Ogata wins the argument, and Serizawa reluctantly agrees to use the device, burning his notes to prevent it from being weaponized.

to study the creature are rejected by authorities more concerned with economic and diplomatic survival, and as the death toll mounts, Yamane ceases resisting plans to kill the monster. Emiko and Ogata are a typical young couple attempting to start a hopeful life in postwar Japan, but their dreams are repeatedly dashed by Godzilla-related emergencies. Takarada, a young actor making his starring debut, plays Ogata as a soldierlike figure driven by latent revenge (his shipping company was attacked by Godzilla) and a duty to defend the country: "Godzilla's no different from the H-bomb still hanging over Japan's head." Ogata's strident stance comes into conflict with his would-be father-in-law, who throws him out of the house. Emiko provides the film with its one true monster-movie cliché—a screaming close-up as Godzilla roars in her direction—but her importance lies in a heartbreaking decision to betray Serizawa, her lifelong friend, to save humanity.

Though he appears in just a handful of scenes and has relatively little dialogue, Serizawa is the truly pivotal character in *Godzilla*, a post-Hiroshima scientist faced with the grim realization that his idealistic

ABOVE: In a makeshift medical triage center, Emiko (Momoko Kochi) attempts to comfort a young girl whose mother has perished in the aftermath of Godzilla's attack. Note the high-contrast lighting and cinematography by Masao Tamai. ■ **RIGHT:** Dr. Serizawa (Akihiko Hirata) clutches the terrifying Oxygen Destroyer as he prepares for his fateful dive to confront Godzilla. Emiko (Kochi) and Dr. Yamane (Takashi Shimura) look on.

pursuit of knowledge has opened a deadly Pandora's box. (Serizawa's dilemma is timely: In 1955, a group of nuclear physicists and scientists, similarly alarmed that their search to understand the nature of matter had produced the ultimate weapon of war, would sign the Bertrand Russell–Albert Einstein manifesto against nuclear weapons.) He wears a white coat and works in a dark basement laboratory, yet he is not a mad scientist, but rather a scientist driven to despair. Hirata, then a young character actor who would develop a long association with Toho's genre films, delivers a career-defining performance.

"Serizawa was a war survivor, and he carried that trauma with him," recalled Hirata. "I thought he wouldn't be interesting if I played him as too sentimental. I tried to keep his trauma just below the surface but still visible." Serizawa's pain is physical and emotional; he bears facial scars and wears an eyepatch due to war injuries. His love for Emiko is unspoken, yet he trusts her above all others. In a dramatic climax, Ogata demands Serizawa use the Oxygen Destroyer against Godzilla, and the scientist must confront his fear. "As long as I'm alive, who can say I won't be coerced into using it again?" On a TV broadcast, a children's choir sings the mournful "Prayer for Peace" over images of Godzilla's victims. The sadness of the vigil is overpowering, and Serizawa is moved.

ELEGY FOR MAN AND MONSTER

"Prayer for Peace" is characteristic of the deep emotional power of composer Akira Ifukube's compelling, propulsive, and resonant musical score. From the stirring main title theme, which alternately drives the heroic military response and serves as the monster's signature motif, to the thundering, guttural dirges that accompany Godzilla's reign of destruction, this is a masterful suite that supplies the film's dramatic pulse and reinforces Godzilla's size and irrefutable power—it is arguably among the most memorable and recognizable scores of any genre film. Even with his esteemed background in classical music, and as a composer of dramatic films, Ifukube—like Tsuburaya and Honda—embraced the novel, risky proposition of a monster movie even when contemporaries urged him not to do it. "Something monstrous comes out and makes you jump out of your wits!" Ifukube said. "It is sheer fear, not an abstraction, and it is global. . . . I couldn't sit still when I heard that in this movie the main character was a reptile that would be rampaging through the city."

In the final moments, Serizawa and Ogata dive into Tokyo Bay. The heavy atmosphere remains; this is the antithesis of a typical monster movie climax. There is no exciting showdown, only anticipation as to whether the plan will succeed. In its natural habitat, Godzilla is peaceful and vulnerable, displaced in time by man's nuclear hubris. The pacing is slow and deliberate until Serizawa, now alone at the bottom of the sea, detonates the Oxygen Destroyer. Then, unexpectedly, he bids sayonara to his friends above, cuts his lifeline, and takes the secret of his deadly discovery to the grave. Serizawa's suicide saves the world and ends his personal hell of regret and heartbreak and allows Emiko and Ogata to marry without

ABOVE: Dr. Serizawa (Akihiko Hirata) prepares to activate the Oxygen Destroyer on the ocean floor. ■ **LEFT:** In concluding its long Tokyo rampage, Godzilla enters the Sumida River and, while heading back toward Tokyo Bay, the monster flips over the Kachidoki Bridge. The bridge was built in 1940 and is one of few double-leafed drawbridges in Japan. It was designated a national Important Cultural Property in 2007. Here, the special effects team assists Godzilla actor Haruo Nakajima (*inside the suit*) during filming of the scene.

ABOVE: *Godzilla* ends with a fateful message from Dr. Yamane, predicting Godzilla may return. "I wasn't thinking about a sequel," said screenwriter Takeo Murata. "I thought if we continued testing the H-bomb, maybe another Godzilla would appear again and other tragedies would occur. That's why I wrote a line at the end like that." ■ RIGHT: As the film ends, mourners offer a farewell salute to the sacrifice of Dr. Serizawa.

trace of dishonor. And Godzilla, the indestructible menace born of the bomb, dies a pitiable, agonizing death in a bubbling liquid mushroom cloud. Ifukube's requiems well up; the military salutes the lost man, and a prayer seems to be offered for Godzilla as well. There is no rejoicing, only a profound sense of loss.

Godzilla harbors almost none of the clichés common to the 1950s-era science-fiction and monster movies that it is often associated with. It stands alone as a cautionary tale born of history and tragedy, and a worthy bookend to Christopher Nolan's acclaimed *Oppenheimer* (2023), the story of the Manhattan Project and its dire legacy, made nearly seventy years later. Upon its release in Japan in November 1954, *Godzilla* became an entertainment sensation, owing to its social relevance and its extraordinary and dramatic use of special effects. Reviews were nevertheless mixed to negative, with some critics objecting to allusions to the atomic bombings and to the *Lucky Dragon*, accusing the filmmakers of exploiting a crisis. ("They called it grotesque junk," director Honda lamented.) Despite its commercial success and technical achievements, the film was received as merely a monster movie rather than a serious work of cinema. Yukio Mishima was among the few writers who praised its message, calling *Godzilla* "a film with the power to criticize civilization." In the 1954 edition of "10 Best Japanese Films," a survey of critics published by the film magazine *Kinema Junpo* (*Seasonal Cinema News*), *Godzilla* was not even ranked among the top twenty. However, acceptance and appreciation among film scholars and critics slowly grew. Thirty-five years later, when the same magazine published its list of the best films in Japanese cinema history, *Godzilla* was ranked twentieth best of all time.

On its opening day, *Godzilla* sold thirty-three thousand tickets at four Tokyo cinemas, setting a new record. Overall, the film sold 9.6 million admissions during its 1954–55 theatrical run across Japan and placed eighth at the domestic box office for the year. Kobayashi's plan to reinvest in marquee entertainment pictures was an unqualified success, as both *Seven Samurai* and *Musashi Miyamoto* also ranked among the year's top ten performing films. Thus, *Godzilla* helped relaunch Toho to the forefront of the Japanese movie industry, and although there was no hint of the dramatic changes that the monster was destined to undergo, the success of this film marked the beginning of a new and uniquely Japanese science-fiction cinema that would long outlast the type of Hollywood films that inspired it. The career trajectories of the personnel behind the camera were similarly catapulted: Tsuburaya and Honda forged a close creative partnership across more than a decade of internationally successful genre pictures (with Tsuburaya winning numerous awards for his work), Ifukube's film music would be closely identified with Godzilla, and Tanaka would become one of Toho's most powerful and successful producers, shepherding the Godzilla franchise for more than forty years. "Tanaka was a big shot," said actor Shigeo Kato, who appeared in *Godzilla* and many Toho special effects films. "He rose to prominence."

Audiences had watched as the Oxygen Destroyer dissolved Godzilla's flesh and bone at the bottom of the ocean. But Godzilla, as it turned out, was immortal. Its cinematic life had only just begun.

LOST IN AMERICA, LOST IN JAPAN

GODZILLA, KING OF THE MONSTERS!
RELEASED: APRIL 4, 1956 (USA)

Godzilla's worldwide popularity began with one of the great curiosities of cinema history, when Hollywood drastically reshaped the monster's first appearance into something resembling a typical 1950's B-movie.

After a landmark Supreme Court antitrust ruling in 1948 ended the movie industry's monopoly over production and distribution, independent art-house theaters and drive-ins soon flourished. The demand for highbrow foreign films and low-budget genre flicks soared just as Toho made its fortuitous entry into the American market. International interest in Japanese cinema was piqued after Akira Kurosawa's *Rashomon* (1950) won the grand prize at the Venice Film Festival in 1951. Soon after, in 1953, Toho opened a foreign sales office (Toho International) in the Little Tokyo section of Los Angeles. The first Toho film sold to a US

CLOCKWISE FROM TOP LEFT: Rare B-style US release poster for *Godzilla, King of the Monsters!* ▪ Reporter Steve Martin (Raymond Burr) in a publicity shot for *Godzilla, King of the Monsters!* ▪ Steve Martin (Burr) is questioned by security officer Iwanaga (Frank Iwanaga, *left*) upon his arrival in Japan. ▪ Lobby card for the original US release of *Godzilla, King of the Monsters!*

distributor was Kurosawa's *Seven Samurai*, which Columbia Pictures released in November 1956. The second, *Godzilla*, took a more unusual path but was actually released earlier, in April 1956, with the hyped-up new title *Godzilla, King of the Monsters!* In what is now a minor Hollywood legend, *Godzilla* was heavily re-edited to include a new protagonist, an American journalist who, while en route to Cairo, makes a stopover in Japan and is caught in Godzilla's path.

Was *Godzilla* a foreign film or an exploitation picture? The professionals credited with acquiring, modifying, and releasing it had experience in both types of movies, which proved valuable. Edmund Goldman had imported Hollywood films to Japan for Columbia during the occupation; Harold Ross and Richard Kay were exploitation producers whose hits included *Untamed Women* (1952); Terry Morse was an ex-Warner Bros. B-movie editor and director reputed as a "film doctor"; Paul Schreibman was an attorney and deal man who would later represent Toho in foreign sales for many years; and Joseph E. Levine was a multifarious producer-exhibitor who, in his long career, would be at the vanguard of many aspects of postwar cinema. After Goldman acquired the *Godzilla* rights (for a mere $25,000) in September 1955, it was Ross, Kay, and Morse who rewrote and heavily reworked the film to include a moody, film noir–like flashback scenario with reporter Steve Martin (Raymond Burr) recounting the events of Godzilla's Tokyo rampage. Though hurriedly and inexpensively filmed, these inserted scenes of Burr appearing to interact with the original cast—doubled by English-speaking Asian actors cleverly filmed over the shoulder and wearing wardrobe matching that of the Japanese cast—worked surprisingly well and gave the film an American perspective, enhancing its commercial potential. Voices for all Japanese characters were dubbed by just three performers: Chinese American actors James Hong and Sammee Tong, and Japanese American actress Amy "Emiko" Iwanabe. With the addition of Burr's scenes and corresponding cuts to the Japanese footage, Morse created a Tokyo-Hollywood hybrid cut running about eighty minutes long. More than one-third of the original film was excised; scenes were shortened or deleted altogether, including key references to the atomic bombing of Japan, Godzilla's relationship to hydrogen bomb testing, and political squabbles over whether to make this information public. Notably, Dr. Yamane's final speech about the dangers of nuclear testing and the likelihood of another Godzilla was removed, and the American cut ends with Burr instead declaring that "the whole world could wake up and live again."

Because the film arrived in theaters at a time when the US and USSR conducted hundreds of hydrogen bomb tests, these changes to the film have fueled speculation that the American distributors neutered the antinuclear message for political reasons. "No," responded producer Richard Kay. "We weren't interested in politics, believe me. We only wanted to make a movie we could sell." Kay noted that the film was released just eleven years after World War II. "At that time, the American public wouldn't have gone for a movie with an all-Japanese cast. That's why we did what we did. We didn't really change the story. We just gave it an American point of view." They also created a tremendous ad campaign and media blitz. Levine, known for outlandish salesmanship, employed the suffix "King of the Monsters" to draw direct comparisons to *King Kong* (publicity materials said the big gorilla was "like 'Peter Pan' by comparison"). Trailers and newspaper ads proclaimed, "It's alive! A gigantic beast! Stalking the Earth! Crushing all before it in a psychotic cavalcade of electrifying horror!" In its US theatrical run, *Godzilla, King of the Monsters!* earned (per *Variety*) more than $2 million, a then-sizeable sum for a black-and-white, low-budget exploitation film.

TRAILBLAZING TERROR

Many movies have cannibalized footage from other films; Alain Resnais's *Hiroshima Mon Amour* (1959), which borrows from Hideo Sekigawa's *Hiroshima* (1953), is just one well-known example. However, one would be hard-pressed to cite another film so thoroughly reworked into an alternate version for foreign markets as *Godzilla*. Thus, Japanese audiences must have been bemused when *Godzilla, King of the Monsters!* was shown in a very limited release in Japan in May 1957, less than three years after the original version debuted. Publicity materials rationalized the extensive changes. "Why re-edit a film that was already considered good and enjoyable for us Japanese viewers?" asked the film's program booklet, and posited: "The answer lies in the fact that fantasy or horror films always demand an element of 'plausibility' . . . viewers should sense true power and be able to immerse themselves in the lifelike portrayals of 'unrealistic' scenes."

Godzilla, King of the Monsters! remained the only version of the first Godzilla film officially available in the US and other Western territories until 2004, when the original Japanese cut of *Godzilla* was commercially released for the first time via a fiftieth-anniversary art-house theatrical run in major American cities. The more immediate and longstanding impact of *Godzilla, King of the Monsters!* was the opening of Japanese entertainment to the West. Science-fiction films from Toho and other studios would soon be exported successfully around the globe, followed not long after by Japanese animated programs and films, TV shows, anime, manga, and other content. While it can be debated whether *Godzilla, King of the Monsters!* is a cleverly reengineered cult classic or a bowdlerization of a classic Japanese film, this version inarguably paved the way for Japan's eventual global pop-culture dominance. With the help of Raymond Burr, the monster—spawned as a cinematic symbol of the horrors unleashed by the United States' death blow to Japan—conquered America and the world.

ABOVE: Japanese release poster for the American cut of the film, which played in only a handful of theaters. To add novelty effect, the film was cropped to simulate widescreen ratio.

(*GOJIRA NO GYAKUSHU / GODZILLA'S COUNTERATTACK*)
RELEASED: APRIL 24, 1955 (JAPAN)

GODZILLA RAIDS AGAIN

"I can't believe that Godzilla was the last of his species. If nuclear testing continues, then someday, somewhere in the world, another Godzilla may appear."

Dr. Yamane's closing words in *Godzilla* issued a plea for sanity amid the insanity of nuclear proliferation. They also proved to be prophetic: Mere months later, in April 1955, another Godzilla did in fact appear when Toho released *Godzilla Raids Again*. This often-overlooked entry in the series featured a new Godzilla, with quicker reflexes and more animallike traits, facing off against the ferocious quadruped Anguirus. This film set the stage for the menagerie of kaiju that would come forth from Toho and established a template for numerous monster-versus-monster epics.

Eiji Tsuburaya was rewarded for the success of *Godzilla* with an unprecedented honor that began with this production: the official title of director of special effects (*tokugi kantoku*). Tsuburaya was Japan's first filmmaker to be recognized for the achievements and contributions of *tokusatsu* in this way; not even Hollywood counterparts such as Willis O'Brien, whose special effects work on *Mighty Joe Young* (1949) had earned an Oscar, was given a director title. It was an acknowledgment of the power Tsuburaya now wielded, essentially putting him on equal footing with the principal director and conferring decision-making authority over special effects scenes.

Because the sequel was rushed into production, and with Ishiro Honda already working on the abominable snowman thriller *Half Human* (1955), directorial duties were assumed by Motoyoshi Oda, a prolific company-man director who had joined Toho's precursor, PCL Studios, in the 1930s and risen through the assistant director corps. Oda was perhaps chosen because of his prior associations with Tsuburaya: the two had collaborated on Oda's sci-fi thriller *Invisible Man* (1954), and Oda had served as an assistant director on Ishiro Honda's war epic *Eagle of the Pacific,* which featured Tsuburaya's elaborate simulations of air and naval warfare. More than any other entry in the original series of films, *Godzilla Raids Again* showcases the aerial battles that were one of Tsuburaya's cinematic trademarks dating back to the 1930s.

Set against a rapidly rebuilding Japan, *Godzilla Raids Again* is a straightforward drama that ruminates on themes of bravery, love, and friendship, interjected with action and destruction sequences that serve as reminders of war's looming power to disrupt normal life, and concludes with an exciting showdown between Godzilla and a squadron of fighter pilots. The screenplay, by Takeo Murata and Shigeaki Hidaka, was again adapted from an original treatment commissioned from genre author Shigeru Kayama. A young ex-military airman, Tsukioka (Hiroshi Koizumi), now employed as a fish-spotting pilot for a large Osaka cannery, is dispatched to rescue fellow pilot Kobayashi, who is stranded on a tiny island. The men are terrified when Godzilla and Anguirus suddenly appear, deadlocked in a heated battle; the pilots narrowly escape just as the monsters tumble into the sea and disappear. Despite having saved his friend, Tsukioka wrestles with self-doubt, having been shaken with fear by the monsters. (Many of the film's themes would resurface in *Godzilla Minus One* sixty-eight years later.)

Oda's film reflects the then-current debate over the role of Japan's new military, acknowledging the tensions between a longing for peace and stability versus fears of another devastating conflict. Tsukioka and his sweetheart, Hidemi (Setsuko Wakayama), daughter of the wealthy cannery boss, are eager to marry, but the monsters' swath of destruction interrupts their promising young lives. Happy scenes of Osaka nightlife quickly pivot to a city on war footing, with chaotic evacuations and a complete blackout to avoid attracting Godzilla ashore. When Godzilla and Anguirus make landfall, their fight to the death topples factories and office buildings, symbols of Japan's economic resurgence. The main characters are part of that resurgence—as the masses flee on foot with their belongings on their backs, Tsukioka and Kobayashi whisk Hidemi to safety in a big American sedan. But prosperity is no shield from the perils of war. As the men rush back into the battle zone, Hidemi is left alone at her family's mansion on a hill. Osaka is in flames, the plumes of smoke resembling a mushroom cloud.

PREVIOUS SPREAD: Godzilla and Anguirus clash near Osaka City Hall in the Yodoyabashi district. ∎ **LEFT:** Godzilla and Anguirus devastate the Osaka industrial area.

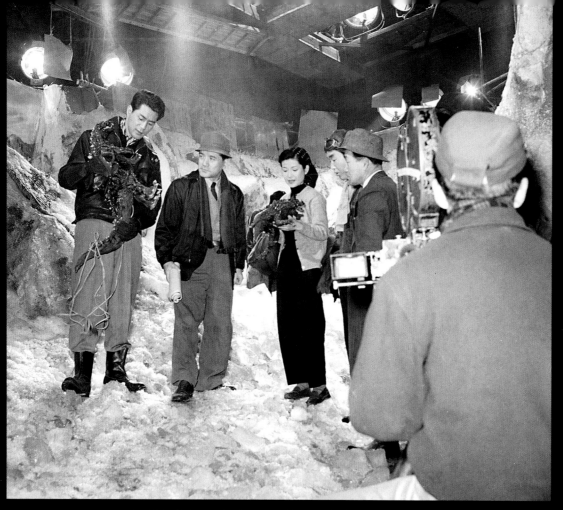

ABOVE: Minoru Chiaki (*left*) as Kobayashi and Hiroshi Koizumi (*right*) as Tsukioka. ■ **LEFT:** On the Kamiko Island set (*left to right*): Koizumi, director Motoyoshi Oda, Setsuko Wakayama (Hidemi Yamaji), Chiaki, and special effects director Eiji Tsuburaya. ■ **BELOW:** Godzilla and Anguirus locked in mortal combat on the miniature harbor set.

Godzilla Raids Again marks the first genre appearance of two actors with long and important associations with kaiju films: Hiroshi Koizumi and Yoshio Tsuchiya. Koizumi was a frequent leading man in romantic dramas and comedies; he would also star in Ishiro Honda's *Mothra* (1961) and many genre pictures. Tsuchiya, a favorite of Akira Kurosawa, is Tajima, leader of the Japan Self-Defense Forces (JSDF) fighter squad and Tsukioka's old military pal, a gung-ho role far removed from the aliens and villains the actor would later become associated with. The fine cast also includes Kurosawa regular Minoru Chiaki as the good-hearted but bashful pilot Kobayashi, while Takashi Shimura reprises the role of Dr. Yamane, recounting Godzilla's first attack and positing that the world is now irreversibly inhabited by giant monsters. With the Oxygen Destroyer off the table, mankind has no obvious solution. "We now face a threat even greater than nuclear weapons," Yamane says.

Oda's direction is effective if unremarkable. His most significant contribution may have been the selection of composer Masaru Sato, who propels *Godzilla Raids Again* with an eerie, ominous soundtrack that subtly amplifies the danger and uncertainty. In contrast to the stirring motifs of Akira Ifukube, Sato's music provides an unnerving layer of psychological tension, even as his themes remain somewhat ambiguous.

Sato would go on to become one of Japanese cinema's most prolific and important composers through a ten-year association with Akira Kurosawa, contributing to Toho's science-fiction films, and scoring more than three hundred movies and TV shows during his career.

Like Ifukube's work on the prior film, Sato's music is especially impactful when it breaks through silence. A long military buildup along the waterfront anticipating the monsters' arrival is accompanied by no music and only sparse dialogue and the intermittent roar of jet squadrons patrolling the airspace (a nod to the nascent Japan Air Self-Defense Force's [JASDF]) acquisition of F-86 fighters and T-33 trainers— both seen in the film—from the US that year). When Godzilla surfaces offshore, Sato announces its arrival with brash, shimmering cymbals. Low, guttural orchestral sounds rumble as the JSDF lights up the sky with flares, luring Godzilla back out to sea but inadvertently drawing Anguirus ashore, where the beasts clash. Sato skillfully mutes the orchestra during a lengthy destruction sequence as the monsters are bombarded by artillery fire and lay waste to the industrial sector, then underscores the kaiju clash with a low horror motif. Utilizing then-new magnetic tape technology, Sato manipulated recordings of gongs, cymbals, harps, and other instruments via reverse playback and altered speeds, enhancing traditional instruments with inorganic sounds.

This was Sato's first major score assignment, but he received no instructions from director Oda, which was "quite unnerving," as he recalled. Given the enormous success of the previous film, the young composer felt tremendous pressure in taking on such a high-profile project. "They were looking for someone new. *Godzilla* was not something to be taken lightly. Even if it didn't have an all-star cast, the film was still like Toho's cleanup hitter [as in baseball] for the year. My clear thought was that I should avoid doing the same thing Ifukube did; I had to do something completely different. So I thought of the kind of music that sounds more like American movies, with some type of mechanical sound, but I couldn't quite get the hang of it."

The new Godzilla is motivated not by vengeance and destruction but by territorial aggression and an instinctive drive to exterminate a

---

LEFT: Godzilla challenges Anguirus as the monsters near Osaka Castle. ■
ABOVE: Director Motoyoshi Oda and actress Setsuko Wakayama.

mortal enemy of a rival species. It moves with speed and agility, in stark contrast to the slow, deliberate creature that stalked Tokyo a year earlier. For publicity purposes, Toho's exhibitors in Kansai had begged the studio to set the story of the new Godzilla movie in their region. Godzilla and Anguirus lunge at, tackle, and bite each other, their fierce battle decimating entire sections of Osaka. As the fight moves to the historic Osaka Castle, Godzilla sinks its teeth into its spiny adversary's neck. Both monsters fall onto the crumbling landmark, and Godzilla finishes Anguirus off, sending the creature's carcass into the castle moat and incinerating it with a blast of its heat ray.

The quicker, more fluid movements of the monsters were made possible through improved costume design, as the suits were created with a lighter latex material and made to fit the actors' bodies this time out. During the Osaka battle sequence, the monsters move noticeably faster at times, with a lightning swiftness owing to an unintended change in camera speed that was, as it turned out, a happy accident. "There were three cameras—A, B, and C—and it was ordinary to shoot Godzilla at high speed" to create the slow movement associated with such large creatures, said special effects cameraman Sadamasa Arikawa. "But camera C wasn't set at high speed. . . . When we saw the dailies, cameras A and B were on the right setting, but camera C's Godzilla moved quicker." Eiji Tsuburaya was alarmed, but after examining the footage closely, he concluded, "Wait a minute. That movement's not that bad. Maybe we can use it." Tsuburaya also employed frame removal to accelerate the monster action, a technique he would later use to great effect in *Mothra vs. Godzilla*.

As evidence of Tsuburaya's growing respect for Haruo Nakajima's dedication to playing Godzilla, the stuntman was given full responsibility for choreographing the monsters' struggle. "There was a sword-fighting choreographer for *jidai-geki* (samurai movies), but there was no monster-fighting choreographer back then," Nakajima recalled. "So I was the first one. Tsuburaya told me, 'Do whatever you want.' It was such a responsibility! I was freaking out, but I was happy that he trusted me that much. . . . I choreographed the monsters moving up and down, glaring at each other, lunging and wrestling, etc., just like a *jidai-geki* fight."

Prior to the start of production, Toho held a big party to celebrate the opening of Stages No. 8 and No. 9 on the studio lot, two enormous buildings dedicated to shooting special effects scenes; this was evidence of Tsuburaya's growing influence and the studio's plan to ramp up production of *tokusatsu* films and expand into widescreen productions. The stages took about a year to complete and totaled about 1,000 *tsubo* (roughly 35,000 square feet/3,252 sq m), with high ceilings and vast, open interiors that enabled Tsuburaya to build bigger miniature sets and film them from higher and wider angles. The Osaka cityscape was constructed inside Stage No. 8, a 1/25 scale miniature set encompassing the Osaka Castle, police headquarters, Yodoya Bridge, Osaka Bay, and the city's Nakanoshima district of government buildings and museums. It took the special effects team about a month to complete work on the project.

The final act of *Godzilla Raids Again* features one of the most imaginative special effects sequences in the entire Godzilla series, a climactic confrontation between man and monster on icy Kamiko Island, north of Hokkaido. Reminiscent of the final act of *King Kong* (1933), Godzilla's battle with fighter planes, partly shot on an outdoor set, includes innovative views of the monster, filmed at low angles, with snow-capped peaks towering above, alternately highlighting the monster's immense size compared to man and its relative small-ness in the scheme of nature. The battle is masterfully edited, with overhead shots zooming past Godzilla, viewed from the pilots' perspective, and fine wire manipulation of the model planes as they maneuver through and above the white canyons. Godzilla's optically animated ray turns steamy in the icy air, and the bombardment of the mountain and ensuing avalanche, filmed at high speed, are well staged. The frozen tomb covering Godzilla was made by crushing huge ice blocks and then using a snowmaking machine, borrowed from a ski resort, to blanket the set. Unable to kill the monster, the airmen succeed in burying it alive, but not before Godzilla shoots and swats down numerous planes in the tense, protracted battle.

Like its predecessor, *Godzilla Raids Again* is an entertainment picture informed by the realities of 1950s Japan and a story of families and friends banding together to rebuild after total destruction. It ponders how a country devoted to peace and recovery might respond if war were to break out again. In the end, Tsukioka confronts his demons and delivers the final, decisive shot against Godzilla, but only after his devoted friend Kobayashi is killed in action. The film seems to ask: Could young men be sent into battle again, and if so, at what cost?

TOP: Eiji Tsuburaya (*left*) and Anguirus suit actor Katsumi Tezuka share a lighter moment in between takes. ■ **ABOVE:** A new set of legs, worn with suspenders, was created for filming close-up shots of Godzilla's feet. ■ **OPPOSITE TOP:** Anguirus strikes a defiant pose. ■ **OPPOSITE BOTTOM:** Long shot of the monsters facing off in Osaka Castle Park.

LEFT: Haruo Nakajima gets into the Godzilla suit. Suit maker Teizo Toshimitsu is holding the head. ▪ **BELOW LEFT:** Katsumi Tezuka as Anguirus (*right*) goes over the battle plan with Nakajima (*inside Godzilla*) and suit maker Toshimitsu (*center*). ▪ **OPPOSITE TOP:** Eiji Tsuburaya discusses a scene with Nakajima as Godzilla. ▪ **OPPOSITE BOTTOM:** The effects crew creates the snow-covered mountains of Kamiko Island for the finale using a snowmaking machine. ▪ **FOLLOWING SPREAD, CLOCKWISE FROM TOP LEFT:** Jets fly past Godzilla and bombard the mountainside to create an avalanche. Huge miniature mountains were built on an open set. ▪ The large indoor set of icy Kamiko Island—the oil drums are about to be ignited to block Godzilla's escape from the island. ▪ Godzilla reacts as Kobayashi's plane flies past.

Godzilla Raids Again was one of Toho's top earners for 1955, selling 8.3 million tickets. But the studio did not immediately commit to a continuing series of Godzilla movies. In the second half of the 1950s, it would instead enable the talents of Eiji Tsuburaya and his special effects artists to flourish in a wide-ranging slate of science-fiction and fantasy films, exploring new techniques made possible by color photography and the widescreen process, newly available to Japanese studios. Godzilla's survival left open the possibility of more sequels, but writer Shigeru Kayama made it clear he would not be back. "What had started as a symbol representing his fear of atomic weapons had morphed into a character that produced feelings of intimacy and closeness from the viewing audience," writes Kayama biographer Jeffrey Angles. "Viewers sympathized with the monster [when it] was destroyed." Kayama, too, felt sorry for the way Godzilla suffered; watching the monster melted by the Oxygen Destroyer and then covered in ice had given him nightmares. "I have firmly decided not to write any sequels," Kayama concluded. "No matter how much the film studio may ask."

GIGANTIS, THE FIRE MONSTER

RELEASED: JUNE 2, 1959 (USA, WARNER BROS. PICTURES INC.)

The success of *Godzilla, King of the Monsters!* opened an export market for inexpensively acquired and highly profitable science-fiction films, but the pathway from Japan to Hollywood could be problematic. As Toho successfully gained a foothold in the US and the West, it struck a Faustian bargain wherein many of its genre pictures were altered via dubbing, reediting, music replacement, and changes to titles and credits. Among the most extensively modified Toho films was *Godzilla Raids Again*, which reached US theaters in 1959 in a highly doctored form under the new title *Gigantis, the Fire Monster*. In arguably one of the most questionable marketing decisions in movie history, the US distributors changed Godzilla's name.

The US rights to *Godzilla Raids Again* were originally acquired by some of the same individuals responsible for *King of the Monsters!*, but this time their plans were more ambitious. Utilizing only Tsuburaya's effects footage, the producers intended to create an entirely different film with an American cast titled *The Volcano Monsters*, based on a script by writers Ib Melchior and Ed Watson, wherein Godzilla and Anguirus were referred to as "tyrannosaurus" and "ankylosaurus," and the city of Osaka, site of the creatures' big battle, was to be masqueraded as San Francisco's Chinatown. Toho's special effects team sent new Godzilla and Anguirus suits to Hollywood to enable the producers to shoot additional monster footage. "The idea was that we didn't want anyone to know this was a Japanese film," Melchior recalled, "so we eliminated the entire Japanese story and cast."

ABOVE: The Godzilla and Anguirus suits that were specially created for *The Volcano Monsters*, pictured with the Toho suit-making team: Teizo Toshimitsu (*kneeling*), Kanju Yagi (*left*), Eizo Kaimai (*center*), and Yoshio Suzuki (*right*). This Godzilla is a hybrid: Its face resembles the 1954 Godzilla, the basic form and fins are similar to the suit from *Godzilla Raids Again*, and it foreshadows the suit for *King Kong vs. Godzilla*. It was made of lighter and more durable materials, and Godzilla's body is 8 inches (20 cm) taller to accommodate the height of an American performer. No footage utilizing these suits appears to have been shot, and the suits vanished after the cancellation of the project.

Plans for *The Volcano Monsters* were shelved when AB-PT Pictures, the production company behind the project, folded. Then, in 1958, the *Godzilla Raids Again* rights were acquired by another group of producers, who treated Oda's film to a low-budget reworking for American cinemas. It was dubbed into English (actor Keye Luke portrayed the main character and narrator) and heavily reedited with newsreel clips and stock footage from low-budget science-fiction movies; much of Masaru Sato's music was replaced with library cues, and the Hokkaido University song "Miyabi," sung by Tsukioka and his military buddies, was inexplicably overdubbed with "For He's a Jolly Good Fellow." *Gigantis, the Fire Monster* was released through Warner Bros. on a double bill with the cult classic *Teenagers from Outer Space* (1959).

The title *Gigantis* was intended to masquerade this as an all-new monster film rather than a sequel. "We called it *Gigantis*," recalled producer Paul Schreibman, "because we didn't want it to be confused with *Godzilla*." *Gigantis* faded into obscurity, while Schreibman, an entertainment attorney, would forge a long and successful relationship with Toho, helping facilitate the sale of US rights for numerous films.

(*KINGU KONGU TAI GOJIRA*)
RELEASED: AUGUST 11, 1962 (JAPAN)

KING KONG VS. GODZILLA

B y the time Godzilla returned from a seven-year hiatus, much had changed. Japan was now enjoying its historic "economic miracle," one of the most dramatic periods of growth and prosperity in modern history. During these boom years, the Japanese movie industry flourished with record numbers of films and record-breaking attendance. Simultaneously, the number of households with television sets, once considered a luxury item, also exploded. But there were trade-offs. Lowbrow TV programs were accused of dumbing down the populace, and among the most popular was *puroresu* (professional wrestling), with live broadcasts of violent, bloody bouts between Japanese heroes, such as the legendary Rikidozan, and their villainous opponents (often Americans) tossing one another around the ring.

No wonder, then, that the star monsters of *King Kong vs. Godzilla* do judo flips, hurl and kick boulders, and mock one another like wrestlers putting on a show. The third Godzilla film is a lighthearted satire, a hybrid of Toho's popular white-collar salaryman comedies and *tokusatsu*, two genres that had helped restore the studio's commercial supremacy in the second half of the fifties. Post-*Godzilla*, Ishiro Honda and Eiji Tsuburaya had collaborated on a string of successful giant monster and alien-invasion spectacles including *Rodan* (1956), *The Mysterians* (1957), and *Battle in Outer Space* (1959). In particular, *Mothra* (1961) signaled new directions for kaiju films, with a sympathetic

"IT WILL BE A CLASH BETWEEN THE MASSIVENESS OF GODZILLA AND THE AGILITY OF KONG. LIKE A HEAVY-WEIGHT-CLASS PRO WRESTLING MATCH."

—Eiji Tsuburaya, director of special effects

hero-monster and a family-friendly story that incorporated comedy, fantasy, and popular music. Toho's sci-fi films were increasingly made with an eye toward foreign sales; *Mothra* marked the studio's first significant collaboration with Hollywood. Columbia Pictures had invested in the production and, for overseas marketability, asked that the ending take place not in Japan but a fictitious city resembling New York. *Mothra* was a big hit, one of Japan's most highly attended films of the year.

King Kong vs. Godzilla was part of Toho's much-hyped slate of thirtieth anniversary films and the first Godzilla movie in color, Toho Scope (the studio's widescreen format), and with a stereophonic soundtrack. It embraced the comic side of kaiju, with a story that is part monster mash and part *manzai,* a traditional style of straight man–funny man comedy. Tako (Ichiro Arishima), the manic publicity manager of Pacific Pharmaceuticals, tries to boost the rating of an unpopular TV program his company sponsors by dispatching hot-headed cameraman Sakurai (Tadao Takashima) and his bumbling soundman sidekick, Furue (Yu Fujiki), to tiny Faro Island, located in the Solomon Islands chain, to investigate rumors of a "mammoth evil spirit," which turns out to be the mighty Kong. The men and their goofy interpreter (Senkichi Omura) appease the island natives (Japanese actors in dark makeup), then tow a sedated Kong back to Japan with plans to exploit the creature on TV. Meanwhile, Godzilla, glowing with radioactivity, bursts out of an iceberg in the Arctic, destroys a United Nations submarine, then trashes a military out-post (which appears to be Soviet) and heads south. Godzilla's territorial traits are explained by Shigezawa (Akihiko Hirata), a government scientist, who says Godzilla has a "homing instinct" and will "return to Japan without fail." It's a brief but important rationale for much of Godzilla's behavior through the decades. Kong plows through Japan; Godzilla heads for a confrontation with the simian.

Given Eiji Tsuburaya's admiration for the original *King Kong*, there is a bittersweetness to the story behind *King Kong vs. Godzilla* and the fact that Kong—by necessity—was created via suitmation rather than model animation. In 1960, Willis O'Brien, now relegated to working on low-budget pictures, sought to revive his great ape in a proposed film titled *King Kong vs. Frankenstein*. O'Brien partnered with independent producer John Beck, who tried unsuccessfully to sell the idea to Hollywood studios. Beck then pitched the idea to Toho, which seized an opportunity to pit its own marquee monster against an even more famous foe in

PREVIOUS SPREAD: Special effects director Eiji Tsuburaya (*right*) gives directions to monster actor Haruo Nakajima (*inside the Godzilla suit*) before filming a scene. Fellow suit actor Katsumi Tezuka (*with headband*), providing support to Nakajima, listens in. ■ **ABOVE:** Tako (Ichiro Arishima) rejoices at the publicity that Kong has brought to the company. ■ **LEFT:** Making contact with the Faro Island natives: (*left to right*) Senkichi Omura (Kono, the interpreter), Tadao Takashima (Sakurai), and Yu Fujiki (Furue).

ABOVE: A bon voyage party for the explorers heading to Faro Island; (*left to right*) Cameraman Osamu Sakurai (Tadao Takashima), Tamiye (Akiko Wakabayashi), Fumiko Sakurai (Mie Hama), and sound man Kinsaburo Furue (Yu Fujiki). ■ **RIGHT:** The giant octopus attacks the islanders prior to its fatal fight with Kong. Depending on the scene, Tsuburaya employed one of several live octopi (the crew would eat them for lunch after filming), a rubber octopus prop wrapped in cellophane (for a slimy look), stop-motion tentacles that interacted with the actors via blue-screen compositing, or live-action tentacles suspended by wires (shown here). ■ **BOTTOM RIGHT:** Filming the Faro Island native ceremony to calm the great devil god Kong.

"I WROTE THE TITLE AS *GODZILLA VS. KING KONG*, BUT THEY CHANGED IT TO *KING KONG VS. GODZILLA* TO HONOR THE AMERICAN STAR."

—Shinichi Sekizawa, screenwriter, *King Kong vs. Godzilla*

an East-versus-West epic. The project became *King Kong vs. Godzilla,* with Beck brokering a deal with RKO Pictures for Kong to appear in the movie, while discarding O'Brien's original treatment.

Screenwriter Shinichi Sekizawa had a knack for light comedy, likable characters, and big monster showdowns that was well matched to Ishiro Honda's easygoing directing style. Seikizawa later recalled the excitement surrounding the production. "I remember thinking, *I might get to write about that guy who climbed the Empire State Building,*" he said. Though the tone is far removed from the original *King Kong,* Sekizawa included homages to it, such as the wooden ramparts on Faro Island that protect the natives from their monster-god and Kong beating his chest. "Instead of goofing around and trying to come up with something new, I thought it would be better to keep what's already there. Those things were a must," he said. Certain references to the 1933 film—Kong snatching a female in his hand and climbing atop a building—were stipulated by RKO.

After dividing the late fifties between genre pictures and comedies and dramas about life in postwar Japan, Honda was now firmly established as Toho's foremost director of science-fiction films. He maintains a brisk tempo throughout, with characters alternately chasing after or fleeing the monsters when not capturing their fights for the TV cameras. Takashima and Fujiki have a natural on-screen chemistry, and their bickering and banter contrasts well with Arishima's frantic energy; all three actors were among Toho's top comedy stars. A subplot has Sakurai's sister, Fumiko (Mie Hama), as a damsel in distress whose train travel is twice interrupted by monsters. Passengers aboard an express on the Tohoku Main Line are forced to disembark in the mountains and flee as Godzilla approaches beneath a moonlit sky and tramples the train. Fumiko is delirious with fear, splashing desperately through a streambed until she's rescued by her boyfriend, Fujita (Kenji Sahara). In an homage to Fay Wray, Kong spies Fumiko through the window of the Tokyo Metro Marunouchi Line, then snatches the woman in his palm.

The memorable Godzilla-versus-train sequence is a fine example of the coordination between the Honda and Tsuburaya teams, shooting the live-action drama—in this case, on location at Gotemba, near Mount Fuji—and special effects footage on a Toho stage. By now the two directors had an established system involving advance planning and storyboarding, constant communication via assistant directors, and one-on-one meetings. Colleagues said the men developed an unusually close understanding in which words were not required. "They could almost read each other's minds," remembered Haruo Nakajima. "When I went to Stage No. 9 every morning at 9 A.M., they were already there, discussing the connections between the drama and effects parts. . . . Mr. Honda goes, 'How do you want to handle this part?' and Oyaji-san answers, 'I think it'll work out like this.' They understood one another just by saying 'this part' and 'that part.' I had no idea what they were talking about."

TOP: Godzilla prepares to attack a military base in the Bering Sea. ■ ABOVE: The comic trio: (*left to right*) Tadao Takashima (Sakurai), Yu Fujiki (Furue), and Ichiro Arishima (Tako). ■ BELOW LEFT: Eiji Tsuburaya (*foreground*) and team prepare the miniature set for the giant octopus's attack on a hut. ■ BELOW RIGHT: The giant octopus comes ashore on Faro Island. ■ OPPOSITE: (*clockwise from top left*) Assorted materials from the original theatrical release of *King Kong vs. Godzilla* and subsequent rereleases: 1970 Champion Matsuri poster; 1977 Champion Matsuri poster; 1962 countryside poster; 1962 standard poster; and 1977 Champion Matsuri lobby card. ■ FOLLOWING SPREAD: Godzilla attacks the Tsugaru Express train.

Asi anaroi a seke samoai
Asi anaroi a seke samoai
Ke keletena ke keletena
Ina mang fanadoro sa qu tia
Ina mang fanadoro sa qu tia
*Ke keletena ke keletena**

When Godzilla battles the military or Kong stomps Tokyo, Honda and Tsuburaya set comic antics aside and *King Kong vs. Godzilla* temporarily becomes a straightforward giant monster movie. These tonal shifts are relatively seamless, thanks in large part to the music of Akira Ifukube, which lends an unironic and cohesive sense of pathos and scale. "Song of Faro Island," the main theme, is a recurring motif of chanting and percussion with lyrics reportedly culled from actual folk songs of the Solomon Islands, elevating a studio-bound scene in which the Faro islanders lull a drugged Kong to sleep with a big production number led by a beautiful dancer (Akemi Negishi). This is Ifukube's first monster-versus-monster score, and the composer writes distinctive themes for each creature. Notably, the first iteration of his "Terror of Godzilla" motif is introduced, with low brass and a series of chromatic phrases that would become synonymous with Godzilla's appearances over time.

A KAIJU COMEDIAN

By now, Haruo Nakajima's physical strength and willingness to accept any challenge were well known. However, inside the Godzilla suit, nothing was easy.

"At the end of the movie, when King Kong and Godzilla are intertwined and fall into the sea from a cliff, there wasn't enough planning. They just told us to fall together, so we did, into the Big Pool, in one take. This time out, the Godzilla suit had a motor in its head to operate the mouth movements by radio control. When I fell into the water, Godzilla sank headfirst. I had to wait upside down in the water [to be pulled out]. It was not a big deal because I could hold my breath for quite a long time."

In the first encounter between the two monsters near Mount Nasu, there is a noticeable change in Godzilla's behavior. It taunts its opponent and waves its arms, suddenly displaying an intelligence and personality to match Kong's. "By this time Godzilla had become quite anthropomorphic, as if to please the audience," Nakajima recalled. Playing Kong was burly Shoichi Hirose, a fellow B2 actor nicknamed "Solomon" for having fought in the 1942 Battle of the Eastern Solomons with the Imperial Navy. Nakajima was again charged with choreographing the monster battles, but Hirose's first outing in a kaiju suit was challenging. "'Without the suit on you make a great King Kong, but once you put the suit on, you aren't Kong,'" Nakajima remembered telling Hirose. "His acting, movement, and expression were mediocre. . . . Mr. Tsuburaya whispered, 'Well, there's no future for Mr. Hirose as a monster actor.'" (Hirose would, however, later play King Ghidorah.)

The final showdown is the first Toho monster battle to take place, significantly, beneath Mount Fuji, the tallest mountain in Japan and the nation's sacred symbol, surrounded by temples and shrines. In this revered spot, the monsters engage in a battle alternately fierce and silly. They tumble downhill and volley

"WE'LL LET THEM DESTROY EACH OTHER."

—Dr. Onuki (Somesho Matsumoto)

boulders, and after Kong KO's himself by slamming headfirst into a rock, Godzilla buries the ape and ignites a forest funeral pyre. The momentum shifts when Kong is super-charged by a lightning storm; a line of dialogue notes the likeness to Popeye, the spinach-eating cartoon sailor, and the fight rages downhill to the seaside town of Atami, where Nakajima and Hirose trash touristy Atami Castle before falling into the sea. Tsuburaya's team built three beautiful miniature models of the castle and town to enable filming both indoors as well as at the Big Pool, on an open set.

Tsuburaya's work had earned recognition outside Japan, including profiles by *American Cinematographer* magazine and the Associated Press. He now felt compelled to create work that not only played well at the Japanese box office, but internationally; there was little margin for error. Godzilla and Kong's climactic ocean dive was shot by three cameras in a single take, but when one cameraman worried aloud that he may have framed the shot incorrectly, Tsuburaya fumed. "He said, 'What the heck are you doing? People all over the world are watching!'" Nakajima remembered. "It was very unusual that the normally calm [Tsuburaya] got that upset." Honda, meanwhile, had concerns about shifting audience expectations and Godzilla's evolution into a movie star. "I did the best I could with it, and Mr. Tsuburaya did his best as well," Honda later said. "It was about that time that Godzilla movies started to move toward a younger audience. [But] to make Godzilla act like a human showed off the fact that it was a man in a suit."

A MONSTER HIT

"People were making a big deal out of [TV] ratings," said Honda. "But my own view of TV shows was that they took the audience for granted." *King Kong vs. Godzilla* partly succeeds as a critique of television, but the monsters take center stage by the third act. Messages aside, the film was a runaway hit, selling 11.2 million tickets and placing fourth in annual box office rankings. To date, it remains the most-attended live-action Japanese science-fiction film of all time, and its success set the stage for a continuing Godzilla

OPPOSITE, TOP & BOTTOM: A river of fire herds Godzilla toward a poisoned pit trap. Rather than optical composition, here actors in military uniforms were filmed in the foreground on set, creating a forced-perspective view of Godzilla in the distance. ■ **RIGHT:** Kong (Shoichi Hirose, *off-screen*) swings Godzilla by the tail—with Haruo Nakajima inside the Godzilla suit!

THE UNUSED ENDING

***

Early drafts of *King Kong vs. Godzilla* ended with an epilogue. Announcers report that no trace of either monster can be found, then the scene abruptly shifts to Kong and Godzilla fighting, and Tako is heard shouting, "No, no, no, that's no good!" The monsters remove their heads to reveal they're really Sakurai and Furue in costume, shooting a commercial. Sakurai suddenly remembers that his sister's wedding is today, and the men rush out the door, still in costume, and jump onto a flatbed truck that drives wildly to the wedding hall, causing panic and alarm. Responding to reports of an infant Godzilla and Kong, a squad of police cars gives chase, and the scene fades out. More outright farce than comic satire, this ending was deleted from the final script.

franchise. Even so, it remains something of a one-off. Though Godzilla would continue to develop anthropomorphic traits, no future Toho kaiju movie would be an out-and-out comedy again.

It should be noted that this chapter covers the original, Japanese-language version of *King Kong vs. Godzilla*, which first became available in the US in 2019 through the Criterion Collection. For the preceding fifty-six years, the film was seen in America and certain Western territories only in a drastically altered version produced by John Beck and released theatrically in 1963 by Universal-International. Scenes were deleted and reordered, Ifukube's music was largely replaced with library cues, and Honda's TV satire was obfuscated by frequent inserts of actors portraying newscasters. This cut is largely responsible for the criticism the film has received outside Japan. The existence of different versions across the globe also led to a legendary rumor that each edit had a different ending, with Kong winning the fight in America and Godzilla in Japan. In truth, both versions end the same way: ambiguously, with Kong swimming 3,000 miles (4,828 km) back to Faro Island and Godzilla disappearing below the depths.

THANK YOU, GODZILLA

"After *King Kong vs. Godzilla* was released, I was summoned by the chief of the studio," Nakajima remembered. "I thought I did something wrong and expected to be scolded, but as it turned out, he gave me a bonus envelope. Inside was ¥50,000, probably equivalent to ¥500,000 nowadays. He gave one to Solomon [Shoichi Hirose] too, who played King Kong. It was the one and only time that they gave us a bonus. The film was that big of a hit."

LEFT: The special effects director works with monster actors Haruo Nakajima (*inside Godzilla suit*) and Shoichi Hirose (*inside Kong suit, behind Godzilla*) during the filming of the end battle scene at Mount Fuji.

CLOCKWISE FROM TOP: Sakurai, Tako, and Furue react in horror as Kong is roasted by Godzilla during the battle in Nasu. ▪ In the film's climactic moments, Godzilla (Haruo Nakajima) taunts Kong at Atami Castle, an elaborate miniature set. Although the set appears to be built on a table, the visible structure represents real support beams built into the mountainside next to Atami Castle. ▪ The "Godzilla suit handlers" assist monster actor Nakajima (*facing camera, in T-shirt, emerging from the Godzilla suit*) out of the Big Pool after the monsters' tumble into the ocean. ▪ The special effects team makes preparations for the final showdown scene at Atami Castle, filmed on an open set next to the Big Pool on the Toho lot. The backdrop surrounding the pool can be seen here.

(*MOSURA TAI GOJIRA*)
aka *Godzilla vs. The Thing*
RELEASED: APRIL 29, 1964 (JAPAN)

MOTHRA VS. GODZILLA

In September 1959, Japan was hit by Super Typhoon Vera, the deadliest tropical storm in its history. Originating near Guam, the cyclone tracked northward across the Pacific and struck the southern coast of Honshu, Japan's main island, with winds exceeding 160 mph (257 kph). The coastline was pounded, farms and industries were destroyed, the harbor was ruined, and parts of Nagoya city were submerged. More than five thousand people were killed, forty thousand injured, and 1.5 million left homeless. Temporary pumps were deployed to return water to the sea, and recovery efforts lasted five years.

Mothra vs. Godzilla opens with Eiji Tsuburaya's dramatic staging of a disaster closely resembling Typhoon Vera, from the location of the destruction to the pumps that drain the flood zone. Torrential rains crash down, the sea roils, and walls of water demolish the shoreline. It's an exciting start to the fourth Godzilla movie, one of the most entertaining entries in the original series, with big-scale special effects set pieces, a snarling Godzilla battling an unexpectedly formidable opponent, and memorable characters in a fast-moving story that satirizes rising commercialism and greed even as it optimistically calls for goodwill among humankind. This arguably represents the high point of Tsuburaya's collaboration with director Honda, as well as the

"MOTHRA'S ROLE WAS A MESSENGER OF PEACE. I THINK THE IDEA OF MOTHRA SHOWED WHAT MR. HONDA WAS LIKE AT HEART BETTER THAN GODZILLA DID."

—Hiroshi Koizumi (Professor Miura)

creative contributions of screenwriter Sekizawa and composer Ifukube, whose suite of stirring motifs again propels the pathos and drama.

Godzilla ceases the humorous and humanized antics of the previous outing and slowly stalks Japan with menacing purpose, motivated by territoriality and resembling the emotionless, destructive force of 1954. The monster fells major landmarks and rebuffs attempts by the Self-Defense Forces to repel it with tanks, napalm bombs, air-dropped nets, and an "artificial lightning" field. In contrast to the malice of Godzilla, the elegant, graceful Mothra assumes the role of a benevolent, deified monster that dies for the misdeeds of man and is reborn to save Japan from Godzilla's wrath. The two battles between the kaiju are surprisingly dramatic; adult Mothra fearlessly defends its offspring from Godzilla's aggression, and the outmatched larva display cunning intelligence in rendering Godzilla powerless.

The agreement with John Beck for production of *King Kong vs. Godzilla* effectively granted Toho a five-year exclusive negotiation window for the right to make more King Kong movies. Thus, following that film's incredible success, the studio began preparations for a sequel under the working title *King Kong vs. Godzilla 2* or *Continuation: King Kong vs. Godzilla*. In the treatment by Shinichi Sekizawa, an airliner crashes in the jungle and the only survivor, a baby, is raised by King Kong. When the child is discovered by explorers and brought to Japan, Kong follows. Meanwhile, a dormant Godzilla is found at the sea bottom near Atami and thought to be dead. The operators of a nearby amusement park advertise Godzilla as their main attraction, and while they attempt to revive the monster with electrical shocks, Kong arrives. Godzilla awakens and the monsters fight, trashing the amusement park, then go their separate ways, licking their wounds. Kong tracks the child all the way to the southern tip of Kyushu, until Godzilla emerges from Mount Aso (Japan's largest active volcano) for the final battle. This was one of several interesting Toho films announced in 1963–64 but ultimately canceled; others included *Frankenstein vs. the Human Vapor* (a sequel to *The Human Vapor*, Honda's 1960 tale of a murderer who transforms into gas) and *Frankenstein vs. Godzilla* (which evolved into *Frankenstein Conquers the World* in 1965). The amusement park setting was timely, for Japan was in the midst of a postwar leisure boom that saw parks like the Disney-inspired Nara Dreamland flourishing. Sekizawa would reuse the concept when he began writing *Mothra vs. Godzilla* in late 1963, and Toho announced the film on January 10, 1964, as part of its annual slate. It was fast-tracked for release just three and a half months later, yet it arguably stands as Tsuburaya's most ambitious and fully realized entry of the original Godzilla series.

PREVIOUS SPREAD: Godzilla is challenged by its most formidable foe, Mothra. ■ **BELOW LEFT:** Fishing boats approach Mothra's egg. ■ **BELOW RIGHT:** When the giant egg suddenly appears in their fishing waters, the villagers gather on the beach while a Shinto priest performs a ritual to ward off misfortune.

MERCIFUL MOTHRA

A gigantic egg, dislodged from Infant Island by the typhoon, floats to Japan and, in scenes masterfully executed by Tsuburaya via both miniature work and composite photography (utilizing Toho's new Oxberry optical printer, acquired from the US), the egg is brought ashore by local fishermen. The villagers exploit the situation for profit, selling the egg to oily businessman Kumayama (Yoshibumi Tajima), whose silent partner is the cash-hoarding young financier Torahata (Kenji Sahara). The men are constructing an amusement park, with plans to charge admission to watch the egg hatch in a big incubator ("The entire world will be watching!"—with no thought to what dangerous thing might emerge!). When newsman Sakai (Akira Takarada), rookie photographer Junko (Yuriko Hoshi), and scientist Miura (Hiroshi Koizumi) investigate the egg's appearance, the *shobijin* (Small Beauties), Mothra's tiny fairy muses from Infant Island (The Peanuts singing duo, Emi and Yumi Ito), appeal to the heroes for help bringing the egg home. Kumayama refuses to cooperate; instead, he crassly tries to buy the fairies for his amusement park. The fairies depart, saddened "that certain people cared so little for our feelings." Soon all hell breaks loose when a dormant Godzilla, washed ashore by the typhoon and buried under mud and earth, reawakens and heads for the egg.

After Japan joined the United Nations in 1957, Ishiro Honda pivoted to themes of global cooperation to confront world-threatening crises in films such as *The Mysterians* (1957), *Battle in Outer Space* (1959), and *Gorath* (1962). *Mothra vs. Godzilla* shares a similar idealism, but instead of an international alliance, it is expressed through an emotional appeal to humanity. As Godzilla destroys the Yokkaichi petrochemical complex and advances on Nagoya, the situation grows dire, and so the heroes decide to humbly ask Mothra's help to defeat Godzilla. "Infant Island may despise us," Miura says, "but I'm willing to accept their scorn and make a sincere appeal." The primitive islanders—turned away by Japan, their world despoiled by "the devil's fire" of nuclear tests, and likely having been occupied during the war—at first shed no tears for the "divine retribution" Japan faces. The heroes' plea expresses Honda's ideal: "We too want a world where we can trust one another," Sakai says. "Please don't be quick to judge us." Moved to compassion, the fairies beseech their spirit god and, though dying, Mothra sacrifices its remaining life to aid Japan and protect its progeny.

> ## "FROM THE APPEARANCE OF THE ADULT MOTHRA, WHICH EXUDES A SENSE OF LIFE, TO THE SPECTACULAR ENTRANCE OF GODZILLA, THIS FILM TRULY MARKS THE GOLDEN ERA OF GODZILLA FILMS MADE BY TSUBURAYA."
>
> —Koichi Kawakita (SFX crew member)

GODZILLA THE BELIEVABLE

Special effects in this Godzilla film take a significant leap forward, with numerous Tsuburaya flourishes: a stunning aerial view of Mothra's egg awash on a beach, a widescreen landscape with Godzilla and the adult Mothra battling, and Godzilla looming above the city or suddenly appearing over a ridgeline. The meshing of effects and live action is smoother, thanks to clever intercutting and advancements in composite photography that enable Tsuburaya and Honda to put humans in the path of monsters with greater believability. In contrast to the set-bound look of previous films, an unprecedented amount of footage shot on location enhances the sense of realism. Large-scale location shoots were conducted in and around the Yokkaichi refinery—where the production was granted access to the grounds, personnel to act as extras, work clothes, helmets, and even the firetrucks that respond when Godzilla sets the plant ablaze—and Nagoya city, where a throng of two hundred extras flees the real-life Nagoya TV Tower (Japan's first broadcast tower) and the historic Nagoya Castle (destroyed in the war, but mostly restored by 1964) just before Godzilla wrecks them in miniature.

As the heroes survey the typhoon-battered coastal area for radiation, the mud flats begin rumbling in the distance. A giant steam cloud spouts up, and suddenly Godzilla's tail erupts from the ground! The dead-eyed monster slowly emerges and shakes the loose earth from its body. Filming this now-classic entrance scene was yet another physical test for Haruo Nakajima inside the suit. "Tsuburaya knew that Nakajima's work could be dangerous," scripter Keiko Suzuki remembered. "They buried Godzilla in dirt, and he was supposed to rise out of it. It was scary just to watch. They didn't bury his head until the very last moment; as soon as his head was covered, they started filming right away. Everybody was worried about him, and they all kept asking, 'Are you OK?' Then his back rises out of the dirt. He had tremendous strength."

The battle with adult Mothra presented a different challenge—instead of choreographing a fight with another actor, Nakajima first practiced the action outside the suit, pantomiming with the large Mothra puppet, which hung from wires attached to a moving brace that was operated from above. Nakajima recalled, "The wire staff moved Mothra in response to my actions, like when Godzilla tried to attack Mothra, Mothra flapped its wings and went backward. It was all about planning and working together. It was the first time Godzilla fought a wire-controlled monster." In a symphony of Tsuburaya effects, Mothra drags

ABOVE: The US fleet bombards Godzilla.

THE FRONTIER MISSILE MYSTERY

At a joint Japan-US military tactical conference, it is announced that a new weapon, the Frontier Missile, will be deployed to stop Godzilla's rampage. US battleships spot Godzilla walking along the coast and launch a blistering attack. But when the smoke clears, the monster emerges unscathed.

For viewers in the West, the Frontier Missile sequence has remained a highlight of *Mothra vs. Godzilla*. But when the film was first released in 1964, and for decades afterward, Japanese audiences never saw it.

Why would this memorable sequence have been omitted from the Japanese release? Some have speculated that its depiction of US military action on Japanese soil was problematic, but the reasons appear to be more practical than political. On March 17, 1964, while the film was in production, Toho dropped the sequence from the shooting schedule to avoid jeopardizing the release date of April 29, the start of Golden Week holidays. In an unprecedented move, the sequence was rescheduled and shot later and included in the export version only.

The Frontier Missile attack appeared in Toho's first two shooting schedules and all three versions of Shinichi Sekizawa's screenplay, indicating that it was to be part of the domestic version if scheduling had allowed. Nevertheless, after production was finished on April 15, the sequence was completed over the following weeks. At Toho's Big Pool, Tsuburaya's special effects team filmed long shots of Godzilla walking on the beach and the American fleet launching missiles; next, the Godzilla suit was taken to the Nakatajima Sand Dunes in Hamamatsu to supplement explosion footage previously shot there in February. Tsuburaya then edited the effects footage before leaving for Hawaii to work on Frank Sinatra's war film *None but the Brave* (1965). Concurrently, director Honda filmed the military conference and scenes aboard the American destroyer on Toho's Stage No. 6. Dubbing and editing were completed on May 9, two weeks after the film had hit Japanese cinemas.

Meanwhile, *Variety* reported on May 6, 1964, that United Productions of America paid a then-hefty $225,000 fee, equivalent to over half the film's reported production budget, to acquire the US theatrical and TV rights from Toho. UPA retitled the film *Godzilla vs. The Thing* and released it through American International Pictures in August of that year.

Significant changes were made before the Frontier Missile attack was shot. As originally written, the naval fleet was from the United Nations, and the missiles were provided by Rolisica, the fictional US/Russia stand-in of Honda's *Mothra*. The attack took place not at the beach but at the Tenryu River, with an explosive force so great that it hurtled military personnel and equipment backward and created a deep crater; amid the smoke and debris, Godzilla appeared vanquished, then climbed out of the hole, as in *King Kong vs. Godzilla*.

Given UPA's investment, were these late-breaking revisions made at its behest? Did UPA president Henry G. Saperstein believe an assault by the US Seventh Fleet (with the stars and stripes rippling in the wind) would better appeal to American audiences than an international effort by the United Nations and fictional Rolisica? These questions remain mysterious.

The JSDF usually goes it alone against Godzilla; despite America's postwar commitment to protect Japan's security, the US military is almost never asked to intervene. The Frontier Missile bombardment is a rare and interesting exception, but it remained unreleased in Japan until 1993, when the US cut of *Godzilla vs. The Thing* was a bonus feature on Toho's *Mothra vs. Godzilla* laserdisc.

CLOCKWISE FROM TOP: UPA president Henry G. Saperstein. ▪ The suit team, led by Katsumi Tezuka (*far left*) prepares for shooting at the Big Pool. Haruo Nakajima is in the Godzilla suit. ▪ Godzilla walks across the beach as the pyrotechnics crew sets off charges planted just beneath the surface of the sand. ▪ Preparing to shoot at the Nakatajima Sand Dunes. Godzilla rests on a box as Tezuka adjusts the tail. Eizo Kaimai (*white hat*) talks to Nakajima, who is inside the suit.

Godzilla far away from the egg—achieved via high-speed filming and frame removal, giving the winged creature a smooth, stop-motion-like movement—then pins Godzilla down and attempts to asphyxiate the big reptile with pollen clouds. Though Mothra fights bravely, a strike from Godzilla's heat ray proves fatal.

Akira Takarada, now a top-billed movie star, returns to the series for the first time since his breakout role as Ogata. ("It's been ten years since the first *Godzilla*. I sort of missed it; my feelings are rather complicated," he mused at the time.) The banter between his jaded reporter and the youthful, greenhorn photographer played by Hoshi is charming, but the gleeful grifter Kumayama and the smirking, cigar-chomping slickster Torahata are the real scene-stealers. Actors Tajima and Sahara, both playing against type, relish their roles; Sahara went so far as to research the part by hanging out with pushy real estate speculators. Unlike *King Kong vs. Godzilla*, those responsible for the disaster pay the price. Realizing he's been swindled, an enraged Kumayama storms into Torahata's hotel suite and beats him up. Dazed, Torahata spies Godzilla approaching outside the window and, panicking, shoots Kumayama and tries to escape with a bagful of cash. Godzilla smashes the building, burying the villains.

MELANCHOLY MELODY

Pop music sister act The Peanuts reprise their dual role as the Small Beauties from *Mothra*, wearing fashionable attire and speaking in unison. Arguably the story's greatest highlight is the sisters' performance of the mournful melody "Sacred Spring" ("Seinaru Izumi"), with music and lyrics written in Tagalog by Akira Ifukube. They sing at the last remaining beautiful spot on Infant Island, a lush garden hidden among the barren rocks and beaches scarred by explosions. Director Honda lamented that he wasn't afforded sufficient resources to fully depict the tragedy of the island (the sets are rather undetailed), but the contrast of this verdant, life-sustaining oasis—Honda described it as a "paradise within hell"—is certainly underscored by the fairies' melancholy harmonies. Tsuburaya also employs some new tricks to make the fairies believably tiny, including oversize furniture props—an inversion of the miniaturization techniques that create the illusion of giant monsters.

Mothra vs. Godzilla is perhaps Honda's most fully realized collaboration with composer Ifukube, who contrasts the brash, raw power of Godzilla and the grace of Mothra in operatic clashes of chromatic and diatonic themes that stir the emotions. Here, Ifukube perfects the "Terror of Godzilla" piece introduced in *King Kong vs. Godzilla*; this new, revised composition is heard during the opening credits and several times after, and it would become synonymous with the monster in perpetuity. Ifukube also incorporates Mothra's signature theme, composed by Yuji Koseki for the 1961 eponymous film.

TOP LEFT: Godzilla warily approaches Mothra's egg inside the giant incubator.
■ **TOP RIGHT:** The movement of the Mothra puppet's wings was controlled with an overhead brace mechanism.
■ **ABOVE, TOP TO BOTTOM:** Mothra risks its life to protect the egg. ■ As Godzilla approaches, Torahata kills Kumayama and attempts to escape with the money. Godzilla destroys the building, burying the greedy businessman and his loot beneath the rubble.

CLOCKWISE FROM ABOVE: The Small Beauties of Infant Island look to escape from the greedy businessmen. ▪ (*left to right*) Kumayama (Yoshibumi Tajima) and Torahata (Kenji Sahara) of Happy Enterprises. ▪ Emi and Yumi Ito prepare for a scene on the oversize set of Torahata's hotel room. ▪ Shooting the scene at the Sacred Spring on Infant Island, where the heroes appeal to the Small Beauties for Mothra's help to save Japan from Godzilla. An electric fan is placed in the foreground, off camera, to provide the cast with an eyeline as they pretend to interact with the twin fairies. ▪ "I wanted to visualize the terror and the power of the atomic bomb," director Ishiro Honda later said. "The first Infant Island scene was supposed to be more graphic and realistic, [but] the art department didn't have enough budget to make the set that I wanted. As a director, I should have been more stubborn. The proper way of making a movie is to visualize the director's idea, [but] the businesspeople thought the scene was not important because you could still follow the story without seeing that." ▪ Filming the Infant Island ritual to hatch Mothra's egg.

"CALLS TO BAN NUCLEAR WEAPONS ARE A DIME A DOZEN NOW."

—Sakai (Akira Takarada)

After the villains are killed off, the drama hinges on whether Godzilla will be stopped. The JSDF tries using electricity yet again, and it almost works until an overzealous commander blows the "artificial lightning" transformer. In a third-act twist, Mothra's egg hatches not one but two caterpillars, which pursue Godzilla to Iwato Island for the final showdown. Though overmatched, the twin larvae coordinate their strategy, gradually encasing Godzilla in a cocoon. Ifukube's thundering, eight-minute battle opus turns this lopsided fight into a compelling struggle between darkness and light that ends with a straightjacketed Godzilla—"a white daruma doll wrapped in silk," recalled crew member Hideaki Miyazaki—tumbling into the sea and vanishing. (This required yet another precarious stunt by Haruo Nakajima; a medical doctor was standing by on set, just in case.)

CHILD'S PLAY

By now, the fear that hung over the original *Godzilla* was fading into memory as Japan continued to focus on its economic future. Godzilla still made the Geiger counter click, but this would be the last film of the Honda–Tsuburaya era to portray the monster as an out-and-out threat to humankind. Godzilla was about to enter a reluctant alliance with humanity, defending Japan and the planet from terrestrial and alien threats, and the monster's strong appeal to children in the audience would influence the series' evolving tone and direction. "Kids were becoming the majority of the audience by this time, so it was generally thought that we shouldn't make the monsters too scary," remembered Honda. "No one ever said that to my face, but it was the general feeling that since our films were shown during [holidays], children were coming to see them, so we should make movies for them."

PREVIOUS SPREAD, LEFT TO RIGHT: Sculptor and monster modeling artist Teizo Toshimitsu adding textures to the head of Godzilla from *Mothra vs. Godzilla*. ▪ Godzilla approaches the Hamakaze Hotel. ▪ BELOW, CLOCKWISE FROM TOP LEFT: Plan B: Leading Godzilla into the electrical net trap. ▪ (*three-image sequence*) Godzilla struggles with conductive nets as the military attacks with artificial lightning.

ABOVE: Akira Suzuki uses a fan to shoot Mothra's cocoon at Godzilla. Like *King Kong vs. Godzilla*, this film ends with Godzilla plunging into the sea and vanishing. ■ **RIGHT:** The newly hatched Mothras follow Godzilla to Iwa Island. ■ **BELOW:** The twin caterpillars encase Godzilla in a silken prison. "While we were shooting the climactic showdown scene, I accidentally got some of the Mothra larvae's web [an oil-based substance] in my eye," remembered assistant special effects director Teruyoshi Nakano. "The upper part of my eye swelled up, the pain didn't go away for two or three days, and I worried that I might go blind."

三大怪獣
地球最大の決戦

(SAN DAIKAIJU CHIKYU SAIDAI NO KESSEN /
THREE GIANT MONSTERS: THE GREATEST BATTLE ON EARTH)
RELEASED: DECEMBER 20, 1964 (JAPAN)

GHIDORAH, THE THREE-HEADED MONSTER

While the plot of a kaiju movie serves as a framework for monster action, these stories often mirror the real world in interesting ways. The events that set *Ghidorah, the Three-Headed Monster* in motion recall the *Kashmir Princess* incident of 1955, in which assassins bombed a plane over the South China Sea in a failed attempt to kill Chinese premier Zhou Enlai, who had declined to board at the last minute. *Ghidorah* is a fast-paced mix of international intrigue, doomsday prophecy, monster mayhem, and—signaling a major trajectorial shift—kaiju diplomacy. The eponymous dragon is an unstoppable force, unleashing destruction on par with Godzilla's original rampages a decade earlier. The world's fate hinges on whether Godzilla, Rodan, and Mothra can settle petty differences and join forces.

Princess Salno (Akiko Wakabayashi) of the tiny kingdom of Selgina flees to Japan to escape an assassination plot; en route, she is beckoned by an otherworldly spirit to jump from the plane just before it explodes. She is

"GODZILLA SITS LIKE HE'S BORED—THAT'S MY ACTUAL POSE, WHEN I TAKE A REST INSIDE THE SUIT. IT LOOKED QUITE COMICAL, SO (EIJI) TSUBURAYA DECIDED TO USE IT. ACTING LIKE A HUMAN, KICKING ROCKS, THROWING ROCKS. THE FIRST GODZILLA WAS REALLY SCARY, BUT IT WAS GRADUALLY TURNING INTO A LOVABLE, POPULAR CREATURE."

—Haruo Nakajima, Godzilla suit actor

assumed dead, but soon appears in Yokohama wearing an old fisherman's clothing. The princess remembers nothing of her royal status and instead proclaims herself a visitor from Venus who has visions of imminent disaster for Japan. She accurately predicts the return of Rodan and Godzilla and warns of the arrival of King Ghidorah, which destroyed Venusian civilization eons ago. Selginan killers arrive to finish off the princess-prophetess, who is protected by police detective Shindo (Yosuke Natsuki) and his journalist sister, Naoko (Yuriko Hoshi), who is reporting on a spate of foreboding events: a destructive winter heat wave, an outbreak of deadly encephalitis, global meteor showers, and UFOs in the skies. The heroes are aided by the Small Beauties of Infant Island. Geology professor Murai (Hiroshi Koizumi) investigates a gigantic meteor that has crashed into the Alps and witnesses the emergence of King Ghidorah, which destroys Matsumoto Castle (one of Japan's oldest structures) and launches a series of aerial city attacks. Military officials rule out atomic weapons to kill the monsters. With a crisis looming, the Small Beauties beckon Mothra to intervene; perhaps the caterpillar can convince Rodan and Godzilla to help stop the menace.

Ghidorah represents Toho's genre cinema at the height of its creative power. Scenes were shot on location across Japan, and Eiji Tsuburaya's ambitious effects sequences include monster battles on big landscape sets that fill the widescreen frame, renewed emphasis on urban destruction, and impressive landslides and forest fires. Made during the excitement surrounding the Tokyo Olympiad in October 1964, the film showcases Japan's postwar economic boom, with glimpses of new highways and hordes of visitors fleeing the monsters at tourist sites around the country, including the Mount Aso volcanic crater, Mount Fuji, and historic Matsumoto Castle. The idea for an all-star monster epic first surfaced in April 1964, around the time of *Mothra vs. Godzilla*'s release, when producer Tomoyuki Tanaka told a newspaper, "We want to produce a story where Mothra, Godzilla, and King Kong hold a summit meeting at Mount Fuji." (Toho was still considering a sequel to *King Kong vs. Godzilla*.) Other reports announced a possible New Year's season film featuring Godzilla, Mothra, and Rodan, though plans were still vague. In August 1964, Toho released an early synopsis that mostly resembled the film that would be made, save for a few details; Godzilla emerged from melting ice in the Arctic, an unnamed and undescribed "space monster of unparalleled ferocity" came from a meteor that had been formed "by an exploding planet," and the monsters were confronted by an Earth Defense Force. Rather than keep fighting one another, Tanaka

PREVIOUS SPREAD: Coming to Mothra's aid, Godzilla attacks King Ghidorah. ■ **BELOW LEFT:** The prophetess, aka Princess Salno (Akiko Wakabayashi), warns Japan of impending disaster at the Mount Aso volcanic crater. ■ **BELOW RIGHT:** The Peanuts (Emi and Yumi Ito) reprise their role as the Small Beauties of Infant Island, who now willingly befriend Japan and offer to ask Mothra for help against King Ghidorah.

reckoned that, in an era of Cold War tensions, Earth's monsters must work for world peace. "We liken the monsters to the three major nations of the Soviet Union, the United States, and the United Kingdom," he said. (Indeed, Mothra would play the role of a kaiju Winston Churchill.) He compared the forthcoming monster summit to the US-USSR summits, most recently held in Vienna in 1961; as part of this transformation, Tanaka noted, the monsters would adopt more humanlike, distinct personalities.

Though unconfirmed, *Ghidorah* may have been influenced by *Beautiful Star*, a 1962 novel by Yukio Mishima about a Japanese family whose members believe they are from other planets (their daughter claims to be from Venus), with a mission to save Earth from nuclear destruction. A news item about a music teacher in Kanagawa who claimed to be a reincarnated Venusian may also have provided fodder. The inclusion of a UFO enthusiasts club, scanning the sky with rooftop telescopes, was likely inspired by similar groups (e.g., the Japan Flying Saucer Research Society and the Space Friendship Association), some of whom had attempted to influence the content of *Battle in Outer Space* (1959).

Shinichi Sekizawa's first-draft script, dated August 27, 1964, was titled *Four Monsters: The Biggest Battle in Earth's History;* it differed from the finished film in significant ways and included several references to international affairs. In it, the protagonist, Detective Shindo, is a narcotics investigator pursuing Aikawa, a member of a drug syndicate, who jumps from a rooftop during a UFO club meeting and vanishes, later reappearing near the site of a fallen meteor; he now claims to be a Venusian and foretells the arrival of King Ghidorah (described as having a griffin-like body, giant wings, a single dragon-like head with a horn, and a sharp beak). Godzilla sinks a drug smuggler's ship, and Rodan attacks military bases on both sides of the 38th parallel dividing North and South Korea. King Ghidorah destroys New York, and NATO urges using the world's entire nuclear arsenal against it, but the prophet Aikawa warns against this because the Venusians used all their weapons against King Ghidorah and wiped themselves out. Tripartite talks are held among Japan, NATO, and Aikawa; the prophet beckons Godzilla, Mothra, and Rodan to unite against the space invader. The final script, dated October 7, 1964, ended differently than the completed film—the commander of the international forces flies from New York to Japan to plan an attack against Earth's monsters, but the Small Beauties advise that the creatures will be gone before any action takes place. The closing scene had Godzilla and Rodan vanishing into a dense fog around Mount Fuji.

Ghidorah begins with an opening credits montage of Godzilla, Mothra, and Rodan fighting, backed by a medley of composer Akira Ifukube's stirring monster motifs, a clear acknowledgment of the monsters' star power. King Ghidorah's visage is not revealed until after the midpoint, and it is something to behold. The three-headed dragon is a departure from previous Toho creatures based on prehistoric or extant animals. King Ghidorah resembles the multiheaded Hydra of Greek mythology and the supernatural dragons

THE MAN WHO DREW KING GHIDORAH'S RAY

During the golden age of Toho genre cinema, creating animated rays and other optical effects was the responsibility of Sadao Iizuka, known as the "Man Who Keeps Drawing Rays." *Ghidorah, The Three-Headed Monster* showcased Iizuka's talents like no other film.

For the scene in which King Ghidorah emerges from a meteor, Eiji Tsuburaya told Iizuka, "I want Ghidorah to be born from a fireball." Simply overlapping footage of an actual fireball wouldn't look very interesting, so instead, Iizuka utilized animated flames to transition from a fireball to the fully formed creature, using the character known as the Monster from the Id from 1956's *Forbidden Planet* as his inspiration. By reversing the fireball to make it appear as if King Ghidorah's form is coalescing, and by adding flashes and dissolving the animated flames, Iizuka created one of the most impactful moments in kaiju history.

Tsuburaya thought of King Ghidorah as a fire monster and wanted the creature to exhale straight fire, like a flamethrower. However, with the constant and random movement of King Ghidorah's necks, this would not work. Instead, Iizuka created King Ghidorah's "antigravity ray," its signature lightning-like energy bolts. "If we made the rays like electrical discharges, then it didn't matter which way the necks were pointing. We also realized that a straight-fire type of ray dragged the sense of speed down."

Then came the finishing touch. "When I started working at Toho on *The Mysterians* (1957), I just connected rays to the explosions. Later I realized that [buildings] exploding as soon as they're hit by the ray—no, that would never happen! The [impact] spot should be heated first, then it blows up. So if I hold it for about three frames before the explosion, it's more believable." This subtle change makes the destruction sequences in *Ghidorah* all the more effective.

Iizuka's work dominates the screen in *Ghidorah*. "It had a ridiculous number of cuts, about two hundred and forty. I'd never done a film like that. There were so many composites in this film, but the schedule was the same as usual."

LEFT: King Ghidorah blasts a village near Mount Fuji.

of Chinese lore; it was specifically intended as an homage to Yamata no Orochi, the evil, eight-headed serpent from the tale of Shiga, the legend of the birth of Japan. King Ghidorah's birth via an otherworldly fireball and its strafing of Yokohama are spectacular; the monster's iconic, warbling trill is heard constantly as its wiggling heads wildly spit antigravity beams, sending exploding debris in all directions. The oversize King Ghidorah suit required numerous wire puppeteers in the rafters to direct its constantly moving three heads, two tails, and wings; when King Ghidorah touches down for the final battle, its movements are limited, and its primary tactic is to shoot ray beams. "King Ghidorah's appearance was flashy indeed, but it was huge, and with so many wires, it had no mobility at all," recalled Godzilla actor Haruo Nakajima. "It was a troublesome opponent to deal with. Except for minor movements that the actor inside could make, King Ghidorah couldn't do anything. Godzilla had to be the one to attack, get hit, chase, get bopped, etc. . . . On top of that, the wires controlling its necks got snagged on Godzilla and snapped. It was so much trouble!"

Roughly the final half hour of *Ghidorah* is dominated by monsters, while the dramatic storyline resolves with Detective Shindo's heroic thwarting of repeated attempts on the princess's life, until she is grazed by an assassin's bullet and regains her royal memory. The fight between Godzilla and Rodan moves to the Mount Fuji foothills and involves much comic horseplay (tail biting, a judo flip, boulder kicking, and volleying—the latter a nod to the Olympic gold medal–winning Japan women's volleyball team) before Rodan keeps Godzilla at bay with a wing-flapping windstorm. Mothra arrives and attempts to end the juvenile antics by spraying Godzilla, then Rodan, in the face with silk, each monster laughing at the other's suffering. In the long-awaited kaiju summit, the monsters communicate in a cross-species dialect; Mothra's appeal to the others falls on deaf ears at first. "Godzilla's saying 'We have no reason to help humans,'"

"IT WAS A MISCALCULATION. . . . IT WAS A SCENE WITH FALLING ROCKS, SO IT WASN'T REALISTIC FOR HIM TO BE ABLE TO GRAB A HUGE BOULDER, BUT ITO-KUN (ACTOR HISAYA ITO) INSTINCTIVELY CAUGHT IT, AND TO MY SURPRISE, WE COULDN'T CUT THAT TAKE."

—Director Ishiro Honda on the assassin Malness's unintentionally funny death scene

TOP LEFT: Psychiatrist Dr. Adachi (Takashi Shimura) attempts to restore the amnesiac princess's memory with shock treatments as Shindo (Yosuke Natsuki) and Naoko (Yukio Hoshi) look on. ∎ **TOP RIGHT:** In a memorable scene, the tiny twin fairies peek out from behind a mirror as they watch the Selginan thugs threaten the princess. To create the illusion, a blue-screen panel representing the mirror was placed in front of the stagehands (shown in this behind-the-scenes photo), and footage of the villains and the princess was composited onto the panel.

report the Small Beauties, acting as interpreters. "'Humans are always bullying us.'" Rodan and Godzilla harbor a mutual grudge, stubbornly demanding an apology and refusing to budge. But when Mothra confronts King Ghidorah alone, the pair relent and join the fight. The Earth monsters prevail via clever teamwork, Godzilla holding King Ghidorah back while Mothra—assisted by Rodan—cocoons the dragon in sticky silk.

YOKOHAMA HOLIDAY: THE INCOGNITO PRINCESS

Ghidorah's appeal also derives from spirited performances by a cast of familiar Toho actors. Hoshi and Koizumi essentially reprise their *Mothra vs. Godzilla* roles (though their characters have different names); Hoshi prepared for her part by conducting man-on-street interviews with a tape recorder outside the Yoyogi National Gymnasium during the Olympics. Up-and-coming star Natsuki is pitch-perfect as the straitlaced, earnest cop assigned as the princess's bodyguard. Interestingly, the film's two standout parts were both recast just prior to filming. Wakabayashi plays the amnesiac princess in a catatonic, monotone fashion: "I tried to [portray] someone who was sleepwalking," the actress said. "I tried not to look at each person's face. [The princess had] the look of a homeless person; she really had a boy's style. That was actually my favorite kind of look in private." Toho siren Kumi Mizuno was originally cast in the role but pulled out because of a medical condition. Hisaya Ito is similarly dead-on as the steely, sunglasses-clad assassin, Malness; Yoshio Tsuchiya was originally cast but canceled due to scheduling overruns on Akira Kurosawa's *Red Beard* (1965). Takashi Shimura and Akihiko Hirata, the two scientists at the heart of *Godzilla,* have small but memorable parts as a psychiatrist and police chief, respectively. The Peanuts return as the Small Beauties, again playing a decisive role. The Infant Islanders are no longer reluctant to help the outside world, and the Beauties embrace their celebrity status, singing the pop song "Call Happiness" on Japanese television.

In prerelease publicity, producer Tanaka pegged the budget for *Ghidorah* at twice that of a typical kaiju film. The actual figure was reportedly about ¥133 million, or ¥10 million less than *Mothra vs. Godzilla*; thus, certain effects shots and sequences in early drafts were omitted, including buildings and sea tornadoes being sucked into the air by King Ghidorah's beams, and King Ghidorah's New York attack. Nevertheless, the film was a major success. It was paired with the Crazy Cats comedy *Edo Flower of Irresponsibility* (in those days, Toho's A pictures were released on double bills), and the program earned ¥375 million (just over $1 million) in its release; trade paper *Kinema Junpo* listed *Ghidorah* as the fourth-highest earning domestic film of the 1964–65 season. Prerelease publicity efforts emphasized this was a film for

ABOVE: In an example of Eiji Tsuburaya's creative shot composition, reminiscent of eighteenth-century traditional Japanese woodblock prints, King Ghidorah prepares to destroy a temple gate with its antigravity beams, one of the film's memorable moments. ■ **RIGHT:** This film features unprecedented use of monster puppets and props, particularly for the battle between Godzilla and Rodan. Tsuburaya (*in bucket hat*) inspects a shot in which the puppet Rodan drops Godzilla onto high tension towers.

all ages: "Please avoid the impression that it is primarily aimed at children," theater owners were asked. "This is an ultra-entertaining film that adults can enjoy without reservations." Still, much of the campaign did target children. Haruo Nakajima wore the Godzilla suit at meet-and-greet events for kids at amusement areas on department store rooftops in Tokyo and Nagoya; for the first time, Godzilla plastic models were sold, and a manga adaptation of the film was published in a children's magazine.

Ghidorah's script is threaded with an homage to William Wyler's *Roman Holiday* (1953), a perennially popular foreign film in Japan, and rereleased there in 1963. *Ghidorah* pretends that, just as Audrey Hepburn did, a gorgeous foreign princess can hide in plain sight with only a slight change in appearance. The final scene mirrors the ending of Wyler's film: As her highness bids farewell to the shy policeman who saved her life, there are hints of feelings in Wakabayashi's eyes and Natsuki's stammer that give the scene much charm.

For director Honda, who viewed Godzilla from the beginning as a cautionary symbol, the further humanizing of monsters—and the idea that they would talk to one another and join forces to save man, was difficult. "I used The Peanuts as Mothra's interpreters, but [it] was something I had to force myself to do," Honda later said; however, "the producer liked how it turned out. . . . It was a big success." As the battle ends, Japanese villagers cheer while the good monsters expel King Ghidorah back into space, signaling the series' future. The once-mysterious and dangerous monsters were now familiar, and for the first time—significantly—Godzilla remains in Japan. The monster was not yet truly a hero—it still held no sympathy for humankind, but it was now sworn to protect its homeland from outside threats as a reliable if unpredictable guardian.

LEFT: After the space monster knocks Godzilla backward into the bridge, Rodan launches an aerial attack on King Ghidorah from behind. ■ **BELOW:** Surprisingly, Godzilla does not use its heat ray in the final four-way battle with King Ghidorah. Mothra's silk once again proves to be the decisive weapon.

TOP: A number of women assisted the Toho suit-making staff as part-time helpers. Here they pose (joined by unidentified children) with the Godzilla and Rodan puppets, as well as the yet-unpainted King Ghidorah suit, its bluish-green hue clearly visible. ■
ABOVE: The very first publicity photo of King Ghidorah. The monster has a dark bluish-green body with rainbow-patterned wings.

KING GHIDORAH: CHAMELEON?

King Ghidorah is an awe-inspiring golden dragon from outer space, one of Toho's most inspired kaiju creations. Along with its menacing three heads and imposing wingspan, the monster's brilliant color is essential to its otherworldly power. But early publicity photos, taken while the film was in production, show the monster with a dark bluish-green color and a rainbow pattern on its wings. Was the golden dragon originally not gold?

"The King Ghidorah suit was done, and it was just getting dried off, so I went to see it," remembered scripter Keiko Suzuki. "There was King Ghidorah hanging from the ceiling, and it was kind of greenish blue. I told Tsuburaya that I thought King Ghidorah should be gold since it came from Venus. I didn't think it should have a dark tone like that. Tsuburaya thought for a while, and then he went to the suit makers. I went with him. He said to Teizo Toshimitsu, 'I hate to ask, but can you change the color to gold?' I've never told anyone this story because I really did not think anyone would believe that Tsuburaya changed his mind just because of something I said."

However, according to suit maker Keizo Murase, the suit simply hadn't been painted yet. "We never painted it blue," he said. "The latex was mixed with black ink, which creates a bluish tone. It got sticky when it was curing, so I put baby powder on the surface to prevent the latex from getting sticky, which turned it to this [blue] color. So this wasn't even a finished product; it's before the color was put on. The first I heard about the color was when Toshimitsu told me to paint it gold."

As far as the rainbow pattern on the wings, Murase surmised, "This could've been a test of whether the wings were see-through. The pattern is painted directly on the fabric, but they did such an uneven paint job. . . . This can't be the finished suit. There is no one [still alive] who can remember at this point, so it's unknown who did it or why. But I wonder why they ever used this kind of picture for an ad."

A TRADITION OF ARTISTRY

THE TOHO SPECIAL EFFECTS DEPARTMENT IN THE GOLDEN AGE OF JAPANESE CINEMA

"Compared to [the James Bond movies], the monster movies we make are done with about 1 percent of that budget. In general, our techniques are born out of poverty."
—Eiji Tsuburaya, special effects director

Long before the advent of computer-generated imagery, the artists and craftsmen of Toho Studios created Godzilla and its fellow kaiju from scratch and built the make-believe world in which the monsters exist using the tools, materials, and technology of the day. Necessity, it's been said, is the mother of invention; with the exception of certain trick-photography techniques, the magic of Toho special effects was almost entirely handmade, through trial and error.

The Toho Special Effects (SFX) Department was originally founded in 1937 and was infamously involved in the production of wartime "national policy" films, which garnered technical awards and earned prestige on the studio lot for Eiji Tsuburaya and his crew. After the war, Tsuburaya was among those temporarily expelled from the industry for making those same war films, and the department was disbanded. When Toho resumed making films with special effects in the early 1950s, Tsuburaya returned and assembled a ragtag group of old hands and new recruits, most of them non-studio employees and part-time workers, who were now viewed as misfits and outcasts on the lot. "When we were working [on *Godzilla*], everybody, including the company itself, was making fun of us, and no one took us seriously," recalled Eizo Kaimai, a monster-suit sculptor. "Anyone who wanted to do special effects was considered a crazy person."

Toho's special effects department was officially relaunched in 1957. Led by Tsuburaya and SFX producer Masami Sueyasu during its heyday (late 1950s to mid-1960s), it grew into the biggest and most accomplished group of its type at any Japanese studio, earning several technical awards for Tsuburaya. A core of about one hundred studio employees was augmented by dozens upon dozens of contractors, part-timers, and trainees, many of them young men who were mentored by the old guard. It was hard work: Due to short filming schedules, team members often slept at nearby lodges or at the studio rather than go home—or didn't sleep at all—to complete a project on time. They subsisted on take-out sushi and endured the all-nighters through love of their work and a family atmosphere that centered around Tsuburaya himself, as well as his art director, Yasuyuki Inoue, both demanding but beloved bosses.

"[Inoue] wasn't just all words, he actually did things himself," recalled assistant art director Jiro Shirasaki. "He was an amazing artist, and we had so much respect for him. . . . Our department probably worked the longest hours in the entire company, more than any other department. But still we had the joy of making things. And when we did a good job, he always complimented us. We had mutual respect and built a relationship together." As their efforts paid off at the box office, the SFX team's status soon improved. "I joined Toho [in 1961]," Shirasaki said. "It was the best time. *Godzilla* was a hit, and then *Rodan* and *Godzilla Raids Again*, all those films. The department was now fully respected and accepted. We were like the kings of the studio."

Within the studio's seniority system, Tsuburaya—older than directors such as Ishiro Honda and Akira Kurosawa—wielded considerable influence. ("All the money and budgets we got were because of him," Shirasaki recalled.) But Tsuburaya's death in 1970 left a void in leadership. The SFX department's formal structure was again dissolved, though it regrouped on a project-by-project basis. Toho's Stage 11, exclusively used for shooting effects scenes, was soon demolished. Longtime staffers now divided time between film projects and television, where *tokusatsu* programming exploded in popularity. During the transitional period of the seventies and eighties, Tsuburaya proteges Sadamasa Arikawa (briefly) and Teruyoshi Nakano served as SFX director; later, roughly from 1989 to 1997, the team would be led by Koichi Kawakita, and included new recruits and a dwindling number of veterans from the Tsuburaya years.

Describing the work of his talented team, Tsuburaya said, "From natural disasters like earthquakes, fires, floods, and typhoons, to imaginative creations like sea and aerial battles, monsters, or even the splitting of the Sea of Japan, special effects in movies encompass depicting any scene required in visual form." The following is a snapshot of the department structure circa 1965, an overview of primary teams and roles, as well as some key studio facilities. Select personnel are identified here, but it should be noted that the size and organization of the department evolved over time, and many more individuals contributed to the success of Toho's special effects films.

ABOVE: Cameraman Sadamasa Arikawa.
■ BELOW LEFT: Assistant director Teruyoshi Nakano with the monster Gabara on the set of *All Monsters Attack*. ■ BELOW RIGHT: Script supervisor Keiko Suzuki (*fore-ground*) on the set of *Son of Godzilla*.

THE SFX TEAM

Assistant directors maintained coordination between the SFX and live-action teams to ensure seamless transitions between filmed sequences. They managed the shooting schedule and activity on the set, freeing the director to focus on filming. Nakano was the primary assistant director during the 1960s.

The **cinematography** team, made up of cameramen and assistant cameramen, was led by Arikawa during this period. They were experts in shooting at high speeds (e.g., 48 or 72 frames per second), which was necessary to make the monsters' movements appear appropriately slow, and at simulating depth of field even when shooting miniature sets in confined spaces.

The **lighting** team handled the blazing, high-powered lights that were required in large numbers due to the high-speed filming process. They used arc lamps to simulate the glow of lightning strikes and to create other on-set light effects.

After Toho acquired an Oxberry optical printer from the US in the early 1960s, the **optical photography** team, supervised by Hiroshi Mukoyama, began producing stunning images combining live-action footage with other elements, such as matte paintings (e.g., the crowds surrounding Mothra's egg and other masterful shots in *Mothra vs. Godzilla*). The optical art team, including prolific animator Sadao Iizuka, made hand-drawn animated effects, such as the rays and beams emitted by Godzilla, et al., and traveling mattes for composite shots.

The **script supervisor** was responsible for tracking the special effects crew's daily shooting and documenting any instructions that needed to be sent to the **editor**, who would assemble the effects sequences. There was also a **still photographer** on set, the most well-known of whom, Takashi Nakao, snapped hundreds of thousands of behind-the-scenes images for publicity purposes or internal reference material. Many of Nakao's photos appear in this book (see "Takashi Nakao: A Legacy of Kaiju Photography" on page 314).

SPECIAL ART

"Japanese people are skilled. That's why they're good at making models."
—Eiji Tsuburaya

A subset of the SFX department, the special art section (*tokusyu bijutsu*, or "toku-bi" for short) was a group of highly specialized artists and craftsmen that consisted of several teams.

The **design** team designed and oversaw the construction of all aspects of miniature sets, using detailed sketches and blueprints. This team was originally supervised by Akira Watanabe, and later by Inoue, both supremely talented designers. The **carpentry** team built the sets from the floor up and also created buildings and other miniatures. Some of Toho's master carpenters had prior expertise building temples and shrines, and their skills were apparent on-screen. The **plaster shop** created buildings to be stomped or smashed by monsters, as well as collapsing roads, rock formations, and more.

The **wire works** or **operations** team operated not only flying monsters such as Rodan, King Ghidorah, and Mothra, but also model planes, trains, ships, and more. Even Godzilla's tail was manipulated by

TOP LEFT: Eiji Tsuburaya (*center, wearing fedora*) supervises construction of the miniature high tension towers (from 1954's *Godzilla*). ■ LEFT: The miniature Iwa Island coastline. The studio's reflection shows in the indoor pool (from *Mothra vs. Godzilla*). ■ OPPOSITE TOP: The sprawling miniature Yokohama Harbor set (from *Ghidorah, the Three-Headed Monster*). ■ OPPOSITE BOTTOM: An overmatched Mothra challenges King Ghidorah alone. The miniature village set shows intense attention to detail (from *Ghidorah, the Three-Headed Monste*r).

overhead wires. They also employed large fans and pumps to create wave effects and used dirt and sand to simulate the smoke of collapsing miniature buildings. Fumio Nakadai supervised this team for many years.

The **modeling** team designed and built the miniature tanks, planes, ships, and spaceships and created the motors and mechanical devices that propelled them across the set. Electricians created remote-controlled systems to open and close Godzilla's mouth and put lights in miniature buildings for night scenes.

The **physical effects** team employed a variety of methods to simulate destruction via pyrotechnics and explosions, as well as atmospheric smoke. Everything from piped-in steam, fog machines, and canned smoke to acid, gasoline, "black powder," and gunpowder were in their arsenal. They used electrical mechanisms that triggered pyro effects and air cannons to simulate explosions caused by monsters or the military.

The **sculpture** and **modeling** team designed and built monster suits by hand, often from clay prototypes, evolving and improving their methods and materials over time. The main monster creators from 1954 through the mid-1960s were chief sculptor Teizo Toshimitsu, along with the Yagi brothers, Kanju and Yasuei, and sculptors Eizo Kaimai and Keizo Murase. Noboyuki Yasumaru joined the suit-making team in 1967, creating Gorosaurus, Hedorah, Anguirus (for *Destroy All Monsters*), and Gigan, then took over as chief Godzilla suit maker in 1973. Yasumaru continued the tradition until his protege, Tomoki Kobayashi, served as chief suit maker from 1991 to 1995.

Backdrop painters rendered spectacular skies, mountains (including Mount Fuji), clouds, and even outer space to create depth and realism behind the miniature sets, as well as various matte paintings. Fukutaro Suzuki was chief painter, while artist Fuchimu Shimakura was known as the "god of cloud painting."

BELOW, CLOCKWISE FROM TOP LEFT: Only the side visible to the camera of this miniature of Osaka Castle from *Godzilla Raids Again* was built. The plaster team and carpenters rigged the castle with wires to be pulled on cue, making the structure collapse—barring any mishaps. "There were about five or six men pulling ropes to make the structure collapse," remembered Haruo Nakajima. "They pulled too soon, and it didn't match [the monsters'] movements. The castle fell apart at the wrong time. Rebuilding the castle cost ¥500,000. My salary was half that." ▪ Putting the finishing touches on the Kachidochi Bridge on the set of *Godzilla*. ▪ Actress Keiko Sawai watches sculptor Teizo Toshimitsu making the Godzilla suit for *Invasion of Astro-Monster*. ▪ A pyrotechnic explosion in *Mothra vs. Godzilla*. ▪ The wire works crew suspending King Ghidorah in *Ghidorah, the Three-Headed Monster*.

ABOVE: Fuchimu Shimakura painting the backdrop of Jupiter for *Invasion of Astro-Monster*. ■ RIGHT: Shimakura's magnificent backdrop painting of Mount Fuji in *Destroy All Monsters*. ■ BOTTOM LEFT: Stage No. 9, where many classic special effects scenes were lensed, reflected in the waters of the Big Pool. ■ BOTTOM RIGHT: Keizo Murase (*left*) and Haruo Nakajima (*right*) help Katsumi Tezuka (*inside Godzilla suit*) get out of the Big Pool during the filming of *King Kong vs. Godzilla*.

THE STAGES

Most special effects scenes were filmed inside the drab concrete walls of Stage No. 8, Stage No. 9, or Stage No. 11 on the Toho lot. In the early years, none of these buildings had heating or air-conditioning, and temperatures inside could be brutally hot or freezing cold depending on the season. Stage Nos. 8 and 9, built just prior to the filming of *Godzilla Raids Again*, were expansive structures spanning about 14,000 square feet (1,300 sq m), large enough that several miniature sets could be constructed concurrently. Stage No. 11 was reserved exclusively for SFX work and had unusually high ceilings, which allowed for erecting tall horizon backdrops.

THE BIG POOL

Prior to production of the war film *Storm Over the Pacific* (1960), Tsuburaya asked Inoue, chief of the special art staff, to design a giant water tank where naval battle scenes could be filmed. Inspired by a similar pool at Rome's Cinecitta Studios, Toho's SFX team constructed the Big Pool on the lot, and over the next several decades it would serve as the setting for countless water scenes in many types of films. Difficult to maintain, the pool could be a treacherous workplace; actors who portrayed Godzilla nearly drowned due to slippery algae or debris on the pool's floor. Despite its important role in special effects history, the Big Pool was paved over after the production of *Godzilla Final Wars* (2004) and replaced by a screening room and ADR facility.

怪獣大戦争

(KAIJU DAISENSO / THE GREAT MONSTER WAR)
aka *Monster Zero, Godzilla vs. Monster Zero*
RELEASED: DECEMBER 19, 1965 (JAPAN)

INVASION OF ASTRO-MONSTER

Science fiction flourished in Hollywood during the early to mid-1950s, when essential films such as *The Thing* (1951), *The Day the Earth Stood Still* (1951), *The War of the Worlds* (1953), *Invasion of the Body Snatchers* (1956), *It Came from Outer Space* (1953), *The Incredible Shrinking Man* (1957), and *Them!* (1954) were made. Over the course of a single decade, however, the genre fell from inventive heights to low-budget lows. Copycat films followed, featuring giant atomic creatures and flying saucers rendered with crude effects, often set in barren deserts and starring once-popular actors on the downside of their careers now playing archetypes (scientists and astronauts) in stories targeting juvenile audiences; by the 1960s, these films had essentially run their course. Meanwhile, in Japan, Toho's science-fiction cinema followed a parallel but different path. *Godzilla* beget fellow travelers *Rodan* (1956) and *Varan the Unbelievable* (1958), as well as ambitious space-invader epics like *The Mysterians* (1957) and *Battle in Outer Space* (1959), and sci-fantasy hybrids *Mothra* (1961) and *Atragon* (1963). While American sci-fi pictures faded, Toho's genre fare thrived at the domestic box office and found audiences overseas; the pictures were bound not by common stories or characters but by Eiji Tsuburaya's distinctive special effects visual aesthetic, and they borrowed tropes and stars from the studio's other genres (e.g., war films, corporate comedies, and spy thrillers). The classic Godzilla movies, though often considered a stand-alone set, were part of this larger "Tohoverse."

> ## "I WAS THINKING ABOUT HOW TO COMBINE MONSTERS AND SCIENCE FICTION. I ALSO FOCUSED ON MAKING THIS COMPLETELY BIZARRE STORY VISUALLY BELIEVABLE AND INTERESTING."
> —Eiji Tsuburaya, special effects director

Invasion of Astro-Monster, the sixth movie starring Godzilla, is a surreal throwback to classic 1950s-era American sci-fi, with rockets and flying saucers that recall *Destination Moon* (1953) and *Earth vs. the Flying Saucers* (1956), and a fading Hollywood star—onetime Oscar nominee Nick Adams—in a leading role. It is also an update of Toho's own *The Mysterians*, with aliens from a devastated planet targeting Earth for its natural resources. But whereas *The Mysterians* was a sober sci-fi drama with themes of nuclear war, scientific ethics, and international alliances, *Astro-Monster* is a breezy blend of space adventure, light comedy, kaiju fury, and a hint of romance, in keeping with the Godzilla series' tonal shifts. Godzilla performs a loopy victory dance, and the alien invaders—wearing wraparound sunglasses and behaving like yakuza thugs—use advanced technology to weaponize the monsters; this plot device would be revisited, with variations, in numerous movies and television shows produced by Toho and others.

Invasion of Astro-Monster functions as a direct sequel to *Ghidorah*, though it is set in a future several years later when interstellar travel is common. The film was a co-venture with Benedict Pictures and producer Henry Saperstein, who had distributed *Mothra vs. Godzilla* in the US two years earlier and then coproduced Toho's 1965 *Frankenstein Conquers the World*. Like *The Mysterians* and *Battle in Outer Space*, the story (written by Shinichi Sekizawa) portrays resurgent Tokyo as a key partner in the space race, with American and Japanese astronauts Glenn (Adams) and Fuji (Akira Takarada) leading the way. Investigating a mysterious transmission from Planet X, a newly discovered body near Jupiter, the heroes encounter a race of computer-controlled, standoffish, but seemingly benevolent aliens driven underground by King Ghidorah—known there as "Monster Zero"—which has ravaged their surface world. Though the film is light entertainment, it hints at the perils of a fascist society where technology supplants free will and science supplants biology; all the women are identical, genetically engineered replicants. "That was the basis," director Ishiro Honda said, "that genetic engineering of humans was possible. We need to beware of that."

The Xiliens (Planet X people) ask to borrow Godzilla (dubbed Monster Zero One) and Rodan (dubbed Zero Two) to help repel King Ghidorah, as the monsters (with Mothra's help) did previously on Earth. It's

PREVIOUS SPREAD: King Ghidorah (aka Monster Zero) attacks Planet X. The monster's appearance is unchanged from *Ghidorah, the Three-Headed Monster*, though its animated antigravity beams are less detailed, and their electric tendrils are no longer visible.
■ ABOVE: Setting up a shot of the huge P-1 rocket model. ■ LEFT: Toho's international sales poster (B3 size) for *Invasion of Astro-Monster*. The poster has promotional still images from the film and a trilingual (English, French, and Spanish) plot summary printed on the reverse side.

It went unobserved by the astronauts, but··········
THE MOST GIGANTIC MONSTER EXPLOSION OF THE SPACE AGE NOW BEING BLASTED INTO FILM

PRESENTED BY
TOHO COMPANY, LTD.
14, 1-CHOME, YURAKUCHO, CHIYODAKU, TOKYO, JAPAN
Cable address "TOHOFILM TOKYO"
Overseas Office in New York · Los Angeles · San Francisco · Honolulu
Paris · Rome · Hongkong · Bangkok · Manila · Sao Paulo · Lima
MOST-AWARDED COMPANY AT 1965 FESTIVALS

STARRING
NICK ADAMS · AKIRA TAKARADA · KUMI MIZUNO
and
directed by INOSHIRO HONDA · special effects by EIZI TSUBURAYA

all part of a double-cross to gain control of the two kaiju and use them, plus King Ghidorah, to dominate Earth and poach its supply of water, which is scarce on Planet X. The story has a wonderfully naive logic—the technologically superior aliens could simply attack Earth, but instead create an elaborate ruse, pretending to offer humanity a cancer cure in trade for the monsters. The aliens could easily dispose of nerdy inventor Tetsuo (Akira Kubo, playing against type), but instead they create a sham corporation to keep his Lady Guard buzzer—which emits an audio frequency that's deadly to the aliens—off the market. The climax has the heroes broadcasting the buzzer's harsh sound to incapacitate the Xiliens, while Japan's defense forces quickly assemble a convoy of A-Cycle Light Ray cannons—among the first of the many techno-superweapons that would become a hallmark of Toho's genre pictures—to disable the invaders' monster control, allowing Godzilla and Rodan to expel King Ghidorah from Earth once again.

Both of the Toho–Saperstein kaiju coproductions feature a romance between characters played by Adams and Kumi Mizuno, an actress with an atypically strong screen persona and known for playing urbane, "Westernized" women. Mizuno is Namikawa, an alien posing as a fashionable Japanese business-woman. She is assigned to monitor astronaut Glenn but instead falls hard for him, and the two plan to marry. Their scenes together are brief, but the love affair has unusual heat for this type of film: a kiss is glimpsed (the only kiss in any live-action Japanese Godzilla movie), and Glenn hints that they've spent the night together. The Xiliens exterminate Namikawa for getting too close to the earthling; her final, redemptive act helps save both her lover and humanity from ruin. (The Mizuno–Adams relationship was reportedly more arm's length in Sekizawa's screenplay, but Honda amplified their attraction for dramatic effect.) Adams, meanwhile, injects American swagger and attitude throughout, even though he's basically a sidekick, billed beneath Takarada in the Japanese credits. Since appearing in major films such as

"THE DIRECTOR TOLD ME TO FALL IN LOVE WITH HIM AS A HUMAN, NOT AS AN ALIEN. . . . THE LOVE SCENES WERE VERY REALISTIC. I THOUGHT PERHAPS THAT WAS THE HOLLYWOOD WAY, BUT HE (NICK ADAMS) WAS VERY GOOD AT IT."

—Kumi Mizuno (Namikawa)

"(ADAMS) HAD A HABIT OF SHIFTING UP HIS PANTS. I TOLD HIM TO TIGHTEN HIS BELT, BUT IT WAS (HIS) HABIT. YOU SEE HIM DOING IT THROUGHOUT THE FILM."

—Yoshio Tsuchiya (Planet X controller)

Rebel Without a Cause (1955) and starring in the TV series *The Rebel* (1959–61), the prolific actor's stock in Hollywood had fallen, and he was now making genre pictures and occasional TV guest spots. Adams nonetheless delivers an enthusiastic performance, channeling James Dean and, in his intense final scene with Mizuno, quoting Humphrey Bogart's "hill of beans" speech from *Casablanca* (in the English-language version only). Adams's chemistry with Mizuno and Takarada is remarkable given the unusual way his scenes were directed, with Adams delivering his lines in English. Adams's dialogue was overdubbed for the Japanese release, while his voice remained (and everyone else's dubbed into English) in the US cut.

ASTROFUTURISM

Astro-Monster's special effects sequences are a mix of impressive visual ideas, inventive new filming angles and techniques, and—for the first time in the series—significant use of stock footage from earlier films. The aliens' arrival at Lake Myojin features the spectacular appearance of a retro flying saucer that rises from the steaming waters and effortlessly glides to a landing on the lakeshore, achieved via excellent compositing thanks to Tsuburaya's Oxberry optical printer. The Xiliens transport Godzilla and Rodan across the galaxy to Planet X in electromagnetic spheres, with the creatures in suspended animation, an insanely fun and improbable sight. (In an early story draft, the monsters were frozen and shipped with rockets attached to them; Godzilla's transport was hit by a meteor and damaged.) The first battle pitting Rodan and Godzilla against King Ghidorah is fought on the barren surface of Planet X. In this environment's lighter gravity and atmosphere, Godzilla leaps through the air at King Ghidorah. Jupiter's massive presence on the outer-space horizon is later paralleled by Mount Fuji looming over the monsters as they attack Japan, both rendered as striking backdrops by the SFX art department. When Godzilla, Rodan, and King Ghidorah are unleashed against Japan, creative compositing shows the monsters approaching from the foothills around Mount Fuji as villagers flee in the foreground while saucers hover above. A giant Godzilla foot prop repeatedly crushes traditional-style houses via rapid editing. Rodan fans windstorms, and the camera is perched above its shoulder as roof tiles fly off buildings below. Spliced into these exciting

ABOVE: SFX director Eiji Tsuburaya instructs cameraman Sadamasa Arikawa (*right*) on how to film the huge P-1 model rocket ship. ■ **BELOW LEFT:** Godzilla takes cover behind a rock formation to avoid King Ghidorah's ray beams during the three-way monster battle on Planet X. ■ **BELOW RIGHT:** Filming a close-up of Rodan (Masaki Shinohara) on the Planet X set. Both Rodan and special effects cameraman Arikawa (*seated*) are on raised platforms in order to capture the huge, stunning view of Jupiter on the horizon backdrop.

BELOW: The Toho special effects crew shooting the three-way monster battle on the surface of Planet X. The multiple wires that control King Ghidorah's heads, wings, and tails can clearly be seen descending from the rafters above the stage.

scenes are numerous shots of destruction and tank gunfire from *Rodan*, *Mothra*, and *The Mysterians*; these cuts are well integrated, though the older footage is noticeably grainier.

Aside from Godzilla performing boxing moves inspired by Muhammad Ali and Japanese bantamweight champion Masahiko Harada (aka "Fighting Harada"), the monster action is played mostly straight, with one glaring exception. After besting King Ghidorah on Planet X, Godzilla celebrates by jumping up and down while flexing its arms and legs, a move borrowed from the award-winning comedy manga *Osomatsu-kun* by Fujio Akatsuka, wherein it was performed by a character who shouted "*Sheeeh!*" Amid the postwar manga boom, the "*sheeeh*" became a fad, with people everywhere striking the pose. "I didn't know anything about this '*sheeeh*,' because I didn't read mangas," remembered suit actor Haruo Nakajima. "[Tsuburaya said], 'It's so popular now. Let's do it! I'll decide later whether or not to use it. Let's film it anyway.' It wasn't difficult because the suit was pulled up by wires. . . . I actually enjoyed doing humanlike actions more than the heavy-looking monster actions. But even when we were filming a comical scene like that, no one laughed. Everyone was serious about their job."

Composer Akira Ifukube's familiar themes create a brisk tempo, and two pieces stand out. As the saucers capture Godzilla and Rodan for transport, Ifukube alternates between an eerie, low-volume motif with hints of theremin, and a figure played by brash horns, emphasizing the mystery and power of the Xilien's technological might. The main title theme, by contrast, is a reworking of the heroic frigate march from 1954's *Godzilla*. By this time, Ifukube had begun to reuse music from previous films and from his

"TSUBURAYA-SAN ASKED, 'HEY GUYS, DO YOU KNOW ABOUT THIS "*SHEEEH*" THING?' IT WAS FUN TO SEE IT ON THE SCREEN. BUT THE AUDIENCE'S OPINION WAS DIVIDED."

—Teruyoshi Nakano, assistant special effects director

classical works in order to maintain his busy film-composing schedule. "It would be easier if I had plenty of time, but it usually doesn't work that way," Ifukube later recalled. "I tried my best, but there are time constraints. . . . That's why some of my film music pieces may sound similar to one another."

Invasion of Astro-Monster was tenth in the *Kinema Junpo* rankings for 1965–66, earning ¥210 million (about $580,000) against a budget of ¥132 million. Foreign films now dominated the Japanese box office, with *Thunderball* (1965, ¥1 billion) and *My Fair Lady* (1964, ¥428 million) outperforming all domestic releases. The popularity of American films and the continuing growth of television were shrinking the audience for Toho's Showa-era Godzilla pictures, none of which reached the yearly top ten again.

Outlandish and entertaining, *Invasion of Astro-Monster* endures as a nostalgic piece of sci-fi kitsch. It also represents another turning point for Godzilla and the genre. Tsuburaya Productions would soon launch *Ultraman*, creating a type of popular *tokusatsu* teleseries that would see the genre's audience gravitate to the small screen. Meanwhile, in the US, Saperstein's company—for reasons that remain unclear—would not release *Astro-Monster* until 1970, when it was retitled *Monster Zero* and double-billed with *The War of the Gargantuas*; the pairing had a profitable run in drive-in theaters and matinees. Adams had passed away suddenly, at age 36, in 1968, thus his name was omitted from posters and trailers. Both films were syndicated to independent US TV stations during the 1970s and became international cult-film favorites.

In 1946, Japan's Ministry of Economy, Trade, and Industry founded the Institute of Japanese Film Technology Awards to recognize technical achievements in cinema. Tsuburaya had first received this award for *Godzilla*, and then several times since; in 1966, he was honored for the final time for his work on this film.

PREVIOUS SPREAD: Rodan, Godzilla, and King Ghidorah, under the control of the Xiliens, face off against the armed forces. ■ ABOVE: Yoshio Tsuchiya gives a tour de force performance as the steely controller of Planet X. Tsuchiya improvised the alien despot's quirky hand gestures and combined French, German, and author Ryunosuke Akutagawa's *Kappa* language when speaking the Xilien dialect. ■ LEFT, CLOCKWISE FROM TOP LEFT: Astronauts Glenn and Fuji (*left*, portrayed by Nick Adams and Akira Takarada) meet with Fuji's sister, Haruno, and her boyfriend, inventor Tetsuo Tori (*right*, portrayed by Keiko Sawai and Akira Kubo). Tori fails to impress his girlfriend's disapproving brother (and surrogate father figure), a recurring theme in Japanese dramas and comedies of the period. ■ Kumi Mizuno (Namikawa) and Adams (Glenn) in a light off-camera moment while shooting the star-crossed lovers' final scene. With Namikawa now revealed to be from Planet X, Mizuno wears the aliens' funky vinyl body costume and sports a black nylon wig. ■ The P-1 interstellar rocket returns to Earth, landing at the World Space Authority space center. The P-1 is reminiscent of the Luna rocket from producer George Pal's *Destination Moon* (1950). ■ OPPOSITE, CLOCKWISE FROM TOP LEFT: After having been shuttled from Earth to Planet X and all the way back again, Godzilla (Haruo Nakajima) and Rodan (Masaki Shinohara) await the controller's order to attack. ■ In the final battle for Earth, Godzilla (Nakajima) restrains King Ghidorah (Shoichi Hirose) while Rodan (*shown here in puppet form*) prepares to deliver the coup de grace, an aerial body slam that sends not just King Ghidorah but all three monsters tumbling into the sea. ■ Under control of the aliens, Godzilla and Rodan begin their attack in the foothills of Mount Fuji as the Planet X saucers keep watch.

南海の大決闘

(GOJIRA EBIRA MOSURA NANKAI NO DAIKETTO /
GODZILLA, EBIRAH, MOTHRA: GREAT DUEL IN THE SOUTH SEAS)
aka *Godzilla vs. the Sea Monster*
RELEASED: DECEMBER 17, 1966 (JAPAN)

EBIRAH, HORROR OF THE DEEP

After twice battling King Ghidorah for the fate of the world, Godzilla retired to a small island for a much-needed slumber, only to be rudely awakened by a band of castaways, a rogue nation building nuclear bombs, and a gigantic lobster-monster that guards the villains and their secret base of operations. The highly entertaining seventh Godzilla movie, *Ebirah, Horror of the Deep*, steers the series into uncharted waters with a setting and story influenced by early James Bond films. Driven by fresh creative talent behind the camera, *Ebirah* truly is a change of pace. It moves quicker, sounds more modern, has youthful energy, and reveals some new tricks up Godzilla's scaly sleeve.

Godzilla, however, wasn't supposed to be in this movie at all. The project originated when Rankin/Bass Productions, known for its popular holiday television specials, approached Toho sometime in 1965 or '66 to coproduce a film promotionally tied to Rankin's animated series *The King Kong Show*, which would debut on ABC-TV in the US in September 1966. Shinichi Sekizawa's screenplay, *Operation Robinson Crusoe: King Kong vs. Ebirah*, was completed on July 13, 1966; the script bore no resemblance to the cartoon series, causing Rankin to reject it, but rather than drop the project altogether, Toho quickly

"STARING AT EBIRAH FROM THE SHORE, EXPRESSING ANGER BY THROWING MY ARMS UP IN THE AIR, AND LUNGING IN THE WATER. THIS TIME, GODZILLA WAS REALLY FULL OF EMOTION."

—Haruo Nakajima, Godzilla suit actor

pivoted. A few weeks later, on August 8, it announced the revamped production: King Kong was out, Godzilla and Mothra were in, and Toho proceeded without foreign involvement. Shooting began on August 31, 1966, for a New Year's season release date

"I didn't get deep into the details, but I always used current events in the background of the story," Sekizawa once recalled. In October 1964, the People's Republic of China had successfully tested its first atomic bomb, triggering concerns across Asia and the world. The story of Japanese theoretical physicist Shoichi Sakata, a Marxist who visited China around this time, also intrigued Sekizawa. His screenplay is not a political thriller, however, but a lively hybrid of the kaiju genre and Toho's popular action comedies of the mid-sixties. The Red Bamboo is a thinly veiled Chinese stand-in for Bond's terrorist nemesis SPECTRE; the organization's secret plutonium-producing facility on fictional Letchi Island, and the exciting climax with the heroes racing against the clock to flee before a nuclear bomb explodes, bring to mind *Dr. No* (1962) and *Goldfinger* (1964).

Jun Fukuda was a versatile and accomplished craftsman from Toho's roster of mainstream directors, adept at crime dramas, youth pictures, actioners, and comedies. A year earlier, Fukuda had spoofed the Bond films with his slyly titled *Ironfinger* (1965, aka *100 Shot, 100 Killed*), starring Akira Takarada as a tourist mistaken for a spy. In *Ebirah*, Takarada plays a fugitive safecracker unwittingly swept up in a South Pacific adventure to rescue a young fisherman who has disappeared in a typhoon. In a far-fetched and amusing *Robinson Crusoe*–like tale, the crook and a trio of teenagers set sail on a stolen yacht, are shipwrecked by the gigantic crustacean Ebirah, and wash up on a remote island. The heroes are hunted by the Red Bamboo, and one boy is enslaved alongside natives kidnapped from Infant Island. As a diversionary tactic, the protagonists awaken Godzilla, and the sleep-deprived monster faces off with the big shrimp, a giant condor, fighter jets, and Mothra as she swoops in to rescue her people. Sensing a threat, Godzilla demolishes the terrorists' base, triggering the nail-biter of a final act. The heroes escape and, in a memorable endnote, the thankful humans beckon Godzilla to leap into the sea just before the island goes kaboom.

Ebirah is a film made up of replacements: Godzilla replaces Kong, Fukuda assumes the director's

PREVIOUS SPREAD: Ebirah (Hiroshi Sekita) challenges Godzilla (Haruo Nakajima) to a duel. ■ ABOVE: The Infant Island natives perform a ritual dance in the hope of awakening Mothra to help rescue their kidnapped brethren. ■ BOTTOM LEFT: (*left to right*) Akira Takarada (Yoshimura), director Jun Fukuda, Toru Ibuki (Yata), and Toru Watanabe (Ryota) on location.

CLOCKWISE FROM ABOVE: Pair Bambi (Yuko and Yoko Okada), as the Small Beauties, pray to Mothra on an oversize set. ▪ Godzilla smashes the Red Bamboo secret base on Letchi Island. ▪ Acting special effects director Sadamasa Arikawa (*right*) and assistant SFX director Teruyoshi Nakano (*in dark glasses*) discuss a scene involving the flying Mothra puppet. ▪ Mothra arrives to rescue the humans from the doomed island and must fend off an attack from Godzilla. The battle is reminiscent of their titanic struggle in *Mothra vs. Godzilla*.

chair from Ishiro Honda, and longtime assistant Sadamasa Arikawa becomes the de facto special effects director, stepping into the sizeable shoes of Tsuburaya (credited as SFX director for the last time in the Godzilla series, though actually serving as an editorial supervisor). The resources afforded to Arikawa are noticeably reduced; miniature sets are fewer and smaller, the Godzilla suit and Mothra puppet (both a bit worse for wear) and giant condor (a redressed Rodan prop) are all retreads. "I was told that they could not make director Tsuburaya work with such a low budget, so they would have me work on the smaller projects with less money and they would keep the bigger projects for Tsuburaya," remembered Arikawa. "Actually, I thought this was a good thing. If I only imitated Tsuburaya's work, just on a smaller scale, then my movies would have no originality; I wouldn't be putting my own stamp on them."

Arikawa frames Godzilla from new angles to illustrate its gigantic size. More than once, characters come dangerously close to Godzilla's giant feet. Arikawa's camera assumes a monster's vantage point as Ebirah emerges from the sea to fight Godzilla, and when Godzilla broils Ebirah—blasting its heat ray into the camera lens—it's both a new twist on an old trick and an expression of Arikawa and Fukuda's go-for-broke approach. The filmmakers' attention to unusual details—the sight and sound of Godzilla sleeping, and the electric crackling of its dorsals and twitch of its toe when awakened—likewise lend a welcome feeling of experimentation.

This is the first time since 1954 that Godzilla is shown submerged underwater. The majority of the undersea confrontation with Ebirah was filmed on a dry set, with the monsters behind a water tank. Arikawa simulates rays of sunlight filtering through the sea surface, and Godzilla's roar is appropriately muffled in the simulated depths. For scenes actually shot in the water, Nakajima labored mightily because the Godzilla suit would absorb moisture, making it heavy and difficult to move. "It took at least a week to wrap up the water-related filming," Nakajima recalled. "I worked overtime until about eight o'clock every day. I lived in the water! Even though I wore a wet suit under the costume, I got cold. But I never got sick because I was so tense during the filming."

Why a giant shrimp? "It wouldn't be interesting to have two humanlike creatures with two legs," a studio official reportedly mused at the time. "So I thought one should have pincers." Other sources say writer

Sekizawa was inspired by his love of fried shrimp. Either way, Ebirah is a kaiju outlier, a giant animal rather than a fantasy creature. Its inability to fight on land and lack of special powers make it a rather unchallenging foe, yet its aggressive attacks on ships and feasting upon swimmers and sailors make this one of Toho's most terrifying monsters. Designed by SFX art director Yasuyuki Inoue, Ebirah was portrayed by stuntman Hiroshi Sekita in a half-suit, worn from the waist up, when the big red shellfish stands erect in the surf; a tail was attached to the bottom when Godzilla judo-flips the (empty) Ebirah suit or pulls it underwater. The creature's gigantic pincer claw rising from the ocean, set against the night sky amid a raging storm, is a masterfully chilling sight.

"REMEMBER THE SCENE WHEN GODZILLA SCRATCHES HIS NOSE? IT WAS A NOD TO YUZO KAYAMA'S *WAKADAISHO (YOUNG GUY)* SERIES, WHEN HE USED TO SAY, 'BOKAA, SHIAWASE-DANAA!' ('I'M SO HAPPY!') (TSUBURAYA) TOLD ME TO DO IT BECAUSE THOSE MOVIES WERE POPULAR BACK THEN."

—Haruo Nakajima, Godzilla suit actor

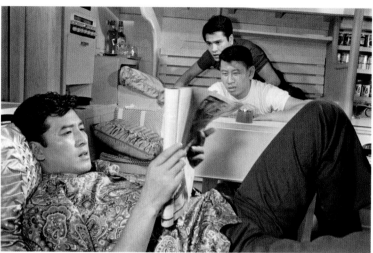

JAZZING IT UP

Since his early work on *Godzilla Raids Again*, Masaru Sato had become one of Japanese cinema's most prominent composers, having scored numerous Kurosawa masterpieces. Here, Sato transports Godzilla into a world of adventure and fantasy with a score that is at times lush and beautiful, or brash and mechanical, or fast-driving, with surf-rock guitars and jazzy horns. "My Godzilla [music] is playful," the composer said. "It's all in good fun." Sato also creates a beautiful vocal piece for the Small Beauties of Infant Island, portrayed here by a new twin-sister act, Pair Bambi (another replacement!). The only real off-key moment comes when the jets attack Godzilla, scored with go-go source music originally recorded for a nightclub in Kurosawa's *High and Low* (1963). It's an odd cue for such an exciting scene; this music was wisely omitted when *Ebirah* was later shown on American television.

AN APPEALING ENSEMBLE

Because King Kong was swapped out at the last minute, Godzilla plays a role written for the ape with apparently few script changes. This may explain why Godzilla sleeps inside a cave and takes an almost Kong-like interest in the native girl. Godzilla continues to gradually evolve from an instinctive, destructive force into a thinking creature with personality and motivation; after tearing off Ebirah's claws, Godzilla taunts the fleeing crustacean, clacking the pincers like castanets. This characterization of the monster meshes well with Fukuda's direction of the actors and his skillful balancing of drama, action, and comedy.

For the first time since 1954, stars Takarada and Akihiko Hirata appear together in a Godzilla movie. Takarada is once again the brave hero and Hirata the eyepatch-wearing adversary, but similarities end there. Hirata chews scenery as an over-the-top Red Bamboo commander leading his gun-happy troops in hot pursuit of the heroes. Kumi Mizuno spends the film in a tropical skirt, playing a role for which she was—of course—a replacement. Actress Noriko Takahashi was originally cast as Dayo, but when she developed appendicitis, producer Tomoyuki Tanaka begged Kumi Mizuno—who was about to quit acting after getting married—to step in. Mizuno performed her own stunts, running and crawling over craggy rocks on location. "I was young enough, so I could do things like that," she recalled. "The only problem was the dark skin color makeup that I had to wear because she was supposed to be a native woman of the South Seas islands, and my skin couldn't breathe. You couldn't wear it for a long time."

Ebirah also swaps Godzilla's usual stomping grounds in Japan for an island setting. While this may have been a cost-cutting move, it signals another evolution in the monster's mythology. The term "monster island" had not been coined yet, but *Ebirah* establishes that Godzilla—like King Kong and Mothra—resides on islands inhabited by inhospitable giant creatures. Although the script does not explicitly say so, Japanese writers have speculated that contamination from the nuclear plant may have lured Godzilla there and/

PREVIOUS SPREAD: The fight between the monsters begins with long-distance boulder volleys from the shore and escalates into hand-to-claw combat in the sea. ■ CLOCKWISE FROM TOP LEFT: Kumi Mizuno as Dayo. ■ The safecracker Yoshimura (Akira Takarada) and castaways Nita (Hideo Sunazuka, *in white shirt*) and Ichino (Chotaro Togin) aboard the ill-fated stolen yacht, the *Yahlen*. ■ Special effects director Sadamasa Arikawa readies Godzilla suit actor Haruo Nakajima for the Red Bamboo air force attack.

CLOCKWISE FROM TOP: The battle between Godzilla and Ebirah is filmed with a handheld camera in the indoor water tank. ▪ Haruo Nakajima: "In the last scene, Godzilla jumped off a cliff into the water. . . . I didn't think about it, I just did it. When I jumped in, Godzilla completely disappeared underwater for a moment. I guess the pool was really deep." ▪ Nakajima makes the leap from the cliff into the indoor pool.

or caused Ebirah to grow into an oxymoronic giant shrimp. And although this is not a political story, the setting nevertheless conjures politically charged images. The total destruction of Letchi brings to mind the US nuclear tests at the Marshall Islands or even the deadly island battles of World War II; the enslavement of Infant Island natives is an unintentional reminder of the subjugation of island peoples during the war.

JUN FUKUDA'S LAMENT

Toho and Rankin/Bass would make *King Kong Escapes*, which had a vaguely similar plot about a rogue nation making nuclear bombs, in 1967. The Honda–Tsuburaya–Ifukube nucleus was reunited, but Toho's effects cinema—and the Godzilla series specifically—was entering a transition period when new, younger talents brought fresh ideas even as economic pressures on the film industry forced them to work under budgetary and creative limitations. "All I can remember is that making [*Ebirah*] was like pouring two cups of water into one," Fukuda remembered. "I had to cut one sequence after another." Fukuda would direct five Godzilla movies in all, and he took a dim view of his own work, telling an interviewer, "The original [*Godzilla*] is the only one that's successful, that's really good. I give all of my Godzilla films a minus score." Yet Fukuda was truly an important contributor to the series, giving Godzilla a jolt of creative energy that would have lasting influence through the end of the Showa cycle in the mid-seventies.

怪獣島の決戦
ゴジラの息子

(*KAIJUTO NO KESSEN: GOJIRA NO MUSUKO /*
SHOWDOWN ON MONSTER ISLAND: SON OF GODZILLA)
RELEASED: DECEMBER 16, 1967 (JAPAN)

SON OF GODZILLA

The sixties saw tremendous conflict and social upheaval around the world. Wars, protests, struggles for equality, assassinations, and environmental concerns fueled uncertainty about the future of humankind and the planet. Postwar population growth reached historic global levels worldwide, and anxiety grew about the global food supply. Would the population explosion cause a deadly mass famine within a few decades?

In 1967, Japan witnessed another type of explosion, a "kaiju boom" wherein all movie studios released at least one *tokusatsu* film, and monster-themed TV shows were simultaneously on the rise. Children had proved to be a dedicated audience, and the genre was now targeted more directly at them. With *Son of Godzilla*, director Jun Fukuda strikes an interesting balance between a straight-ahead science-fiction story about the misuse of technology to manipulate nature and a documentary-like view of monsters living in their natural environment. A baby Godzilla is born and raised, and Godzilla's humanlike attributes continue evolving as the monster becomes a stern but caring parent.

"We wanted to take a new approach," said Fukuda. "So we gave Godzilla a child. We thought that it would be a little strange if Godzilla had a daughter, so we instead gave [the monster] a son. We focused on [their] relationship."

> # "I THOUGHT, *HOW COULD A MALE HAVE A SON?* I THOUGHT GODZILLA WAS MALE, AND I HAD NEVER THOUGHT OTHERWISE. AND IF SOMEONE SAYS, 'MINILLA LOOKS LIKE GODZILLA,' I COMPLETELY DISAGREE."
>
> —Haruo Nakajima, Godzilla suit actor

The original concept was somewhat different, however. An early treatment titled *The Two Godzillas: Japan SOS!!* was penned by writer Kazue Shiba, an associate of screenwriter Shinichi Sekizawa. The story began with a meteorological experiment that goes haywire and awakens Godzilla and Godzilla Junior, who head for Japan and fight a giant mollusk en route. The monsters wreak havoc until a plan is devised to lure them out to sea and explode bombs to create a gigantic artificial whirlpool, which sucks them deep into the Japan Trench.

Son of Godzilla follows a team of United Nations–backed Japanese scientists stationed on fictional Solgell Island in the South Pacific to conduct a climate-control experiment aimed at averting a global food crisis. Dr. Kusumi (Tadao Takashima) and his men are joined by Goro Maki (Akira Kubo), an uninvited reporter who parachutes onto the island, and beautiful Saeko Matsumiya (Bibari Maeda), who is the orphaned daughter of a Japanese scientist and has survived alone on Solgell for years. Saeko befriends Godzilla's adopted offspring, Minilla, who soon grows from a defenseless hatchling into a timid juvenile and eventually learns to fight like a monster. The villains are the island's predatory invertebrates, which pose a more direct threat to humans than typical kaiju. These monsters are essentially giant versions of extant animals: The Kamacuras (aggressive giant mantises) bully and harass and try to eat Minilla; Kumonga (an effectively terrifying giant spider) stalks the scientists, preys on the mantises, attempts to kill Minilla, and blinds Godzilla in one eye.

Sekizawa (who shared screenplay credit with Shiba) again keeps things fast-paced and light, even while using real-world concerns as a backdrop. The weather-control operation mirrors controversial cloud-seeding experiments aimed at boosting rainfall for crop production, or even the US military's secret efforts to create flooding rains and disrupt enemy supply lines during the Vietnam War. Kusumi is a figure of scientific altruism and hubris; he wants to reshape "worthless" deserts and jungles without

PREVIOUS SPREAD: Special effects director Sadamasa Arikawa prepares to shoot the film's ending, in which Godzilla and Minilla attempt to stay warm as Solgell Island rapidly freezes over. ■ TOP: Jun Fukuda's *Ebirah* and *Son of Godzilla* were the first two Godzilla movies to bypass a theatrical release in the US and go straight to TV distribution. This prologue of Godzilla swimming to Solgell Island was cut from the US TV release; it's also the first of several times the 1965–66 Godzilla suit would be redeployed for water scenes in this film, as well as *Destroy All Monsters* and *Godzilla vs. Hedorah.* ■ ABOVE: Minilla amuses itself while Godzilla rests. ■ LEFT: The ensemble cast reacts to a Kamacuras attack. (*left to right*) Akihiko Hirata, Akira Kubo, Bibari Maeda, Tadao Takashima, Yoshio Tsuchiya, and Kenji Sahara (*behind Tsuchiya*). ■ OPPOSITE TOP: Minilla is bullied yet again by the aggressive Kamacuras. Godzilla repeatedly bails the lad out of trouble. ■ OPPOSITE BOTTOM: Godzilla comes to the newborn Minilla's rescue, facing off with three hungry Kamacuras.

regard to the ecosystems that would be radically altered. His work is a meteorological Manhattan Project, a world-changing test conducted at a remote location in secret for fear it could be weaponized in the wrong hands and "freeze the entire planet." Like the H-bomb that birthed Godzilla, it has unforeseen consequences. A glitch causes the experiment to malfunction, and instead of snow, the island is flooded with boiling rains. When the torrent breaks, radiation released by the mishap has mutated the mantises to enormous size.

SMALL WONDER

By this time, Toho was receiving ample fan mail from children fond of its *tokusatsu* films. Fittingly, the name of Godzilla's son was chosen by kids through a public submission campaign, and the winning selection of "Minilla" (often pronounced "Minya" in the West) was announced in a ceremony at Toho Studios, with children on hand to celebrate. With its wide eyes, pug nose, plump middle, and chubby thighs, Minilla resembles a cross between a young Godzilla and a human toddler, and behaves more like the latter. The little monster is alternately playful, friendly, and afraid, and its vexing habit of getting into harm's way turns Godzilla into a beleaguered parent always bailing its adopted son out of trouble.

Minilla is played by the diminutive Masao Fukazawa, a former wrestler and entertainer known by the stage name Kobito no Machan ("Machan the Dwarf" or "Little Man Machan"). Though in his mid-forties, Fukazawa gives a childlike, charming, and comical performance. Minilla clumsily skips rope over a napping Godzilla's twitching tail, and it rubs its tummy when it's hungry for the tropical fruits that Saeko lobs into its maw. Minilla's rite of passage is one of the most beloved scenes in the entire series. When Godzilla attempts to teach its young to exhale a heat ray, the tyke can only muster puny smoke rings (an idea suggested by Eiji Tsuburaya); the lesson concludes when Godzilla steps on the kid's tail and a startled Minilla suddenly emits a powerful blast.

"[Fukazawa] was a veteran comedian who had performed with overseas troupes and in cabarets in Japan," remembered Haruo Nakajima. "Minilla's costume was thin and light, but it was really difficult for Machan because he was a bit older. He was sweating a lot, and I could tell he was struggling. He took it very seriously and tried so hard, and his acting was really good. He came up with all of Minilla's

"GODZILLA AND SON, KAMACURAS, KUMONGA. THIS SHOULD BE CALLED 'MONSTER ISLAND!'"

—Goro Maki (Akira Kubo)

TOP: Special effects director Sadamasa Arikawa (*left*) directs Masao Fukazawa (as Minilla). ■ **ABOVE:** Saeko Matsumiya (Bibari Maeda) befriends Minilla, tossing the young kaiju a melon treat. ■ **LEFT:** Minilla skips rope over Godzilla's twitching tail as a tired-out dad tries to grab a much-needed nap.

CLOCKWISE FROM TOP LEFT: The serrated arms of the mantises were fashioned from sheet metal to give these deadly weapons a sense of sharpness and weight. "There's a scene where they crack open an egg," said effects team member Noboyuki Yasumaru. "I wanted to show the moment it really breaks." ▪ The crew puts finishing touches on the large Kumonga spider puppet, controlled with multiple piano wires for each of its multi-jointed legs, operated by technicians from above. ▪ *Son of Godzilla* special effects supervisor Eiji Tsuburaya (*left*) and director Jun Fukuda (*right*).

movements, waddling like a toddler, etc. With his chubby body, he was very cute. Minilla was really like Machan himself."

With *Son of Godzilla*, Sadamasa Arikawa graduates from his apprenticeship to be officially credited as special effects director for the first time, and he continues to experiment with new ideas and techniques beyond Tsuburaya's typical style. The giant mantises and spider are not men in suits, but large, articulated puppets masterfully brought alive by a team of wire works technicians working in unison.

"The audience believed that monsters needed someone inside to make them move, and I wanted to change that perception," Arikawa recalled. "Even with the low budget, I wanted to do something different so it would be remembered. To move these puppets, so many piano wires were needed. Kumonga had three joints in every leg, each of which needed a wire, and there were eight legs. So to move them all independently, we needed twenty-four wires; along with the body, we had thirty-five wires in total. Kumonga was 13 feet (4 m) wide. In order to get movement in all directions, we had to have operators on all sides, so we required a lot of space. To control the legs, we had a platform above the set with twenty people on it. I was down on the set, yelling out the numbers as to which joint should move and how it should move. It was like a human computer control; when Kumonga moved, I felt we really accomplished something.

"I remember being warned that the wires would show up on the screen. I could see them on the set myself, of course. We did our best to hide them. In the case of Kamacuras, there were only six wires, but you could see them pretty easily. So the 'son of Godzilla' was not able to surpass his father. This is how I felt about my work in this film compared to that of Eiji Tsuburaya. Still, it was something special."

NONTRADITIONAL MONSTER CASTING

Haruo Nakajima plays Godzilla in just two scenes: a prologue wherein an aerial navigator spots the monster at sea, and later, an exciting moment when Godzilla swims ashore. Before the start of filming, Eiji Tsuburaya had visited Nakajima at the Toho B2 actors' room. There would be a little Godzilla, and to make parent Godzilla appear to tower over the child, Tsuburaya wanted to cast actor Seiji Ohnaka, who was about 6 inches (15 cm) taller. "He came to explain to me, just out of respect," Nakajima said. "I always appreciated his thoughtful, kind gesture."

Ohnaka typically played background parts like cops and soldiers; in *Rodan*, he was a photographer killed by the monster. His first kaiju role was grueling. "[The Godzilla suit] was so heavy, and I thought I would just die," Ohnaka later recalled. "Inside the suit, I said, 'Son, come here, it's dangerous there,' or 'This is how to shoot the radioactive ray.' Of course, the audience can't hear my voice, they can only see the action. That was really tough work, but the pay was very good." After filming began, however, Ohnaka injured his hand while playing baseball, and the Godzilla scenes were completed with Hiroshi Sekita, who had previously played Ebirah, in the role.

Though he was not on set, Tsuburaya was credited as special effects supervisor and oversaw the editing of special effects scenes. "Arikawa showed the rushes to Tsuburaya for confirmation, and Tsuburaya edited them," recalled script supervisor Keiko Suzuki. "When he was editing, I heard him say things like, 'It doesn't connect well here. It needs this kind of cut for better continuity.' Then he called up Arikawa and said, 'Film such-and-such to insert here. Otherwise, it won't work.' I'm sure it was a good experience for Arikawa because he was becoming a director himself, yet he still had much to learn from Tsuburaya."

In the second half of the sixties, Toho produced multiple special effects movies per year. These included not only sci-fi and monster films, but also war films and an occasional fantasy or comedy picture. *Son* is the second straight Godzilla movie not made by the Honda–Tsuburaya–Ifukube A-team, which was instead assigned to coproductions with foreign investors, such as *The War of the Gargantuas* (1966), *King*

Kong Escapes (1967), and *Latitude Zero* (1969). Explaining his absence from the series during this time, Honda said, "One [reason] was scheduling conflicts. The other was Toho's concern that people would feel monster films had to be directed by me."

Like *Ebirah*, this film is better suited to Fukuda's skillful, action-driven style. The likable cast is an ensemble of Toho special effects film stars, including not only Takashima, but Kenji Sahara and Akihiko Hirata as scientists, and Akira Kubo as the reporter. The versatile Yoshio Tsuchiya stands out as Furukawa, a scientist driven to the brink of madness by the island's intense heat. Fukuda shot exteriors on Guam, lending the beaches, jungles, and hills of Solgell a lush beauty. (Takashima, the nominal leading man, declined to visit Guam for fear of flying; his scenes there were shot with a body double.) *Son of Godzilla* also features an unprecedented amount of composite photography employing location and studio footage, matte paintings, and matte work to place humans and monsters into the same shot, in ways that are often breathtakingly convincing. Composer Masaru Sato again provides a lively tableau of distinct motifs for the island, the various monsters, and the suspenseful buildup to the experiment and its outcome.

Fukuda creates another memorable ending, a melancholy coda amid a man-made blizzard. Godzilla and son vanquish the horrible Kumonga and briefly celebrate, only to struggle through the snow as the island rapidly freezes over. With no place to hide, Godzilla and Minilla embrace on the shore, father affectionately shielding son from the subzero onslaught as they drift into hibernation. Never again would Godzilla transcend the norms of monster behavior quite so profoundly as in *Son of Godzilla*.

ABOVE: The giant spider Kumonga proves to be one of Godzilla's most aggressive and dangerous opponents. ■ RIGHT: Kumonga is distracted from its deadly pursuit of Minilla (*foreground, in webbing*) as Kamacuras looks to snatch the spider's meal away.

怪獣総進撃

(KAIJU SOSHINGEKI / MARCH OF THE MONSTERS)
RELEASED: AUGUST 1, 1968 (JAPAN)

DESTROY ALL MONSTERS

One of the most unforgettable sequences in Godzilla's entire filmography comes in the early moments of *Destroy All Monsters*. The viewer is taken on a documentary-style flyover of the Ogasawara Islands, where all the Earth's giant creatures are now held safely in captivity in Monsterland. One by one, a narrator introduces the monsters, which almost seem to acknowledge the camera. An offshore marine ranch keeps the kaiju well fed, and security devices prevent them from escaping. In an underground research facility, an international team of scientists studies these majestic creatures that once endangered humanity but are now tamed by technological prowess. Suddenly this monster utopia is shattered: A mysterious gas floods the island, and everything on it—human and leviathan—succumbs.

Destroy All Monsters is a watershed in kaiju cinema history, an unprecedented assembly of creatures from across the Tohoverse—eleven of them in all—brought together for a spectacular apex of the studio's long and successful run of special effects pictures. With a simple, good-versus-evil story and a spirited musical score, this film has remained a nostalgic cult favorite, remembered by many as the last hurrah of the classic era. It also represents a final bow for the collective talents of special effects master Eiji Tsuburaya (credited again as supervisor), director Ishiro Honda, composer Akira Ifukube, and producer Tomoyuki Tanaka. Fourteen years after 1954's *Godzilla*, the founding quartet reunites for what was intended, according to many sources, to be a coda. "They

PREVIOUS SPREAD: The Monsterland containment system includes a gas barrier that prevents Godzilla and other creatures from leaving the island. This is the last Godzilla suit made by original suit maker Teizo Toshimitsu. ▪ ABOVE, CLOCKWISE FROM TOP LEFT: Manda wraps its body around the monorail, its movement achieved via intricate manipulation with wires above and on each side of the puppet. A brief battle between Godzilla and Manda was also filmed but omitted from the final cut. ▪ Rodan feeds on marine life from Monsterland's undersea ranch. The care, feeding, and study of the captive monsters were an early concept in the story development by director Ishiro Honda and cowriter Kaoru Mabuchi. ▪ The Baragon suit from *Frankenstein Conquers the World* had subsequently been loaned to Tsuburaya Productions and modified into several different monsters that appeared in television programs. The suit was in such poor overall condition that it appears only briefly. ▪ King Ghidorah is brought to Earth as the Kilaaks' ultimate weapon. ▪ Godzilla exhorts the monsters to attack the city. ▪ When Gorosaurus destroys the Arc de Triomphe, a newscaster misidentifies the creature as Baragon, the subterranean monster. This apparent gaffe has caused long-standing confusion as to whether Baragon was supposed to appear in this scene, but storyboards indicate the filmmakers always intended Gorosaurus to do the deed.

ABOVE, CLOCKWISE FROM TOP LEFT: Anguirus surveys its lair in Monsterland. Anguirus is one of just two original monster suits created by Noboyuki Yasumaru for this film. ■ Earth's monsters team up to punch, kick, choke, stomp, and finally cocoon King Ghidorah into submission. Kumonga's webbing was made of rubber cement used to fix flat tires. ■ The original Varan puppet from the monster's debut in 1958's *Varan the Unbelievable* is refurbished and used in two brief scenes. ■ The Kilaaks' preferred mode of transportation is a traditional, round-shaped flying saucer. In the film's climax, the aliens unleash the Fire Dragon—which is really just a flying saucer in burning mode—as a final gambit against the Earth. ■ Godzilla and Minilla celebrate the Earth monsters' hard-won victory over King Ghidorah. ■ *Destroy All Monsters* continually raises the monster stakes. Just when it seems Godzilla, Manda, and Rodan have Tokyo vanquished, suddenly Mothra bursts onto the scene.

"THIS MONSTER FORCE WITH GODZILLA AT ITS HEAD IS A SIGHT TO SEE!"

—Newscaster

were going to end the Godzilla series then," remembered special effects director Sadamasa Arikawa. "Tanaka figured that all the ideas had just run out."

Not exactly. Honda and cowriter Kaoru Mabuchi (aka Takeshi Kimura) were given a simple directive: "Show all the monsters." In addition to Godzilla, Rodan, Mothra, Anguirus, King Ghidorah, Minilla, and Kumonga, they recruited four Toho creatures from beyond the Godzilla series: Gorosaurus (a dinosaur from *King Kong Escapes*, 1967), Manda (a sea serpent from *Atragon*, 1964), Varan (*Varan the Unbelievable*, 1958), and Baragon (*Frankenstein Conquers the World*, 1965), Appropriately, the film was developed under the working title *Monster Chushingura*, a reference to the historical tale of a gang of forty-seven ronin avenging their master's unjust death. Mabuchi, a veteran Toho genre scribe whose works were often marked by gloomy, misanthropic themes, instead delivers a colorful, effects-centric popcorn extravaganza that combines most everything that made the studio's classic-era kaiju romps and space-invader epics exciting and fun. Aliens from planet Kilaak—rocklike beings who take the form of Japanese women—deploy the monsters as remote-controlled drones, smashing cities worldwide and demanding humanity's surrender. Moscow, Beijing, Paris, London, New York, and Tokyo are all attacked. Astronauts and aliens engage in a series of chase scenes on Earth and the moon, with kitschy flying saucers

CLOCKWISE FROM TOP LEFT: The Kilaak queen (Kyoko Ai) issues an ultimatum to the people of Earth. ▪ Dr. Otani (Yoshio Tsuchiya) welcomes Kyoko Manabe (Yukiko Kobayashi) to her first day on the job in Monsterland. Under Kilaak mind control, Kyoko will transform into a coldhearted villain who does the aliens' evil bidding. ▪ Close-up of Manda, the serpent protector-god of the Mu Empire, originally seen in Toho's *Atragon* (1963).

ABOVE: Gorosaurus and Mothra in peaceful coexistence in Monsterland.
■ RIGHT: Mothra tests the Monsterland containment system.

and a futuristic spaceship-rocket, the SY-3. The final battle is an unprecedented ante upper. Godzilla leads Earth's monsters in an all-versus-one war against King Ghidorah at the foot of Mount Fuji, the army of mighty creatures assembled spectacularly across the widescreen vista, while a TV newscaster provides dramatic commentary.

Destroy All Monsters is set in 1999, three decades into the future, and showcases director Honda's idealized vision of a harmonious, rational, international coalition. Scientists rather than politicians are in positions of authority, and the United Nations serves as a science-centric, quasi-governmental global organization that manages aerospace and military matters. (This is the only Toho film in which Godzilla attacks the US; the aliens order the monster to destroy not Washington, but the real power center: the UN headquarters.) Reminders of past conflicts become idealistic symbols of peace: The film was made amid worldwide anticipation of the Apollo 11 lunar mission, and rockets to the moon are launched from a space center on Iwo Jima, the island where the US planted its flag in 1945. In June 1968, roughly one month before the film's release, America officially ended its twenty-three-year occupation of the Ogasawara Islands; Honda sees this archipelago not as a former war outpost but as a scientific Xanadu, where humankind and monsters coexist. Early concepts had the researchers raising monsters in a bio-technology research project, Honda recalled; the director had hoped to explore the imaginary science of the creatures—their behaviors, their languages, even the possibility of communicating with them—more thoroughly, if not for practical limitations.

"[Mabuchi] and I agreed it would be crazy to make each of the monsters just somehow appear," Honda said. "Eventually, we came up with an island on which all the monsters had been collected for scientific study. We imagined that undersea farming would be required to feed all of the monsters. . . . I thought about the idea of a marine ranch scientifically, it would be what we now call aquaculture. From there, we started to develop the storyline.

ABOVE: The Moonlight SY-3 was designed by Mutsumi Toyoshima, whose previous work included the Maser Cannons from *The War of the Gargantuas.* Toyoshima based the spaceship-rocket on the F-14 fighter aircraft. He often referred to NASA designs for inspiration. The modeling crew made the SY-3 in three different scales. ■ **LEFT:** Special effects director Sadamasa Arikawa and Manda on the Tokyo miniature set. ■ **BELOW:** The Tokyo assault marks the last time Godzilla would attack Japan in the original series of films.

"Initially, I had a lot more underwater scenes in the script. I was going to use special effects and set filming to depict them. But because of financial as well as time constraints, what you ultimately see is what we were able to do—the bare minimum. In a way, those things [that I could not do] were the scenes I wanted to film the most. Back then, the notion of aquaculture and biotechnology was already there, and we knew that things were going in that direction in the future."

HIGH-WIRE ACT

Arikawa had been a key member of the Toho special effects team since the birth of Godzilla. This would be Arikawa's last effort as the series' special effects director, as he would soon depart Toho to begin working in television productions, and once again he demonstrates a particular mastery of wirework effects. The climactic monster melee may appear to be a free-for-all but was meticulously choreographed, performed, and edited. The unusual number of actors in monster suits on the set, coupled with a multitude of wires required to control the movements and flight of King Ghidorah, Rodan, and Mothra, plus all the other monsters' tails, amounted to an unprecedented challenge. Rather than pulleys operated from the floor, the monsters were manipulated by crew members balancing on a narrow wooden walkway 20 to 30 feet (6 to 9 m) above, handling piano wires that could slice off a finger if not properly handled; down below, the suit actors struggled to avoid getting tangled up in the wires or breaking them.

"Even if things went well in rehearsals, it didn't mean we'd get a good take," said Haruo Nakajima. "There were so many monsters, and each one had to get a spotlight. On top of that, Godzilla is the main monster, so it was really hard to determine how to stage the fight, the composition, that kind of thing. You couldn't just fight without planning. You had to plan first, then fight." Arikawa also offers a few new creative flashes that again distinguish his work from Tsuburaya's. The arrival of King Ghidorah at Mount Fuji, sailing over the waiting monsters below, and the Fire Dragon's dive-bombing confrontation with Godzilla are two brief-but-exciting moments.

The studio reportedly allocated a budget of ¥200 million for the production—¥80 million more than recent efforts—yet with the throng of monsters, numerous effects scenes, and the requisite sets, props, and staffing, resources were nonetheless stretched. New-look Godzilla and Anguirus costumes were created by the suit-making team, but the other nine monsters were portrayed via suits and/or props reused from

"THE MONSTERS ARE ON OUR SIDE NOW. THEY'LL OBEY OUR COMMANDS."

—Dr. Otani (Yoshio Tsuchiya)

ABOVE: Suit maker Teizo Toshimitsu repairs the Rodan suit—which was previously seen in *Invasion of Astro Monster*—for use in this film. ■ **RIGHT:** Under Kilaak control, Kyoko Manabe (Yukiko Kobayashi, *center*) and her henchmen (Kazuo Suzuki and Susumu Kurobe) threaten the heroes in an attempt to steal the body of Dr. Otani.

past productions. Some of these (Gorosaurus, Minilla, Kumonga) were practically new, while others required refurbishing. For long-distance or flyover shots, puppets of the monsters were created.

The excesses of *Destroy All Monsters* were apparently intended as a response to the popular *tokusatsu* television programs, such as Tsuburaya Productions' *Ultraman*, that saw aliens sending monsters to conquer Earth on a weekly basis and giant, kaiju-fighting heroes aligned with space-traveling organizations such as the Science Patrol defending Japan and the planet. It's also notable that *Destroy All Monsters* would be the last of Toho's original wave of monster movies to receive a standard theatrical release, and that it hit cinemas on a double bill with Toho's undersea fantasy *Atragon*, which was cut to seventy-five minutes to quicken the pace and emphasize kaiju scenes. Beginning with the following year's *All Monsters Attack* and continuing through *Terror of Mechagodzilla*, all new Godzilla movies would be part of the Toho Champion Matsuri, a recurring children's entertainment marathon that typically featured a main attraction accompanied by cartoons, shorts, an episode of a *tokusatsu* TV show, and often an older kaiju film that was similarly shortened.

The Kilaaks meet their end when Godzilla, freed from all external control, locates the aliens' secret base at Izu Peninsula and destroys it, fighting alongside humankind in a way that would have been unimaginable in 1954. This is effectively the end of one era and the start of a new chapter, in which Godzilla would be cast unambiguously as Earth's hero and guardian. The movie then concludes with another flyover of Ogasawara, where the monsters are corralled once again. The protagonists happily wave goodbye to the creatures, but in hindsight, the scene feels unintentionally somber. Godzilla and adopted son, Minilla, and all the rest, are confined to a tiny island, all-powerful giant creatures now rendered unthreatening and small. Ifukube's music has driven the film's many high points with animated marches and a titanic battle opus of monster themes. But in these final moments, as the monsters appear to bid farewell to the camera, the composer offers a parting lament.

Rumors of the series' demise were, as it turned out, premature. *Destroy All Monsters* was a significant hit, the twelfth-highest-grossing domestic release in Japan for 1968, according to *Kinema Junpo*, thus the series would continue. "I'd heard that the plan was to show all the monsters together and to make it the last one, at least for a while," Nakajima remembered. "I don't know if it was true, but after all, Godzilla just kept going."

PREVIOUS SPREAD: Godzilla charges as King Ghidorah takes to the air in the climactic battle. ■ **ABOVE:** Hero astronaut Katsuo (Akira Kubo, *center*) and team destroy the Kilaaks' transmitter, hidden on the moon. ■ **BELOW:** Godzilla, under alien control, defends the Kilaak base when the Earth forces attack.

RIGHT: The King Ghidorah costume last seen in *Invasion of Astro-Monster* was given a new gold paint job, and its fabric wings were redone in vinyl. The monster's movements are smoother overall than in previous films, and its dramatic landing at Mount Fuji for the showdown—with Earth's monsters reacting in lifelike fashion—is a memorable moment. ■ **BOTTOM RIGHT:** Godzilla leads the charge into the final battle. Artist Fuchimu Shimakura created the majestic backdrop of Mount Fuji that looms above. "I've painted Mount Fuji so many times that I don't need to look at anything. Our job is to paint quickly, so I don't bother with references," Shimakura said.

PRODUCTION DESIGN: SHOWA SERIES

Godzilla's rampages and battles begin as words on the pages of a screenplay, but they are brought to cinematic life through a long process that begins with production design, an essential yet often underappreciated aspect of moviemaking. Design sketches specify the look of each character, set designs indicate the layout of the miniature sets, and storyboards represent the flow of the film in drawings that capture each shot in a sequence. These are the blueprints used by the artists and craftspeople of Toho's special effects department to translate the story from script to screen.

LEFT: Art school students were hired part time to draw the extensive storyboards for *Godzilla*, resulting in a mixture of styles and depictions of the title character. ■ **BELOW LEFT:** Concept design of Ebirah for *Ebirah, Horror of the Deep*. Note that the placement of the human figure inside the suit is roughly drawn in by Yasuyuki Inoue. ■ **BELOW RIGHT:** Image board of Godzilla asleep inside a cavern on Letchi Island for *Ebirah, Horror of the Deep* by Inoue. ■ **OPPOSITE, CLOCKWISE FROM TOP:** Preliminary sketch by Inoue of the Monster Island inhabitants for *All Monsters Attack*. ■ Image board for the final battle in *Destroy All Monsters* by Inoue. ■ Image board by Inoue of the battle between Godzilla and Kumonga in *Son of Godzilla*. ■ Set design of the hill where Minilla's egg is buried for *Son of Godzilla*. Godzilla and Kamacuras are shown for scale. This plan by Inoue shows a full breakdown of materials and cost needed to create the set.

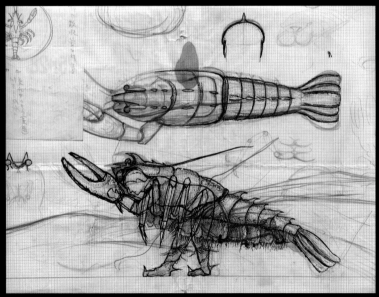

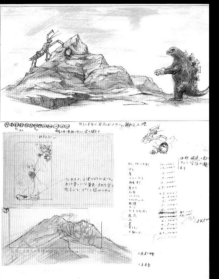

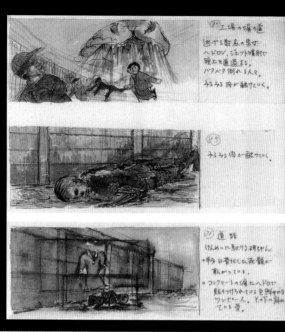

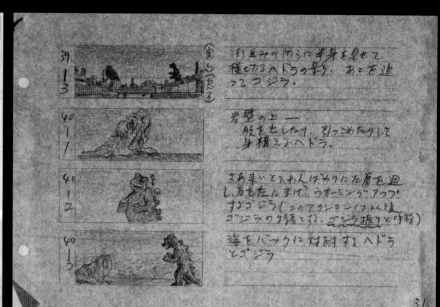

CLOCKWISE FROM TOP LEFT: Image board for *Godzilla Raids Again* of Godzilla on Kamiko Island by Yasuyuki Inoue. ▪ Rough storyboards for *Destroy All Monsters* of the Tokyo attack by Inoue. ▪ Original design sketch of King Ghidorah by Akira Watanabe for *Ghidorah, the Three Headed Monster*. ▪ Set design by Inoue for the meteor that brings King Ghidorah to Earth in *Ghidorah, the Three-Headed Monster*.

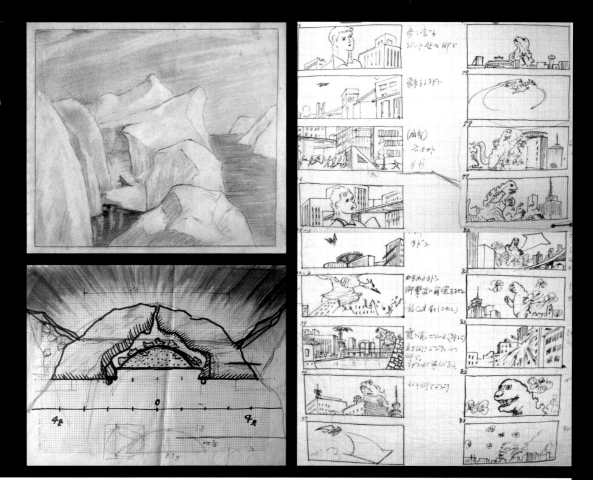

(*GOJIRA MINIRA GABARA ORU KAIJU DAISHINGEKI* /
GODZILLA, MINILLA, GABARA: ALL MONSTERS ATTACK)
aka *Godzilla's Revenge*
RELEASED: DECEMBER 20, 1969 (JAPAN)

ALL MONSTERS ATTACK

In March 1968, Eiji Tsuburaya invited about one hundred children to meet the creatures from Monsterland on the set of *Destroy All Monsters*. Minilla was introduced, wearing a typical grade-schooler's outfit, with a yellow hat and backpack and carrying a yellow flag. The little monster taught the children about pedestrian road safety: walking home along busy streets, using crosswalks, and using hand signals to stop motorists. Then the kids posed for a photo with their kaiju friends.

The real-life embrace between monsters and youngsters becomes the stuff of dreams in the kaiju fable *All Monsters Attack*. A troubled schoolboy escapes to an imaginary Monster Island, where he is befriended by Godzilla's talking son, and the pair learn essential life lessons together. This character-driven monster movie isn't actually a monster movie at all but a metafiction set in the real world, where monsters exist only in the movies and in a kid's fantasies. There is no destruction, no aliens, no scientists, no military. Long misunderstood, *All Monsters Attack* is a clever departure from the standard formula, a sixty-nine-minute children's entertainment gem.

"The company wanted a lot of monsters, but they told us that they had no [budget]," director Ishiro Honda recalled. "We decided to take on one of the

"GODZILLA SAYS I HAVE TO LEARN TO FIGHT MY OWN BATTLES."

—Minilla (voiced by Midori Uchiyama)

social problems of that time, the latchkey kid. We set it up that the kid liked monsters, so he pretends and makes it all real. This one got to be really popular and made a lot of money, and it is one of my favorites as well."

The setting is Kawasaki, a major industrial hub and a symbol of the uneasy trade-offs of rapid postwar growth, blighted by smoky factories and noisy, smoggy, congested highways. Working-class people struggle and strive to make ends meet. Local police search for two bank robbers hiding in the neighborhood. Against this bleak backdrop, the story follows good-natured but diminutive Ichiro (Tomonori Yazaki), a lonely kid whose parents work long hours and who's routinely harassed by the neighborhood bully. Minilla is his reflection, a lonely monster boy always pushed around by a big, green, ugly ogre with a hyena laugh. Dreams and reality blur: Ichiro's nemesis and Minilla's tormentor are both called Gabara.

Japan's film industry attained its commercial apex in the late fifties, but from 1960 to 1970, national attendance would plummet from about one billion to two-hundred-and-fifty million annually. More televisions meant there was less incentive to go to the movies; kaiju films in particular competed with

PREVIOUS SPREAD: Gabara terrorizes the diminutive Minilla. Japanese promotional materials for the film declared, "The furious new monster Gabara appears, challenging for the throne of Monster Island!" ■ CLOCKWISE FROM LEFT: Eisei Amamoto, an actor usually known for playing oddball characters, is the warmhearted toy inventor and neighbor who acts as Ichiro's (Tomonori Yazaki) surrogate parent. ■ The child cast of *All Monsters Attack*. ■ Schoolchildren greeted by Minilla, Godzilla, and the rest on the *Destroy All Monsters* set. ■ OPPOSITE TOP: Godzilla actor Haruo Nakajima (*center, with headband*) helps direct Gabara suit actor Hiroshi Sekita. Special effects technician Teruyoshi Nakano (*in white hat*) and crew members observe. ■ OPPOSITE BOTTOM: Gabara is an upright, warty, toad-like, evil kaiju that looks a bit like the creatures from *Where the Wild Things Are*. This was the only new kaiju suit created for the film.

monster-themed TV shows. The end of the drive-in era and changes in the American film market reduced opportunities for overseas coproductions and distribution. As the studio resumed the Godzilla series, it pivoted to a more economical and child-focused approach. A Godzilla cartoon series was planned to be coproduced with Hollywood-based Filmation, but the deal fell through. Then, in the fall of 1969, screenwriter Shinichi Sekizawa proposed a different style of Godzilla movie—a children's fantasy repurposing monster scenes from prior films, thus requiring a very low budget. The project was fast-tracked, and the movie began shooting on October 11, 1969, to be released just over two months later.

Previous entries were made for general audiences, with children in mind, but *All Monsters Attack* is the first created expressly for kids. The difference is apparent from the very beginning. "March of the Monsters," a zippy vocal theme song written by Gendai Kano, who penned tunes for actor-singer Akira Kobayashi, plays under a montage of Godzilla film clips; the "Go, Go, Gojira!" melody is a recurring musical theme. The soundtrack by composer Kunio Miyauchi, better known for *tokusatsu* TV themes, is a fun, sixties-era jazz-pop hybrid with a small band rather than a traditional big orchestra—some instruments were performed by Miyauchi himself—and effortlessly pivots from one childhood emotion to another.

Like the film adaptation of *The Secret Life of Walter Mitty* (1947), Ichiro steps into scenes from his favorite monster movies. Godzilla's battles with Kumonga, a giant condor, Kamacuras, fighter jets, and Ebirah the sea monster are all taken—in edited form—from Jun Fukuda's *Ebirah, Horror of the Deep* and *Son of Godzilla*. Screenwriter Shinichi Sekizawa had included Rodan and a giant octopus in his original draft, presumably to be included via footage from previous Honda films, but the director decided to use the Fukuda material instead because its island settings suited the story better. (Curiously, Minilla's fire-breathing lesson from *Son of Godzilla* was refilmed; the new version has Godzilla as an even more stern parent.) Other than some noticeable changes in Godzilla's appearance from scene to scene, or an abrupt shift from day to night, these stock scenes are smoothly integrated, with cutaways showing Ichiro and Minilla watching and reacting from a distance. Bits and pieces of stock footage had appeared in previous Toho films, but this is the first to reuse nearly entire scenes, an approach previously tried by Daiei Studios' economy-minded Gamera series.

TOP: Ichiro's visits to Monster Island are achieved via a "computer" composed of scavenged junk radio parts and headphones. ▪ ABOVE: The tormentor Gabara (which, according to the script, is supposed to be a mutated toad) searches for the easily bullied Minilla. ▪ OPPOSITE, CLOCKWISE FROM TOP LEFT: Motoyoshi Tomioka's camera captures the battle between Minilla and Gabara on Monster Island. ▪ Minilla is raised on a platform to shoot the scene where the child monster jumps down for a surprise attack on Gabara. ▪ In dreamland, Minilla is alternately a human-size talking monster (voiced by actress Midori Uchiyama) and a kaiju-size creature whose growing pains mirror those of Ichiro.

For much of 1969, Tsuburaya (respectfully credited as special effects supervisor) and his effects technicians were creating a major audiovisual exhibit for the upcoming Expo '70 event in Osaka, therefore Tsuburaya and many of his staff were unavailable for *All Monsters Attack*. For the first time, there was just one crew, working under Honda on both the human drama and a handful of new monster scenes. "I directed almost [everything]," Honda said, because of "the limited size of the production budget and time constraints. In addition, the movie was shot on a very small sound stage, so it was decided not to separate the filming of the special effects and the standard footage." Veteran assistant effects director Teruyoshi Nakano was on set to advise, as well. "[The director] would say to me, 'I do not know how to go about directing the effects, so please, go ahead and do it for us,'" Nakano said. "I even went on locations with him. We were always moving together. . . . The difference was that there was only one schedule, based on the entire film as a whole."

In another change, effects cinematographer Motoyoshi Tomioka was director of photography for the entire film, lending visual continuity across disparate settings. A polluted stream where kids fish, barren lots where they play, and the dingy interior of a condemned factory are Ichiro's reality; his dreamworld is colorful and bright. A symbolic rabbit hole on Monster Island and a parallel hole in the floor of a deserted building form a motif, each leading Ichiro into and out of danger. Ichiro longs for more time with his parents, and in scenes between the boy and his sympathetic but overworked dad (Kenji Sahara), Tomioka's camera deftly emphasizes the space separating them.

This is a compact, sincere drama about the social problem of bullying, made several years before serious research was published on the subject. Told almost entirely from a child's point of view, the film is well-directed and features a fine performance from Yazaki, a natural young actor who conveys Ichiro's sadness and isolation without wallowing in sentimentality.

With changing economic realities impacting the Godzilla series and filmmaking in general, some crew members were already feeling wistful. "[We] had to draw the line, suck it up, and take it for what it was," recalled Koji Hashimoto, an assistant director. "There was a feeling of disappointment for those who were involved in creating really heavy kaiju films in the past. But we couldn't do anything about the passing of time." More significant changes were forthcoming. Still, *All Monsters Attack* ends with optimism and hope. As strict-but-caring daddy Godzilla teaches Minilla to fight like a monster, Ichiro also learns to fend for himself. Kidnapped by the crooks, the boy bravely fends them off and escapes, leading to their arrest. He becomes a local celebrity for solving the crime and heroically dispenses with the local bully. With its positive message and whimsical charm, the film remains unique among the entire series.

GODZILLA VS. HEDORAH

Godzilla flies!

No, really—*Godzilla flies!*

Godzilla vs. Hedorah is indisputably the most offbeat of all Godzilla movies: A serious-minded effort to revisit the monster's origins as a cautionary symbol, infused with environmentalism, sixties-era counterculture, psychedelic rock, a Woodstock-style outdoor jam, hallucinations, 007-style opening credits, and unprecedented suffering wrought by a horrific monster that rains down deadly pollution. It is also a sincere children's story about a young boy with a telepathic relationship to Godzilla, told with colorful cartoon interludes. A heroic, battle-scarred Godzilla saves the day, taking flight in one of the most oft-discussed moments in the series.

This radical departure came to be via a confluence of seismic events in the film industry and the personal convictions of first-time Godzilla series director Yoshimitsu Banno. Eiji Tsuburaya's untimely death at sixty-eight of a heart attack on January 28, 1970, stunned Toho's special effects team and brought an outpouring of tributes to the master; Ishiro Honda's retirement later that year further lent an air of uncertainty about the future. Meanwhile, economic pressures led Japan's film studios to undergo major restructuring in order to compete. Toho created several subsidiaries, including Toho Eiga (Toho Pictures), the main production arm; the special effects department

"THINKING ABOUT THE MESSAGE OF THE ORIGINAL GODZILLA, I BELIEVED THE BIGGEST THREAT TO MODERN CIVILIZATION WAS POLLUTION."

—Yoshimitsu Banno, director, *Godzilla vs. Hedorah*

---

was shuttered on March 1, 1970, and *tokusatsu* productions would subsequently continue beneath the new banner of Toho Eizo (Toho Visual), under producer Tomoyuki Tanaka's supervision. "[*Hedorah*] was the first Godzilla film after Tsuburaya's death," recalled Teruyoshi Nakano of the effects team. "Everyone had mixed feelings about what should happen now. But we had to keep going."

Banno was an experienced assistant director who had worked on numerous films, including several by Akira Kurosawa. In 1969–70, Banno directed *The Birth of the Japanese Islands*, the short film produced by Tanaka for the Mitsubishi Group's exhibition hall at Expo '70. During the expo, "Tanaka told me to think about ideas for the next Godzilla film," Banno recalled. "At that time, there was a news story about high school girls in Suginami who got sick from breathing smog." He personally witnessed the industrial pollution of Japan's coastline, fouled with chemicals and garbage. "I told [Tanaka] that a pollution monster would be very timely. He liked the idea."

Banno had grown up near the sea and was ecology-minded. He admired biologist Rachel Carson, whose 1962 bestseller, *Silent Spring,* helped inspire the environmental movement; Banno's lyrics for the film's theme song, "Give Back the Sun," would be inspired by Carson's writing. However, *Hedorah* is more specifically a response to the plague of pollution-related illnesses that struck Japan in the 1950s and '60s. These included Minamata disease, caused by mercury poisoning of coastal fisheries; Yokkaichi Asthma, resulting from factory emissions of sulfur dioxide; and *itai-itai* (ouch-ouch) disease, linked to cadmium dumped in rivers by mining companies. The film would mirror the victims' suffering and the public outcry that followed: beautiful Mount Fuji watching over smoke-belching factories; trash and scum floating on waterways ("Banno was so into it, he even brought rotten fish to the studio—it was so stinky!" recalled Nakano); a crying baby covered in mud; political protests; irate citizens; oxygen masks for sale; a young boy washing pollutants from his eyes; reports of mass casualties. Though released during the Champion Matsuri film festival for children, Banno's film is the only Showa series entry that might truly be labeled a polemic. "I wanted to make a movie not just for kids, but also something an adult could enjoy," Banno said.

The project was greenlit, yet in this new climate, the neophyte was afforded a lower budget, a short shooting schedule of thirty-five days, a cast without stars, just two live-action sets, and as with *All Monsters Attack,* there would be one crew for both the drama and effects rather than the traditional dual-team system. A first draft by veteran writer Kaoru Mabuchi focused on a child, a fisherman, and an older scientist; Banno and Kimura sequestered ("at a cheap hotel, with lots of discussion and arguments," Banno remembered) for heavy rewrites. Banno oversaw the entire film, while Nakano (credited simply as "special effects") assisted. SFX art director Yasuyuki Inoue and his team would pull double duty to visualize Banno's concepts, not only designing and creating Hedorah and other effects, props, and sets, but also the groovy go-go nightclub, modeled after a real-life disco in Tokyo's Roppongi nightlife district. Amazingly, even under these conditions, Banno brought his unusual vision to fruition, incorporating split screen, animation, a moody visual style, and all without relying on stock footage.

POLLUTION AND PESSIMISM

If *All Monsters Attack* was a kaiju-loving kid's dream, this is the stuff of nightmares. Young Ken Yano's (Hiroyuki Kawase) first encounter with Hedorah leaves him with a burned hand and wondering if his

"GODZILLA CURLS UP AND FLIES, EMITTING ITS HEAT RAY. THIS SCENE, NOT ORIGINALLY IN THE SCRIPT, AND CONTROVERSIAL FOR LONGTIME FANS, WAS DREAMED UP BY DIRECTOR BANNO AND NAKANO. THEY WANTED TO DO SOMETHING UNEXPECTED."

—Koichi Kawakita, assistant director of special effects

scuba-diving father has been killed; Ken, standing alone on a beach and calling out "Papa!" is among the saddest sights in any Godzilla film. His dad, the scientist Dr. Yano (Akira Yamanouchi), remains bandaged from his monster-inflicted injuries. Hedorah is an alien spore that regenerates by feeding on industrial pollution; the seemingly unkillable creature's battles with Godzilla result in deadly ooze and toxic gas killing thousands. In another unforgettable scene, a tongue of monster mud descends the stairs of the nightclub, fouling a helpless kitten. Hedorah's flyover coats Ken's toys in slime and kills the fish in his aquarium (recalling Dr. Serizawa's experiment in the original *Godzilla*). The boy witnesses charred human bodies in the streets, survives a massive explosion, and watches his uncle die. Child actor Kawase previously played the beggar's son in Kurosawa's tragic poverty fable *Dodes'ka-den* (1970); here he delivers a remarkably stoic performance as a child exposed to innumerable traumatic events. Godzilla, meanwhile, suffers massive burns and injuries in its fights with the amorphous Smog Monster: a hand almost turned to bone, blinded in one eye, and nearly drowned in toxic crud.

"I killed lots of people, including one of the protagonists," Banno said. "Some were turned into skeletons, and people playing mah-jongg were attacked. I wanted to create the fear of pollution spreading everywhere. Producer Tanaka didn't object. During the last half of the shoot, he was hospitalized [Tanaka was reportedly treated for exhaustion after concluding the Expo '70 project], but he was there when I was

CLOCKWISE FROM TOP LEFT: Keiko Mari performs the film's theme song while dancing in a nightclub, one of only two sets built for the film. ■ Yoshimitsu Banno directing the go-go club scene, where environmental desecration and a few good cocktails cause Ken's uncle to have hallucinations of dancers transforming into fish. ■ Whereas *All Monsters Attack* acknowledged Godzilla as a fictional monster, in this film, Godzilla exists both in the real world and in the movies, as illustrated by Ken Yano (Hiroyuki Kawase) playing with Godzilla toys. ■ Director Banno with Kawase on location.

ABOVE: To make Hedorah appear dark and filthy—yet colorful enough to stand out—the suit makers added sparkling dust to the paint. So much paint and latex were applied to create this slimy look that the suit's weight increased by almost 50 pounds (23 kg). ■ ABOVE RIGHT: Hedorah was designed by special effects art director Yasuyuki Inoue (*center*). The final-stage Hedorah suit was the largest and heaviest of the Showa era, clocking in at 250 pounds (113 kg). ■ BOTTOM RIGHT: In one of the film's animated segments, Hedorah flies in and consumes a factory that is polluting the environment.

filming the go-go scene. He must've thought, *What the heck is he filming?* but he didn't say anything. Even for the flying Godzilla scene, he didn't object. If he had, I was prepared to change it."

"I felt that society was escalating toward more gruesome things, so I thought that kids were accustomed to those kinds of images," said Nakano. "It may have been too much. I heard that some kids felt sorry for Godzilla. . . . But I just wanted kids to understand the really dark part of this story."

Kenpachiro Satsuma, a young, athletic actor who routinely appeared as a background player in samurai action pictures for Mifune Productions, reluctantly accepted the arduous task of playing Hedorah in a gigantic, octopus-like costume. "After thinking about it for a while, I decided to accept the role for this one monster movie," said Satsuma, then known by the stage name Kengo Nakayama. "I saw it as a chance to learn about the 'instinct' of acting and, above all, the pay was good." (He would go on to a major career as a monster actor, playing Gigan twice and later Godzilla.) Haruo Nakajima, in his penultimate turn as Godzilla, gives a more animated and emotional performance than ever. Godzilla's role as hero is cemented (Ken calls the monster "a superman"), but the characterization here is played relatively straight, flying scene notwithstanding. When an exhausted Godzilla finally rips Hedorah's eyeballs from its corpse and turns them to dust, Nakajima's monster is truly disgusted by the mess humankind has created. Bloodied and battered, Godzilla stares in judgment at the humans—a warning?—before exiting across the horizon. A somber refrain is sung by a male chorus, accompanied by more images of fouled air and water: "Polluted seas / polluted skies / all life is gone / the fields and mountains are silent."

The soundtrack by Riichiro Manabe, who previously scored works by new-wave director Nagisa Oshima and numerous genre films, is distinctively different from anything heard previously, and a key element of Banno's unusual vision. Manabe veers from a strangely unforgettable Godzilla theme with blaring,

PREVIOUS SPREAD: The final showdown between Hedorah and Godzilla. ■ **LEFT:** In the flying scene, the Godzilla suit was suspended on wires. Godzilla and Hedorah props also appear. "We used CFC gas for Godzilla's flight," said crew member Akinori Takagi. "Back then, no one knew it hurt the ozone layer. So Godzilla emitted toxic gas to destroy the Smog Monster!" ■ **ABOVE:** Hedorah peers menacingly from the polluted waters of Suruga Bay. ■ **BOTTOM LEFT:** The monster battles are marked by long-distance standoffs, with a wary Godzilla gesturing while maintaining distance. This was largely due to the immense size and weight of the Hedorah suit, which was nearly impossible for actor Kenpachiro Satsuma to move in.

staccato horns to a zippy, upbeat march for Godzilla's sortie, and composes multiple variations on the main theme. "I thought consciously of avoiding Akira Ifukube's style," Manabe said. "I made sure none of my pieces sounded like his."

UPENDING A TOY BOX

Even the ending of *Godzilla vs. Hedorah* is singularly different, the first to offer an overt hint at a sequel. The historic Hokusai woodblock painting, *The Great Wave Off Kanagawa*, flashes across the screen, followed by the question, "Will there be another?" and an image of Hedorah resurfacing. Banno had plans for a direct sequel partly set in Africa, but he would never direct another feature again. "It was maybe too early," Banno said of his film. "People weren't ready for it. The reason I never got to do another Godzilla movie was because I did too much of everything. It was like I turned over a toy box, I think. They may have worried what I would come up with next."

RIGHT: Yukio (Toshio Shiba, *far right*) forms the All Japan Youth League and calls for a million-man protest against pollution. It turns into a party instead, with about thirty revelers dancing near Mount Fuji. The youths throw torches at Hedorah, which responds with toxic mudballs, killing Yukio and a few others. **BELOW:** Godzilla stomps on Hedorah's carcass. The idea to dehydrate Hedorah with electrodes was suggested by sci-fi writer Masami Fukushima, who noted that big electrodes had been used to dry out rice fields.

(CHIKYU KOGEKI MEIREI GOJIRA TAI GAIGAN /
EARTH DESTRUCTION DIRECTIVE: GODZILLA VS. GIGAN)
aka *Godzilla on Monster Island*
RELEASED: MARCH 12, 1972 (JAPAN)

GODZILLA VS. GIGAN

Godzilla speaks!

Yes, *Godzilla speaks!*

The opening frames of *Godzilla vs. Gigan* make abundantly clear that the twelfth Godzilla movie is intended as a straightforward crowd-pleaser. Over the signature thunder of Akira Ifukube's "Terror of Godzilla," the mighty monster stands alone in a windstorm on its Monster Island home. The king rears back and bellows its inimitable roar, then fires its heat ray straight into the lens. Roll credits!

Following the dreams and nightmares of the previous two films, *Godzilla vs. Gigan* is an effort to revisit Toho's familiar aliens-and-monsters formula of the sixties, albeit on a decidedly smaller scale and under ever-challenging circumstances. As if symbolizing the changing fortunes of the film industry at large, and of special effects productions specifically, the studio's expansive Stage No. 11, where many ambitious effects sets had been erected, was demolished after *Hedorah* wrapped. "With the death of Eiji Tsuburaya and the decline of the movie industry," remembered effects technician Jiro Shirasaki, "things started getting cut back right away."

> "USUALLY TOHO'S ARTISTS DESIGNED OUR CREATURES, BUT THIS WAS THE FIRST TIME THAT WE USED A DESIGNER FROM OUTSIDE IN ORDER TO INJECT SOME NEW BLOOD. DRAMATICALLY, WE NEEDED SOMETHING MORE POWERFUL THAN GODZILLA. GIGAN WAS ONE OF THE BEST-LOOKING MONSTERS, IN TERMS OF SMALL DETAILS."
>
> —Teruyoshi Nakano, special effects director

Godzilla vs. Gigan marks the revival of the traditional two-team approach, with Jun Fukuda returning as director and Teruyoshi Nakano elevated to special effects director. Working with smaller sets and diminished resources, and targeting an ever-younger audience, they deliver an action-heavy battlefest featuring the resurrection of King Ghidorah and introducing sleek and powerful Gigan. The space monsters are summoned by a race of alien cockroaches from M Space Hunter Nebula, who plot the takeover of Earth while disguised as the benevolent developers of a Godzilla-themed children's amusement park. Godzilla and Anguirus "talk" in kaiju language, comic book–style, and defeat the invaders in a tag-team match, aided by a band of heroes that includes a bumbling manga artist, his karateka girlfriend, and a goofy hippie who scarfs corn and bananas.

Even while *Hedorah* was in production, plans for another film were underway. Sometime in early 1971, Toho contracted artist Takayoshi Mizuki, known for colorful magazine illustrations of characters and monsters from the Tsuburaya Productions *Ultra* universe, to design a new Godzilla foe based on ideas by Nakano. Nakano conceptualized a futuristic monster with scythe-like hands and a rotating buzz saw in its abdomen—an impractical weapon that nonetheless proves effective at close range; Mizuki submitted two design concepts, one of which was Space Monster Gigan, a vaguely dinosaur-shaped cyclops cyborg.

In an usual move, the studio commissioned two competing story treatments from prominent genre writers Kaoru Mabuchi and Shinichi Sekizawa, and both submitted drafts for consideration in September 1971. Mabuchi's *Earth Defense Order: Godzilla vs. the Space Monsters* was an over-the-top space-invasion story with ideas recycled from

PREVIOUS SPREAD: The Gigan suit (*left*) was modeled by Noboyuki Yasumaru and worn by Kengo Nakayama (aka Kenpachiro Satsuma), who previously played Hedorah. Nakayama struggled inside the heavy suit; it was near impossible to lift Gigan's scythe hands, which were cast in fiberglass. ▪ **RIGHT:** Even working within a smaller stage than previous productions, the special effects team still managed to create an expansive refinery set. The battle features impressive explosion and smoke effects, trademarks of new SFX director Teruyoshi Nakano.

Destroy All Monsters. A scientifically advanced alien intelligence called Miko sends King Ghidorah and new monsters Gigan and Megalon to conquer Earth, threatening not only Japan but the US and USSR; Earth is defended by Godzilla and Anguirus. From a hidden transmitter on the moon, Miko controls the space monsters as well as the humans who do its bidding; the alien wants to "make a better world, free of traffic accidents and wars." The action is focused on Science Land, a children's theme park with a Godzilla Tower at its center (in one scene, Godzilla stares at its own likeness in amusement), and big battles among the monsters and military in and around Tokyo. Miko is revealed to be a disembodied alien brain; Godzilla and Anguirus defeat the invaders with the help of a legendary sword-wielding stone idol god from the Andes Mountains that suddenly comes to life. Meanwhile, Sekizawa's treatment, *Godzilla vs. Gigan: King Ghidorah's Great Counterattack*, was closer to the final product, though it featured a six-way showdown pitting Gigan, King Ghidorah, and a new monster called Mogu against Godzilla, Rodan, and Varan. Sekizawa's version was approved, though the Godzilla Tower was borrowed from Mabuchi's draft and rewritten as the villains' base of operations, and the roster of monsters was reduced to four, with Anguirus making the cut.

Godzilla vs. Gigan has almost no original music and incorporates a smorgasbord of stock footage from several previous Godzilla films and other Toho pictures. Ray beams and explosions seen during Gigan and King Ghidorah's assault on Tokyo are extracts from *Ghidorah* and *Invasion of Astro-Monster*, but as the attack moves from city to countryside, Nakano displays inventive traveling camera work, following the monsters' path of destruction. The four-way battle is at times well-choreographed and framed, with the monsters using their environment rather than merely grappling and wrestling; King Ghidorah cleverly creates a windstorm as cover for Gigan's aerial buzz saw attacks. Somewhat unbelievably, actual gasoline fire and explosions were set off in the small studio environment, to impressive effect. The battle eventually becomes lengthy as the creatures flip, kick, and smack one another repeatedly. Tsuburaya's long-standing taboo against graphic monster bloodshed is abandoned: Godzilla's shoulder is sliced open, and an injured Anguirus spurts blood into the camera lens.

As with *Hedorah*, the cast has no stars of the bygone era but does feature familiar faces from *tokusatsu* television shows. The simple plot follows the heroes as they investigate the villains' background and rescue a computer programmer who's been kidnapped by the aliens to provide IT support for their invasion.

TOP: Script discussion on the World Children's Land office set, with the architectural model of the amusement park. (*left to right*) Toshiaki Nishizawa (Kubota), Hiroshi Ishikawa (Gengo), director Jun Fukuda, and an unidentified assistant director. ■ ABOVE: Gigan and King Ghidorah rampage across the countryside as Maser tanks attempt to repel the invaders. ■ BELOW: Anguirus became Godzilla's sidekick, "because we found the suit in storage, and it was in good shape," said SFX director Teruyoshi Nakano. "We thought a four-legged, not-too-strong partner was ideal."

ABOVE: Ghidorah and Gigan lure Godzilla to the Godzilla Tower, where the aliens attack Godzilla with lasers.

"DESPITE THE LIMITATIONS, THERE WAS A DETERMINATION TO KEEP THE FLAME OF *TOKUSATSU* ALIVE, UTILIZING THE TREASURE TROVE OF TSUBURAYA'S GOLDEN-ERA (FOOTAGE)."
—Koichi Kawakita, assistant effects director

"PERSONALLY, I DON'T LIKE THE USE OF STOCK FOOTAGE. (THE AUDIENCE) COMES TO THE THEATER BECAUSE THEY LIKE THESE MOVIES, AND IT IS VERY CLEAR TO THEM WHEN STOCK FOOTAGE IS USED."
—Haruo Nakajima, Godzilla suit actor

GHOST NOTES:
SCORING *GODZILLA VS. GIGAN*

With budgetary matters an increasing concern, producer Tanaka and director Fukuda asked assistant producer Kenji Tokoro (who usually worked closely with a film's composer) about the possibility of using music tapes of previous Akira Ifukube soundtracks rather than allocate the resources required to create a new score for *Godzilla vs. Gigan*. Tokoro calculated that ¥1 million could be saved by doing so, but he first needed permission from composer Ifukube. Initially hesitant, Ifukube agreed to the usage of his past works, but only if Tokoro himself would select the tracks. Both Ifukube and Fukuda told Tokoro, "We won't nitpick; we'll leave it to you."

Tokoro visited the Toho Recording Center, where the master tapes were stored. Using a duplicate set of tapes, he secluded himself in a nearby studio to listen to Ifukube's scores. Working mostly at night after his daytime duties were done, Tokoro made extensive notes, classifying each track into categories such as action, mood, suspense, etc., and identifying bridge cues for each group; then he watched edited rush films and selected suitable cues. For an all-rushes screening with Ifukube and Fukuda, Tokoro prepared a tape with his selections arranged in sequence. When the time came for each piece, he would press "play."

Tokoro said, "I managed to synchronize everything well. It went so smoothly that they told me, 'It's almost like it's finished.' Ifukube-sensei had no complaints with my choices." Ifukube was pleased not to have to create a new score, as the physical and mental stress was becoming more difficult. Just one change was made: Instead of the theme from *Battle in Outer Space* (1959) for the opening credits, director Fukuda requested Ifukube's music from the volcano scene in *The Birth of the Japanese Islands*, the short created for Expo '70. The finished film would include several cues from the Expo '70 film, as well as from several Godzilla films and other Toho pictures, including *Atragon* (1963), *Frankenstein Conquers the World* (1965), and *King Kong Escapes* (1967).

While the *Godzilla vs. Gigan* music lacks the organic connective tissue of an original score, it illustrates how ubiquitous Ifukube's genre music had become, carrying the narrative along and complementing the action as if written specifically for this film, at times giving the production a sense of drama and scale far exceeding its limitations.

The soundtrack does include one original piece, the heroic "Godzilla March" end title song composed by Kunio Miyauchi, in the style of *tokusatsu* TV themes, with lyrics by director Fukuda: "He has his targets in his sights / he'll defeat the evil monsters / that's our Godzilla / go get 'em!"

LEFT: Maestro Akira Ifukube in 1993, conducting the recording session for the *Godzilla vs. Mechagodzilla II* score.

Fukuda connects the human and monster threads, though the story forgoes the action-adventure ethos of the director's 1960s genre pictures. Stock footage of scummy oceans from *Hedorah* offers a bit of social commentary; the peace-preaching space roaches are opportunists who travel the universe, wiping out civilizations despoiled by pollution and nuclear contamination.

The film ends with a victorious Godzilla swimming away, the heroes waving goodbye from shore. In hindsight, as Godzilla turns back to roar farewell, the moment carries a melancholy weight. This would be Haruo Nakajima's final performance as Godzilla, though he was unaware during the shoot. As the film industry moved away from long-term employment for actors and others, his tenure inside the suit came to an end, and he went to work at a bowling alley owned by a Toho subsidiary instead. "I had no idea [that it was my last Godzilla movie] at the time," Nakajima said. "I was forty-three, and I thought I could still play Godzilla until I was fifty. . . . I had hopes that I would be called back, but in the end, they continued to make Godzilla movies—beginning with *Godzilla vs. Megalon*—without me."

TOP: The 1964 King Ghidorah suit was refurbished again, this time with three newly sculpted heads by Noboyuki Yasumaru. The suit would make its final screen appearance in a 1973 episode of Toho's *tokusatsu* teleseries *Zone Fighter*. ■ **ABOVE:** SFX director Teruyoshi Nakano (*pictured*) used a seven-color gradient from Gigan's chest to its lower section, inspired by the traditional Japanese twelve-layer ceremonial kimono. "They used to stagger the layers so you could see multiple colors," he said. "Beautiful, big, and strong. That was the idea for Gigan." ■ **TOP RIGHT:** The battle's pivotal moment: Godzilla is pinned down by lasers from Godzilla Tower while the enemy monsters prevent Anguirus from helping. Nakano frequently places three or four monsters in the widescreen frame. ■ **RIGHT:** A revived Godzilla pounds its chest, ready to fight again. Suit actor Haruo Nakajima gives another spirited performance in this, his last turn as Godzilla.

THE ROAR HEARD 'ROUND THE WORLD

CREATING GODZILLA'S CLASSIC SOUND EFFECTS

Japanese science-fiction and fantasy cinema is a primarily visual medium, but the sight of giant monsters rampaging and the resulting cataclysm of destruction would have little impact without the cacophony of noises that makes up its epic soundscape. In the classic years of Toho's special effects movies, this was the work of the studio's imaginative, highly skilled sound effects engineers. Not to be confused with foley work, which re-creates the normal and ambient sounds of everyday life, sound effects produce special, out-of-the-ordinary audio for use in a film. The sounds of monsters roaring, spaceships streaking, death rays, and much more—they all came from the creative ingenuity of these technicians.

"I've been in this profession for a long time, but looking back, *Godzilla* was the most challenging," said Ichiro Minawa, who joined Toho as a sound effects artist in 1942 and worked in that capacity until 1971, creating sound effects for nearly nine hundred movies. "It involved depicting a creature that was entirely fictional, and moreover, it was gigantic, so we struggled a lot with conveying its size."

Godzilla's roar was created by Minawa and recording engineer Hisashi Shimonaga via a trial-and-error process. They first mixed together recorded sounds of large animals, such as lions, tigers, bears, and condors, but no matter how they processed and combined them, the results failed to create the desired impact. Next, they experimented with musical instruments. Wind instruments didn't work—their sound was too simple, not enough like the voice of a living creature. After testing different instruments, they settled on the extreme low-register sound of a contrabass (string bass).

"To eliminate its instrument-like quality, we loosened all the strings and played various parts of it, resulting in a very rough sound," recalled Minawa. "We did not use leather gloves, as has long been rumored. We recorded hundreds of variations of this sound onto tape, selected usable takes, and further processed them by changing the tape speed or adding echo." They altered the tape speed not by mechanically turning the reels, but by pulling the tape itself by hand. "For the beginning [of the roar], we wanted sharpness and volume, so we sped up the beginning and gradually slowed down the rest." Toho's in-house musicians would leave their instruments in the rehearsal room when they were not performing, so Minawa and Shimonaga would borrow these instruments and use them for their sound effects recordings— not only for Godzilla's roar, but for other monsters' cries in later films.

Godzilla's footsteps are the first thing the audience experiences at the very beginning of the first film; the ominous sounds are heard even before the main title appears on-screen. These footsteps are key to establishing the story's drama and suspense—along with the roar, they are the only manifestation of Godzilla's presence until the creature's visage is later revealed on Odo Island. Through the years, conflicting accounts have emerged as to how Godzilla's footsteps were created. Some sources, dating to the 1970s, say the sound is the result of a large knotted rope striking a kettle drum. Composer Akira Ifukube has said it was an echo-like sound produced through a then-new type of electronic amplifier. However, according to Minawa, the footsteps were made by manipulating and adding echo to the sound of an explosion. "We used only the head of that explosion sound, cut it off, recorded it on film, cut it to about two frames, added an echo to the reverberation, and played it back. It just went, 'Bang!' Then we added an echo to make it go 'Bang! Bang!'" There was no echo machine, so in order to create this effect, Minawa used an empty staircase between Toho's Stages No. 1 and No. 2, playing the original sound through a speaker on the first floor and recording it with a microphone on the third floor, working at night when the outside noise level was low.

Godzilla's heat ray, another signature sound effect, was created by mixing together the sounds of a 6.5-foot- (2-meter-) diameter ventilation fan in the studio, cylinders releasing steam, and a volcanic eruption. Minawa felt pride at what his team accomplished in 1954. "It was time-consuming and challenging to create something from nothing, but I feel like we gained a lot of experience in the struggle and joy of turning nothing into something with just that one film."

In subsequent years, the pitch of Godzilla's original roar was manipulated on tape to make it slightly higher. "This was because Ifukube's music primarily featured low tones, and having Godzilla's roar too low would diminish its impact," Minawa explained. "All Godzilla roars [from *Godzilla Raids Again* through *Terror of Mechagodzilla*] were modifications of the original. We didn't create entirely new ones." When the series was rebooted in *The Return of Godzilla,* the original 1954 vintage roar was heard again.

Minawa continued creating sound effects for Godzilla and all of Toho's monster and science-fiction films. For explosions, buildings crumbling, gunfire, vehicles, and other incidental sounds, he utilized Toho's rich library of recordings collected during the war in cooperation with the military. For out-of-the-ordinary sounds, Minawa recalled, "I watched film rushes and came up with ideas for what kind of voice or sound would be suitable for the monster. It was mostly based on intuition."

Godzilla was the first film for which Minawa used musical instruments to create sound effects, and he would rely heavily on this technique going forward. In *Godzilla Raids Again*, he used a French horn and bass clarinet to create the roar of Anguirus. "Since Godzilla was created with string instruments, we thought we'd go with wind instruments for the opponent. We asked musicians to play it, but it didn't work. They could only play it musically, not like a monster."

The Yamaha Electone split electric organ was utilized to create many classic monster sounds, including the cries and flying noise of Mothra and King Ghidorah, the sound of Mothra spraying its cocoon, and King Ghidorah firing its antigravity beams. The clavioline, an early electronic analog synthesizer, was frequently used for mechanical sound effects, such as spaceships seen in *Invasion of Astro-Monster* and *Destroy All Monsters*. The "combo organ," a type of portable transistorized electric organ capable of varying pitch and speed of musical notes, was used extensively in the 1970s. Jet Jaguar and Gigan's cries were created with a combo organ, while Megalon's roar combined the sounds of a combo organ and a contrabass. Mechagodzilla's roar was realized via a melding of the combo organ and the scratching of a glass pane and then varying the playback speed.

The contrabass, combined with other sounds, gave voice to many other Toho creatures. Rodan's roar combined the rubbing of a contrabass with a sped-up human voice, which was then oscillated. Roars for the monsters Varan and Baragon were created with the same basic combination of sounds, played back at different speeds. Texture was added to Baragon's cry by rubbing the strings of a toy violin. Gorosaurus's cry was a variation of Baragon's, with extra echo effects added.

Practical devices, real animals, and even the human voice were the basis for many other sounds. The mighty bellow of Toho's King Kong was created by mixing recorded lion and elephant roars together with sounds of thunder; the tape was then manipulated back and forth and then processed with echo effects. King Caesar's roar was essentially the same as that of Kong but played at a slower rate and lower pitch. Minilla's voice was a sped-up version of Godzilla's roar; depending on the young monster's mood, its texture was altered by mixing in the sounds of a monkey, a seal, a cat, a bear, a lion, and even a pig. Titanosaurus's cry was based on an elephant roar, with King Kong's mixed in, and the tape shaken back and forth to achieve a warbling effect. The snorts of a horse doubled for Titanosaurus's growling.

Another technique used in the late sixties and early seventies involved scratching a pane of glass with the cover of a tea kettle. The voices of Ebirah, Kamacuras, and Hedorah were all created this way. For Ebirah, the screeching voice was echoed, the tape shaken back and forth, and then combined with the scraping of a wooden oar to simulate its limb movements. Hedorah's sounds combined glass screeching and the squealing of a machine, and the recordings were jogged back and forth. Sometimes sound engineers creatively utilized everyday items. The movements of Kumonga and Kamacuras were created by pumping an automotive grease can, mixing the sound with music, then manipulating the speed and direction of playback.

(*GOJIRA TAI MEGARO*)
RELEASED: MARCH 17, 1973 (JAPAN)

GODZILLA VS. MEGALON

I n the early 1970s, the world of Japanese sci-fi and fantasy entertainment experienced another "kaiju boom" when Japan's TV airwaves exploded with the *Ultraman* series and other kaiju-fighting heroes in *Kamen Rider, Android Kikaider, Spectreman, Mirrorman, Inazuman,* and other programs. With bizarre monsters and traditional *tokusatsu* effects, these shows brought a new generation of young viewers to the genre. In 1973, Godzilla stepped into the fray via *Godzilla vs. Megalon,* a monsters-first film that was part of a crossover strategy connecting the worlds of big-screen monster movies and small-screen heroes. Godzilla teams up with a bravehearted, size-shifting robot in a four-way match against the insect monster Megalon, aided by Gigan. Made quickly and inexpensively, with ample stock footage, *Godzilla vs. Megalon* nonetheless introduced Godzilla to a legion of new young fans, particularly in the US, where it received wide exposure in theaters and on TV.

It all begins with a nuclear test on the Aleutian Islands (alluding to a controversial test there by the US in 1971) that causes widespread earthquakes and threatens to wipe out the undersea kingdom of Seatopia. The normally peaceful Seatopians send monster-deity Megalon to attack the surface dwellers in retaliation; they also steal Jet Jaguar, a radio-controlled flying robot built by young inventor Goro (Katsuhiko Sasaki), and use it to guide Megalon to destroy cities. Soon the robot is freed from Seatopian

"MEGALON! MEGALON! WAKE UP, MEGALON! COME ON, RISE UP NOW, TO THE EARTH'S SURFACE! DESTROY THE EARTH! DESTROY OUR ENEMIES! RISE UP! GO ON! MEGALON!"

—Antonio, King of Seatopia (Robert Dunham in English-dubbed version)

---

control and reprograms itself, growing to gigantic size and fighting the invader. Godzilla and Gigan provide backup for the hero and villain, arriving for the final battle. The story takes place in an almost surreal, childlike bubble, where the three main characters—Goro, his little brother Rokuro (Hedorah's Hiroyuki Kawase), and their race car driver best friend, Hiroshi (Yutaka Hayashi)—appear to be the last people on Earth, save for the Seatopian henchmen assaulting and chasing them. There are no parents, no women, no cars on the streets, and only a few military men. A huge army buildup consists entirely of stock footage, and the assault against Megalon involves fighter planes resembling a model kit that Rokuro finds in a hobby shop. The roughly half-hour-long kaiju showdown transpires without military interference, while the protagonists watch safely from a hill, with no parallel human drama.

Plans for *Godzilla vs. Megalon* originated in late 1971 with a monster design contest for kids, cosponsored by Toho and the Seiyu store chain. The grand prize winner was revealed on live TV: Red Aron, a winged humanoid with a colorful red, blue, and yellow design; it was also announced that the character would appear in a Godzilla movie. Special effects director Teruyoshi Nakano supervised significant changes to the design, giving it an angular, diamond-shaped head, retaining the basic color scheme and

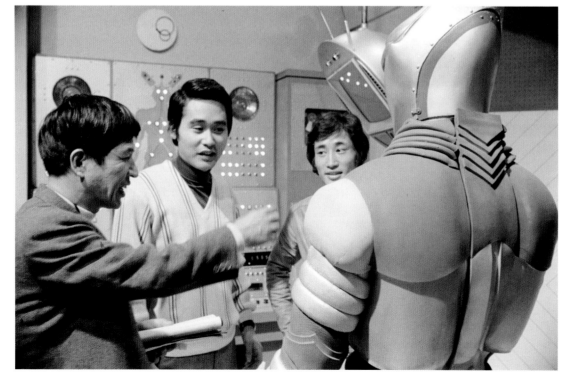

PREVIOUS SPREAD: Earth's heroes, Godzilla and Jet Jaguar, stand ready to repel the invaders. ■ CLOCKWISE FROM FAR LEFT: Seatopia, inspired by lost continent legends such as Mu and Atlantis, is a victim of nuclear testing, and goes to war to protect itself. The king of Seatopia is played by Robert Dunham, a nonprofessional actor, stuntman, stunt driver, and author who was part of a small community of foreigners appearing in Japanese films in the 1950s through '70s. The king beseeches Megalon, aided by a formation of trance-induced dancing females. ■ US nuclear tests cause worldwide destruction and open a fissure beneath a lake, where Rokuro (Hiroyuki Kawase), riding a "dolphin cycle," is nearly pulled under. The fissure leads to Seatopia, providing a path for the monster Megalon to later reach Earth's surface. ■ Director Jun Fukuda with Katsuhiko Sasaki (*center*) as Goro and Yutaka Hayashi (*right*) as Hiroshi. Sasaki, son of Kurosawa veteran Minoru Chiaki, was a theater actor who had recently joined Toho. "It was a really low-budget movie, and the time passed very quickly," Sasaki recalled of *Megalon*. "I was just so happy to be a leading man in a Godzilla movie." Hayashi was a twenty-five-year-old ex-drummer for the band the Village Singers just starting his long acting career. He didn't recall *Megalon* being low budget. "I thought that films for children would be made on a low budget with a small crew, but I was greatly mistaken. There was plenty of enthusiasm on the set, and a sufficient budget," Hayashi said. Director Fukuda gave him "all kinds of freedom in performing. He was a very kind director. . . . I didn't have enough experience, so I just basically played myself."

little else. The character would be described as a "Kamen Rider–like robot" in the script, and a costume was constructed with a wetsuit-based design à la Ultraman-style heroes. In September 1972, screenwriter Shinichi Sekizawa submitted multiple drafts of a treatment titled *Godzilla vs. the Megalon Brothers: The Undersea Kingdom Annihilation Strategy* and *Insect Monster Megalon vs. Godzilla: The Undersea Kingdom Annihilation Strategy*; the monster Megalon was a holdover from Kaoru Mabuchi's unused story for *Gigan*. Nakano modeled Megalon after the Japanese rhinoceros beetle, a large bug often captured and kept as pets by children and elementary school classes, popular for its large horns and jaws and hard outer wings.

The film began shooting in December for a March release, just before the start of the Japanese school year. "I remember it was a very short shoot, probably about three weeks," said Nakano. "It went into production without enough preparation. There was no time to ask Sekizawa to write the script, so he kind of thought up the general story, and director Fukuda wrote the screenplay. The screenplay was completed right before crank-in [the start of filming]."

NEW REALITIES

From 1969 to 1975, when Godzilla movies were part of the Toho Champion Matsuri film festival, the economic realities of Japan's film industry were increasingly challenging. Whereas the budget for *Destroy All Monsters* was reportedly ¥200 million (about $550,000 in 1968), the company is said to have discussed reducing Godzilla budgets in the early seventies to about ¥30 million (roughly $100,000 in 1973) to offset the impacts of decreased attendance and revenue sharing with other production companies on the marquee. While the actual *Megalon* budget is unknown, the filmmakers clearly worked with reduced resources, evidenced by just two live-action sets (Goro's funky 1970s inventor pad, and the idol altar of Seatopia), deserted and remote locations, and the increasing use of special effects stock footage. Shots from the most recent entry, *Gigan*, reappear, as do entire stock sequences that had been reedited for that film. And yet the film also includes extended new special effects content, including the lengthy end fight that is entertaining for its newly playful approach to monster violence. The entire film is

SELLING *GODZILLA VS. MEGALON*

US RELEASE (1976)

GIANT AGAINST GIANT... the ultimate battle!

Godzilla vs. Megalon is perhaps the most infamous of all Godzilla movies, but it nonetheless enjoyed a very successful and well-received theatrical run across the United States, owing to an inventive and lighthearted publicity blitz by its independent distributor, Cinema Shares International. Beginning in the spring and summer of 1976, the company launched a series of Godzilla-themed stunts: In New York, a big Godzilla footprint appeared on the sidewalk outside Madison Square Garden for the Democratic National Convention, and "Godzilla for President" buttons and banners appeared through-out the city; in other markets, Godzilla and Megalon cutouts rode atop cars parading through downtown streets. The film was lightly edited to be even more family friendly (scenes of mild violence, including the kidnapping of Rokuro and the deaths of two Seatopian agents, were cut), thus earning a G rating from the Motion Picture Association of America. Matinee-style press screenings brought positive reviews from major critics, including Vincent Canby of *The New York Times*: "It's wildly preposterous, imaginative and funny (often intentionally). It demon-strates the rewards of friendship, between humans as well as monsters, and it is gentle." According to Mel Maron, head of Cinema Shares, the film played on more than two thousand screens over a period of many months, earning around $5 million, a then-sizable sum. *Godzilla vs. Megalon* was also the first and only Godzilla movie to have a primetime US network television premiere, airing March 15, 1977, on the NBC network. The broadcast was hosted by comedian John Belushi in a Godzilla suit.

ABOVE: Souvenir button given to theatergoers during the US theatrical release of *Godzilla vs. Megalon*. ■ **LEFT:** The one-sheet poster for Cinema Shares' release was one of many audacious publicity stunts. The monsters battle atop the Twin Towers of the World Trade Center, capitalizing on a similar ad campaign for Dino De Laurentiis's much-higher-budgeted *King Kong* (1976), released later the same year. ■ **BOTTOM LEFT:** Excerpt from the Cinema Shares promotion and advertising press kit for *Godzilla vs. Megalon*, showing the variety of souvenir giveaway buttons that were available to theater operators.

BUTTON, BUTTON, Who's got the button?

Boost your box-office grosses with these exciting *Three Color Buttons*. Order them early and arrange for give-aways:

(1) Give out buttons to every patron (as long as supply lasts) — make sure you plug this item in all of your pre-opening ads, on radio and TV.

(2) Arrange with either Radio or TV stations to distribute these buttons, in exchange for free time. They can either run contests or merely have viewers or listeners call in.

(3) Arrange with local merchants to distribute buttons (and have them run ads on your behalf) — tie in with MONSTER SALE, etc.

(4) Have the buttons passed out on the streets. Make sure that they also have heralds to give out with theatre name, day and date. (Artwork for herald shown on this page.)

Price: $42.44 per thousand — (shipping $1.75 per shipment of 4,000 — 1,000 of each of 4 styles — Under 4,000 shipping $3.00) ORDER FROM: VERNON CO., NEWTON, IOWA 50208 (515) 792-2880

"THEY WROTE DOWN HOW MANY FEET OF FILM SHOULD BE EXPOSED FOR EACH SHOT, AND WE WERE EXPECTED TO FINISH WITHIN THAT RANGE. THAT'S WHY WE DID EVERYTHING IN ONE TAKE. THERE WERE NO NG ('NO GOOD') SHOTS, NO RETAKES."

—Katsuhiko Sasaki (Goro)

whimsically unreal: the inventor rescues his little brother with a handy rocket launcher; Megalon launches a shipping container with Goro and Rokuro inside over a mountain, yet they are unharmed; and the big battle ends with Godzilla performing an impossible flying kick—twice!—for the coup de grâce.

The team behind *Megalon* nonetheless boasts considerable talent. Cinematographer Yuzuru Aizawa was an assistant cameraman on 1954's *Godzilla* and shot Akira Kurosawa's noir masterpiece *The Bad Sleep Well* (1960). New-wave veteran and *Hedorah* composer Riichiro Manabe contributes another offbeat score highlighted by electric guitar, Jew's harp, and flute. And director Fukuda brings hints of his trademark action style in the form of car chases (unusual for Japanese films at the time) handled in a tongue-in-cheek style. It is to Fukuda's credit that, despite its limitations, *Godzilla vs. Megalon* is an uncynical effort made only to entertain and has a charming innocence about it. "I had hated watching or hearing about [*Godzilla vs. Gigan* and *Godzilla vs. Megalon*], but later I realized that they really are popular among children," Fukuda said years later. "Godzilla's popularity is pretty amazing."

PREVIOUS SPREAD: Godzilla and Jet Jaguar prepare to engage Megalon and Gigan. During the 1970s, the battlefield sets often became empty, featureless countrysides due to reduced production budgets. ■ CLOCKWISE FROM TOP LEFT: The final battle between Megalon, Godzilla, Gigan, and Jet Jaguar resembles a tag team *puroresu* (professional wrestling) match. Extremely popular in Japan during the sixties and seventies, *puroresu* is a cultural phenomenon marked by popular heroes and villains, though it is different in style from Western pro wrestling, and distinct also from sumo and amateur wrestling. ■ Jet Jaguar (Tsugutoshi Komada) follows the tradition of radio-controlled robots of *Tetsujin 28-Go* (aka *Gigantor*) and *Giant Robo* (aka *Johnny Sokko and His Flying Robot*). "We couldn't help but focus on the new character, Jet Jaguar, so Godzilla was kind of a sidekick," said SFX director Teruyoshi Nakano. "There were complaints that Godzilla didn't appear in enough scenes." ■ The film is a showcase for the launch of Jet Jaguar as a new character. After Godzilla departs, the heroes are reunited, and the film ends on the theme song "Godzilla and Jet Jaguar: Punch! Punch! Punch!" performed by Masato Shimon, a vocalist known for *tokusatsu* TV show themes. ■ Megalon deploys its red napalm grenades to encircle Godzilla and Jet Jaguar in fire. Curiously, both Godzilla and the robot fear the flames; however, moments later Godzilla uses its white-hot breath (rendered here via low-resolution animation) to repel the villains.

EXPANDING THE GODZILLAVERSE
METEOR MAN ZONE aka *ZONE FIGHTER*

Godzilla vs. Megalon was part of a crossover strategy to introduce Godzilla to the world of popular superhero programs on Japanese TV. As head of the newly formed subsidiary Toho Eizo (Toho Visual), which took over the studio's special effects productions, Tomoyuki Tanaka planned for the new superhero Red Aron (which evolved into Jet Jaguar) to debut in *Megalon* and then assume the lead role in a program to be produced by Toho Television and broadcast on the Nippon TV (NTV) network. Godzilla would appear as a frequent guest star, thus creating a shared kaiju universe.

The plan was revised, however, after Kimihiko Eto, a representative from the Mannensha advertising agency who had helped launch Toho TV's *Rainbowman* and similar programs, advised the producers that the TV network preferred all-new superheroes rather than preexisting characters. Toho Eizo subsequently pivoted to a new project titled *Meteor Man Zone* (*Ryusei Ningen Zone*), commonly known as *Zone Fighter*.

The series follows three refugees from the planet Peaceland, which was destroyed by the evil Baron Garoga, leader of a band of aliens out to conquer the universe. The refugees adopt the human alter egos of a Japanese family; the main character is Hikaru Sakimori, a young man in his early twenties who becomes the Zone Fighter in times of crisis by shouting "Zone! Fight! Power!"; his teen sister and little brother also transform into heroes. Every week, Garoga unleashes one or more kaiju called "Terror Beasts." Godzilla comes to the aid of Zone Fighter when summoned.

The show followed on the heels of *Godzilla vs. Megalon*, airing for one twenty-six-episode season from April to September 1973. Godzilla appeared in five episodes, with monster actor Toru Kawai performing inside the suit from *Megalon*; King Ghidorah and Gigan also made appearances. When victorious, Godzilla beats its chest like King Kong; in one episode, Godzilla lives in a cave with retractable doors; in another, its heat ray was created not with optical animation, but a spray mist from a nozzle in its mouth. Veteran Toho directors Ishiro Honda and Jun Fukuda helmed a few episodes, and special effects were provided by Teruyoshi Nakano and future Toho SFX director Koichi Kawakita. The series marked the beginning and end of Godzilla's short-lived *tokusatsu* TV career.

CLOCKWISE FROM TOP LEFT: Godzilla, champion of justice, comes to the aid of Zone Fighter. ▪ Godzilla engages Gigan in combat. Both monsters appear in the suits used in *Godzilla vs. Megalon*. ▪ After vanquishing the enemy, Zone Fighter and Godzilla shake hands. ▪ Godzilla and Zone Fighter battle tag-team style against the monsters Wargilgar (*left*) and Spylar (*right*) in an episode directed by Ishiro Honda.

(GOJIRA TAI MEKAGOJIRA)
aka *Godzilla vs. the Cosmic Monster; Godzilla vs. the Bionic Monster*
RELEASED MARCH 21, 1974 (JAPAN)

GODZILLA VS. MECHAGODZILLA

O n May 15, 1972, after twenty-seven years of postwar rule by the United States, Okinawa prefecture was reverted back to Japan. Stretched across 400 miles (644 km) of ocean south of Kyushu, the territory comprises a chain of more than sixty islands, anchored by the largest: Okinawa Island. Prior to its annexation in 1879, the archipelago was home to the independent Ryukyu Kingdom for four centuries, thus its indigenous people, language, and culture are distinct from mainland Japan. Following the handover, preparations began for a massive celebratory event: Expo '75, an oceanographic-themed World's Fair that would be held on Okinawa Island beginning in July 1975. *Godzilla vs. Mechagodzilla,* the twentieth-anniversary Godzilla movie, is set during this time and place of historic transition, with a familiar Toho alien-invasion plot that incorporates Okinawan scenery and customs, while introducing one of Godzilla's most formidable opponents. The film is something of a return to form; although released via the children's Toho Champion Matsuri, *Godzilla vs. Mechagodzilla* is a more ambitious effort than the previous four films, weaving prophecy and mystery and violence in between the requisite kaiju battles and destruction.

Mechagodzilla is an inspired creation, a sleek and angular doppelgänger with an electronic brain, a powerful arsenal of ray beams and missiles, and the ability to take to the skies and strafe its opponents. It follows a tradition of giant robots appearing in manga, anime, and live-action entertainment, but unlike its predecessors, Mechagodzilla is programmed to destroy Japan, not to defend it. "It was twenty years since the first *Godzilla*, so we had to think of a really strong enemy," remembered special effects director Teruyoshi Nakano. "We thought, *nothing is stronger than Godzilla, so its enemy would have to be itself*. Why not Mechagodzilla? That's how this character came up." Mechagodzilla was designed by artist Akihiko Iguchi, who had previously created monsters for Tsuburaya Productions and would design Toho's Titanosaurus a year later. The robot's formidable powers create several highlight-reel moments, including an explosive "beam lock" between cyborg and kaiju that leaves Godzilla seriously wounded. In response, Godzilla summons its own lighting-fueled superpower (last hinted at in *Ebirah*) and turns itself into an electromagnet, overpowering Mechagodzilla and ripping its head off (with the sound of metal creaking) for the coup de grâce, another all-time memorable moment.

The plot went through several variations leading up to the film's production. An initial story by screenwriter Shinichi Sekizawa, titled *Great Showdown: Giant Monsters Assemble at Cape Zanpa*, involved the M Space Hunter Nebula aliens from *Godzilla vs. Gigan* plotting to colonize Earth and flip it like real estate, selling it to aliens from other worlds. From their underground base at Cape Zanpa on Okinawa (site of a former US military facility), they build the mechanical monster Gargan; in response, Godzilla, Mothra, and Anguirus rise to defend Earth. In a second draft, *Great Showdown: Godzilla vs. Mechagodzilla*, the invaders were changed to aliens from Planet R, who send Mechagodzilla and Gigan to do their nefarious bidding. This version introduced a legendary Okinawan kaiju deity called King Barugan, covered in golden scales, which allies with Godzilla. The idea of Mechagodzilla is attributed to science-fiction author

PREVIOUS SPREAD: "[The Mechagodzilla design] started from the idea that we should replace all the curved lines of Godzilla and make them into straight lines, as if you took a tin toy of Godzilla and hammered its curved lines down," said SFX director Teruyoshi Nakano. "I wanted to make the shoulders bigger, because in this form, it's no different from Godzilla's narrow shoulders, [but] it would have made it much harder to move the arms. Instead, we put folds on the shoulders, accordion-style. . . . [We also made] the eyes much bigger and sharper." ■ CLOCKWISE FROM TOP LEFT: When Mechagodzilla first appears—disguised as Godzilla—Anguirus instinctively attacks it and suffers a bloody beating. Mechagodzilla displays surprisingly non-robot-like behavior, viciously beating Anguirus and nonchalantly brushing itself off. The "fake" Godzilla's roar is mechanical and metallic sounding. ■ Godzilla's body is riddled with missiles from the cyborg's attack. ■ Koichi Kawakita served as assistant director for both the live action and special effects. "The underlying principle was to use your wits when you didn't have money," he recalled. "So I handled everything from live-action footage to compositing—anything and everything."

Masami Fukushima, who shared on-screen writing credit with Sekizawa for the original story. "Monsters born from unconventional ideas, shaped by unique concepts, must continually emerge, diverging from the Godzilla-inspired dinosaurian mold," Fukushima was quoted as saying. In the final screenplay, cowritten by director Jun Fukuda and prolific genre writer Hiroyasu Yamaura, the location of the final battle shifted from Zanpa to the cliffs, beaches, and rock formations of Manzamo, one of Okinawa's paradise tourist spots; Gigan was dropped; the invaders—simian-like beings cloaked in human form—now hailed from Black Hole Planet 3; and King Barugan became King Caesar, based on the shisa, a traditional Ryukyuan idol from Okinawan mythology, inspired by Chinese guardian lions. The shisa is a ward, believed to protect homes and structures from evil; the statues are commonly displayed across the islands, and resemble a cross between a lion and a dog. In the film's reality, King Caesar is an ancient god that once protected Okinawa from Japanese invaders.

The film's opening credits are akin to an Okinawan tourism advertisement, with views of beautiful, historic coral and limestone structures with red-tile roofs, and shisa ever-present. At the Nakagusuku Castle ruins, tourists snap photos as the traditional female priestess Nami (Beru-Bera Lin) performs a ritual of song and dance. A descendant of an ancient royal family, Nami wears a Chinese robe and hat, the attire of Okinawan nobility; she faints mid-song after experiencing a prophetic vision of a giant monster attacking Japan. (Confusingly, the vision is depicted via images of King Ghidorah, though King Ghidorah never actually appears in the movie.) A mystery begins to unfold: Masahiko Shimizu (Kazuya Aoyama, star of Toho's *Meteor Man Zone* teleseries) visits another tourist site, the stalactite and stalagmite formations of Gyokusendo Cave, where he discovers a clue that will lead to a secret underground alien base there; elsewhere, his brother, Keisuke Shimizu (Masaaki Daimon), a construction supervisor for Expo '75, stumbles onto another, related prophecy, scrawled in cave paintings, foretelling of two monsters that will defend the world against the threat. When "Godzilla" (a disguised Mechagodzilla) appears in Japan, an Okinawan elder (Masao Imafuku) believes divine vengeance has been visited upon the mainlanders who once subjugated his people. As the alien-invasion plot is revealed and the battle moves to Okinawa, priestess Nami awakens long-dormant King Caesar by singing a catchy pop ballad while standing on a gorgeous beach; the shaggy, red-eyed monster comes to life just as Mechagodzilla attacks.

For Godzilla's twentieth outing, a larger budget appears to have been afforded. On the special effects side, there is more sophisticated optical composition and optical animation; Mechagodzilla's multicolored

LEFT: For certain shots, such as when the disguised Mechagodzilla (*left*) and the real Godzilla (*right*) are both on camera, the cloaked robot is represented by a Godzilla "attraction suit" created for promotional appearances and not originally intended for filming. ▪ **BELOW:** After shedding its disguise, Mechagodzilla (Kazunari Mori) confronts Godzilla (Isao Zushi). *Godzilla vs. Mechagodzilla* was the first Godzilla film in which the suit actors were identified by their respective roles in the opening credits.

GODZILLA FACT: In 2022, local officials launched "Godzilla vs. Okinawa," an annual event promoting tourism and sightseeing at locations where *Godzilla vs. Mechagodzilla* was filmed, including the Gyokusendo Cave, the beach and cape of Nago Bay, the Nakagusuku Castle ruins, and more.

Space Beam was created by assistant SFX director Koichi Kawakita, based on a similar effect he'd designed for the show *Ultraman Ace*. There are larger miniature sets for the destruction sequences, owing to the availability of leftover buildings from Toho's hit disaster movie *Submersion of Japan* (1973), released earlier that year. On the drama side, the primary cast is populated by younger actors, but several veterans of Toho's classic period make welcome returns, including Akihiko Hirata and Hiroshi Koizumi as scientists and Kenji Sahara as a ship's captain. More so than the previous two entries, *Godzilla vs. Mechagodzilla* has the markings of a 1960s-style Jun Fukuda action picture: chase scenes, fisticuffs, handheld camera work, colorful art direction and lighting (e.g., the interiors of the alien base), and most significantly, a tongue-in-cheek sense of humor. Alien commander Kuronuma (Goro Mutsumi) is a cigar-smoking, brandy-drinking scene-stealer; the sunglasses-wearing, trenchcoated, always-smoking Interpol detective Nanbara (Shin Kishida) is in his own private film noir. No stock footage was utilized for the monster scenes; however, the film does evince the era's budget restrictions, including the noticeable use of an "attraction" Godzilla suit for a few shots. There are no military-versus-monster confrontations, owing to

CLOCKWISE FROM TOP LEFT: Mechagodzilla forces its finger missiles into King Caesar's mouth in a bid to defeat the monster. ▪ Filming Nami's (Beru-Bera Lin) performance of the song "Miyarabi's Prayer" (composed by Masaru Sato, with lyrics by Jun Fukuda), beseeching King Caesar to revive and protect the Okinawans. ▪ King Caesar defends its homeland against the alien invader. ▪ Director Jun Fukuda inspects the star of the film: Mechagodzilla. ▪ **FOLLOWING SPREAD:** Setting up the scene in which electrical energy absorbed by Godzilla during a lightning storm enables the monster to transform into a giant electromagnet.

the spirit of US-Japanese cooperation during the handover—and, perhaps, to avoid any reference to the tens of thousands of US troops controversially remaining in Okinawa post-reversion. "It was right around the time of [Okinawa's] return, so I actually avoided any military type of scene for either the SDF or the American military," Nakano said.

Masaru Sato's score lends a fast and energetic tempo, ideally suited (as with *Ebirah* and *Son of Godzilla*) to Fukuda's action- and adventure-oriented style. Unlike the past four films, which featured either a smaller ensemble or recycled music, Sato is afforded the resources of a full orchestra. His main title theme is a lush tribute to Okinawan folk music, set to a typically Sato Western-style pop-jazz arrangement (according to some sources, the piece employs Ryukyuan scales, though this is unconfirmed); appropriately, the melody becomes King Caesar's theme. The final battle theme (titled "Showdown Between the 3 Large Monsters in Okinawa")—as Mechagodzilla unleashes its eye and chest beams and launches projectiles from its fingers, knees, and toes, nearly killing both Godzilla and Caesar—is a joyous rapture of powerful percussion and swinging horns. This would be Sato's fourth and final contribution to the series; he ends on a high note.

In time, Mechagodzilla would acquire a cult following in its own right, resurrected in several later Toho pictures, making a cameo in Steven Spielberg's *Ready Player One* (2018), and costarring in *Godzilla vs. Kong.* More immediately, it would reappear in a direct sequel the following year, to be directed by Ishiro Honda, whose dark approach to the cyborg would be a world apart from Fukuda's freewheeling action. "The first one was made for kids, but for the second one, we also thought of the adults in the audience," recalled Nakano. "They picked the right type of director for the kind of films they were aiming to make."

ABOVE: Godzilla strikes the decisive blow against Mechagodzilla, ripping its head off and tossing it into the ocean. ▪ RIGHT: Mechagodzilla takes to the skies to launch an attack on its kaiju namesake. ▪ BELOW: Mechagodzilla's ability to fully rotate its head enables the robot to simultaneously unleash a two-way fusillade against Godzilla and King Caesar in the final showdown.

(MEKAGOJIRA NO GYAKUSHU / MECHAGODZILLA'S COUNTERATTACK)
aka *The Terror of Godzilla*
RELEASED: MARCH 15, 1975 (JAPAN)

TERROR OF MECHAGODZILLA

Godzilla was now a matinee star, but some of the series' creators longed to make the monster relevant for general audiences once again—to revisit the gravitas of the early days. This nostalgia led producer Tomoyuki Tanaka to lure director Ishiro Honda out of retirement and bring back esteemed composer Akira Ifukube in an effort to restore lost luster. At the same time, Tanaka introduced a talented new writer, Yukiko Takayama, who brought a darker viewpoint influenced by modern science fiction. The result was *Terror of Mechagodzilla*, a direct follow-up to *Godzilla vs. Mechagodzilla* that takes a very different turn. Whereas Jun Fukuda's film was a lively monster mystery, the sequel is a sci-fi metaphor for the mechanization of humankind, wedded to an atypically character-focused story: a fateful Romeo–and–Juliet romance. Themes of scientific ethics, duty and obligation, vengeance, family, love, honor, and self-sacrifice are entwined within a monster melee. "The idea was to bring Godzilla back to its origins," said special effects director Teruyoshi Nakano. "The character had been an idol for children, but we'd started to question whether it should continue that way. We wanted, somehow, to try to bring [the series] back to its basics, to how it was in the beginning. That's how the project began."

The story begins with a brief, mysterious shot of Katsura Mafune (Tomoko Ai), the beautiful and tragic figure at the heart of the drama. Katsura is devoted to serving and protecting her father, Dr. Mafune (Akihiko Hirata), a disgraced biologist expelled from academia for wild theories about a living dinosaur and his ability to control its actions. That dinosaur—Titanosaurus—is indeed real, and Mafune is hell-bent on using it to exact revenge on the world in mad-scientist fashion. Mafune's research is secretly funded by the Black Hole Planet 3 invaders, who need his dinosaur-controlling technology to steer Mechagodzilla in their renewed world-domination plan. Mafune's misguided and dangerous quest leads to his daughter's death not once, but twice. The aliens revive her each time, first by turning her into a coldhearted cyborg, and later by seizing the opportunity to surgically implant the Mechagodzilla control system in her body, where Interpol can never find it. Katsura wrestles with what remains of her conscience and emotions as she is wooed by Ichinose (Katsuhiko Sasaki), a good-hearted biologist investigating the Titanosaurus mystery. The aliens and Mafune send Mechagodzilla 2—a bit worse for wear yet more powerful and imposing than before—and Titanosaurus to blast Tokyo. Godzilla (absent from the first half) prevails, but only after Katsura takes her own life, destroying the Mechagodzilla controller to save the world and her paramour.

After the release of *Godzilla vs. Mechagodzilla*, Toho received about fifty submissions to a contest soliciting story ideas for the next film. Takayama, a screenwriting student, penned the

PREVIOUS SPREAD: Titanosaurus (Tatsumi Nikamoto) punches Godzilla (Toru Kawai). Despite the straightforward approach to the drama, the big battle includes some typical 1970s-era anthropomorphism (e.g., Godzilla dusting off its shoulders), impossible camera angles, and improbable monster stunts. ■ LEFT: Mechagodzilla 2's (abbreviated as "MG2") missile attack causes a Tokyo street to "jump" up—an on-set accident (caused by excessive explosives) that was retained in the final edit. "After the street settled back down, we shot additional cuts that make it look like it was supposed to happen," said crew member Jiro Shirasaki. "It wasn't the first time that something unplanned happened, but we would often just go with it and modify something else [to make it fit]. Especially for *Terror of Mechagodzilla*, there was no budget or time to shoot it over again. Being able to adjust on the fly was important."

winning entry; her treatment featured Titan 1 and 2, male and female dinosaur monsters with the ability to merge. To reduce costs and instill new energy, Tanaka commissioned a full script from Takayama rather than hire an established writer, thus making her the first female in the series to receive sole screenplay credit. Through four drafts, she made gradual changes in response to studio cost-cutting notes: the twin dinosaurs became a single Titanosaurus, and city destruction was downscaled. However, the writer was undaunted. "Katsura had been turned into a cyborg by aliens," Takayama said. "Even after she had been altered, she [still] had emotions. As long as this idea was not removed from the script, I didn't care all that much."

Aliens and robots and cyborgs are a world apart, yet Honda draws certain parallels to the first *Godzilla* by hinging the decisive outcome on a doomed love, staging Titanosaurus's first attack on Tokyo in the dark of night (with the classic trope of hordes fleeing, carrying their belongings), and directing in a downbeat, sober fashion, without the childish trappings of recent films, nor the lightness of his own 1960s efforts. Some moments seem peculiar in a children's film: there is brief, nonsexual nudity during Katsura's surgery; evidence of torture (the aliens hold kidnapped prisoners in a grim dungeon, their vocal cords severed); and the alien leader sadistically whips subordinates. As with *All Monsters Attack*, Motoyoshi Tomioka serves as director of photography for the entire film, consistently lending a dreary veneer to the dramatic scenes, the interior of the Mechagodzilla hangar (with repairmen working on scaffolds), the monster battles (some filmed in day-for-night fashion, and on a mix of indoor and open sets), and so forth.

Dr. Mafune is another throughline to 1954, analogous to the ill-fated Dr. Serizawa; both live in seclusion in an old, creepy house, and most significantly, are played by Hirata twenty-one years apart. Playing opposite Hirata, twenty-year-old Ai is excellent in her first feature film role, the deeply troubled Katsura.

CLOCKWISE FROM TOP LEFT: Aliens always seem to need the help of human scientists to fulfill their ambitions. Dr. Mafune (Akhiko Hirata, *center*) gets his first glimpse of Mechagodzilla courtesy of Tsuda (Toru Ibuki, *left*) and Commander Mugar (Goro Mutsumi, *right*). Although Mutsumi played the alien leader in both Mechagodzilla movies, they are two different characters. ■ Dr. Mafune (Hirata) is overcome with grief as he realizes that the aliens have transformed his daughter Katsura (Tomoko Ai) into a cyborg. ■ The Black Hole aliens monitor Godzilla's location with their Super Geiger. ■ After her life is saved for a second time by the aliens (whose surgeons are always standing by), Katsura (Ai) survives as a cyborg, with the Mechagodzilla controller implanted in her body, compelled to do the invaders' evil bidding.

CLOCKWISE FROM TOP LEFT: Titanosurus actor Tatsumi Nikamoto inspects the suit's head during a break between takes. ■ Set to Akira Ifukube's chilling music, the Tokyo attack features impressive effects. Both monsters strike Noh drama–inspired poses. For scenes of Titanosaurus bending backward, the actor stood in reverse inside the suit. ■ Using its tail, Titanosaurus (Nikamoto) unleashes hurricane force winds against Godzilla. Mechagodzilla 2 stands ready to attack. ■ Mechagodzilla 2 sets Tokyo ablaze with its rainbow-colored Space Beam attack.

"I hardly showed any energy at all," said the actress. "I recall especially that [Honda] told me to speak without changing my facial expression. . . . [Katsura] isn't supposed to smile."

The film's cold opening establishes continuity with the present and the past: a credits recap of the previous year's monster battles set to a thundering and brooding opus of old and new Akira Ifukube themes. The three-note motif of the original *Godzilla* is heard for the first time since 1954. Ifukube's dark new themes for Mechagodzilla—an antithesis to Masaru Sato's zippy interpretation of the robot—and Titanosaurus are a return to form, driven by aggressive percussion and brash brass, a reminder of the composer's unparalleled ability to imbue special effects films with tremendous power and emotion, transcending the images on-screen.

Takayama's original story included a scene in which Godzilla attacks Tokyo—but, as in the prior film, it's actually Mechagodzilla in disguise. Two boys are alarmed. "Godzilla, what's wrong?" they ask. "You're supposed to save us!" Despite attempts to re-center the monster in a more adult scenario, Godzilla was now a superhero, not an existential threat. Titanosaurus is an interesting contrast, a gentle sea serpent—an attractive coral red, with a fishtail and frills—that is forced to do evil against its nature; Mafune's great discovery is another victim of his madness, and Godzilla kills the poor beast. As for the special effects, Godzilla makes a dramatic nocturnal entrance, and the attacks on Tokyo feature the most impressive city destruction since *Ghidorah*, yet the composited monsters are sometimes out of scale. The lengthy end battle includes some seventies-era monster silliness, and another Godzilla "attraction suit" is glimpsed. Still, Honda concludes the film in dramatic yet downbeat fashion. Interpol storms the villains' hideout, bulldog Godzilla foils the aliens' escape, and as the monster swims off into the horizon, Ichinose lays Katsura to rest.

The Toho Champion Matsuri featuring *Terror of Mechagodzilla* drew the lowest theatrical attendance of any Godzilla film to date. Going forward, this seasonal children's program would soon pivot from Toho science-fiction films to showcasing classic Disney movies and, beginning in the eighties, films starring Doraemon, a time-traveling cartoon robot cat whose popularity in Japan is comparable to Mickey Mouse. In hindsight, the ambitious and uneven *Terror of Mechagodzilla* would mark the end of the directorial career of Honda (though he would go on to work with Akira Kurosawa on five films) and the beginning of an extended hiatus in Godzilla's film career.

CLOCKWISE FROM TOP LEFT: For close-ups of Titanosaurus performing biting motions, an articulated hand puppet of the monster's head and neck was used. ▪ Special effects director Teruyoshi Nakano discusses fight choreography with Godzilla (Toru Kawai) and Titanosaurus (Tatsumi Nikamoto). ▪ Suit actors Kazunari Mori (as Mechagodzilla 2) and Kawai (as Godzilla) rehearse a battle scene. ▪ When Dr. Mafune sends Titanosaurus to attack the city, Godzilla suddenly appears to repel the threat.

RIGHT: As Godzilla runs through a gauntlet of explosions and fire during the final battle, the suit briefly catches fire.

■ **BELOW:** As with the previous film, the scale of the miniature sets is enhanced via the use of leftover buildings, many of them originally created for *Submersion of Japan* (1973).

GODZILLA IN TRANSITION: 1975-1984

After *Terror of Mechagodzilla* concluded its theatrical run, Godzilla seemed to vanish from public view. *King Kong vs. Godzilla* was rereleased in March 1977 (the second time that film was featured in the Toho Champion Matsuri), but the annual parade of new Godzilla movies came to a halt.

Soon, however, the worldwide phenomenon of *Star Wars* (1977) launched a science-fiction boom, prompting Toho to rush Jun Fukuda's alien-invasion picture *The War in Space* into production for a December 1977 release. With sci-fi and special effects movies on the rise once again, producer Tomoyuki Tanaka convened a meeting of media and industry professionals on February 4, 1978, to discuss reviving the Godzilla series. Tanaka had commissioned a script from screenwriter Ryuzo Nakanishi (whose credits included *The War in Space* and the 1967 Nikkatsu Studios kaiju film *Gappa: The Triphibian Monster*), which was later revised by screenwriter Akira Murao. Titled *King of Monsters: Godzilla's Resurrection* and based on ideas by Hachiro Jinguji (Tanaka's pen name), the story introduced concepts that would eventually surface in 1984's *The Return of Godzilla*, including giant bloodsucking ticks that attach to Godzilla's body, and Godzilla seeking nuclear energy for food. It begins with a shipwreck at Bikini Atoll and the discovery of a huge cave where Godzilla, until recently, had hibernated. It is learned that the monster was revived by an explosion at a Soviet nuclear weapons facility; it then attacked a Japanese ship illegally dumping nuclear waste. Godzilla appears in Japan and stops a group of nuclear terrorists out to destroy Yokohama using plutonium stolen from a reactor. Godzilla attacks a nuclear power plant and then destroys multiple cities before it is lured to Mount Mihara, where an eruption is artificially triggered to trap it. Godzilla is wounded but narrowly escapes; it soon surfaces at Bikini and is attacked by US and Soviet forces and is believed killed by a nuclear bomb. Later, the "resurrected" monster reappears on the west coast of the US and, as the story concludes, approaches another nuclear power plant. Jun Fukuda was initially attached to direct. Then, in August 1979, the Associated Press reported that the project, now titled *The Return of Godzilla*, would be produced in 1980, with veteran director Ishiro Honda at the helm. "It will be a serious film, just like the first movie, which was a reaction to uncontrolled atomic bomb testing," Tanaka told AP. Further drafts of the story had Godzilla battling another monster, but the project never materialized.

BELOW, LEFT TO RIGHT: Yuji Kaida's dynamic painting graces the poster for the concert "A Night of Special Effects Music" held on August 5, 1983. ■ The advance poster for *The Return of Godzilla* featured a giant shadow. Godzilla's appearance was well known; the aim was to create mystery and anticipation surrounding its return. "Presenting it as if a formidable being was approaching was enough," said Koichi Kawakita, who designed the poster. "This felt fresh." ■ Poster for Godzilla Festival 1983, featuring six Godzilla titles as well as other Toho science-fiction and monster films.

Meanwhile, also in the late seventies, producer Henry Saperstein pushed for a Japan-US coproduction. "Four story ideas from the Japanese side and eleven from the American side were exchanged with [Saperstein], and scripts were also written, but unfortunately, nothing came to fruition," recalled producer Fumio Tanaka. Reportedly among these proposals was a film titled *Godzilla vs. Gargantua*. But the idea that seemed to gain the most traction was *Godzilla vs. the Devil*, in which Godzilla would have battled monsters awakened by evil human thoughts. Saperstein wanted the film to be written and produced entirely in America; when Toho insisted the special effects be done in Japan, the idea was abandoned.

Over time, public interest in Godzilla slowly grew. In mid-1978, Asahi Sonorama published *Fantastic Collection No. 5: Godzilla*, the first in a series of books to reveal previously unknown background information about the Godzilla series. This launched a mini-boom in Godzilla- and *tokusatsu*-related books, LPs, and videos over the next few years as publishers discovered a viable niche market. In August 1979, in honor of the monster's twenty-fifth birthday, Toho held a twenty-one-day film festival in Tokyo, showing numerous Godzilla and other special effects films, including *Godzilla, King of the Monsters!* with Raymond Burr.

In the early eighties, a grassroots organization called the Godzilla Revival Committee began publishing Godzilla fanzines in Japan. Tomoyuki Tanaka traveled the country to meet with committee members, promoting screenings of old films and holding lectures. "It was Tomoyuki who triggered the spread of Godzilla fans' voices in the streets," said *The Return of Godzilla* director Koji Hashimoto. From 1981 to 1983, the committee helped organize the Japan SFX Convention, in which guests such as Honda appeared, and actual special effects props from Toho genre films were displayed. In 1983, Toho organized a Godzilla film festival and participated in the concert event "A Night of Special Effects Music" on August 5, 1983, which featured the premiere performance of Akira Ifukube's *Symphonic Fantasia*, a suite of the composer's special effects movie music. The concert was hosted by Tanaka, with appearances by Ifukube, Honda, and actor Akihiko Hirata.

Of all the ideas discussed during Godzilla's hiatus, the one that apparently came closest to realization was *Godzilla: King of the Monsters in 3-D*, an entirely American production proposed in 1983 by director Steve Miner, who had previously helmed two entries in the *Friday the 13th* series. The exciting script by writer Fred Dekker had a dead baby Godzilla washing ashore on a beach after a nuclear accident, and an enraged Godzilla destroying San Francisco after discovering its offspring's corpse; the action was set against a Cold War plot pitting an American hero against a Soviet villain, with the threat of nuclear war looming in the background. Godzilla was to be rendered via stop-motion modeling and the latest effects technology, and the picture's budget was estimated as high as $30 million. In 1984, *Variety* reported that Miner was pursuing a deal with Universal Pictures to produce the film that year, but this project also fell apart.

The long drought, however, was nearly over. By January 1984, Toho had formed the Godzilla Revival Preparation Committee, with every department within the company dedicated to producing a new Godzilla film that year. Committee member Koichi Kawakita recalled a sense of urgency to bring the monster back before it was too late: "Without new Godzilla films being made, there wasn't much opportunity for a new generation to become fans."

TWO

RESURRECTIONS:
1984 TO 1995

(GOJIRA / GODZILLA)
RELEASED: DECEMBER 15, 1984 (JAPAN)

THE RETURN OF GODZILLA

Amid the towering steel canyons of Tokyo's Shinjuku ward, Godzilla faces off with the Japan Self-Defense Forces' flying tank, the Super X. Godzilla roars, and the Super X fires cadmium missiles into the monster's open mouth—a direct hit, then another. Blood oozes from Godzilla's jaws. The stunned monster's chest heaves, and it loses consciousness, collapsing against a crumbling skyscraper. Godzilla is vanquished. A large crowd gathers to gawk at the fallen beast. Just then, a nuclear explosion in the stratosphere above Japan ignites an electromagnetic storm. Lightning strikes Godzilla! The monster is resurrected—and enraged.

The Return of Godzilla marks the monster's comeback on the big screen. A snarling, new-look Godzilla is brought to life via updated special effects in a story that places Japan and the monster at the center of a Cold War crisis, mirroring real-world fears of a nuclear catastrophe as tensions between the US and USSR escalated. During his tireless nine-year-long effort to bring Godzilla back, producer Tomoyuki Tanaka had insisted that Godzilla return to its original intent; he strongly wanted to reconnect the monster with its antinuclear message and, in doing so, to make Godzilla fearsome once again. This would be Toho's most costly genre production to date. According to *Variety*, its budget climbed to $6.25 million due to extensive miniature sets and the construction of a robotic Godzilla; thus, veteran special effects director Teruyoshi Nakano, who had labored through the lean-budgeted films of the 1970s, would now

"DESPITE BEING BAPTIZED BY NUCLEAR WEAPONS, JAPANESE TODAY ARE CAREFREE ABOUT NUCLEAR ISSUES. I THINK NUCLEAR WEAPONS ARE THE GREATEST TRAGEDY OF HUMANITY, THE GREATEST TRAGEDY OF THIS CENTURY. SO I THOUGHT OF DEPICTING THE NUCLEAR ISSUE IN *THE RETURN OF GODZILLA*."

—Producer Tomoyuki Tanaka

have greater resources to pursue more ambitious visuals. Tanaka initially asked director Ishiro Honda to lend his steady hand to this pivotal project, but Honda felt it was time to step aside for the next generation. Koji Hashimoto, a longtime assistant director who had recently codirected his first feature, the science-fiction saga *Sayonara Jupiter* (1984), was then selected, much to Hashimoto's surprise. "I never expected it," said Hashimoto. "*Sayonara Jupiter* didn't get good reviews, after all."

The core team of Tanaka, associate producer Fumio Tanaka (no relation), Hashimoto, Nakano, and screenwriter Hideichi Nagahara all agreed that the superhero Godzilla of the 1970s was finished. There was disagreement, however, on whether to put the heavy themes of nuclear weapons and nuclear energy front and center. Both Nagahara and Hashimoto were strongly opposed; they admired the lighthearted, entertaining Godzilla films of the sixties, with monster action and touches of comedy. For his part, Hashimoto wanted to take Godzilla movies in a new direction—the original *Godzilla* "pushed too much on the nuclear issue," he said. But Tomoyuki Tanaka insisted on a return to the sober seriousness of 1954; he saw Japan's increasing reliance on nuclear power and the animosity between nuclear superpowers as urgent matters. In the 1950s, Japan had embarked on an ambitious yet controversial nuclear energy program to meet the rising electricity demands of its rapid economic growth. By the 1970s, there was an expanding network of nuclear power plants, though citizen protests were widespread, especially after the meltdown at the Three Mile Island reactor in Pennsylvania in 1979 raised concerns about the safety of nuclear power. Meanwhile, the Soviet invasion of Afghanistan in 1979 led to a dangerous phase in US-USSR relations; President Ronald Reagan deployed nuclear missiles in West Germany and announced the Strategic Defense Initiative, or "Star Wars" program, a proposed satellite-based laser weapon system that would shoot down intercontinental ballistic missiles. The threat of nuclear war loomed.

A fearsome Godzilla, however, would be a sharp contrast to the monster's family-friendly image of the previous decade. "We had great difficulty in terms of how to convey the fear of nuclear weapons and radioactivity," recalled special effects director Nakano. "Children nowadays go to sleep hugging Godzilla plush toys. For the peace-blinded Japanese people, the fear of nuclear radiation has completely disappeared. So what happens if you revive Godzilla as a child of the nuclear age in this peace-blinded, stable era? How can we create fear?" Nevertheless, Nakano envisioned making Godzilla scary again by situating the monster in a true horror film with greater realism. He proposed radical ideas, such as eliminating Godzilla's heat ray altogether and emphasizing the fear of death represented by the monster: "For me, radiation was just a convenient setup." Ultimately, Tomoyuki Tanaka won out. "He thought it wouldn't hit Japanese people

PAGES 204–205: Godzilla confronts its biological brethren in the final showdown of *Godzilla vs. Biollante*. ■ PREVIOUS SPREAD: Godzilla feeds off the reactor core of the Mihama Nuclear Power Plant. Godzilla's biological need for radiation (a recurring theme throughout the Heisei series) is established in this film, a dramatic change from the Showa series. ■ ABOVE: After being temporarily disabled by the EMP (electromagnetic pulse) from a Russian missile, the Super X desperately tries to escape from Godzilla. ■ BELOW LEFT: Godzilla surveys the smoking remains of the military convoy sent to confront the monster at the waterfront. ■ BELOW: Director Koji Hashimoto (*with hat*) discusses the cabinet meeting scene with Keiju Kobayashi (*standing*), who plays Prime Minister Mitamura. ■ OPPOSITE TOP: The Super X flies in between skyscrapers and launches attacks on Godzilla. ■ OPPOSITE BOTTOM: Godzilla crushes the Super X by toppling the Shinjuku Sumitomo Building onto the flying battle tank.

unless it's serious, that Japanese people would feel a bit awkward if it's done tongue in cheek," said Fumio Tanaka. Added Hashimoto, "Godzilla belongs to [Tomoyuki] Tanaka. He was determined to do it his way, and ultimately, we just had to give in to his forcefulness."

Screenwriter Ryuzo Nakanishi's proposed *King of Monsters: Godzilla's Resurrection* (see the "Godzilla in Transition" section) tied Godzilla to nuclear power but was written before the Cold War threats of the early eighties came into focus. A revision by screenwriter Akira Murao featured a battle between Godzilla and Bagan, a new monster that controlled the actions of three divine beasts, but this story was dropped due to budget considerations. Tanaka next turned to Nagahara, whose genre film credits included Toho's *The War in Space* (1977) and the aforementioned *Sayonara Jupiter*.

"I tried really hard to get the image of the original Godzilla out of my head," Nagahara recalled. "What would it be like if Godzilla showed up in Japan today? That's the reality I was chasing." Nagahara saw Godzilla not as a monster, but as a living creature. "Godzilla has no animus for human beings," he said. "Godzilla is just Godzilla. I tried to dispense with the idea that Godzilla is evil."

THE FIRE WITHIN

One of Nagahara's most significant contributions was to portray Godzilla as a biological organism, a living nuclear animal. To neutralize the monster, the military deploys bombs made of cadmium—a highly poisonous substance used for absorbing neutrons and dampening nuclear reactors. The bombs appear to kill Godzilla, but here Nagahara ties together the movie's parallel threads of monster action and Cold War tension. Earlier, when Godzilla first appears, a diplomatic meeting is quickly held, and the American and Soviet envoys pressure Prime Minister Mitamura to permit a nuclear device to be used in Japan to kill the monster. Mitamura steadfastly refuses, lecturing the diplomats on Japan's Three Non-Nuclear Principles

ABOVE: An iconic view of Godzilla as reflected in the mirrored windows of the Yurakucho Mullion building. This shot was unfortunately deleted from *Godzilla 1985*, the reedited version of the film released in the US by New World Pictures.

"IF GODZILLA REAPPEARS IN JAPAN OR IN JAPAN'S COASTAL WATERS, YOU MUST AGREE TO LET US USE NUCLEAR WEAPONS!"

—US Special Envoy Rosenburg (Walter Nichols)

that prohibit the country from possessing, producing, or permitting the introduction of nuclear weapons. However, unbeknownst to all, the Soviets have hidden a remote ICBM launcher on a cargo ship in Tokyo Bay. Godzilla's attack accidentally triggers the launch of a satellite-based missile (in this fictional reality, a "Star Wars"–type program already exists) toward Tokyo, and—for the first time in the series—Japan asks the US for help, not from troops stationed there, but to launch another ICBM and intercept the death blow. The explosion releases radiation that turns the sky an eerie red and, as in 1954, man's nuclear hubris inevitably gives rise to Godzilla. Nagahara also introduced the novel idea of Godzilla feeding on radiation. As Tomoyuki Tanaka said, "Frankly, Godzilla doesn't make any sense since it doesn't want anything. It's just walking around. We had to make radiation attract it or else the story wouldn't work."

There are many homages to the original *Godzilla*. As if predestined, Godzilla attacks a resurgent Japan— a nation now fully bearing the progress and prosperity that were in their infancy thirty years before. Its dramatic entrance occurs at a nuclear power plant, where it feeds on the energy of Japan's Faustian bargain with the atom. Godzilla's arrival in Tokyo is a spectacular update of its 1954 assault—the country's once-threadbare military is now a robust array of ground and air might, but the new, nuclear-powered Godzilla is unstoppable; this is arguably the most exciting Godzilla-versus-military exchange in any film to date. In the end, the biophysicist Prof. Hayashida (Yosuke Natsuki) exploits Godzilla's prehistoric lineage, using bird sounds to lure it into the mouth of the Mount Mihara volcano, seemingly entombing it forever. The threat is over, but there are tears of sadness for the mythic, tragic creature.

OLD TALENTS AND NEW FACES

The Return of Godzilla is not a character-driven film, but distinguished actor Keiju Kobayashi delivers a memorable turn as the embattled prime minister who exhibits poise and resolve while the American and Soviet envoys spout bellicose rhetoric; the prime minister's reverence for Godzilla also provides the film with its most emotional note. The unethical-journalist-turned-hero Goro Maki is played by popular actor Ken Tanaka, while nineteen-year-old Yasuko Sawaguchi, a recent Toho Cinderella appearing in just her second film, is the nominal ingenue Naoko Okumura; she would go on to become one of Toho's most popular actresses. There are several familiar faces: Natsuki, the young detective in *Ghidorah, the Three-Headed Monster,* returns as the stoic Prof. Hayashida, a role originally intended for Akihiko Hirata, who fell ill with cancer and was replaced before filming began. Series veterans Hiroshi Koizumi and Yoshibumi Tajima, both enthusiastic to take part in Godzilla's revival, have smaller roles.

Director Hashimoto felt the constant scrutiny of producer Tomoyuki Tanaka, who frequently visited the set and offered suggestions. "When the politicians [were] engaged in a heated discussion, Tanaka suddenly walked in during rehearsals and said, 'This is not working. Put more tempo into it. Be more lively,'" remembered assistant director Takao Okawara. "It was amazing how he could assess the scene so quickly." As a novice director, Hashimoto felt he was not completely trusted. Perhaps his biggest clash

ABOVE: (*left to right*) Goro Maki (Ken Tanaka), Naoko Okumura (Yasuko Sawaguchi), and Professor Hayashida (Yosuke Natsuki) prepare to test the plan to attract Godzilla using magnetic waves. ■ **RIGHT:** Maki (Tanaka) and Naoko (Sawaguchi) flee Godzilla's rampage. An actual-size Godzilla prop foot was constructed of kapok and controlled by a huge construction crane. It appears in only a few scenes.

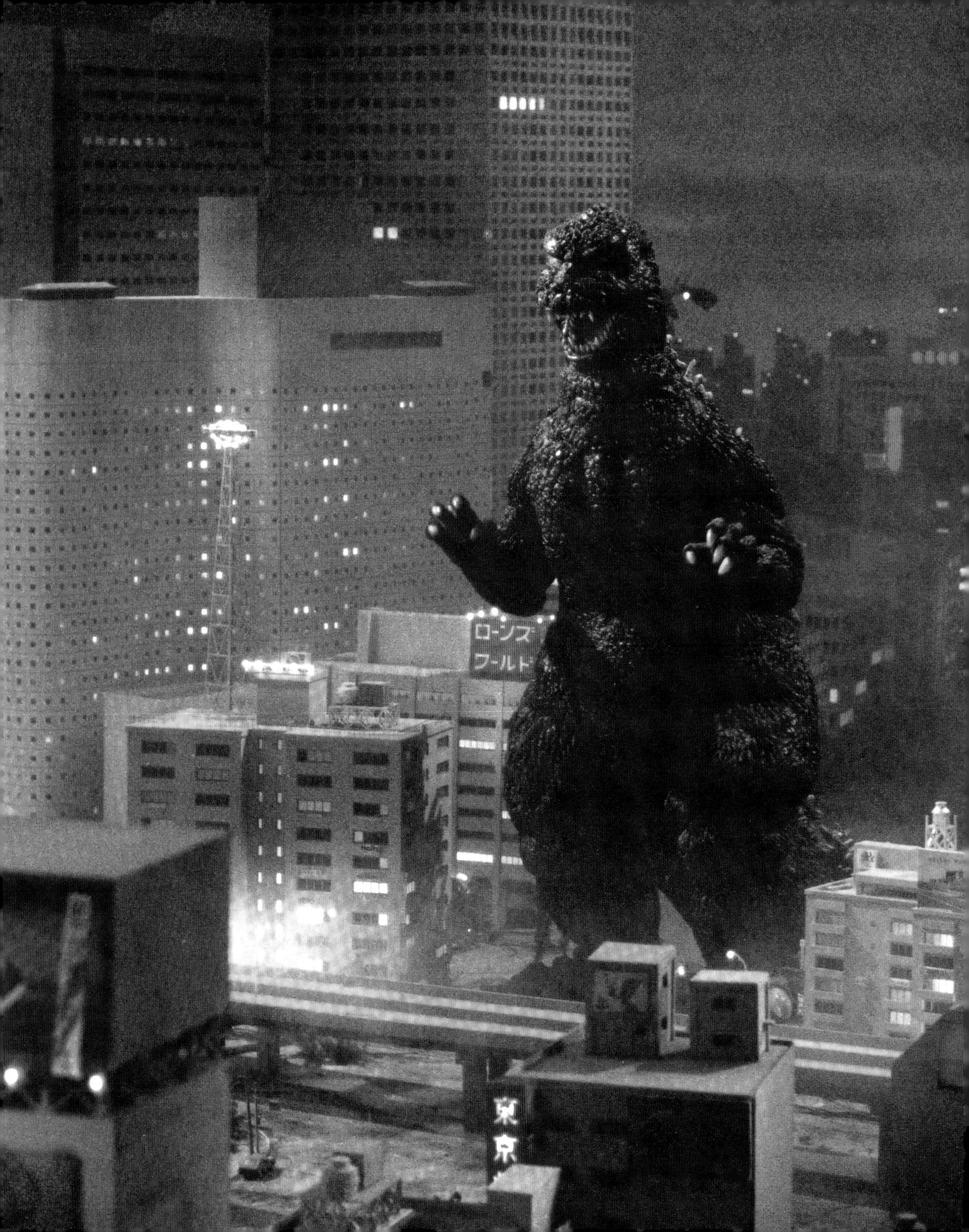
ローンズ
ワールド
東京

with Tomoyuki Tanaka was over a scene featuring actor and folk singer Tetsuya Takeda as a vagrant, a bit of comic relief in an otherwise straightforward film. The character was inspired by a homeless person encountered while the team was location hunting in Shinjuku. Takeda ad-libbed most of his lines, mocking Godzilla. Hashimoto liked the results, but when Tanaka viewed the rushes, he was displeased by the silliness.

In recent decades, large skyscrapers had sprung up in Tokyo. Recognizing that Godzilla would be dwarfed by these modern structures, Tomoyuki Tanaka decided to double Godzilla's height from 164 to 328 feet (50 to 100 m), thus downsizing the miniature landscape by half from the traditional 1/25 scale to 1/50 scale. To help make this challenging adjustment, Nakano brought in special effects art director Yasuyuki Inoue, who last worked for Toho on *Submersion of Japan* (1973) and had extensive experience in making large, meticulously detailed miniature sets for Eiji Tsuburaya in previous decades. On his own initiative, Inoue instead decided to build sets in a more manageable 1/40 scale, thus pegging Godzilla's corresponding height at 262 feet (80 m) rather than 328 feet (100 m). Shinjuku's forest of high-rises tower above the monster and create an interesting setting for the battle between Godzilla and Super X.

Nakano sought to utilize updated technology to create the new Godzilla, though most of the equipment in use had not changed since the Tsuburaya era; filming techniques also remained largely unchanged, and many crew members were holdovers as well. "There were still plenty of people who had worked with Tsuburaya," said Toshio Miike, then a young recruit on the miniature-making staff. "I heard plenty of stories from them about the old days." Still, Nakano introduced some new ideas. Shooting in 1.85:1 aspect ratio rather than scope, he was able to more fully express the size of a giant monster in the taller frame size, and he utilized a snorkel camera to shoot Godzilla from a ground-level viewpoint.

To better depict even the most minute movements of Godzilla's eyes, mouth, and hands, Nakano secured producer Tanaka's approval to commission the creation of the Cybot Godzilla, a 16-foot- (4.8-m-) tall robot. Unfortunately, the best robotic technology then available did not fully live up to Nakano's aspirations. The cybot's movements were not always smooth, and its design was not a perfect match to the Godzilla suit. In the end, the cybot appears only sporadically, mostly in close-ups of Godzilla roaring; it is most noticeable

PREVIOUS SPREAD, LEFT TO RIGHT: Monster modeling artist Noboyuki Yasumaru sculpting the prototype maquette of Godzilla for *The Return of Godzilla*. ▪ Godzilla's advance through Tokyo brings the monster to the Shinjuku area, with its huge skyscrapers. ▪ **ABOVE:** Godzilla smashes the reactor building of the Mihama Nuclear Power Plant. ▪ **BELOW:** Godzilla advances through the enormous Shinjuku miniature set. Because Godzilla's height was increased to 262 feet (80 m)—compared to 164 feet (50 m) in the Showa series, to enable the monster to stand among Tokyo's modern skyscrapers without being dwarfed—the miniatures were downscaled from ⅟₂₅ to ⅟₄₀, resulting in some loss of detail.

CLOCKWISE FROM TOP LEFT: A closeup of the Cybot Godzilla's face as Godzilla roars at the Super X. ▪ SFX director Teruyoshi Nakano speaks at the film's introductory press conference on August 8, 1984. "I was thinking about how to show off the Cybot Godzilla to the press," recalled Koichi Kawakita, who orchestrated the monster's appearance at the event. "Open up the drapes, put on the smoke. . . . It was a great show." ▪ Adding last-minute details to the Mihama Nuclear Power Plant set for Godzilla's first appearance. This scene is dramatically shot and edited, emphasizing Godzilla's height and size by alternating between the monster's elevated viewpoint and the view from ground level.

in the scene in which Godzilla is shot in the mouth with missiles. Nakano said, "The value of the cybot was in touring all over Japan for promotional appearances rather than in the actual filming."

According to some reports, composer Akira Ifukube declined an invitation to score *The Return of Godzilla*. The job instead went to relative newcomer Reijiro Koroku, a prolific composer of themes for anime, fantasy, and television productions. Koroku's musical style was markedly different and contemporary. From the opening frames, his powerful melodies and orchestrations and use of Hollywood-style motifs propel and transcend the visuals. "They wanted music that would have something in common with the original *Godzilla*, but they still wanted something that was new," Koroku recalled. "For that reason, they wanted a new composer—that was stressed to me." Koroku was largely left to his own creative vision. "Director Hashimoto was a tender, nice person. He was very quiet; he didn't talk much. For the most part, I just decided everything for myself, and he agreed. . . . It was really Tanaka's plan that we followed with the music. We wanted to give the feeling of scariness, but more than that, we were trying to project the feeling of something mysterious, something not understandable." Koroku felt that Godzilla was "absolutely not something evil. On the contrary, Godzilla has every right to think, *Why do these people want to kill me?* That's the kind of image I wanted to convey in the music, particularly in the final scene [of Godzilla's descent into the volcano]. It is not meant to simply convey fear."

The Return of Godzilla was the second-highest grossing domestic film of the 1984–85 season, with returns of about ¥1.7 billion, according to the Motion Picture Producers Association of Japan. It represented a significant leap forward in the series' production values and scope. Nevertheless, Hashimoto and Nakano both felt they had come up a bit short. "We should have let Godzilla rampage more wildly and fully embraced the entertainment aspect of Godzilla as king of destruction," said Hashimoto. "It was halfway done." Nakano agreed. "It might have been enough to simply have a scary Godzilla come out and rampage. We might have been a bit too serious."

THE RETURN OF RAYMOND BURR

GODZILLA 1985

RELEASED: AUGUST 23, 1985 (USA, NEW WORLD PICTURES)

"When they asked me to do [*Godzilla 1985*], I said, 'Certainly,' and everybody thought I was out of my mind. But it wasn't the large sum of money. It was the fact that, first of all, I kind of liked Godzilla, and [when] do you get the opportunity to play yourself thirty years later?"

—Raymond Burr (journalist Steven Martin)

The Return of Godzilla* serves as a direct sequel to the original *Godzilla*, erasing a thirty-year history of intervening movies that varied widely in tone and content. Less than one year after the film was released in Japan, it surfaced in American cinemas—except it wasn't the same film anymore. And yet, something was oddly familiar: The film had undergone significant reediting, and new scenes were inserted to give the story an American point of view. Those new scenes starred Raymond Burr as an old journalist who'd witnessed Godzilla's first attack on Tokyo decades earlier. *The Return of Godzilla* was thus transformed into *Godzilla 1985*, a de facto sequel to *Godzilla, King of the Monsters!*

New World Pictures, originally founded by Roger Corman, acquired the North American distribution rights to *The Return of Godzilla* for a reported $500,000, then spent $200,000 more to film new material featuring Burr reprising his role of reporter Steve Martin (now called Steven). Producer Anthony Randel and director R.J. Kizer initially intended to turn the film into a silly parody, but things got serious once they enlisted the services of Burr, who took Godzilla's antinuclear stance to heart and insisted on playing things straight.

The new scenes are set at the Pentagon, where gruff General Goodhue (Warren Kemmerling) barks out lines like, "What the hell is going on?" and tries to prevent the crisis in Japan from sparking a nuclear war with the USSR. Martin joins the general, a wisecracking junior officer (Travis Swords), and other officials as they watch Godzilla attack Tokyo remotely via video monitors. Burr's role is to comment on the action in grave tones. "Godzilla is like a hurricane or a tidal wave. We must approach him as we would a force of nature."

"Burr is not propelling the story in any way," said Randel. "His scenes absolutely don't need to be there, but somehow it all fits."

Numerous scenes were trimmed, reordered, or deleted, and much of composer Reijiro Koroku's music was replaced with stock themes. A questionable editorial change concerned the depiction of nuclear weapons and turned Godzilla's antinuclear theme into an example of Reagan-era Cold War paranoia. In *The Return of Godzilla*, a Russian naval officer is killed while trying to stop an ICBM from accidentally launching toward Tokyo. New World reworked the sequence, making it appear that the Russian launches the nuclear weapon on purpose; to drive the point home, a new shot of a finger pressing a button was inserted. "Every[one] who was working for New World at that time learned very quickly that this management group was decidedly conservative in its political outlook," said director Kizer. "I said to [producer Randel], 'Wait a minute, why are we having the Russian trying to blow everything up?' And he just turned to me and said, 'This is the company we're working for.'"

New World launched a major promotional campaign for the release, including tie-in commercials for Dr. Pepper (the beverage also appears in the film), public appearances by an actor in a real Godzilla suit, and a media blitz. *Godzilla 1985* would be the last Japanese-made Godzilla movie to be theatrically distributed in the US until the similarly titled *Godzilla 2000.*

Burr reportedly shot all his scenes in one eight-hour session and was paid $50,000. Nevertheless, his dedication to Godzilla's deeper meaning is evident. He reportedly had a hand in writing his character's ending narration: "For now, Godzilla, that strangely innocent and tragic monster, has gone to earth. Whether he returns or not . . . the things he has taught us remain."

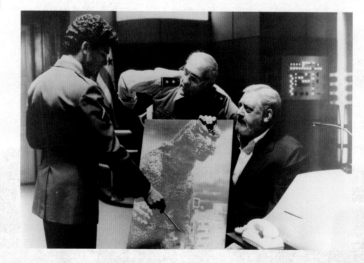

LEFT: Steven Martin (Raymond Burr, *right*) is summoned to Washington to advise General Goodhue (Warren Kemmerling, *center*) during Godzilla's attack on Japan.

"PERSONALLY, I PREFER GODZILLA TO HAVE A MEAN STREAK."

—Tomoyuki Tanaka, producer

ABOVE: Prime Minister Mitamura (Keiju Kobayashi) weeps for Godzilla in the film's final, tragic moments. However, actor Kobayashi's tears were unplanned. "Kobayashi-san cried out of his own feelings," said director Koji Hashimoto. "I thought tears weren't necessary, but a crying face has power. I regretted it later for being overly sentimental." ■ **RIGHT:** Godzilla rampages through the Nishi Shinjuku section of Tokyo.

(GOJIRA TAI BIORANTE)
RELEASED: DECEMBER 16, 1989 (JAPAN)

GODZILLA VS. BIOLLANTE

Bombs explode at the crater of Mount Mihara, triggering an eruption and freeing Godzilla from its volcanic prison. Instinctively, the monster heads across Sagami Bay toward Lake Ashi, lured by the cries of Biollante, a giant reptile-flower creature spawned from the combined DNA of Godzilla and roses— a freak accident of reckless bioengineering. Godzilla cautiously approaches its monster-plant hybrid brethren. Biollante attacks, ensnaring Godzilla in tendril vines; Biollante's Venus flytrap–like mouths spit acidic sap. The night sky glows with military searchlights. Godzilla's fins sparkle, and its heat ray mortally wounds Biollante, which burns to death on the water's surface. The beautiful yet hideous monster vaporizes into a cloud of spores, floating into the heavens.

Godzilla vs. Biollante is an ambitious effort to update the Godzilla formula, made by new, younger filmmakers with something to prove. This is a film jammed with characters and contemporary ideas about genetic engineering, bioweapons, terrorism, and psychic phenomena intertwined with themes of love and loss. It's a hybrid of the kaiju, sci-fi, and thriller genres, with foreign agents vying for possession of a cache of Godzilla skin cells. Coveted for their potential to "neutralize nuclear missiles," according to research magnate Seigoh Okouchi (Ryunosuke Kaneda), these cells are the biological source of Godzilla's strength—and its mortal weakness. A fierce, more animallike

"THERE ARE SO MANY OTHER THINGS IN TODAY'S WORLD THAT ARE TRULY FRIGHTENING. SO MY CONCEPT WAS TO MAKE GODZILLA A POWERFUL AND IMPRESSIVE FORCE AND DERIVE DRAMA FROM THE WAY IN WHICH MANKIND DEALS WITH SUCH AN OVERWHELMING FORCE."

—Kazuki Omori, director

Godzilla wreaks havoc and confronts its half-doppelgänger via ambitious special effects that introduce new innovations while honoring old Toho traditions. Biollante is an inspired creation unlike any other Godzilla foe, a feminine monster born of tragedy.

Audience analysis showed *The Return of Godzilla* had skewed to an older, nostalgic crowd but lacked appeal with the lucrative youth market. Feedback was mixed; those familiar with the monster-versus-monster template of the old days felt something was missing. Some even believed that *Return* marked the conclusion of the Godzilla series rather than its revival. Producer Tomoyuki Tanaka started over, determined to re-create Godzilla for a new generation, to reach a younger crowd via a more Hollywood-style entertainment film. In the fall of 1985, Toho announced a story contest—the winning story would serve as the basis of a sequel provisionally titled *Godzilla 2*. Toho received 5,025 stories, which were judged by a six-member panel that included renowned manga artist and animator Dr. Osamu Tezuka. The winning entry, *Godzilla vs. Biollante,* was penned by Shinichiro Kobayashi, a dentist who had previously written for

PREVIOUS SPREAD: Godzilla emerges from Mount Mihara. ▪ **ABOVE:** Biollante attacks Godzilla at Lake Ashi. Biollante's initial form is an immovable plant, and the vines give the stationary creature the appearance of movement. SFX director Koichi Kawakita attempted to augment the live-action footage with stop-motion animation, but it did not effectively match the live action.

ABOVE: Children at the Psychic Institute show drawings that depict their common vision—Godzilla is returning!

■ BELOW: Biollante attacks, attempting to absorb Godzilla. The action is violent, and green sap is splattered about. SFX director Koichi Kawakita subscribed to Eiji Tsuburaya's philosophy that Godzilla movies should avoid bloodshed; with Biollante's sap, he bent the rule for a more realistic scene.

The Return of Ultraman and other *tokusatsu* productions. Kobayashi's story concerned a biologist studying the crossbreeding of species. His daughter died at a young age, and he attempts to preserve her essence by combining her cells with those of a houseplant.

To help age down the target audience, Tanaka looked outside the Toho system and chose thirty-seven-year-old independent director Kazuki Omori. A medical school graduate turned filmmaker, Omori had found success directing idol movies, a genre of youth-oriented films starring famous pop singers. "I'm not such an enthusiastic fan [of Godzilla]," Omori said at the time. "Although movies are [an] unreal or complete fabrication, Godzilla seems like the biggest fabrication of them all."

Still, Omori and the producer shared a common vision. "Tanaka was looking for someone new," Omori said in a 2021 interview. "He wanted to make this more like an American movie instead of a Japanese-style Godzilla movie. He gave me the top stories [from the contest] and asked which one I thought was the most interesting. One of them was Kobayashi's story; there was another about Godzilla fighting a robot army. Another writer had the idea of different countries fighting for Godzilla cells, so I decided to combine that with Kobayashi's story [and create a scenario] about the fusing of Godzilla and plant cells into a plant monster. That's how we started developing our script."

The film was planned for release at the end of 1986, but it was delayed three years while Omori directed more idol movies and simultaneously worked on the Godzilla screenplay. *Biollante* was officially announced in May 1989, with a December release date, though filming would not start until August, creating a highly compressed schedule and challenging all aspects of the production. Things moved so quickly that Koichi Kawakita, the series' newly appointed special effects director, never paused to celebrate his ascension to the job. "I should have felt more honor and enthusiasm, but I didn't think about it," Kawakita recalled, "because I had no time to stop and think."

REINVENTING GODZILLA

Kawakita was a veteran of Toho's two-director system, having joined Eiji Tsuburaya's special effects team in 1962 in the optical compositing section and slowly worked his way up. His first directing credits were on *tokusatsu* TV shows in the 1970s, and he debuted as a feature-film SFX director on the war drama

"EIJI TSUBURAYA TOLD ME, 'ALWAYS STRIVE TO SHOOT SOMETHING THAT WILL GIVE DREAMS TO THE AUDIENCE WAITING ON THE OTHER SIDE OF THE SCREEN.' THESE WORDS ARE DEEPLY ENGRAVED IN MY HEART."

—Koichi Kawakita, special effects director

ABOVE: Wire works supervisor Koji Matsumoto (*second from left*) and crew setting up the massive system of wires that control the final form of Biollante. ■

BELOW: Preparing for Biollante's charge at Godzilla, the largest-scale stunt of its type ever attempted. Three crew members pulled Biollante's platform with a cable; three pushed from behind, the suit actor inside flailed away, the mouth operator did his thing, the motorized legs pumped away, and a dozen operators ran alongside the suit to control the vines with thirty-two wires.

Samurai of the Big Sky (1976). To a great extent, *Godzilla vs. Biollante* is Kawakita's personal showpiece. He had long aspired to realize his own vision of Godzilla, and he brought creative ideas and enthusiasm to a virtually all-new special effects team that was carried over from the mecha sci-fi film *Gunhed*, released in July 1989. "Most of the staff moved right from *Gunhed* to *Biollante*," Kawakita recalled. "Almost everyone was new, but since we were restarting the Godzilla series, it worked out fine."

"Kawakita realized that an actor's ability to perform inside a 176-pound (80-kg) monster suit is limited," said SFX cameraman Kenichi Eguchi. "By craning, zooming, and so on, the camera should move to support what the suit actor can't do. That idea stuck with me, and I adopted it as my basic approach." Godzilla's fierce battle with the navy in the Uraga Strait and its attack on Osaka by night highlight Eguchi's quick camera work, as well as forced perspective and miniature photography. There are numerous other highlight moments: The first view of rose-form Biollante at Lake Ashi is achieved via a flawless composite shot bearing no evidence of matte lines as the camera pans upward to reveal the creature in full. Kawakita also introduces an important trademark of his work: monsters (and, in later movies, machines) that transform from one stage to another, becoming larger and more powerful. Biollante's second, final form appears as a gracefully animated cloud of spores that descends from the heavens and materializes into a monster that towers over Godzilla. "I prefer to have [monsters] transform," Kawakita said. "It's more entertaining for the audience, and it serves as an identifying characteristic of the [Heisei] Godzilla films."

CLOCKWISE FROM TOP LEFT: Lighting technician Kaoru Saito used backlighting behind Godzilla—an unconventional technique. "Backlighting creates a lot more depth and contrast," he said. "This Godzilla had an especially good silhouette." RC helicopters create more dynamic flying action compared to traditional models on wires. ■ The Fire Mirror enables Super X2 to absorb and then return Godzilla's heat rays back at the monster. ■ On location at Lake Ashi. (*left to right*) Kunihiko Mitamura (Kirishima), Koji Takahashi (Dr. Shiragami), Megumi Odaka (Miki Saegusa), and Yoshiko Tanaka (Asuka Okouchi) with director Kazuki Omori. ■ Cameraman Kenichi Eguchi filming a shot from the Super X2's point of view as the drone approaches Godzilla during the Uraga Strait battle. Moments after this photo was taken, an accident sent Eguchi tumbling into the pool, causing the cancellation of the day's shooting and ruining the ¥20 million camera.

Designing Biollante—an unprecedented flora-fauna kaiju—was especially difficult. Kawakita said, "I wanted Biollante to mutate into a formidable foe, one that could even defeat Godzilla." Due to the time crunch, this was the first-ever monster built by a contractor from outside Toho. But when twenty-nine-year-old designer Fuyuki Shinada delivered the first-stage Biollante—a giant, grotesque rose with a mutated stalk—to the studio for filming, Kawakita's crew scoffed; the creature appeared powerless, and it was virtually immobile. Godzilla actor Kenpachiro Satsuma made the two monsters' battle at Lake Ashi believable as he worked in tandem with the wire works crew to wrestle with Biollante's innumerable vines.

Meanwhile, the design of Biollante's final, second-stage form was not agreed upon until September. With the clock ticking, Shinada set up shop in a Toho warehouse and spent a grueling month of twelve-hour days there; the monster suit was completed just ten days before the production was scheduled to wrap. It was impressively giant and terrifying, with long, razor-sharp teeth jutting from alligator-like jaws; yet the fully evolved Biollante was even more stationary than the first, like a giant stump in the ground.

To avoid rehashing the vine-intensive first fight, Kawakita came up with a wild idea: In the heat of battle, the huge, seemingly immovable monster would charge at Godzilla. "The audience doesn't know the hardships we face behind the scenes," Kawakita reasoned. "All they see is what's on the screen, so we have to give them something to 'ooh' and 'aah' about." The huge costume was put on rollers, and twenty crew members pushed it across the miniature set, the camera shaking violently to simulate the ground quaking as the monster advances. It was the largest monster-manipulation stunt in Toho's history. When it was finished, the entire crew erupted in applause.

GODZILLA CELLS—WHAT COULD POSSIBLY GO WRONG?

Godzilla vs. Biollante is a direct sequel to *The Return of Godzilla* and begins in the burning rubble of the 1984 attack. The story concerns a battle for possession of Godzilla cells, precious samples of the monster's tissue with potentially world-changing self-reproductive properties. As concerns rise that Godzilla may escape from its fiery imprisonment in Mount Mihara, the Japanese military assembles a scientific project, using the monster's cells to develop Anti-Nuclear Energy Bacteria (ANB), a substance that can weaken Godzilla. An assassin from the fictional Republic of Saradia and a pair of terrorists from the American big pharma company Bio-Major, meanwhile, vie to steal and extort the cells from Japanese authorities. Things go awry when Dr. Shiragami (Koji Takahashi), a scientist traumatized by the death of his daughter, Erika, attempts to preserve her spirit by combining Godzilla cells with roses, giving birth to a gargoyle-vine monster. He names it Biollante after Violan, a nymph from Norse mythology.

Omori expressed excitement over producer Tanaka's desire to make a movie along the lines of James Cameron's *Aliens* (1986), with a 007-style chase scene in the opening sequence. It's debatable whether *Biollante* resembles either of those films, or a Hollywood-style production at all. It is more accurately a hyper-plotted traditional Godzilla film that follows many of the expected tropes: evacuations, military rollouts, updated versions of classic Toho mecha (the MBT-MB92 Maser Cannons), the quick construction of a massive anti-Godzilla project—an artificial thunder field, intended to raise Godzilla's body temperature and trigger the ANB's weakening effects—and the updated Super X2 flying tank, now a drone. Omori also introduces several important ideas that would become new genre staples: a Godzilla countermeasures military unit (seen here as an underfunded, one-man operation staffed by the charismatic Colonel Goro Gondo, played by Toru Minegishi), and a central role for a young military officer (Major Sho Kuroki, played by Masanobu Takashima). Most significantly, this film marks the debut of the young psychic girl Miki Saegusa, played by seventeen-year-old actress Megumi Odaka; the character uses her mental powers to delay Godzilla's approach toward Osaka. In five subsequent Godzilla movies, Miki would develop a psychic connection to Godzilla, establishing a semblance of story continuity. With its abundance of people and plot points, *Godzilla vs. Biollante* is inevitably left with some loose threads. But overall, it stands as an ambitious effort . . . perhaps overly so.

DISSONANT NOTES

Omori also sought to take Godzilla in a new musical direction, so he looked to Koichi Sugiyama, a composer of 1970s pop tunes and video game music, notably the wildly popular *Dragon Quest* series. "Our aim is to challenge with a combination of rock and orchestral music," Sugiyama said, describing his approach. Rather than score specific scenes, Sugiyama prepared ten pieces of music. Then, without viewing the film footage, arranger David Howell orchestrated the score and oversaw the recording, thus deferring to the music editor to pair the music with the footage. The film nevertheless opens with a newly rerecorded version of Akira Ifukube's classic Godzilla theme, and Ifukube's powerful motifs are interspersed with

CLOCKWISE FROM TOP LEFT: After terrorists bomb his lab in Saradia, Dr. Shiragami (Koji Takahashi) discovers the body of his daughter, Erika (Yasuko Sawaguchi). Shiragami's traumatic loss leads him to conduct dangerous experiments in an effort to preserve Erika's spirit—with disastrous results. ▪ Scientist Kirishima (Kunihiko Mitamura, *left*), head of the ANB development effort, meets his girlfriend, Asuka Okouchi (Yoshiko Tanaka), at the Godzilla Memorial Lounge in the Shinjuku district, which has been rebuilt since Godzilla's 1984 attack. ▪ Godzilla approaches the Osaka Business Park. This set was built on Stage No. 2, one of the smallest stages on the Toho lot, and forced perspective was utilized to create depth and scale. To the naked eye, the set appeared out of scale, but as SFX director Koichi Kawakita noted, "It is not important that things look real, only that they can be filmed realistically."

CLOCKWISE FROM TOP LEFT: Godzilla marches through Osaka. Production designer Tetsuzo Osawa created partial, single-purpose miniature sets used for just one or two cuts, a new innovation. Traditional SFX productions had utilized fewer and much larger sets that would appear in multiple shots. ■ Colonel Goro Gondo (Toru Minegishi) prepares to shoot Godzilla with Anti-Nuclear Energy Bacteria. ■ Missiles fly across the set (on wires) and seem to explode on contact with Godzilla, all in a single take. This required expert timing by pyrotechnicians to trigger charges placed on Godzilla's body; a moment too soon—or too late—and the effect would fail. ■ Godzilla enters the Thunder Control System field. The microwave towers, vehicles, and activation switches are all built in varying scale and arranged in forced perspective to create the illusion of depth on the miniature set. ■ Kirishima (Kunihiko Mitamura) regards the precious Godzilla cells as Seigoh Okouchi (Ryunosuke Kaneda), CEO of the Okouchi Foundation, looks on.

Sugiyama's jaunty music throughout. The contrast between the two composers' wildly different styles can be noticeable, but this score would pave the way for Ifukube's imminent return to the series.

With so many aspirations, the filmmakers were inevitably forced to jettison numerous ideas. As the end battle winds down, the ANB takes effect and Godzilla collapses on the beach. Kawakita envisioned a finale wherein Biollante would become one with Godzilla and the monsters would assimilate, transforming into a giant rose. The effect was attempted with animation, but the scene was nixed after rushes were reviewed. "We were all dumbfounded," Omori recalled. "It looked like a manga. Kawakita had great ideas, but in the end, we had to settle for the tools that were available. If we had had the right tools, *Biollante* would have been a masterpiece."

"I really put my heart into making *Biollante*, but unfortunately, the box office result wasn't the best," Omori added. "I thought it would be a big hit and even start a new Godzilla boom, but that didn't happen. What a disappointment after such a big production." Though he couldn't have known, Omori was indeed on the verge of starting a new Godzilla boom, just two years later.

(*GOJIRA TAI KINGU GIDORA*)

RELEASED: DECEMBER 14, 1991 (JAPAN)

GODZILLA VS. KING GHIDORAH

In 1992, time-traveling visitors from the future unleash the three-headed monster King Ghidorah upon Japan in a plot to destroy the country and prevent its impending rise to global economic dominance. Godzilla is the only force capable of defeating the dragon—but Godzilla no longer exists, having been erased from history by the duplicitous Futurians under the guise of protecting Japan. In an act of desperation, a plan is hatched to re-create Godzilla by targeting a living dinosaur with missiles secretly used "as shelter for Japan's nuclear waste," according to an official with the Teiyo Group, the mega-corporation harboring the clandestine weapons. Unbeknownst to all, however, the dinosaur has already morphed into Godzilla, having likely been exposed to "a shipwreck loaded with nuclear missiles or a spill of nuclear waste," theorizes the hero Emmy Kano. When the Teiyo Group's sub reaches its target, Godzilla crushes it and absorbs yet more energy. Now larger, more powerful, and more aggressive than ever, Godzilla embarks on an unstoppable, destructive path toward King Ghidorah—and Japan.

This is only a fragment of the plot of *Godzilla vs. King Ghidorah*, yet it makes clear that the eighteenth Godzilla movie is an unabashed attempt to revisit the energy of an earlier era. The creative team of writer-director Kazuki Omori and special effects director Koichi Kawakita return, but the seriousness of *Godzilla vs. Biollante* gives way to a sense of nostalgic fun—even as the story is informed by Japan's contentious economic relationship with the US and the West at the time.

"WITH *GODZILLA VS. BIOLLANTE,* WE WANTED TO AVOID GOING OVERBOARD TO PURSUE AN A-CLASS FEELING. BUT FOR *GODZILLA VS. KING GHIDORAH,* IT WAS MORE LIKE, 'ANYTHING GOES.'"

—Kazuki Omori, director

Faced with competition from television and home video, the Japanese film industry had contracted from its heyday in the early 1960s, when the studios produced more than five hundred films; by 1986, there were just twenty-four domestic studio features. Big-budget movies became increasingly risky; the Nikkatsu studio would go into receivership after the historical drama *The Setting Sun* (1992) performed poorly, and Kon Ichikawa's *47 Ronin* (1994) was widely seen as the end of lavish period films. Meanwhile, family-oriented anime, such as Studio Ghibli's *Kiki's Delivery Service* (1989), *Porco Rosso* (1992), and *Whisper of the Heart* (1995) were at or near the top of the domestic box office. *Godzilla vs. Biollante* had done respectably, earning just over ¥1 billion and ranking eighth among the year's domestic films. (At the time, Toho considered a ¥1 billion return a "passing grade" for a major New Year's–season film; ¥1.5 billion was a major success.) The studio was determined to return the genre to prominence; thus, going forward, Godzilla movies would be family friendly. Audience surveys showed that the most popular Toho monster among children (besides Godzilla) was Mothra; the one they most wanted Godzilla to fight was King Ghidorah. Mechagodzilla and Rodan were also popular.

This data shaped the future of the series. The first post-*Biollante* project to be considered was *Mothra vs. Bagan*, with a script by Omori. A loose remake of *Mothra* (1961), the story pitted Mothra against a new adversary, with the action set in Calcutta, Singapore, Bangkok, and other locations, and included plot ideas that would eventually resurface in *Godzilla vs. Mothra*. Bagan had first appeared in early unmade drafts of what became *The Return of Godzilla*; now, producer Tomoyuki Tanaka hoped to introduce the new kaiju alongside Mothra and then follow up by pitting it against Godzilla in the next film. "Bagan was Mr. Tanaka's favorite potential monster since 1984," Omori recalled. Preparations and design work began; casting was discussed, and the female pop idol duo Wink was considered for the Infant Island fairies. "In the end, they decided to do Godzilla instead, and everything was tossed," Omori said.

FUTURE TRENDS
Back to the Future Part II had a record opening in Japan in December 1989. It played next door to *Biollante* at the Toho Nichigeki Cinemas, and Omori took notice. "Seeing that movie drawing crowds while ours

PREVIOUS SPREAD: A nuclear-armed submarine, secretly owned by the Teiyo Group of Japan, is dispatched to restore Godzilla to the timeline of history, only to find that the monster already exists. ■ LEFT: "We decided to rethink the whole image and design of King Ghidorah," said SFX director Koichi Kawakita (*pictured*). "I thought we should use the image and design of a Western-type dragon instead of an Eastern or Chinese type of dragon." Still, the new design largely resembles the old version from 1964 except for its heads—the hair was eliminated to avoid difficulties with composite shots, and it has long, straight spikes around the face rather than the original monster's crescent-shaped horns.

wasn't, I wondered, *Why is it getting the audience?* The answer was, 'Because it involves time travel.'" That gave producer Shogo Tomiyama—an emerging figure in the Godzilla franchise who would exert tremendous creative influence over the Heisei series and beyond—an idea. "I wanted *Godzilla vs. King Ghidorah* to be a monster story involving time travel rather than an invasion from space," Tomiyama said. "That was the twist—making it seem like they were aliens, but revealing they were actually people from the future."

The Futurians—led by Wilson (Chuck Wilson), Grenchiko (Richard Berger), and Emmy Kano (Anna Nakagawa), representatives of the Earth Union Organization (EUO), arrive from the year 2204 to warn Tokyo of Godzilla's imminent return and the country's resultant destruction. They offer to save Japan by traveling back in time to 1944 and teleporting a living dinosaur—a "Godzillasaurus"—away from Lagos Island in the South Pacific to prevent it from being exposed to the H-bomb tests at Bikini Atoll a decade later, thus averting its transformation into Godzilla. But it's all part of a devious double-cross to bring Japan to its knees, for the Futurians use those same H-bomb tests to create King Ghidorah instead; with the three-headed monster under their control, Wilson and Grenchiko dispatch it on a massive rampage. Alarmed by the devastation, Emmy (the lone Japanese among the time travelers) reveals that the Futurians'

GODZILLA FACT: Director Kazuki Omori's ideal actor for the part of Morris, an elder Earth Union member who assists Emmy with retrieving King Ghidorah from the bottom of the sea, was Orson Welles. "I thought we could go to Hollywood to shoot some close-up shots of him, but the budget didn't allow [for] it," Omori said. The role was instead played by Ginnosuke Azuma.

CLOCKWISE FROM TOP: *(left to right)* The Futurians—Emmy Kano (Anna Nakagawa), Wilson (Chuck Wilson), and Grenchiko (Richard Berger)—arrive for a meeting with Japan's prime minister. ▪ Godzilla's ancestor was originally written as a tyrannosaurus, but designer Shinji Nishikawa "couldn't accept that a tyrannosaur could become Godzilla" and devised the Godzilla-dinosaur hybrid. ▪ During the heroes' visit to Lagos Island in 1945, Emmy leaves behind three Dorats, genetically engineered animals that she has raised as pets. They later fuse into King Ghidorah after being exposed to American weapons tests at Bikini Atoll. "In my synopsis, I had described the Dorats as 'something like the creatures from *Gremlins*,' but they came out nothing like the way Shinji Nishikawa had designed them," said director Kazuki Omori. "We didn't know what to do with them, so we tried not to show them too much in the film."

true aim is to stop Japan from becoming a corrupt, dominant world power that buys up entire continents in the future. The plan, she was led to believe, was to threaten Japan, not actually destroy it; and so, she turns against her comrades and teams with the paranormal journalist Terasawa (Kosuke Toyohara) to foil the plot and save her ancestors from ruin.

In a radical departure from the canon, the origins of both Godzilla and King Ghidorah are rewritten. Godzilla is inevitable; even when removed from the mythology and tragedy of 1954, it is born as an unavoidable consequence of doomsday weapons. Omori's early story draft went even a step further, with the clandestine submarine owned by the Teiyo Group actually firing a nuclear missile at the Godzillasaurus to create Godzilla, but he changed the scene upon producer Tanaka's objection. "Tanaka said, 'It's not a good idea for Godzilla to come back because of a nuclear weapon that Japan owns!'" said Omori. "He said it would contradict the antinuclear message." As for King Ghidorah, "We made its origin related to the H-bomb, whereas it was originally a space monster," Omori said.

PREVIOUS SPREAD: Godzilla is dwarfed by tall office buildings in Tokyo's Shinjuku district. The depth of the miniature set is enhanced by the placement of larger-scale buildings in the foreground, creating a forced perspective. ■ ABOVE: Writer-turned-action hero Terasawa (Kosuke Toyohara), Emmy (Anna Nakagawa), and android M11 (Robert Scott Field) prepare to storm the MOTHER time machine and foil the Futurians' plan to destroy Japan. ■ BELOW: King Ghidorah's rampage begins in the city of Fukuoka (*shown here*) and follows a destructive path across the island of Kyushu. As the monster heads north toward Hokkaido, it is briefly seen flying over Hiroshima, making it the first Toho monster to attack that city.

"DURING THE BUBBLE ECONOMY, JAPAN WAS GOING OVERSEAS AND BUYING UP AMERICAN COMPANIES, AND I WANTED TO PUT THESE THINGS THAT WERE REALLY HAPPENING INTO THE STORY. PEOPLE WERE SAYING THAT JAPAN WAS GOING TO BECOME THIS SUPERPOWER IN THE FUTURE, AND I DIDN'T BELIEVE THAT WAS GOING TO HAPPEN."

—Kazuki Omori, director

CLOCKWISE FROM TOP LEFT: Filming Godzillasaurus's appearance on Lagos Island. Special effects director Koichi Kawakita (*next to camera*) and assistant director Kenji Suzuki (*center*) ready the scene. ■ Godzilla advances upon the city of Sapporo, where it is confronted by a group of updated Maser Cannons. Fierce battles between Godzilla and the JSDF would be a recurring highlight of the Heisei series. ■ Director Kazuki Omori and Yoshio Tsuchiya (as Yasuaki Shindo) prepare to shoot the scene in which Shindo and Godzilla meet face-to-face for the final time in Shinjuku in 1992. ■ In a time-travel scene set forty-eight years earlier, during World War II, Commander Shindo (Tsuchiya) pays tribute to the fallen Godzillasaurus after the creature is severely wounded while defending Japanese troops from a US assault at Lagos Island.

REFLECTIONS IN A MONSTER'S EYE

Fueled by a stock market and real estate boom, Japan's status as an economic juggernaut skyrocketed beginning in the mid-1980s. Investors spent billions acquiring overseas assets, including Rockefeller Center, Columbia Pictures, and the Pebble Beach Golf Links; Japan's banks became the biggest in the world. Anti-Japan sentiment grew in the West, while at home, many Japanese became uneasy with the country's newfound extreme wealth. Made just as the "bubble economy" was about to burst, *Godzilla vs. King Ghidorah* personifies this paradox in Yasuaki Shindo (Yoshio Tsuchiya), CEO of the Teiyo Group, a corporate übertitan and symbol of Japan's hyper-growth. In the 1944 flashback scenes, Shindo is leader of a battalion stationed on Lagos; when he and his men are attacked by US forces, the Godzillasaurus comes to their aid and wipes out the enemy, nearly dying of its wounds in the process. Commander Shindo salutes the dinosaur-savior and maintains a lifelong reverence for the beast. Later, in 1992, Shindo watches as Godzilla destroys the economy he has rebuilt; in one of the most poignant scenes in

GODZILLA FACT: Artist and stuntman Hurricane Ryu pulled triple duty on the film: drawing storyboards, performing inside the King Ghidorah suit, and acting as a wire works technician for Mecha-King Ghidorah, which was operated like a marionette, with no suit actor inside.

the series, man and monster silently meet, and Godzilla passes judgment, incinerating Shindo with its heat ray. "I wanted to create a kinship between Shindo and the Godzillasaurus," said Omori. "Forty years later, the dinosaur has turned into Godzilla [and] Shindo has turned into an economic monster—he represents Japan's economic aggression. Godzilla could not accept that, so he kills Shindo."

Omori said he fought hard to cast Tsuchiya, whose last Godzilla movie was *Destroy All Monsters*, despite the studio's desire for a more well-known, contemporary actor. For his part, Tsuchiya—known for unusual genre roles—said Shindo was his favorite character of all time. "I was [cast] because I am the only one who can talk to Godzilla," Tsuchiya said. "I understand where he comes from and what is in his heart, just like Shindo does. Even though Godzilla is a fictional character, he is very real to me. I have an affinity for him that is difficult to describe."

Godzilla vs. King Ghidorah shows Omori's love of American films—there are nods to *Back to the Future*, the *Terminator* films, and even 1971's *Dirty Harry* ("Make my day" was reportedly improvised by the actor). And it has its share of time-travel conundrums: If Godzilla was deleted from the history books, how is it that everyone still remembers the monster? Regardless, the filmmakers opted to focus on entertainment rather than relativity. "Once we decided to do a time-travel story, we accepted that some viewers would inevitably be fixated on the time paradox," Tomiyama said. The climax sees Emmy travel forward

BELOW, TOP ROW: King Ghidorah and Godzilla clash near Abashiri. After the Futurians' monster-control device is sabotaged, King Ghidorah is left to fend for itself. Godzilla's nuclear pulse sends the dragon to the mat, and Godzilla's souped-up heat ray severs its middle head. ■ **BOTTOM:** Showdown in Shinjuku. The Mecha-King Ghidorah suit was created by adding armor to the King Ghidorah suit, increasing its weight to 441 pounds (200 kg) (or, according to some sources, 661 pounds/300 kg). It was too heavy to manipulate with a suit actor inside, so it was operated as a wire-controlled puppet.

ABOVE: Even with Godzilla's height increased to 328 feet (100 m), the monster is overshadowed by the immense skyscrapers of Japan's bubble economy. In the battle with Mecha-King Ghidorah, Godzilla's heat ray knocks down the top half of the forty-eight-story, three-tower Tokyo Metropolitan Government Building (*at left*), completed in 1990 and the country's then-tallest building. Known unaffectionately as the "tax tower," the building, "symbolized the excesses of Japan in the late '80s," according to *The Wall Street Journal*. "I thought everyone would be delighted to see it destroyed," said producer Shogo Tomiyama. Unlike the old method of making taller structures with wood to support the plaster, this giant structure was all plaster, using a building block approach.

"THE FIRST MOVIE I SAW WAS (1962'S) *THE LONGEST DAY*, AND I HAD ALWAYS WANTED TO DIRECT A WAR MOVIE LIKE THAT. IT'S NOT ON THE SAME SCALE, BUT STILL."

— Director Kazuki Omori on the Lagos Island battle between Godzillasaurus and US forces

to 2204 and convert King Ghidorah (nearly killed by Godzilla and resting comatose on the ocean floor ever since) into Mecha-King Ghidorah, an anime-style cyborg that bursts through the sky above Shinjuku in 1992. In a titanic struggle amid Tokyo's biggest high-rises, Emmy pilots Mecha-King Ghidorah and uses its "Godzilla Grip" weapon to end Godzilla's rampage of destruction, dropping the monster into the sea.

SETTLING THE (MUSIC) SCORE

Akira Ifukube had declined requests to score *The Return of Godzilla* and *Biollante* due to health reasons, and this film marks his return to the series after a sixteen-year absence. His highly recognizable themes for Godzilla and King Ghidorah remain powerful; at his insistence, the score was recorded with the orchestra watching the scene on a large projected screen—a practice no longer commonly in use. Cues from various old films are heard, including from *Destroy All Monsters* and *King Kong vs. Godzilla*. "What's the use," Ifukube mused, "of composing feeble, lifeless music that changes meaning in a mere decade or so?"

Godzilla vs. King Ghidorah made its debut at the Tokyo International Film Festival in September 1991 as part of a new strategy to generate buzz for this and subsequent Heisei Godzilla films several months before their commercial release. The film would go on to earn ¥1.45 billion, a significant improvement over *Biollante*, and validating the studio's new family-oriented strategy.

CREATING GODZILLA

THE ART OF MONSTER SUIT MAKING

They all gathered inside Toho's Stage No. 3 for a test fitting and demonstration of the first Godzilla suit. Eiji Tsuburaya, Ishiro Honda, assistant director Koji Kajita, and chief sculptor Teizo Toshimitsu—the man who oversaw the design and building of the suit—watched, along with other assorted crew members, as Godzilla was wheeled into the studio on a cart. Three or four men struggled to hang the suit upright on a scaffold. Katsumi Tezuka, an athletic forty-one-year-old actor from Toho's "B2" group of performers and one of two men chosen to play the monster, climbed inside, and the back was closed. Someone yelled, "OK, walk!"

Godzilla stood motionless. After a moment, it took three wobbly steps, then tipped over. Tezuka climbed out, gasping for air; Tsuburaya and Honda looked at one another, worried. Then they asked twenty-five-year-old Haruo Nakajima—the other man who was cast in the part—to give it a try, but he too could hardly move because of the suit's immense weight. Summoning all his strength, Nakajima slowly paced forward, the sandals nailed inside Godzilla's feet biting into his flesh with each step. "That's enough!" someone shouted. Godzilla had managed to walk about 33 feet (10 m).

"[The first suit] was way too heavy," recalled Eizo Kaimai, a member of the suit-making team. "It took three people to simply pick it up. The actor couldn't even raise his foot. . . . Because this was really the first time we'd ever done something like this, we hadn't thought about those things."

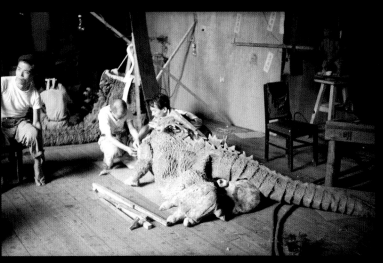 

NECESSITY AND INVENTION

Like so many aspects of the *Godzilla* production, the design and creation of monster suits was a first-of-its-kind effort. When Tsuburaya delegated this crucial task to members of the sculpture and modeling team (a subgroup of the special art section within Toho's special effects department), he was quite literally placing the fate of the entire project in their hands. The team's creativity and ingenuity under pressure brought Godzilla to cinematic life, and their handmade methods became an essential part of the *tokusatsu* filmmaking process.

Charged with leading the effort to create the first Godzilla suit was Toshimitsu, a quiet and reserved artist and an accomplished sculptor and model maker, whose working relationship with Tsuburaya dated back to the wartime action drama *The War at Sea from Hawaii to Malaya* (1942). Using proposed design sketches submitted by several artists—including famed cartoonist Kazuyoshi Abe, who drew a monster with a head vaguely reminiscent of a mushroom cloud—Toshimitsu built a clay prototype of an upright Tyrannosaurus-like figure. The model was approximately 16 inches (40 cm) in height, with a large head and a body covered with fishlike scales. Tsuburaya, Honda, and producer Tomoyuki Tanaka reviewed the prototype, but their consensus was that it was too conventional and not scary enough. Toshimitsu revised the design to incorporate a bumpy skin texture; this iteration was called the "warty" Godzilla. To accommodate the actor who would ultimately don the monster suit, the creature's head became smaller to make it lighter and easier to balance. This model was further refined into the "alligator" version, with small, irregular ridge textures simulating keloid bumps, symbolic of Godzilla's disfigurement from the atomic bomb. The alligator Godzilla was approved by Honda, Tsuburaya, and Tanaka.

Toshimitsu put his modeling team into motion, making the suit at Tsuburaya's Technical Research Institute—an independent facility established by Tsuburaya during the occupation years, when he was barred from working in the studios—located just down the street from Toho. To establish the proportions of the suit, Toshimitsu drew an actual-size illustration on a large slab of plywood, mirroring the physique of a suit actor. While Toshimitsu concentrated on making the monster's head, brothers Yasuei and Kanju Yagi used the plywood drawing to create the body of the suit. Like Toshimitsu, the Yagi brothers had worked with Tsuburaya on *The War at Sea from Hawaii to Malaya*, making dolls for the special effects scenes. After the war, the brothers had worked for a doll company, making traditional chrysanthemum dolls (life-size figures wearing clothes made of chrysanthemum flowers). "First [the Yagi brothers] would make the shape of the monster's body, hands, and feet with bamboo, wire, and mesh," recalled Yoshio Suzuki, an assistant on the project. "Each part would be soldered or welded, and the core of the monster would be completed for each part. They were so skilled that they didn't have to measure every detail precisely; they just went by intuition. We pasted *washi* [traditional Japanese paper] on the surface of the wire mesh, then added several layers of gauze cloth to make the base thicker."

When the basic form of the costume was finished, it was modeler Kaimai's job to find suitable materials and apply the surface details. For the first Godzilla suit, he chose a type of crude rubber that came in pieces about the size of a brick. The material was finely cut with a knife, mixed with oil, kneaded by hand, then heated. "It was harder than oil clay," Kaimai recalled. "Then we would soak it into the fabric core of Godzilla, build it up, and shape it into skin textures. The rubber wasn't thick, just heavy and inflexible. Not as much as a tire, though."

After the skin was applied, the suit would be stepped on and smashed, bending and crushing the wires inside so they could be removed. Afterward, the suit was baked multiple times with infrared lamps in a kiln to harden it. "We tested different baking times, but [each time it] turned out differently," crew member Suzuki said. "Godzilla's surface would become rough, and it would easily peel off. We failed repeatedly."

OPPOSITE: Teizo Toshimitsu sculpting the scaly prototype of the first Godzilla. ■ ABOVE, LEFT TO RIGHT: Yasuei (*left*) and Kanju (*right*) Yagi making fixes to the original Godzilla suit. ■ The *Godzilla Raids Again* suit drying out at the Technical Research Institute. People often came by and touched the suit, causing pieces to fall off, so the Yagi brothers put up a sign that read: ATTENTION, EVERYONE. PLEASE DO NOT BE MEAN TO ME. —GODZILLA.

After baking, the rubber skin turned a white color, so the suit needed to be painted. A mixture of black and white oil-based paint was used, but because the paint reflected light, the suit was finished with a coat of water-based paint. To create the inner lining, the team wrapped cotton in fabric, like a mattress, and then stuffed it inside the body. When the suit was finished, Suzuki felt that "after many failed attempts, we somehow managed to make it work."

Except it didn't work. Because of its immense weight, the suit failed during its initial demonstration. However, anticipating potential problems, and to allow for flexibility throughout the shoot, Tsuburaya had ordered two Godzilla suits be made. As it turned out, only the second suit—somewhat lighter than the original—would be used extensively in *Godzilla*. As for the first suit, "We were so poor, we never threw anything out," Kaimai said. "We cut the first suit in half at the waist and used those sections for close-ups [of the legs and feet or the upper body], like the scene where Godzilla steps on a train or destroys buildings in Ginza."

Once *Godzilla* went into production, Toshimitsu was present on set every day, looking after his creation. Kaimai and Suzuki had the unenviable task of maintaining the suit, loading it onto a cart every night after midnight, covering it with a tarp for secrecy, and dragging it back to the Technical Research Institute and attempting to clean it, dry it off with infrared lamps and hair dryers, and make repairs before the start of filming the next day. Suzuki recalled the grueling task: "Sweat gets absorbed, and it's really, really, squishy and gross. You don't want to get close to it. After finishing, we finally took a bath, had a drink, and quickly went to bed. Sometimes it was already 6 A.M. We'd wake up around noon, then go to the set." This was the routine for forty-five days straight.

As a member of the suit staff, Kaimai also supported the suit actors, mainly Nakajima, with whom he became close friends over the next decade. When he wasn't making or maintaining the suits, Kaimai's job included helping Nakajima in and out of the suit, giving him cues as to when to start acting, and helping him communicate with the crew. Together they would drink and grill snacks—using an empty film can as a makeshift teppan grill—every day in the staff room.

The success of *Godzilla* boosted the reputation of the special effects staff, and for *Godzilla Raids Again*, they had access to more resources. A new Godzilla suit was made using the same processes as before, but much lighter and more flexible, thanks to the introduction of latex rubber for the skin. The modeling team kept busy as Toho continued to produce monster films, and in 1958, they hired Keizo Murase as a part-time crew member. Murase, who specialized in the research and application of new materials, brought innovation to the team. He is credited with finding lighter and more durable latex for the skin, FRP (fiberglass-reinforced plastic) for features such as nails and teeth, and urethane foam to add lightweight bulk to costumes. Among his many creations, Murase was responsible for building the 1961 and 1964 versions of Mothra (adult), the Godzilla 1962 suit, and the Rodan and King Ghidorah suits for *Ghidorah, the Three-Headed Monster.* He loved making monsters, but as the junior member of the staff, he was also assigned maintenance duties, which he did not enjoy. He especially hated sitting and watching over monster suits as they dried under the lights after cleaning (because unattended lights had previously burned holes in the suits, someone had to monitor them at all times).

By the time of *King Kong vs. Godzilla,* the modeling team's workload had grown, putting a strain on Toshimitsu and the Yagi brothers, all of whom were getting up in years. The studio would not hire additional workers, but help came from within. Noboyuki Yasumaru was a newbie in the special effects department's plaster team. In between his duties constructing miniatures of the National Diet Building and Atami Castle for the film, Yasumaru assisted Toshimitsu's team, devising arm extensions for the King Kong suit that enabled the actor to perform simple grasping movements. Although suit making wasn't his job, during his free time, Yasumaru found himself hanging around Toshimitsu, learning by observing. Yasumaru eventually became Toshimitsu's apprentice and a suit maker in his own right, beginning with the dinosaur kaiju Gorosaurus for *King Kong Escapes* (1967).

Despite his advancing age, Toshimtsu remained active through the 1960s, continuing to make Godzilla suits himself through *Destroy All Monsters.* Every Godzilla was different from the last, even though Toshimitsu's reference point continued to be the original Godzilla—the basic model never changed. None of the variations from one suit to the next were intentional; they occurred organically, and Toshimitsu embraced them. "Godzilla is growing, so it's natural that it's changing," he would say.

Toshimitsu continued to focus on sculpting the heads of his monsters, working at his own pace, often finishing well after the rest of the suit was finished. As a result, sometimes the head and body didn't match up precisely, but in retrospect, Yasumaru felt this was a plus. "Maybe that's why we ended up with something interesting," Yasumaru said. "It was a haphazard process to make the head separately from the body. It's unbalanced, but it adds to the character, if you will." SFX art director Yasuyuki Inoue agreed. "It's better if it's not perfectly symmetrical. Besides, symmetrical things don't exist in nature."

Whenever a suit was finished, Tsuburaya would stare at it with his arms folded, rarely offering a comment to the team that created it. "Tsuburaya wasn't much concerned about how the finished product appeared, but rather, he was always thinking about how it would look on film," Inoue said. "That was always his perspective."

Upon Toshimitsu's retirement from Toho in 1970, Yasumaru became head of the suit-making team. An uncompromising and detail-oriented artist, Yasumaru was focused completely on a suit's external appearance, giving little thought to how his monsters would be operated, which led to frequent conflicts with suit actors and SFX director Teruyoshi Nakano that often ended with Yasumaru grudgingly making changes to his designs. The first Godzilla suit to be created solely by Yasumaru appeared in *Godzilla vs. Megalon;* he later sculpted a new, updated Godzilla design for *The Return of Godzilla,* building two costumes while also supervising the design and construction of the 16-foot- (4.8-m-) tall Cybot Godzilla; he would later regret being unable to control this process well enough to ensure the look of the cybot more closely matched that of the suits.

Tomoki Kobayashi joined the suit-making team in 1973 as Yasumaru's apprentice, assisting with the making of the *Godzilla vs. Megalon* suit. On *The Return of Godzilla,* Kobayashi created the polyurethane molds for the Godzilla suit's body parts; these same molds would be used to make every subsequent Godzilla suit through *Godzilla vs. Destoroyah* more than a decade later. Beginning in 1989 with *Godzilla vs. Biollante,* Yasumaru took a reduced role, allowing Kobayashi to take the lead in the suit-making process. Kobayashi completely redesigned Godzilla's head, reducing the size and adding animalistic features.

BELOW, LEFT TO RIGHT: Noboyuki Yasumaru shows off the maquette of the new Godzilla design for *The Return of Godzilla* to SFX director Teruyoshi Nakano (*left*). ∎ Tomoki Kobayashi (*right*) and SFX director Koichi Kawakita (*center*) review the features of the Godzilla suit for *Godzilla vs. Mothra.*

LEFT: Shinichi Wakasa explains construction of the fins on the robot version of Godzilla as seen in *Godzilla 2000: Millennium*.

"I crystallized SFX director Koichi Kawakita's intentions and created the symbolic face for the Heisei Godzilla different from the previous Godzillas," Kobayashi said. After *Godzilla vs. Biollante*, Yasumaru retired, and Kobayashi officially took over as head suit maker. Through the end of the Heisei series, Kobayashi implemented numerous innovations to the suits, enhancing Godzilla's performance. As Godzilla's opponents grew larger, Kobayashi increased Godzilla's size accordingly, which is evident from *Godzilla vs. Mechagodzilla II* through *Destoroyah*. "The upper body alone couldn't be enlarged," he said. "We had to extend the legs as well."

Ever since 1954, Godzilla suits were always created in-house by Toho, even as the studio began to hire outside contractors to make the monster's opponents in later years. That changed during the production of *Godzilla 2000: Millennium*, when Toho tapped Shinichi Wakasa and his independent creature shop, Monsters Inc., to create a new-generation Godzilla. Wakasa had substantial experience with Godzilla and *tokusatsu*; as a contractor, he had previously created the Mechagodzilla, Rodan, Little Godzilla, SpaceGodzilla, and Destoroyah suits for Toho during the nineties, as well as several creatures for other productions. He also brought insights from his own work as a suit actor early his career. Spanning five feature films from 1999 through 2004, Wakasa built multiple Godzilla suits and mechanical Godzillas with new, updated designs that typically evinced catlike facial features and finely sculpted skin textures. Unlike some of his predecessors, Wakasa did not limit his role to making and maintaining suits; having an on-set presence and working with suit actors was equally important. "The filming set is the place where you can really create what the audience will be impressed with in the theater," Wakasa said. "More than the process of creating the suit, being there when filming takes place was important."

The monsters of Shusuke Kaneko's *Godzilla, Mothra and King Ghidorah: Giant Monsters All-Out Attack* are something of a throwback to the kaiju of the early years. The film's dead-eyed, classically inspired Godzilla, along with King Ghidorah, Mothra, and Baragon, were the creations of suit maker Fuyuki Shinada, who, like Wakasa, had first worked for Toho as a contractor (creating both the flower-form and plant-form Biollante for *Godzilla vs. Biollante*, and Godzilla's ancestor Godzillasaurus for *Godzilla vs. King Ghidorah*) and brought a long résumé in monster making. Shinada's Godzilla suit was the tallest and heaviest ever made, emphasizing the creature's dinosaur lineage. Shinada saw Godzilla as a dark and fearful symbol, and his approach to suit making put form before function. "My first priority is the looks," Shinada said. "I would get a lot of complaints from the suit actors, like, 'It's too heavy' or 'I can't see,' and so on."

MAKING THE 1964 GODZILLA SUIT

The creation of the Godzilla suit that appears in *Mothra vs. Godzilla* was extensively documented in photos. While materials and technology advanced through the years, the process and techniques shown here remained basically unchanged throughout the Godzilla series' history.

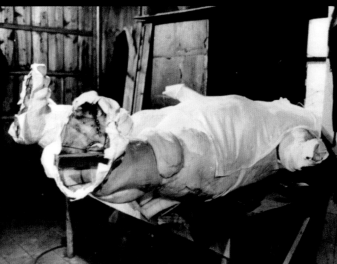

TOP, LEFT TO RIGHT: Head modeler Teizo Toshimitsu sketches a full-size image of the suit on a large sheet of plywood as reference for sizing and proportions. ▪ Using Toshimitsu's sketch, a wire skeleton is built, to which fabric is attached to form an inner layer for the suit. ▪ **MIDDLE, LEFT TO RIGHT:** Urethane foam is cut and glued onto the base skin to create muscles, and to add volume and body contours. ▪ After the foam has been added, an outer layer of cloth is applied, onto which latex skin is attached. This form is baked in a kiln for hardening. ▪ **BOTTOM, LEFT TO RIGHT:** Toshimitsu meticulously sculpts the face. While the rest of the modeling team was building the body, Toshimitsu concentrated on sculpting the head, which could take as long as a month. ▪ Texture is added to the latex skin by cutting small strips of urethane foam and gluing them on individually. ▪ **OPPOSITE TOP, LEFT TO RIGHT:** Giving the detailed body a coat of charcoal gray paint. ▪ Eizo Kaimai (*left*) and the Yagi brothers (Yasue and Kanju), collectively known as the "Yagi Family," attach the feet. ▪ Kanju Yagi adds detail to the feet. ▪ **OPPOSITE MIDDLE, LEFT TO RIGHT:** After removing the internal wire skeleton, the suit is ready for testing. A zipper is added between the large and small rows of fins. ▪ The tail is made as a separate piece, using the same basic process as the body. Built with a series of progressively smaller urethane foam cylinders connected to a central wire core, the tail has excellent flexibility. ▪ Suit actor Haruo Nakajima tries on the under-construction suit and moves around, offering suggestions for improvement. ▪ **OPPOSITE BOTTOM, LEFT TO RIGHT:** To precisely calculate the length of the arms, the hands are attached while the actor is wearing the suit. ▪ The head is attached while the actor remains in the suit to assure accurate positioning. The head, containing control mechanisms for the face, is fitted with a padded metal brace and cap, which sits atop the actor's head. ▪ Toshimitsu inspects the finished suit as it is taken outside for a test.

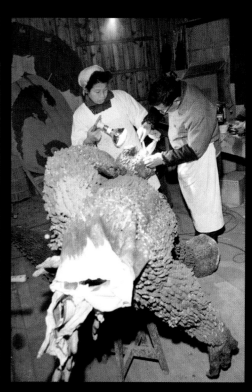

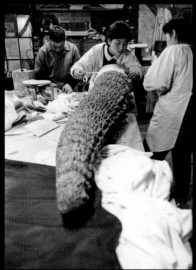

GODZILLA VS. MOTHRA

I n February 1992, Toho's national publicity team reviewed audience questionnaire data from *Godzilla vs. King Ghidorah*. Forty-two percent of all respondents, and 78 percent of schoolchildren surveyed, indicated they wanted Godzilla and Mothra to fight next. Eighty percent of the film's audience was male—the movie was a father-and-son favorite. Statistically, however, a large portion of the overall moviegoing public was female. If the next film could appeal to this largely untapped audience as well, company officials believed box office revenue might top ¥2 billion.

Godzilla vs. Mothra is a back-to-basics movie that steers away from the anything-goes approach of *Godzilla vs. King Ghidorah* and places the work of special effects director Koichi Kawakita front and center. Kawakita was recognized with a special Japan Academy Prize for *King Ghidorah*, and his set pieces and monster battles are showcased here to an even greater extent. Mothra and its evil counterpart, Battra, fight for the fate of the planet, and Godzilla—in one of Kawakita's most visually stunning scenes—rises from the bowels of the earth to wreak havoc. With light environmentalism and a simple story marked by family drama and bits of gentle comedy, wrapped in the familiar music of Akira Ifukube, the nostalgia of *Godzilla vs. Mothra* proved a major success. It was the highest-grossing domestic film of 1993, surpassing ¥2 billion, and second only to *Jurassic Park* at the box office overall.

"I HAD NO DESIRE TO DO GODZILLA AT FIRST. . . . IT SEEMED TOO BIG OF A PROJECT FOR A NEW DIRECTOR LIKE ME—THIS WAS AN INTIMIDATING, FIRST-CLASS PRODUCTION. GODZILLA MOVIES WERE HUGE PROJECTS FOR TOHO AND THEIR NEW YEAR SCHEDULE. IT WAS LIKE BEING THE STARTING PITCHER IN BASEBALL (ASKED) TO OPEN UP THE YEAR. SO I REALLY FELT A LOT OF PRESSURE."

—Takao Okawara, director

Advance planning for a new film began even as *Godzilla vs. King Ghidorah* was still in production. Several proposals were considered, including *The Return of King Ghidorah*, reframing the dragon as a space monster, and *Godzilla vs. Gigamoth*, a treatment by Kawakita, writer Marie Teranuma, and artist Minoru Yoshida that introduced many ideas that would make their way into *Godzilla vs. Mothra*—environmental pollution, typhoons, the unearthing of a giant egg on a remote island, Mothra's evil twin—and the development of an anti-kaiju bacteria weapon reminiscent of the one used in *Biollante*.

The initial plan for *Godzilla vs. Mothra* was to continue with the existing creative team. Kazuki Omori submitted a synopsis in January 1992 that leveraged elements of *Gigamoth* and his aborted *Mothra vs. Bagan* story. Due to a commitment to make a film for another studio, Omori would step aside as director, though he went on to complete the screenplay—a far more restrained scenario than his previous two efforts. Gigamoth and Bagan were replaced with the "black Mothra," dubbed Battra (short for "Battle Mothra"; interestingly, the name Badra, or "Bad Mothra," was also considered).

PREVIOUS SPREAD: Just when it seems Battra has KO'd Godzilla by knocking over the Yokohama Landmark Tower, Godzilla emerges from the rubble—and its revenge is swift and brutal. ■ **ABOVE:** After its spectacular emergence from the volcano at Mount Fuji, Godzilla is intercepted by a battery of Maser Cannons, tanks, helicopters, and jets.

"I was able to write *Godzilla vs. Mothra* because I had already written *Mothra vs. Bagan*," Omori said. "Some people wondered what happened to Godzilla at the end of the previous film, so I connected the two stories by having Godzilla reawakened by the meteor, which also triggered the return of Battra. The meteor at the beginning was inspired by the Tunguska meteorite [a 1908 event in which a large asteroid plunged into Earth's atmosphere and exploded in the skies over Siberia]."

Rather than another independent filmmaker like Omori, Toho pivoted back to the old tradition of tapping in-house talent. Director Takao Okawara had joined Toho in 1972 and ascended through the assistant director ranks on such films as *Submersion of Japan* (1973), *Prophecies of Nostradamus* (1974), Akira Kurosawa's *Kagemusha* (1980), and served as chief assistant director for *The Return of Godzilla*. Okawara's original screenplay, *Super Girl Reiko*, a teen fantasy about a girl with ESP, won a Kido award from the Motion Picture Producers Association of Japan in 1987, prompting Toho to produce the film and

ABOVE: In preparation for water scenes, the Battra suit was set up on a truck, which was then to be pushed through the pool. Battra was designed by assistant SFX director Minoru Yoshida. Due to the large number of suits and props needed for this film, Battra was built by an outside contractor. ■ **RIGHT:** Because Mothra and Battra are airborne adversaries, SFX director Koichi Kawakita ordered the new Godzilla suit to be outfitted with mechanics enabling the monster to raise its head slightly to the sky. "The basic shape doesn't change much, but Godzilla evolves slightly each time," Kawakita said. "Having the gimmick of a moving neck is just one aspect." ■ **BOTTOM RIGHT:** The Mothra caterpillar lunges at Godzilla during their first encounter at sea. *Godzilla vs. Mothra* features extensive use of puppets of all three monsters in various scenes.

promote Okawara to the director's chair in 1991. Although *Reiko* was commercially unsuccessful, producer Shogo Tomiyama felt it was nonetheless a strong first effort and believed Okawara would be a good fit for the studio's increasingly consensus-driven approach to the Godzilla series.

Back in 1983, Toho had established an internal advisory committee to revive the Godzilla franchise. Its members were the heads of film production, film sales, screenings, public relations, music publishing, domestic business, and international business. With *Godzilla vs. Mothra*, producer Tomiyama began to supplement the input of the Godzilla Committee by conducting brainstorming sessions with employees across the company, creating a broad-based, participatory system. "The studio generally doesn't do such things, but regarding Godzilla movies, everyone has various opinions, and I wanted to hear them," Tomiyama said. "We started compiling these ideas and having the screenwriter and director read them from *Godzilla vs. Mothra* onward." Special effects director Kawakita also contributed to the screenwriting phase, providing input on the monsters and battle settings.

A product of this process, *Godzilla vs. Mothra* is essentially a very loose remake-hybrid of *Mothra* (1961) and *Mothra vs. Godzilla*, with a bit of *King Kong vs. Godzilla* for good measure. Familiar situations and scenes are mirrored, and Akira Takarada returns to the series in an extended cameo as a high-ranking government official overseeing Japan's equivalent of the Environmental Protection Agency. The story is a series of episodic setups for the monster battles rather than a plot-driven drama: The freewheeling artifact thief Takuya Fujito (Tetsuya Bessho), his government official ex-wife Masako Tezuka (Satomi Kobayashi), and a sycophantic assistant (Takehiro Murata) to an environment-plundering developer travel to Infant Island to investigate a strange phenomenon. There they discover Mothra's egg and meet the Cosmos, a pair of tiny twin fairies, the last surviving members of an ancient scientific civilization that, long ago, created a device to control Earth's climate. In response, Earth conjured the insectoid monster Battra to destroy the climate machine, but the creature went rogue and wiped out the entire race, provoking a battle with Mothra. The two monsters have been dormant since then, but now Battra has been reawakened, and danger looms. Godzilla is something of a third wheel, a territorial force of nature that resents the presence of the other two monsters. There is also a series of reversals: the thief stops stealing and becomes a good father to his young daughter; the lackey watches his boss's empire crumble and walks away; and Battra reconciles with Mothra to fight Godzilla. Omori's love of Hollywood blockbusters resurfaces via Indiana Jones–type references, and Okawara peppers his direction with ecological messages, lively banter between the ex-spouses, and comic relief from the characters of land baron Tomokane (Makoto Otake) and cabinet member Ryuzo Dobashi (Akiji Kobayashi). "Omori's scenario incorporated family and social matters as a theme, so I thought that bringing comedy into the story was a good idea," Okawara said. "I think that the tone of many Japanese films is too serious. I regard Godzilla films purely as entertainment."

TOP: Battra's Nagoya attack replicates scenes of Godzilla's attack on the city in *Mothra vs. Godzilla*. SFX director Koichi Kawakita became frustrated with the suit actor originally cast as Battra, a diminutive person who struggled to convey powerful movement in the costume. At one point, Kawakita himself climbed into the suit to demonstrate what was needed, saying, "Move your body more vigorously!" The actor was replaced by storyboard artist and suit actor Hurricane Ryu. During filming, Masao Fukazawa (aka Little Man Machan), who played Minilla in the 1960s, visited the set and offered pro tips to Ryu. ■ ABOVE: Director Takao Okawara (*center*) with stars Tetsuya Bessho (treasure hunter Takuya Fujito, *left*) and Satomi Kobayashi (Fujito's ex-wife, Masako Tezuka, *right*). Okawara was insistent that Kobayashi, who had previously appeared in several films from cult director Nobuhiko Obayashi, be cast as the driven yet likable career woman. Kobayashi quipped, "When I heard I got the part in *Godzilla vs. Mothra*, I thought I might be acting inside the Mothra suit, which took me by surprise." ■ LEFT: Mothra spins a cocoon over the National Diet Building to transform into its adult stage. The actions of the heavy Mothra puppet were performed by assistant SFX director Makoto Kamiya, who crawled into a 2-foot (0.6-m) gap underneath the set to stay out of camera view. Mothra showers the capitol building with silk, a stunning sight as the sun sets over the Akasaka section of Tokyo. Kawakita's team experimented with CG effects to enhance Mothra's emergence from the cocoon, but the quality was deemed insufficient, and ultimately only practical effects were used.

CLOCKWISE FROM TOP: In the heat of battle, Mothra renders Godzilla powerless with poisonous scale powder. The SFX team created the effect with gold glitter dust, which sparkled and danced as it fell. The glitter stuck to the crew members' sweaty hands, faces, and skin; they struggled to clean themselves for days. Inside the Godzilla suit, Kenpachiro Satsuma wrapped his head and face with a towel and wore goggles, but dust nevertheless entered the suit's tiny openings and covered Satsuma from head to toe, as well as around his eyes. Dust specks coated the inside of the Godzilla suit, making it difficult to clean; there were still specks inside the Godzilla suit a year later. Here, Godzilla's nuclear pulse blasts Mothra, putting an end to the glitter attack. ▪ (*left to right*) Shigeki Fukazawa, Tohto University geology professor (Saburo Shinoda); Joji Minamino, chief of the Environmental Planning Board (Akira Takarada); Ryuzo Dobashi, cabinet security director (Akiji Kobayashi); and psychic Miki Saegusa (Megumi Odaka, *seated*). ▪ The Cosmos (Seiko Imamura and Sayaka Osawa) are the new fairies of Infant Island, a role originated by The Peanuts. Imamura won the Grand Prize and Osawa won the Grand Jury Prize in the 1991 Toho Cinderella Audition, a periodic actress audition campaign. To make the actresses appear tiny, most of the Cosmos' scenes were achieved via high-definition blue-screen compositing, a technique previously seen in such films as Akio Jissoji's *Tokyo: The Last Megalopolis* (1988), and Akira Kurosawa's *Dreams* (1990).

NOTATIONS AND REINTERPRETATIONS

"Upon reading the script, I realized that this film would require a lot of music," Composer Ifukube recalled. "The task seemed challenging."

"Mothra's Song," composed by Yuji Koseki for the original *Mothra*, is as closely identified with the title character as Ifukube's "Terror of Godzilla" is tied to its namesake. It was a given that Ifukube should include Koseki's piece in *Godzilla vs. Mothra*, yet the classically oriented composer struggled to create an appropriate arrangement. "Koseki's music and mine are as different as water and oil," Ifukube said. In the end, Ifukube opted for a very different interpretation, dropping Koseki's upbeat, South Seas–flavored pop stylings for ethereal, sparse strings, supplementing the Cosmos' vocals with a choir. The kidnapped fairies sing this sorrowful version as they beckon Mothra to their rescue and the monster swims through curtains of fire. Other familiar themes and marches add to the sentimental factor.

The final, extended battle takes place along Yokohama's brightly lit waterfront. Unlike the climax of *Godzilla vs. King Ghidorah,* which pitted the heroine Emmy against Godzilla, this time it's all about the monsters, and everyone watches from a distance. Godzilla barges into the fight between Mothra and Battra, and the two insects join forces for the common good. Godzilla is dispatched into the ocean, although Battra loses its life in the struggle. Good triumphs over bad, but Earth is still in danger—another, deadlier meteor is on a collision course. In the melancholy ending, a reworking of Ifukube's mournful "Sacred Spring" from *Mothra vs. Godzilla* is heard as Mothra and the Cosmos fly into outer space to divert the incoming threat, seemingly sacrificing their lives.

Godzilla vs. Mothra set a new box office record for a New Year's release, thanks to a massive promotional strategy that involved tie-in commercials, manga, a soundtrack CD, a children's TV program called *Adventure! Godzilland*, and other campaigns. For director Okawara, however, an important endorsement came from the series' original director, Ishiro Honda, who attended a prerelease screening at the studio. "You've incorporated social themes well into this Godzilla film," Honda told Okawara. "Keep up the good work."

LEFT: Mothra and Battra perform a cross-strafing run over Godzilla. The final battle scenes employ extended use of miniature sets, as well as compositing of the monster props and puppets into aerial footage of the Minato Mirai 21 district, the Yokohama Bay Bridge, and other locations. "Back then, we didn't have stabilizing equipment like the Wescam, and no digital compositing either," said SFX cameraman Kenichi Eguchi. "Compositing was quite challenging, [but] we managed somehow. That was the technological limit at the time."

■ **BELOW LEFT:** A highlight of the final battle is the toppling of the Yokohama Landmark Tower (*at left*), the third-tallest building in Japan (and still under construction at the time the film was made). Because of the miniature's large size, it was destroyed via an unusual method, with the building suspended from an overhead piano wire, which was then cut on cue. "It was a one-shot deal," said SFX crew member Osame Kume. "We all rallied together for that moment . . . there was a round of applause on set when it collapsed perfectly." ■ **OPPOSITE TOP:** Rehearsing Godzilla's attack on a defenseless Battra. Assistant director Makoto Kamiya provides a visual cue to Godzilla actor Kenpachiro Satsuma.

■ **OPPOSITE BOTTOM:** Suspended by an aerial brace, adult Mothra flies above the Yokohama set. Due to their delicate nature, the Mothra and Battra props and suits sustained numerous accidents, necessitating repairs. The flying monsters' props suffered broken wings in the battle with Godzilla; during Mothra's fight with the JSDF at sea (an homage to the original *Mothra*), repeated plunging into water caused the caterpillar's head to be torn away; and there were many other incidents. ■ **FOLLOWING SPREAD:** The Yokohama waterfront set is effectively crosscut with actual location footage during the extended end battle sequence. Note the effective placement of background and foreground miniatures that, when filmed from the correct angle, make the otherwise sparse miniature set appear detailed.

(GOJIRA TAI MEKAGOJIRA / GODZILLA VS. MECHAGODZILLA)
RELEASED: DECEMBER 11, 1993 (JAPAN)

GODZILLA VS. MECHAGODZILLA II

T hrough the decades, Godzilla has survived varying degrees of punishment and injury in its battles with monsters and humankind. Rarely has Godzilla suffered pain so severe, however, as in *Godzilla vs. Mechagodzilla II*, a kaiju Grand Guignol of sorts that, in its climactic moments, renders Godzilla paralyzed from the waist down and on the verge of death. In anticipation of monster's then-forthcoming Hollywood debut, Toho's twentieth *Godzilla* movie was intended as an all-star finale to the series. It features reimagined and updated versions of Mechagodzilla and Rodan, and introduces Godzilla's new adopted offspring, Baby Godzilla. The series' family-friendly atmosphere continues—this time, the focus is on the reunification of a kaiju family unit—within a violent war for survival among man, monsters, and machines.

Godzilla evolves from a nuclear organism seeking food into a parent protect-ing its adopted young. Kenpachiro Satsuma had by now firmly established the identity of his Godzilla, and he deserves special mention for his performance in this film. Satsuma portrays the monster's emotional and physical pain through movements that are sometimes subtle, sometimes agonized, but always straightforward; even when interacting with Baby Godzilla, the Heisei Godzilla never lapses into the anthropomorphized antics and humor that were trademarks of Haruo Nakajima's Godzilla decades earlier. "Godzilla's

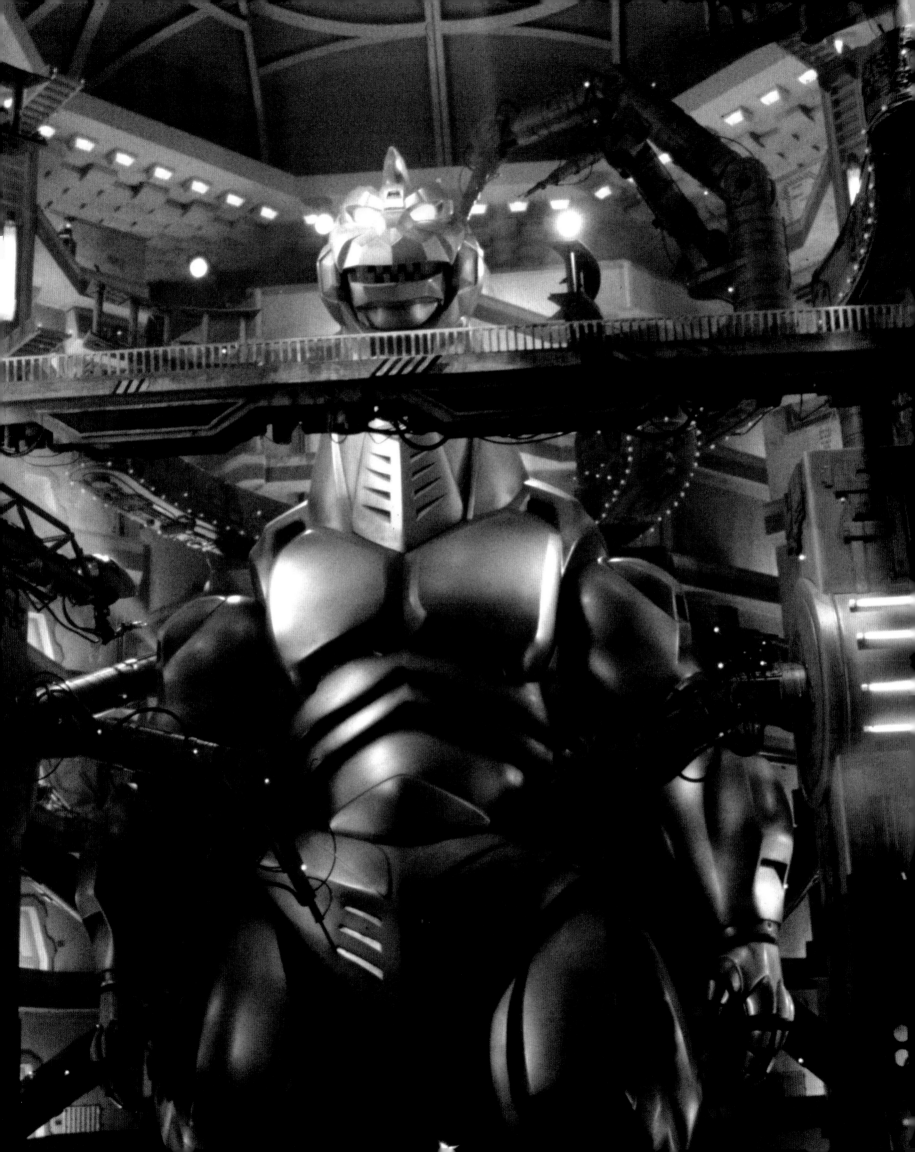

"GODZILLA, FIGHTING TO SAVE ITS OWN KIND, WAS A CHARACTER THE AUDIENCE COULD EMPATHIZE WITH: THE 'SCARY GODZILLA' IMAGE THAT HAD DOMINATED SINCE (*THE RETURN OF GODZILLA*) TOOK A STEP BACK.... THE IDEA OF 'SURVIVAL OF THE SPECIES' HEIGHTENED THE DRAMA, AND IT BECAME ONE OF THE BASIC THEMES OF THE LATER HEISEI GODZILLA SERIES."

—Wataru Mimura, screenwriter

movements in this one are top-notch," said Satsuma. "It doesn't just look like someone in a costume—it's a living Godzilla being portrayed. I was very proud."

Godzilla vs. Mechagodzilla II represents the maturation of the Heisei series and the ways in which it is similar to and different from past Godzillas. The United Nations Godzilla Countermeasures Center (UNGCC) recalls the science-based international coalitions of *Destroy All Monsters* and other movies, with nonprofessional foreign actors in supporting roles as Western officials. The UNGCC, however, has a military branch—G-Force—established to fight Godzilla using internationally funded and developed superweapons. The supporting kaiju are likewise familiar, but different. This Mechagodzilla, smoother in appearance than the original and bearing a humanoid musculature, is not an alien robot but a multi-billion-dollar weapons project, a giant robot mecha operated by a crew of pilots, a nod to anime such as *Mazinger Z* (c. 1972) and many others. Baby Godzilla is cute and sympathetic, and develops an attachment to a human female, similar to what Minilla did, but it eschews the silly antics of the "creature resembling a round cabbage," as composer Akira Ifukube once described it. Baby Godzilla is a Godzillasaur, similar in

PREVIOUS SPREAD: "I thought the new Mechagodzilla should be different," said SFX director Koichi Kawakita. Early design concepts resembled the 1970s iteration—an angular robot made of riveted metal. After struggling to find the right image, Kawakita consulted with Katsushi Murakami, a legendary mecha toy designer for Bandai Co. Ltd. "That's how the idea of a streamlined design came up," said Kawakita. The concept was further refined by Minoru Yoshida, an artist on Kawakita's team. "And so, the image of the new Mechagodzilla was born," Kawakita said. In early story drafts, seven separate armored vehicles would join together, anime-style, to form Mechagodzilla; this idea was eventually dropped due to cost concerns. ■ **BELOW:** The first confrontation between Mechagodzilla (Wataru Fukuda) and Godzilla (Kenpachiro Satsuma) in the Suzuka Mountains near Kyoto.

appearance to Godzilla but less violent. It is a product of brood parasitism, its biological parent having deposited its egg in Rodan's nest. Rodan, believing itself the rightful guardian, and Godzilla, instinctively protecting its own kind, fight for custody of the egg.

After Kazuki Omori declined to return as screenwriter, producer Shogo Tomiyama tapped a rising talent, Wataru Mimura, who had written an unused early treatment for *Godzilla vs. Mothra*. Mimura was a protégé of director Yoshitaro Nomura, a pioneer of Japanese film noir and a frequent collaborator of the great mystery-suspense novelist Seicho Matsumoto. Mimura had written several independently produced films in the 1980s before he was hired to pen an unmade reboot of the *Young Guy* franchise for Toho, with *Godzilla vs. Biollante*'s Masanobu Takashima in the role originated by Yuzo Kayama. Beginning with *Godzilla vs. Mechagodzilla II*, Mimura would be the Godzilla series' most prolific writer for about a decade.

G-Force—the first of many fictional anti-Godzilla military forces in the series—was created by necessity. In the three previous movies, Toho had negotiated with the Japan Self-Defense Forces for actual military hardware and personnel to appear. Those negotiations became more difficult, however, as the military questioned whether its assets should share the screen with fictional weapons such as Maser Cannons and the Super X systems. "I came up with the name G-Force," screenwriter Mimura said. "It might have been problematic for Japan to possess superweapons on its own, but if you portray it as a weapon owned by the United Nations, it becomes more internationally acceptable. For me, it was easier to write about a fictional organization than the actual Self-Defense Forces."

Mimura's script is reminiscent of films such as *Ghidorah* and *Invasion of Astro-Monster,* with two main storylines—handsome but nerdy hero Kazuma Aoki's (Masahiro Takashima) demotion from G-Force and his subsequent atonement for his mistakes, and a scientific team's discovery of the Baby Godzilla egg on Adonoa Island, which sets the monster action in motion—that intersect naturally. Director Takao Okawara maintains an enjoyable balance between the monster action and drama, with light comedy and a hint of romance (involving a flying Pteranodon cycle!) between Aoki and Azusa Gojo (Ryoko Sano), a scientist and Baby Godzilla's caretaker. In an unusual change, Okawara, rather than the special effects team, directed scenes involving Baby Godzilla because of the monster's direct interaction with the cast. "[The producers] originally wanted something cuter and less realistic," Okawara said of the kid kaiju, "but we compromised by keeping the dinosaur form while making his eyes bigger to appeal more to women and children." The idea was to retain the female audience that boosted the prior film's success. Added screenwriter Mimura, "*Godzilla vs. Mechagodzilla II* is a man's world . . . [but] we needed to create something that would appeal to women."

Special effects director Koichi Kawakita's influence is increasingly apparent; as the SFX sequences became longer and more prominent, Okawara struggled to maintain an effective balance. "With special effects, a single line [in the screenplay] can become several minutes long, so it's hard to predict [the film's length]," Okawara said. "We tried to minimize waste, cutting unnecessary parts during the script stage. . . . Still, we ended up cutting nearly twenty minutes [of footage]." Sometimes tensions arose between the two camps. "I was trying to make it work as well as possible," Okawara said. "If I cut a special effects scene in the editing stage, [sometimes] it would be restored the next day."

The power of Mechagodzilla owes much to the awe-inspiring music that accompanies its introductory scenes. A brief prologue connects the story to the events in *Godzilla vs. King Ghidorah*, with UN scientists reverse-engineering the remnants of Mecha-King Ghidorah to develop the ultimate anti-Godzilla weapon. Mechagodzilla's eyes light up, and the massive robot is unveiled inside a cavernous docking area, accompanied by composer Ifukube's slow battle march with thundering percussion and heavy pentatonic phrasing—a melody adapted, ironically, from *Rhythmic Games for Children*, a 1949 suite of simple pieces created to teach music to schoolchildren. Ifukube's score spans the emotional spectrum: Baby Godzilla's hatching is induced

GODZILLA FACT: The UNGCC's moniker was inspired by the United Nations Transitional Authority in Cambodia (UNTAC), an international peacekeeping force that governed Cambodia from 1992–93.

OPPOSITE: Godzilla's attack on the petrochemical complex at Yokkaichi is SFX director Koichi Kawakita's tribute to the monster's attack at the same location in *Mothra vs. Godzilla* nearly thirty years earlier. ■ CLOCKWISE FROM TOP LEFT: Super Mechagodzilla is formed when the Garuda attack craft attaches itself to Mechagodzilla's back. ■ While Godzilla rampages through the city of Kyoto in search of the hatchling, Baby's (Hurricane Ryu) eyes glow red with fear and Azusa Gojo (Ryoko Sano) tries to comfort the young monster. Assistant director Masaaki Tezuka joked, "She [Sano] was always saying to the baby, 'How cute!' and hugging it. . . . She was hugging him so much that I even thought about getting into the suit." ■ Fire Rodan swoops in to attack Mechagodzilla.

by a haunting vocal piece encoded in a prehistoric plant and interpreted by a chorus of psychic children, with lyrics in the Ainu language; a stirring new march accompanies G-Force's heroics; and the requiem that accompanies Godzilla and Baby Godzilla's departure in the finale is an emotional coda. This is among Ifukube's outstanding genre scores, yet his work was fraught with challenges. Although he had composed music for Godzilla, Rodan, and Mechagodzilla previously, the creatures' motivations were fundamentally different than before, and he struggled to write appropriate music. The composer even fell ill from stress for a time. He was determined not to fall back on familiar themes, yet aware of the audience's expectations.

"With Godzilla, I can't keep doing the same things over and over, so I made some changes," Ifukube said. "Godzilla's theme has been used so often that I toned it down a bit. . . . Being involved with Godzilla for forty years is quite a long time. So I included it as part of my legacy. Also, there is quite a dramatic scene toward the end of the film, so the theme just fits there. . . . When you hear those notes, no one expects Godzilla to lose."

The story underwent interesting changes before the script was finalized. Mimura wrote a prologue in which an extinction-level asteroid ends the age of dinosaurs; it ended with a Pteranodon clutching three eggs as snow envelops the earth. The scene at Adonoa Island originally pitted two Pteranodons (male and female) against Mechagodzilla, and Godzilla did not show up until later. In the climax, Godzilla was resuscitated after absorbing radiation from an explosion in the Garuda's nuclear reactor. Other ideas were discarded, including a story with Mechani-Kong (from *King Kong Escapes*) and the death of Godzilla. "What makes the original *Godzilla* so powerful is the fact that Godzilla is killed at the end," Okawara said. "I wanted to kill Godzilla. . . . However, Toho would not permit it."

Godzilla almost dies, however. The final act is staged around the giant Makuhari Messe convention center in Chiba; as with the previous film, Kawakita employs a combination of optical compositing and cross-editing of flyover location footage with a large, detailed miniature sets. Rodan foils the plan to lure Godzilla offshore to Ogasawara, using Baby as bait. A battle between the pterosaur and Mechagodzilla

GODZILLA FACT: Against her wishes, psychic Miki Saegusa (Megumi Odaka) is compelled by G-Force to aid the G-Crusher operation to kill Godzilla. When the plan fails, Miki is relieved; thus begins a new chapter in the character's relationship to Godzilla and its offspring, which would blossom over the next two films. "Miki Saegusa, who senses Godzilla's movements and understands its weaknesses, is Godzilla's greatest adversary in this movie," observed Godzilla suit actor Kenpachiro Satsuma. "At the same time, she understands Godzilla's feelings and she worries about its fate, embodying a woman with a kind heart. That is her true nature."

ensues, and although Rodan damages the robot, it is critically injured. Godzilla comes ashore looking for Baby and is engaged by the cyborg. G-Force attempts to kill Godzilla with the torturous "G-Crusher," using Miki Saegusa's psychic powers to locate Godzilla's secondary brain (an idea based on the double dinosaur brain theory that originated in 1900s-era paleontology) and destroy it. The plan nearly succeeds: Godzilla writhes in agony, spurting blood and foaming at the mouth; Baby Godzilla's tearful cry moves a near-death Rodan to save Godzilla, conveying what remains of its life force to its cross-species kaiju brethren. Godzilla, reenergized and enraged, emits a glittering energy force and spits a glowing red heat ray that destroys Mechagodzilla. Godzilla and Baby are united and depart in peace. Buoyed by another massive promotional campaign, *Godzilla vs. Mechagodzilla* earned almost ¥1.9 billion in admissions and was second at the domestic box office for 1994. With a highly anticipated Hollywood Godzilla production indefinitely stalled in development, Toho's series of films would continue uninterrupted for the foreseeable future.

PREVIOUS SPREAD: Godzilla approaches the iconic Kyoto Kiyomizu-dera Temple landmark. ■ **CLOCKWISE FROM TOP LEFT:** The Garuda flying warship. After being set aside as an ineffective weapon against Godzilla, Garuda is later repurposed as an accessory that turns Mechagodzilla into Super Mechagodzilla. ■ Super Mechagodzilla rains down punishment on Godzilla, using a variety of weapons including the Garuda laser cannons, tranquilizer missiles, and the shock anchor harpoons, which send electrical charges into Godzilla's body. ■ After Godzilla is immobilized by Mechagodzilla's paralyzer missiles, the cyborg launches its shock anchor harpoon weapons.

ABOVE: The battle on Adonoa Island: Rodan swoops in for the attack against Godzilla. ■ **RIGHT:** The G-Crusher nearly kills Godzilla, but after Fire Rodan bequeaths its life force to its fellow kaiju, Godzilla is more powerful than ever. Godzilla's supercharged red heat ray and Super Mechagodzilla's mega-buster ray collide in a midair beam lock (a tribute to 1974's *Godzilla vs. Mechagodzilla*), causing this massive explosion that sends the cyborg hurtling backward. Unlike *Godzilla vs. Mothra*, where the cast watched from afar, the heroes are inside Mechagodzilla and Garuda during the battles, making for a more exciting final act.

GUEST-STARRING GODZILLA

Apart from the Godzilla film series, the King of the Monsters has made numerous appearances in a multitude of other media. Godzilla has had starring roles, guest spots, and cameos in feature films, shorts, television series, commercials, parodies, amusement park attractions, and animated content produced in Japan and abroad. Sometimes the monster is thinly disguised, or its name is changed slightly for comedic effect, but the form and presence of Godzilla is unmistakable.

It all started in the mid-sixties, when Tsuburaya Productions would often borrow monster suits from Toho and re-dress them to inexpensively create creatures for its science-fiction television shows. For the premiere episode of *Ultra Q* (1966), the 1964 Godzilla suit was modified into the monster Gomes by removing the dorsal fins and adding a horn atop its head, oversize claws, and a faux overcoat of scales. Later that year, an episode of Tsuburaya's *Ultraman* (1966) featured the dinosaur monster Jiras, a hybrid kaiju created from the body of the 1964 Godzilla suit and the head of the 1965 Godzilla suit, with the addition of a large, colorful frill around an elongated neck. Despite the modifications to the suits, both Gomes and Jiras were immediately recognizable as an incognito Godzilla.

Godzilla's first (albeit unofficial) foray into animation was the 1969 American parody short-short (less than two minutes) film *Bambi Meets Godzilla*, created by Marv Newland. The first official Godzilla cartoon was Hanna-Barbera's *The Godzilla Power Hour* (1978), a Jonny Quest–like adventure series featuring a green Godzilla that breathed flame and had laser beam eyes, and its flying cousin, the diminutive Godzooky.

Godzilla made several appearances on the NBC television network in the late seventies. In a 1977 *Saturday Night Live* skit, Godzilla (comedian John Belushi in a Godzilla suit originally created by SFX and VFX artist Robert Short for the 1976 comedy film *Hollywood Boulevard*) was interviewed by "Baba Wawa," Gilda Radner's parody impersonation of journalist Barbara Walters. Godzilla returned to *SNL* in 1980 in the skit "Kramer vs. Godzilla," a parody of the film *Kramer vs. Kramer*. In 1981, the ABC television show *Fridays* (an *SNL* knock-off) featured the short film *Zilla, Horrible Monster of the Depths* that had a human-size "Zilla" kick sand on a fisherman at the beach, knock over garbage cans, and terrorize Tokyo before recurring character Vinny the Biker (Michael Richards) fights the monster and knocks its head off, revealing a man inside a monster costume. The dejected man/monster trudges back into the ocean.

When New World Pictures released *Godzilla 1985*, an elaborate advertising tie-in campaign with Dr. Pepper was revealed. The soft drink appeared several times in the movie via product placement shots, and two television commercials showed Godzilla running amok until being tamed by a drink of Dr. Pepper. Around the same time, both Godzilla and King Ghidorah made cameo appearances in Tim Burton's *Pee-wee's Big Adventure* (1985).

Godzilla vs. Charles Barkley, a television commercial for Nike shoes, premiered during the MTV Video Music Awards broadcast on September 9, 1992, and was a major advertising event of the early nineties. Its debut was preceded by an advance trailer that aired several months earlier during the 1992 Major League Baseball All-Star Game, which featured shots of Godzilla battling opponents in classic Toho movies and a narrator intoning, "He's defeated Mothra. He's defeated King Kong. He's defeated Monster Zero and Mechagodzilla. But he's never faced an adversary like this." Produced by Industrial Light & Magic for the advertising giant Widen+Kennedy, the spot pitted Godzilla (in sports goggles) on the court against the then-twenty-nine-year-old NBA all-star. The commercial spawned a tie-in comic book, posters, and other merchandise.

In 1995, an episode of the Kids' WB's *Pinky and the Brain* (an animated sitcom about a pair of genetically enhanced laboratory mice) featured caricatures of Dr. Serizawa and Dr. Yamane creating a miniaturization ray that is reverse engineered by The Brain into an enlarging ray. The Brain's plan is to dress Pinky in a "Gollyzilla" suit, enlarge him with the ray, and then enlarge himself and "defeat" Gollyzilla so that the populace will thank him and anoint him their ruler. But the real Gollyzilla appears and foils the plan. During the climax, Raymond Burr is accidentally enlarged and engages Gollyzilla in battle.

The popularity of the Heisei series generated numerous Godzilla-themed projects in Japan during the nineties. The most prominent of these was *Adventure! Godzilland*, which aired for two months to promote *Godzilla vs. Mothra* in 1992. Hosted by television personality LaSalle Ishii, the show featured trivia questions and cameo appearances by the film's cast members, and typically concluded with an Godzilla attraction costume performing an exercise routine together with Ishii and a cast of kids to the theme song "Gojira So-Fa-Mi-Re-Do." A second season aired the following year as a tie-in for *Godzilla vs. Mechagodzilla II*, featuring frequent appearances (via attraction costumes) of Godzilla, Mechagodzilla, and Baby.

In the mid-2000s, an arcade game produced by NewGin Co. Ltd. featured a short film directed by Koichi Kawakita showing Godzilla (portrayed with the *Godzilla 2000: Millennium* suit) pitted in battle against King Ghidorah (the suit from *GMK*), Gigan, and Anguirus (the suits from *Final Wars*). Following the popularity of *Shin Godzilla*, in 2017, Universal Studios Japan created *Godzilla: The Real 4-D* (a 3D ride with physical effects such as seat motion, water spray, etc.) as part of its "Universal Cool Japan" event series, a seasonal collaboration with Japan's most popular entertainment franchises. In this short film, the audience assumes the role of a fighter pilot trying to shoot a weapon into Godzilla's mouth, a task made difficult when the Universal Studios globe becomes wedged in the monster's jaws. In 2019, the park featured a follow-up ride titled *Godzilla vs. Evangelion: The Real 4-D*.

Godzilla Appears in Sukagawa (2019), a fourteen-minute film made for the Eiji Tsuburaya Museum in Sukagawa City, utilizes a replica of the 1954 Godzilla suit designed by master modeler Yuji Sakai, with traditional suitmation effects directed by veteran SFX director Kenji Suzuki. In the film, Godzilla attacks Sukagawa and is confronted by and obliterates the military.

In 2020, Nijigen no Mori (an amusement park on Awaji Island in the Seto Inland Sea, featuring attractions based on manga, anime, and movies), opened *Godzilla Intercept Operation–National Godzilla Awaji Island Research Center*, an immersive, multipart attraction that begins with a seven-and-a-half-minute film produced by Toho and directed by Kazuhiro Nakagawa (an assistant director on *Shin Godzilla*). Using CG modeling developed for *Shin Godzilla*, the film tells the story of Godzilla's appearances on Awaji Island since ancient times and the operation that trapped the monster on the amusement park grounds, where a giant, life-size Godzilla zipline ride is located.

The list goes on and on. Human-size versions of Godzilla and Megaguirus made cameos in director Koki Mitani's comedy *All About Our House* (2001). Years before directing *Godzilla Minus One*, Takashi Yamazaki opened his film *Always: Sunset on Third Street 2* (2007) with a comedic fantasy sequence set during the early 1960s, in which an all-CG Godzilla destroys Tokyo Tower. Godzilla rode an ATV, went waterskiing, and partied with twentysomethings in a 2014 Snickers candy bar commercial. And the impressive "Snow Godzilla" appeared in the anime *Shinkansen Henkei Robo Shinkalion The Movie* (2019).

These examples, along with others featured in these pages, comprise but a small sampling of Godzilla's innumerable adventures outside the world of Toho's feature films. Beyond the large and small screens, the monster has also appeared in a plethora of other types of media, including manga, comics, toys, books, magazines, souvenirs, art, music, photography, food, clothing, video games, and more. This ever-evolving list of items is evidence of Godzilla's expansive pop culture influence around the world.

CLOCKWISE FROM TOP: (Scenes from *Monster Planet Godzilla*–3D attraction, Sanrio Puroland amusement park, 1994.) Godzilla under attack as it advances on the Marunouchi side of Tokyo Station. ■ Mothra suffers a direct hit from Godzilla's heat ray as they battle in the Ginza district. ■ Megumi Odaka (as Miki Saegusa) appears in the welcome video for the ride at Sanrio Puroland in Tama New Town, Tokyo. The story of the ride had Godzilla, Mothra, and Rodan accidentally transported to Earth from the Monster Planet where they live.

CLOCKWISE FROM TOP LEFT: (*Godzilland* —OVA, 1994–96) *Godzilland* was a series of educational children's OVAs (Original Video Animation) featuring super-deformed versions of Toho monsters teaching kids to read and count. ▪ (*Godzilla Island*—TV, 1997–98) A television series of 256 three-minute episodes filmed entirely with Bandai vinyl toys and a handful of human actors. The story is set one hundred years in the future and features all of Earth's monsters living on Godzilla Island, fighting against an invasion by Xiliens. ▪ (*Gojiban*—web series, 2019–24) Puppet shorts created by puppeteer Hideyuki Kobayashi and coproduced by Toho featuring the charming comic adventures of the Godzilla brothers: big brother Godzilla-kun, Minilla, and Little Godzilla. Featuring guest appearances by many Toho characters. ▪ (*Godzilla vs. Hedorah*—short film, 2021) A five-minute short made for the annual Godzilla Fest (*Gojira-Fesu*), a festival hosted by Toho and celebrated on November 3, the anniversary of the release of the original *Godzilla*. Directed by *Shin Godzilla* assistant director Kazuhiro Nakagawa, the film uses the Godzilla and Hedorah suits from *Godzilla Final Wars*. ▪ (*Godzilla vs. Gigan Rex*—short film, 2022) Premiered at Godzilla Fest, this all-CG film features the invasion of a swarm of Gigan-like creatures and the boss monster, Gigan Rex. They face off against Godzilla (it is implied that this is the regenerated Godzilla from the end of *Godzilla vs. Destoroyah*) in a violent and action-packed battle. Directed by *Godzilla Minus One* VFX artist Takuya Uenishi. ▪ (*Godzilla the Ride*—opened in 2019) Several years before *Godzilla Minus One*, Takashi Yamazaki wrote and directed this 3D CG attraction for the Seibuen Amusement Park in Saitama. The audience is first threatened by King Ghidorah in the ruins of the city. Rodan tries to intervene but is easily defeated by the space monster. Godzilla appears and the audience is buffeted around as the two monsters battle to the death.

RIGHT, TOP TO BOTTOM: (*Gigan Attacks*— short film, 2022) Director Kazuhiro Nakagawa works with a bigger budget and a newly created Gigan costume (made possible by a crowdfunding campaign) for this nine-minute Godzilla Fest short. The action picks up as Godzilla departs following its defeat of Hedorah in the previous *Godzilla vs. Hedorah* short. Suddenly, Gigan returns to Earth and enters into a fierce battle with Godzilla. For the first time, Gigan is shown using the ray emitted from above its visor. ▪ (*Godzilla vs. Megalon*—short film, 2023) Another all-CG Godzilla Fest short by Takuya Uenishi, pitting Godzilla against the Seatopian monster Megalon. Taking full advantage of the design capabilities inherent in CG, the film features breathtaking scene composition and Godzilla's most brutal battle to date packed into its ten-minute run time. ▪ (*Operation Jet Jaguar*—short film, 2023) Director Nakagawa's most elaborate Godzilla Fest short to date, showcasing a new, crowdfunded Jet Jaguar costume (unfortunately, the project came up around 25 percent short of its goal) against the slowly deteriorating Godzilla costume from *Final Wars*. The film ends in a cliffhanger as King Ghidorah (the badly worn *GMK* suit) appears at the climax, ready to take on all comers.

(*GOJIRA TAI SUPESUGOJIRA*)
RELEASED: DECEMBER 10, 1994 (JAPAN)

GODZILLA VS. SPACEGODZILLA

On Birth Island, Little Godzilla is imprisoned inside a cosmic crystal trap by the intergalactic monster SpaceGodzilla. Unable to free its adopted young, and seeking revenge, Godzilla pursues SpaceGodzilla to Japan. Godzilla confronts its doppelgänger at Fukuoka, a city now transformed into a cosmic energy fortress with a network of crystal stalagmite structures. Using the telekinetic power of its Gravity Tornado, SpaceGodzilla suspends Godzilla in midair before sending it crashing into a building. With an arsenal of powerful rays and an impenetrable energy shield, SpaceGodzilla appears unbeatable, so Godzilla must team with G-Force and their latest mecha weapon, M.O.G.U.E.R.A. (Mobile Operations Godzilla Universal Expert Robot Aero-type), to save Little Godzilla—and once again, the world.

With director Takao Okawara and screenwriter Wataru Mimura pivoting to work on *Orochi, the Eight-Headed Dragon* (1994), a historical fantasy-adventure based on the legend of the heroic warrior Yamato Takeru, the twenty-first Godzilla film was instead assigned to two series newcomers, director Kensho Yamashita and writer Hiroshi Kashiwabara. Yamashita was a longtime Toho assistant director who had ascended through the studio system by working on Kihachi Okamoto's *Battle of Okinawa* (1971) and a number of special effects films (including *Terror of Mechagodzilla* and *The Return of Godzilla*), while Kashiwabara was a veteran writer of TV series and anime. Each man had his

"THERE AREN'T MANY GODZILLA FILMS WHERE HUMANS CONFRONT GODZILLA HEAD-ON. I WANTED TO CHALLENGE (THE STATUS QUO) WITH A FAST-PACED ACTION STYLE. I ALSO WANTED TO INTERTWINE ROMANCES OF DIFFERENT AGES BETWEEN MIKI AND SHINJO AND YUKI AND CHINATSU, MAKING THIS A FILM ENJOYABLE FOR BOTH PARENTS AND CHILDREN."

—Kensho Yamashita, director

PREVIOUS SPREAD: The final showdown: Godzilla confronts its evil twin, SpaceGodzilla, in Fukuoka. ■ LEFT: Godzilla protects Little Godzilla from SpaceGodzilla's attack on Birth Island. At the conclusion of this fight, SpaceGodzilla imprisons Little Godzilla in a crystal trap. A scene of Godzilla trying unsuccessfully to free its adoptee from the trap—which would have further illustrated why Godzilla pursues SpaceGodzilla to Japan—was filmed but omitted from the final cut. ■ OPPOSITE TOP: "I envisioned SpaceGodzilla as something like the monster Viras from *Gamera vs. Viras* (Daiei Film, 1968), with a thin and sinister appearance," said screenwriter Hiroshi Kashiwabara. "I imagined it would move around sharply, toying with Godzilla, but it ended up having a strong and angular appearance." ■ OPPOSITE, BOTTOM LEFT: The heroes react to SpaceGodzilla's arrival at Birth Island. (*Back row, left to right*) Chinatsu Gondo (Towako Yoshikawa), Miki Saegusa (Megumi Odaka), Koji Shinjo (Jun Hashizume), and Kiyoshi Sato (Zenkichi Yoneyama); (*in front*) Akira Yuki (Akira Emoto). Scenes on Birth Island were filmed both on studio sets and on location at Okinoerabu Island near Okinawa. Director Kensho Yamashita originally planned to shoot extensively on location at Amami Oshima, an island in southwest Japan, but changed his plans because of the presence of poisonous habu snakes there. ■ OPPOSITE, BOTTOM RIGHT: Little Godzilla was portrayed by pro wrestler Masanobu "Little Frankie" Okamoto. The suit was created by creature designer Shinichi Wakasa and his company, Monsters Inc. "We made three mock-ups: one closer to Baby Godzilla, one slightly deformed, and one like Little Godzilla. It was quite a process to arrive at the final design. Since [SFX director Koichi Kawakita] was inclined toward fantasy, he didn't articulate exactly what he wanted, so I struggled with it," said Wakasa.

own objectives for the new Godzilla movie; ultimately, their ideas would vie for running time with Koichi Kawakita's special effects sequences. *Godzilla vs. SpaceGodzilla* is an anomaly, a monster battlefest peppered with action heroism, latent love, fantasy, psychic powers, and kaiju cuteness.

"I felt that Godzilla films lacked suspense and romance within the human drama," said Yamashita. "I wanted a story where the interaction between the younger generation, represented by members of the G-Force . . . and the older generation becomes a strength as they bravely confront Godzilla and Space-Godzilla [together]. I also wanted to spotlight the heroine, Miki Saegusa, and include moments of gentle romance."

Screenwriter Kashiwabara had somewhat different ideas. An admirer of Hollywood films and classic actors such as John Wayne and Steve McQueen, Kashiwabara envisioned a buddy movie focused on the straight-arrow G-Force lieutenant Koji Shinjo (Jun Hashizume) and his sidekick, Lieutenant Kiyoshi Sato (Zenkichi Yoneyama); he said he wrote the characters with Burt Reynolds and Elliott Gould in mind. Kashiwabara's original story had scenes and ideas that were ultimately cut or changed, either for budgetary or structural reasons. These included a brawl aboard a ship pitting Shinjo and Sato against American military men; the two heroes' misbehavior led to their assignment on Birth Island as punishment. He wrote a funny scene wherein Yuki (Akira Emoto) tries to capture Godzilla with nets, a tribute to Howard Hawks's comedy about big-game hunters, *Hatari!* (1962). When SpaceGodzilla's crystal meteor crashes into Birth Island, it deposits three eggs that hatch a swarm of cosmic dragonflies—SpaceGodzilla's minions— which turn the island's soil and trees into crystals and attack Little Godzilla; as Godzilla defends the youngster, a volcanic eruption damages the crystals, weakening SpaceGodzilla, and the hostile monster departs for Japan.

"We had too many storylines," said Kashiwabara. "Even just sorting out the human relationships and deciding where to focus was difficult. If we had included everything, it would have been a two-and-

a-half-hour movie. . . . But I think we did a good job of tying everything together in the final draft."
To trim the script, Kashiwabara worked with assistant producer Shinchiro Arimasa. "Since I was a
fan of Megumi Odaka, we decided to focus on Miki Saegusa," Kashiwabara added. "If we were to make
another movie, Arimasa and I joked about doing a Miki-centered story like *Aliens*." (Interestingly, before
the production team decided on a space monster as Godzilla's opponent, Anguirus and a new robot called
Super Godzilla were considered; Arimasa also reportedly proposed a story called *Godzilla vs. Godzilla*.)

Miki's feelings about Godzilla and its progeny have evolved; she believes the creatures have the right to
exist and it is immoral to kill or subjugate them. *Godzilla vs. SpaceGodzilla* opens similarly to the previous
film, with G-Force officials unveiling M.O.G.U.E.R.A., the latest anti-Godzilla robot weapon; simultaneously,
the UNGCC has developed T-Project, an effort to control Godzilla with a telepathic transmitter. Mothra,

having flown into space to divert an asteroid at the end of *Godzilla vs. Mothra*, detects a malevolent space monster headed for earth. Mothra's tiny fairies, the Cosmos, telepathically implore Miki—employed as head of the UNGCC's psychic research center—to stop the monster from killing Godzilla and conquering the planet, and she reluctantly agrees to lend her powers to T-Project. Miki is initially cold to the advances of the gung-ho Shinjo, who is dedicated to the anti-Godzilla fight, but after she is kidnapped by villains who want to use her powers to control Godzilla, a dramatic rescue ensues and the two develop a mutual attraction. The film benefits from the casting of Emoto as Yuki, a rogue veteran G-Force operative who is bent on revenge against Godzilla for killing his friend, Colonel Goro Gondo, in *Godzilla vs. Biollante*. A fine actor who later won multiple Japan Academy Prizes, Emoto brings wit and edginess

FAR LEFT: Godzilla and Little Godzilla stalk through the Birth Island jungle.
■ LEFT: SpaceGodzilla looms over the helpless form of Little Godzilla. ■
BOTTOM: The dinosaur-like Baby Godzilla of *Godzilla vs. Mechagodzilla II* has evolved into Little Godzilla, which—although it has grown in size—appears more childlike. "We introduced Little Godzilla because we thought that girls wouldn't come to see a monster movie," said SFX director Kochi Kawakita. "I thought it would be difficult to create a character that would interest girls. I tried to make Little Godzilla reminiscent of Minilla and gave it a catlike appearance."

"IN SOME PAST GODZILLA MOVIES, THE HUMAN CHARACTERS WERE MERELY OBSERVERS OF MONSTER BATTLES, BUT IN THIS FILM, WE INTENTIONALLY HAD SCENES WHERE PEOPLE ENGAGED WITH THE MONSTERS, EITHER IN COMBAT OR (BY) ASSISTING THEM. IF WE HAD CUT A BIT MORE OF THE SPECIAL EFFECTS SCENES IN THE FUKUOKA CLIMAX, WE MIGHT HAVE ACHIEVED A MORE BALANCED STORY. . . . NEVERTHELESS, I BELIEVE WE MANAGED TO CREATE A GODZILLA FILM WITH DEEPER HUMAN DRAMA THAT HADN'T BEEN SEEN MUCH IN THE SERIES UNTIL NOW."

—Kensho Yamashita, director

ABOVE: Chinatsu Gondo (Towako Yoshikawa) and Major Akira Yuki (Akira Emoto) share a tender moment as they watch Godzilla return to Birth Island.

■ **RIGHT:** "Miki Saegusa, possessing abilities beyond the common notion of psychic powers, is an indispensable character for the series," said director Kensho Yamashita (*right*). "We wanted to emphasize her internal growth. . . . Instead of presenting her as a mere psychic girl, we aimed to portray her as a psychic colleague, allowing for more emotional depth. Changing her hairstyle to short hair brought a considerable shift in her image, and [actress Megumi Odaka] embraced the role enthusiastically." Yamashita came up with the idea of illustrating Miki's psychic activity through the movement of her earrings, which have pendants in the shape of Mothra's symbol.

to the outlaw-like character. The threat of SpaceGodzilla eventually unites the heroes and Godzilla in a common purpose, and the movie ends with a romantic ballad on the soundtrack and love in the air between Miki and Shinjo, as well as between Yuki and Chinatsu.

Special effects director Kawakita introduces some new innovations, even as his preferences (transforming monsters or robots, a lengthy battle) remain familiar. Godzilla travels northward across Kyushu in pursuit of its enemy, passing landmarks such as the Shiroyama Hotel Kagoshima, Kumamoto Castle, and Space World amusement park in Yahatahigashi-ku (several citizen groups along this route petitioned Toho to have Godzilla trash their cities). Kawakita employs an unprecedented number of process shots combining the monster with a live-action plate of the city and extras fleeing in the foreground, and films Godzilla via several unusual angles and camera movements.

Director Yamashita faced a problem when filming the action sequence involving Godzilla's approach to Birth Island as Little Godzilla cries for help after stepping on tear gas mines, Yuki scrambles to shoot Godzilla with a lethal blood agent, and the G-Force team readies to tag the monster with the telepathic transmitter. The location was a beautiful coral reef beach in Okinawa—a site used in youth-oriented romance films—but due to a scheduling miscalculation, filming took place during neap tide, when the reefs were exposed above the waterline. This made it impossible to capture wide overhead shots of the characters on

ABOVE & LEFT: The battle among M.O.G.U.E.R.A., Godzilla, and SpaceGodzilla elapses over nearly thirty minutes of screen time. Godzilla and M.O.G.U.E.R.A. work together to destroy the 768-foot (234-m) Fukuoka Tower (*pictured*), Japan's tallest seaside skyscraper, through which SpaceGodzilla channels cosmic energy. SFX director Koichi Kawakita struggled to accurately recreate the Fukuoka waterfront in miniature while excluding the newly built Fukuoka Dome baseball stadium located nearby. The filmmakers had opted not to show the stadium because it was already prominently featured in Daiei Film's *Gamera: Guardian of the Universe* (1995), made at roughly the same time, though released several months after *Godzilla vs. SpaceGodzilla*.

the beach as planned, but the team nonetheless filmed a spectacular wide view of the beach and surf, which Godzilla was later composited into—creating one of the most appealing scenes of Godzilla coming ashore in the entire series.

SpaceGodzilla is a hybrid creature, theoretically born when Godzilla cells were transmitted into outer space (either via the death of Biollante or Mothra's asteroid-intercepting mission) and merged with a crystalline alien life-form. The film features an early score by Takayuki Hattori, who would later become a prolific composer for anime and TV series. Hattori's dissonant motif for SpaceGodzilla adequately captures the demon monster's fratricidal fury. Overall, his music is more Westernized and less distinctive than that of Akira Ifukube, whose signature Godzilla theme is incongruously heard through stock recordings during several scenes.

Godzilla vs. SpaceGodzilla proved successful even with its divisive and uneven mash-up of genre tropes, romance, and the introduction of a cartoonlike, big-eyed Little Godzilla. It earned ¥1.65 billion and was the second-biggest domestic film of 1995, paving the way for the Heisei series to continue.

CLOCKWISE FROM TOP LEFT: "I liked the original Moguera [from Toho's *The Mysterians* (1957)]," said screenwriter Hiroshi Kashiwabara. "This new version showcased its ability to separate into different parts [the Land M.O.G.U.E.R.A. rover, the Star Falcon fighter, and the piloted M.O.G.U.E.R.A. mecha] and recombine effectively. However, I felt its role was somewhat limited, and it ended up as a rather ambiguous character." ■ As the final battle rages, Godzilla (Kenpachiro Satsuma) and M.O.G.U.E.R.A. (Wataru Fukuda) team up against SpaceGodzilla (Ryo Hariya). M.O.G.U.E.R.A. destroys SpaceGodzilla's energy-absorbing shoulder crystals, but SpaceGodzilla retaliates by piercing the mecha with its crystal-tipped tail and hurling it into a row of buildings. Here, as SpaceGodzilla moves in to destroy M.O.G.U.E.R.A., Godzilla intervenes, thus saving the life of Yuki—who had once vowed to kill Godzilla—the last crewman inside the fallen robot. ■ The Fukuoka battle demonstrates SFX director Koichi Kawakita's strategy regarding filming the big climax scenes in the Heisei series. The battle takes place on a single, large miniature set, using forced perspective to create the illusion of depth, and repositioning the camera to film the action from different angles over the course of the fight.

(GOJIRA TAI DESUTOROIA)
RELEASED: DECEMBER 9, 1995 (JAPAN)

GODZILLA VS. DESTOROYAH

G odzilla dies!"
  These unbelievable words anchored the advance marketing campaign for *Godzilla vs. Destoroyah,* the twenty-second Godzilla film and—clearing a path for the much-anticipated Hollywood adaptation, which was at last on the horizon—Toho's last Godzilla movie for the foreseeable future.

"After *SpaceGodzilla,* [SFX director Koichi] Kawakita said we had done everything we could do except kill Godzilla," said producer Shogo Tomiyama. However, this was not a decision Tomiyama and Kawakita could make alone—the final word would belong to executive producer Tomoyuki Tanaka, the father of Godzilla. "Kawakita and I went to Tanaka's house to present the idea," Tomiyama continued. "He said OK, but on one condition: the story must not really end. In the first film, there is the line, 'Somewhere in the world, another Godzilla may appear.' That's a producer's job—to leave the door open so things can continue."

Set in 1996, *Godzilla vs. Destoroyah* brings the series full circle, revisiting ideas from 1954's *Godzilla* and concluding with the monster's tragic, agonizing death and immortal resurrection. After a cluster of uranium deposits explodes and destroys Birth Island, Godzilla's internal nuclear reactor spirals out of control as a result. With its skin covered in glowing lesions, the slowly dying Godzilla becomes a ticking time bomb that could explode in a blast so powerful

> **"THERE IS GREAT SIGNIFICANCE IN THE FACT THAT THIS FILM WAS MADE ON THE FIFTIETH ANNIVERSARY OF THE END OF THE WAR. AND THIS YEAR (1995), WE ALSO HAD AN ISSUE WITH NUCLEAR TESTING BY FRANCE . . . GODZILLA IS ALSO A PRODUCT OF NUCLEAR POWER, AND I WOULD LIKE FOR THE AUDIENCE TO BE AWARE OF AND THINK ABOUT THIS."**
>
> —Momoko Kochi (Emiko Yamane)

it could destroy Earth. The military averts the detonation by temporarily freezing Godzilla—but upon thawing, the monster's organic core becomes unstable, and its temperature approaches 2,192°F (1,200°C), potentially triggering a meltdown that would release catastrophic radiation. Meanwhile, construction of the Tokyo Bay Aqua-Line expressway (which would open in 1997) inadvertently unleashes a dormant monster, Destoroyah [i.e., Destroyer], a prehistoric crustacean mutant created by the aftereffects of the Oxygen Destroyer that was detonated on the seabed in 1954. Godzilla's kaiju adoptee, now renamed Godzilla Junior, becomes a pawn in G-Force's plan to coax Godzilla and Destoroyah into a final battle near Narita International Airport in the hope that the monsters will destroy one another.

DEATH WITH DIGNITY

After securing Tanaka's blessing, Tomiyama presented a rough outline to Toho's Godzilla Committee— an unusual step, but necessary given the unprecedented idea of killing the studio's golden goose. Story meetings were then held in January 1995 between Tomiyama, Kawakita, and screenwriter Kazuki Omori. While Omori initially asked to direct the film, Tomiyama instead wanted to re-create the team behind the success of *Godzilla vs. Mothra*, with Omori writing and Takao Okawara directing. A concept called *Godzilla vs. Ghost Godzilla* was discussed, but the team opted to create a new, all-powerful monster for Godzilla's cinematic finale; Omori scribbled the names "Barubaroi" and "Death-X" as early creature possibilities. Still, Kawakita felt it would be inappropriate for Godzilla to be killed by another monster or by man, and he struggled to come up with a dignified death for the beast. The filmmakers settled on the concept of "Godzilla syndrome," an overload within the nuclear furnace in Godzilla's

PREVIOUS SPREAD: As its body approaches total meltdown, Burning Godzilla arrives for the final confrontation with Destoroyah. ■ ABOVE: Director Takao Okawara (*left*) with Momoko Kochi (*right*), who returns as Emiko Yamane from 1954's *Godzilla*. These scenes take place in the same house where Yamane lived with her father back then, including the study, where a stegosaurus skeleton sits atop a desk. "While it may not be an exact replica of Dr. Yamane's study from the first Godzilla film, it was a meticulously crafted set," said director Okawara. "The dinosaur skeleton model, made by the props team, made a huge difference. I keep that skeleton model at home." ■ LEFT: This film breaks with a long-standing Toho tradition that Godzilla does not appear overseas (the lone exception is Godzilla's brief attack on New York City in *Destroy All Monsters*). Koichi Kawakita had first visited Hong Kong while working as an assistant SFX director on the Shaw Brothers Studio production *The Mighty Peking Man* (1977) and thought it would be an interesting contrast for Burning Godzilla to appear in the city's bright, neon-lit setting. In this behind-the-scenes shot, the sea boils around the monster's steaming body as it enters the Hong Kong harbor.

RIGHT: As the "Perfect Form" (fully evolved) Destoroyah flies away during the battle, its tail maintains a choke hold on Godzilla. Destoroyah transforms into multiple forms and sizes—notably its juvenile form (about 7 feet/2 m tall), aggregate form (about 131 feet/40 m tall), and finally, the perfect form (394 feet/120 m), which towers over Godzilla.

"I WONDERED WHAT 'MELTDOWN' REALLY MEANT. SO I CALLED THE KANSAI ELECTRIC POWER COMPANY AND SAID, 'I'D LIKE INFORMATION ABOUT A NUCLEAR REACTOR MELTDOWN.' THEY SAID, 'PLEASE HOLD,' AND I WAITED ON THE PHONE BUT EVENTUALLY HUNG UP (LAUGHS). I DIDN'T KNOW WHAT A MELTDOWN WAS, EVEN AFTER WATCHING *THE CHINA SYNDROME* (1979). I LATER UNDERSTOOD (FROM NEWS BROADCASTS) DURING THE FUKUSHIMA DAIICHI NUCLEAR DISASTER (IN 2011). BUT AT THE TIME, I WAS WRITING WITHOUT REALLY UNDERSTANDING. VISUALLY, THOUGH, I THOUGHT (SFX DIRECTOR) KAWAKITA EXPRESSED IT WELL."

—Kazuki Omori, screenwriter

body. Tomiyama recalled, "The idea was to end the series with a monster [linked to] the first *Godzilla*, created from the Oxygen Destroyer. Godzilla's death and the concept of a meltdown were decided first because they effectively linked Godzilla to nuclear themes, though the terms 'Godzilla syndrome' and 'Destoroyah' came later."

On January 17, 1995, the magnitude 7.2 Great Hanshin Earthquake wrecked Omori's condominium near Kobe, but he continued writing in the coming months, splitting his time between penning the Godzilla script and directing the drama *Emergency Call* (1995), shot on location in the Philippines. His fifty-page first draft, completed in March, differed from the eventual film in several ways. The story focused on the family of physicist Kensaku Ijuin (Takuro Tatsumi), who discovers the powerful element micro-oxygen, and his father, who had secretly developed a nuclear reactor during World War II; in this scenario, Little Godzilla mutates into Godzilla Junior upon exposure to the reactor. Emiko Yamane, the heroine of *Godzilla*, briefly appears, but as Omori developed a final draft, he shifted the focus from Ijuin to the Yamane family. While watching *Godzilla* for inspiration, Tomiyama and Omori suddenly

MELTDOWN
GODZILLA AS CATASTROPHIC NUCLEAR ACCIDENT

Throughout the production of *Godzilla vs. Destoroyah*, Godzilla's death scene weighed heavily on the mind of special effects director Koichi Kawakita. He interpreted the word "meltdown" quite literally and envisioned the monster's bones and tissue gradually disintegrating from the inside. Dramatic effect was more important than scientific accuracy.

Kawakita and his crew created the meltdown effect by combining shots of a wax-made Godzilla head with CG-generated full-body shots. Toho's CG capabilities were still in the experimental stage at that time, however, thus the sequence was largely created with practical effects, Kawakita noted.

At first, Godzilla's dorsal fins begin to melt. This was accomplished by creating a set of fins made of paraffin and melting them with heated plates. The disintegration of Godzilla's face was achieved with a dummy head made of ordinary paraffin mixed with beeswax and water wax to facilitate melting, and with joints in the neck and jaw that were manipulated by rotating screws. Heated iron plating was placed around the head, causing it to slowly melt. Assistant cameraman Fujio Okawa meticulously calculated the head's range of motion based on the time required for the paraffin to soften and the rotation speed of the screws, enabling him to stop-motion animate Godzilla four frames at a time during the shot. Finally, the entire body was melted via full CG—the skin withered away as the skeleton drooped, then the bones collapsed and vaporized.

When he watched the assembled sequence, Kawakita was not satisfied. The digital effects available in Japan at that time did not match his vision. "CG alone looks too artificial," he said. Kawakita compensated by combining computer graphics with practical methods. As Godzilla's radiation level soars, massive clouds of steam surround the monster. Godzilla lets out a final, agonizing growl as it fades away. Sparkling gold dust was composited into the entire sequence as well. "I thought Godzilla's demise would look more dramatic with internal luminescence as it melts," explained Kawakita.

TOP: Godzilla's body temperature reaches the threshold of meltdown as massive plumes of steam pour out of its body. ∎
ABOVE: Super XIII and the Maser cannons unleash their full arsenal of cryogenic weapons as Godzilla reaches meltdown.

realized that the character of Shinkichi, the Odo Island orphan adopted by Dr. Yamane, offered an interesting link between the present and the past. Reporter Yukari Yamane (Yoko Ishino) and young Godzilla expert Kenichi Yamane (Yasufumi Hayashi) would be Shinkichi's children; a conflict develops in the family as Kenichi advocates for the re-creation of the Oxygen Destroyer in order to kill Godzilla, while his aunt, Emiko—haunted by nightmare flashbacks of the device that killed both Godzilla and her fiancée forty-two years earlier—argues forcefully against it. (Though unstated, Emiko never married following the events of 1954; in honor of Serizawa's memory, she forsook her love for Ogata—notably, it's Serizawa's portrait on her shelf, not Ogata's.)

"[Writer] Kazuki Omori wanted me in the film no matter what," Kochi recalled. "I initially thought, *What, Gojira?* But when I read the screenplay, I realized it had a big antinuclear theme. Yes, the very first film did also, but when you're young, you tend not to be so aware. All I felt back then was how much I didn't want to be in a monster movie . . . It's a small role, but I wanted to tackle the part of this character who voices [an] antinuclear message."

Omori's May 1995 final script underwent significant changes even after filming began. Director Okawara—not Kawakita—added two effects sequences, one with the special forces battling crab Destoroyahs with

GODZILLA FACT: "There was no intention of featuring psychic Miki Saegusa throughout the Heisei series," said *Godzilla vs. Destoroyah* screenwriter Kazuki Omori. "But when she suddenly reappeared in the beginning of *Godzilla vs. King Ghidorah*, everyone took notice. When that happened, we knew we had something." Added producer Shogo Tomiyama, "Every Godzilla movie needs a hero and heroine. . . . But it is not so easy to find [actresses] who like Godzilla. Having Megumi Odaka appear as Miki Saegusa all this time was very valuable in terms of having a woman in a Godzilla movie." As the series progressed, Saegusa's bond with Godzilla and Godzilla Junior deepened, but she was often compelled to compromise her feelings in order to help defend Japan. Saegusa's story spans six films, concluding with her tears of grief as Godzilla Junior lay mortally wounded. And when Godzilla perishes, she bids an emotional goodbye: "My job is done now, Godzilla."

OPPOSITE, MIDDLE ROW: In addition to passing the torch from Godzilla to Godzilla Junior, the film also sees G-Force psychic Miki Saegusa (Megumi Odaka, *left*) beginning to lose her powers and ceding her role to American-trained ESP expert and paleontologist Meru Ozawa (Sayaka Osawa, *right*, one of the Cosmos in *Godzilla vs. Mothra*). Saegusa at first resists using Godzilla Junior as Destoroyah-bait, but Ozawa insists that Earth's survival hangs in the balance. The two psychics join forces to divert the young kaiju from returning to its native habitat in the Bering Sea and lure it to Tokyo instead. ■ Although it is not mentioned, the Super XIII's "elite pilot" was written to be Major Sho Kuroki, the military hero of *Godzilla vs. Biollante*. When actor Masanobu Takashima was unavailable to reprise the role, his older brother, Masahiro (of *Godzilla vs. Mechagodzilla II*), stepped in. "I had hoped that Masanobu would play the role, but our schedules didn't match up," said director Takao Okawara. "However, it turned out well for Masahiro. It was like a gift for him. He even asked, 'Is it OK for me to play such a good role with just two or three days of filming?' His line, 'Our budget for next year will be zero . . . that is, if there is a next year,' was a unique line that only [screenwriter] Omori could have come up with." ■ (*left to right*) Broadcast journalist Yukari Yamane (Yoko Ishino), her younger brother and wunderkind college student (and self-anointed Godzilla expert), Kenichi Yamane (Yasufumi Hayashi), and physicist Dr. Kensaku Ijuin (Takuro Tatsumi, *right*). Ijuin follows in Dr. Serizawa's footsteps, having discovered micro-oxygen, a powerful substance with dangerous potential. ■ **ABOVE RIGHT:** The swarm of juvenile Destoroyahs combine to form the gigantic aggregate-form Destoroyah in front of Ariake Coliseum. ■ **RIGHT:** Godzilla and Godzilla Junior come face to face at Haneda International Airport. Because of the great size difference between Godzilla and its adopted kin, Godzilla Junior is portrayed with a rod puppet rather than an actor in a suit for this scene, enabling both creatures to appear in the same frame.

GODZILLA FACT: In 1917, Japanese scientists founded RIKEN—the Institute of Physical and Chemical Research, to compete with Western organizations such as the Rockefeller Institute. Its mission was to advance science in society, but during World War II, at the direction of the military, RIKEN secretly began developing an apparatus for enriching weapons-grade uranium. "The backstory we had in mind is that Japan lost the war in 1945, and the GHQ [occupation authorities] confiscated a cyclotron, a nuclear weapons research device at the RIKEN institute," said special effects director Koichi Kawakita. "They dumped it in Tokyo Bay in November 1945. This is a true story. I thought that if there was residual radioactivity in the cyclotron when it was dumped, it would affect the crustaceans underground and create a monster." Though unmentioned, this history provides a rich background for *Godzilla vs. Destoroyah*.

---

flamethrowers and another wherein a monster traps the heroine, Yukari, in a car—scenes reminiscent of *Aliens* (1986) and *Jurassic Park* (1993), respectively. ("If the main characters don't get involved in the action, they'll seem detached," Okawara reasoned.) Kawakita embellished the final battle, inserting one scene wherein Destoroyah subdivides into an army of smaller creatures and another in which—at the long-awaited moment when Godzilla is reunited with its wandering adopted kid—Destoroyah snatches Godzilla Junior and drops the youth from a great height, causing it fatal injuries.

A strange tension reportedly hung over the special effects team, many of whom felt sentimental, perhaps even guilty, about burying Godzilla with their own hands. "It was pitiful," remembered crew member Masahiko Shiraishi. "We couldn't help but feel Godzilla's death approaching. It created a joyless atmosphere on set." Even Kawakita's demeanor seemed off; he likely felt the challenges posed both by Daiei Film's recent *Gamera: Guardian of the Universe* (1995), which was praised for innovative effects despite a low budget, and the forthcoming big-budget Hollywood Godzilla film. Moreover, the special effects scenes were particularly difficult to shoot. The final battle between Godzilla and Destoroyah was significantly modified from the script, causing delays; scenes were intermittently filmed over a month and half, from mid-August through early October, and involved monster suits, puppets, and radio-controlled models of Destoroyah's various forms. Kenpachiro Satsuma, in his final turn as Godzilla, labored even harder than usual. "The glowing red Godzilla suit had nearly a thousand LED lights installed, and it required dragging an incredible bundle of wires," Satsuma recalled. "My first Godzilla suit [in 1984] was heavy, but this one weighed 287 pounds [130 kg]."

The action begins with Burning Godzilla's sudden and stunning appearance in Hong Kong, destroying the shoreline with its red spiral heat ray (intensely overheated, Godzilla does not emit its standard-issue ray at any time). As Godzilla vents its fury, composer Akira Ifukube melds Godzilla's traditional theme with a new, guttural horror motif featuring kettle drums and low brass. Vintage katakana characters spelling "Godzilla" appear, giving way to an animated representation of the Oxygen Destroyer, then the main *Godzilla vs. Destoroyah* title card appears. With a flourish of harp, Ifukube transitions to his brash, atonal Destoroyah theme, the music and images tying together decades of history. Ifukube mixes new and familiar themes throughout the film, but it is in the final moments, as Godzilla fades away, that the maestro transcends the visuals with great emotional power. Sound effects and dialogue are silenced; Ifukube's requiem rises, and the human characters soberly watch Godzilla—and, seemingly, their world—coming to an end. "The choral piece during Godzilla's meltdown is not so much about mourning Godzilla's death," Ifukube said. "The intention was to encourage a little contemplation about the consequences of [its] death . . . to make people think about how human actions led to this outcome."

"The [requiem] was one of the most difficult pieces I have ever had to compose. It was as if I was composing the theme for my own death. When Godzilla was born, a phase of my life began. Now Godzilla is gone, and that phase is over. It was very emotional."

ABOVE: Godzilla Junior, its whereabouts unknown since the sinking of Birth Island, finally resurfaces. ■ BELOW, LEFT TO RIGHT: Destoroyah and Godzilla Junior fight in the city. Although the young kaiju at first appears outsized and outmatched, Godzilla Junior fights bravely and succeeds in fending off the deadly crustacean. ■ The aggregate form Destoroyah (Eiichi Yanagida) pins Godzilla Junior (Hurricane Ryu) down and prepares to strike a fatal blow by injecting the young monster with deadly micro-oxygen. ■ A bird's-eye view of the set. Above, Super XIII circles as its crew prepares to unleash the flying tank's cryogenic weapons on Godzilla. Below, Godzilla approaches the dying Godzilla Junior.

CLOCKWISE FROM ABOVE: Godzilla (Kenpachiro Satsuma) and the gargoyle-like Destoroyah (Ryo Hariya) face off in a final battle near the Tokyo International Exhibition Center (aka Tokyo Big Sight). ▪ In the heat of the final battle, the injured Destoroyah suddenly splits into an army of crab monsters that attack Godzilla, an effect created with roughly 2-foot- (.6-m-) tall models. Due to the short production schedule, screenwriter Kazuki Omori handed off his final-draft script to the filmmaking team and said, "Feel free to make changes." This scene was among numerous additions without Omori's input. "When I watched the completed film for the first time, I wondered, *Was this in the script?*" Omori recalled. "Some parts were unclear. . . . When the small Destoroyahs come out in a flurry—that would have been better off omitted, I think. Those parts were more [SFX director] Kawakita's excesses [*laughs*]." ▪ Exposed to a massive amount of radiation released by Godzilla's meltdown, Godzilla Junior is resurrected as the new Godzilla. "I still regret not being able to portray the new Godzilla in the last scene," said suit actor Hurricane Ryu. "The Godzilla Junior suit was designed to have the dorsal fins of Godzilla attached to its back, and initially I was supposed to wear it, but I wasn't called [in] for it." The honor of playing Godzilla in this historic final scene was understandably reserved for Satsuma. As Godzilla roars, Satsuma's long run as king of the monsters concludes.

PUBLICITY MONSTER

Kawakita pushed for *Godzilla Dies* as the film's title. "I felt this was different from anything seen before, and it would lead to big audience numbers," he said. "But unfortunately, we couldn't use that title. It was one of the big regrets of my career." Still, "Godzilla dies" was featured more prominently than the actual title in the long and unusually secretive publicity campaign. The cause of Godzilla's death was kept under wraps, as was the existence of Godzilla Junior, to avoid spoiling the surprise ending (Junior did, however, inadvertently appear on an early prerelease poster). Theaters held a hundred-day countdown to the film's release. Press conferences were kept to a minimum, and there were just two advance screenings. A bronze statue of Godzilla was unveiled in Hibiya, and in Makuhari, a funeral was held for Godzilla, all of which built anticipation and hype. *Destoroyah* was the top grossing domestic film in Japan for 1996, earning ¥2 billion.

Certain historical chapters were closing. This would be the final Godzilla film credited to any of the monster's four original creators; executive producer Tanaka would die on April 2, 1997, aged eighty-six, leaving a tremendous cinematic legacy. And it was Ifukube's last film score, though his music would continue to be an important part of future Godzilla movies.

As Godzilla meets its end, a dense fog shrouds the city. But the radiation quickly dissipates, and the camera moves through the mist to reveal Godzilla Junior has risen—Godzilla lives again. Kawakita suggested that this dramatic conclusion take place after the film's end credits, a nostalgic highlight reel from Godzilla's history set to an adaptation of Ifukube's *Symphonic Fantasia* suite. But, as director Okawara recalled, "Since some people leave the theater when the credits begin to roll, we decided against it."

LEFT: Destoroyah administers its horn katana slash attack, aka "Variable Slicer," against Godzilla.

PRODUCTION DESIGN: HEISEI SERIES

リトルから脱皮するジュニアゴジラ

ABOVE LEFT: Design sketch of Baby Godzilla from *Godzilla vs. Mechagodzilla II* by Shinji Nishikawa. ◼ **LEFT:** Image from an early story version of *Godzilla vs. Destoroyah*: Little Godzilla sheds its skin, evolving into Godzilla Junior. Art by Minoru Yoshida. ◼ **OPPOSITE:** Image board of an early concept from *Godzilla vs. Destoroyah*, with Godzilla facing the enormous Barubaroi. When the story was changed to feature Destoroyah, the basic image of Barubaroi was retained in the aggregate form of Destoroyah, although the monster's size was scaled down to match that of Godzilla Junior. Art by Yoshida.

ゴジラと戦う　バルバロイ成体

TYPE-A

THREE

NEW BEGINNINGS: 1999 TO 2004

(GOJIRA NISEN: MIRENIAMU)
RELEASED: DECEMBER 11, 1999 (JAPAN)

GODZILLA 2000: MILLENNIUM

A lighthouse beacon scans the waters off eastern Hokkaido. BOOM! The lighthouse is shaken by a thunderous jolt, quickly followed by another. The keeper peers out the window and looks straight into the face of Godzilla! At the same time, members of the Godzilla Prediction Network (GPN) speed toward the scene in a Toyota MPV outfitted with tracking devices. As they near the beach, the vehicle screeches to a halt where the road has been sheared away. Searchlights pierce the darkness and reveal Godzilla looming above! Curious, Godzilla bends down to inspect the little car, the monster's breath fogging the windshield. Camera flashbulbs anger the beast. Godzilla roars mightily and stomps forward, its giant feet narrowly missing the fleeing car. The ensuing chase leads Godzilla to the city of Nemuro, where the monster tramples the town and destroys the local electrical power plant.

When Hollywood introduced a new and different take on Godzilla in 1998, some of the monster's creators in Japan feared the iconic, traditional image of Toho's Godzilla might be supplanted by an impostor. "The first Hollywood version was interesting as a movie, but there was a strong feeling that it was not [the true] Godzilla," said producer Shogo Tomiyama. Whereas Hollywood's Godzilla represented a threat to human survival, the Japanese Godzilla had always been something more complex—a creature beyond human understanding, Tomiyama believed. "I was concerned that if we did not resume making

"IF IT WERE UP TO ME, I WOULD HAVE GONE HARDER WITH GODZILLA. I COULD NOT DO A LOT OF THINGS I WANTED TO DO BECAUSE IT WAS A FAMILY FILM. GODZILLA (IS) DEFINITELY NOT SUPPOSED TO KILL ANYONE. HE DESTROYS THE SCENERY AS ALWAYS, BUT THERE COULDN'T BE ANY ACTUAL (GRAPHIC) VIOLENCE. . . . WHEN SOMETHING LIKE GODZILLA BECOMES MORE AND MORE POPULAR, IT HAS TO BE ACCEPTABLE FOR EVERYONE."

—Hiroshi Kashiwabara, screenwriter

Godzilla movies, the world would believe that that other character was Godzilla. I felt the real Godzilla should return as soon as possible."

Godzilla 2000: Millennium is yet another reset for the monster. Although director Takao Okawara and cowriters Hiroshi Kashiwabara and Wataru Mimura were veterans of the Heisei series, the look and feel of this film is considerably different, even as it honors the past. Godzilla itself receives a noticeable redesign: its height is reduced by nearly half, its skin texture is rougher, its dorsals are huge and pinkish in color, its heat ray is now a fiery orange rather than the customary bluish white—and for the first time ever, the monster is green, not gray or black. This is also the first Godzilla movie shot in the 2.35:1 widescreen format since *Terror of Mechagodzilla*. There is unprecedented use of CG visual effects to complement the traditional practical methods, and Godzilla is filmed from interesting new angles and in exciting new situations. (Ironically, some of these—Godzilla dropping a boat, chasing a car, breathing and roaring directly into the camera, getting up close to humans, and walking past a rooftop—mirror the 1998 Hollywood movie.)

Recent changes within the structure of Toho also dictated new approaches behind the scenes. Beginning with this film, the Godzilla series would be produced in a manner closer to a Hollywood-style system, with one director in charge and a more streamlined production management structure. In relaunching the series, producer Shogo Tomiyama envisioned a new way forward, a trilogy in which each film would serve as an original standalone story made by a different filmmaking team to generate fresh ideas. "I wanted the challenge of maximizing Godzilla's potential for the future with [a new] director and other staff [for each film]," he said. "We thought about this [at] an early stage."

PAGES 288–289: As Godzilla approaches Admiral Tachibana's battleship in the harbor, Mothra—its wings still burning from Godzilla's attack—attempts to ambush the monster from behind in this scene from *Godzilla, Mothra and King Ghidorah: Giant Monsters All-Out Attack.*
■ **PREVIOUS SPREAD:** The showdown between Orga (Makoto Ito) and Godzilla (Tsutomu Kitagawa) in Tokyo.
■ **BOTTOM LEFT:** "The Heisei Godzilla by SFX director [Koichi] Kawakita had a black body with whitish fins," creature designer Shinichi Wakasa said. "They asked me to make it completely different; a new Godzilla for the new century. Even so, there is still the familiar image that everyone knows, so I tried to create a different Godzilla without changing the basics. . . . Godzilla is an evolved dinosaur form; it's reptilian, so I added elements of reptiles and lizards. Rather than a real life-form, it is more symbolic."

ABOVE: (*left to right*) Shiro Miyasaka (Shiro Sano), Yuji Shinoda (Takehiro Murata), Io (Mayu Suzuki, *front*), and Yuki (Naomi Nishida) watch from a rooftop as Godzilla goes berserk at the film's conclusion. ■ RIGHT: After temporarily disabling Godzilla and absorbing some of the monster's DNA, the aliens aboard the UFO briefly take the collective form of a silvery, amorphous creature called the Millennian. From this transitional stage, the aliens quickly evolve into the giant, hideous, Godzilla-like life-form Orga. ■ BOTTOM RIGHT: Orga bites Godzilla and attempts to drain the monster's genetic material.

Even so, the role of special effects director remained significant. First-time SFX director Kenji Suzuki brought many creative ideas to the film, seeking to better integrate the dramatic scenes with the monster action. "[Suzuki] had been an assistant director under Koichi Kawakita," said director Okawara. "By comparison, he was much easier to talk to. Kawakita never liked to discuss the drama, he just thought his part was most important—that was his pride. Suzuki would meet with me [often] to discuss the drama. When we started shooting, we couldn't talk often, so we used storyboards instead to keep each other updated."

Okawara and Suzuki's intent to gently break the mold is evident throughout. When Godzilla makes landfall near Tokai, it is confronted by a corps of Type 90 tanks (using actual military hardware, owing to renewed cooperation between the studio and the JSDF). Godzilla is mighty but vulnerable: the military's Full Metal missiles seriously injure the monster, and Godzilla retaliates by unleashing its new heat ray for the first time—a fresh take on a familiar sight, with the energy and heat building to

"YOU REALLY THINK YOU CAN KILL GODZILLA?"

—Yuji Shinoda (Takehiro Murata)

a crescendo in Godzilla's mouth before the iconic blast. "We reduced the number of [heat ray] scenes to make it more effective and added [anticipation] before each shot," said Suzuki. A *Top Gun*–like air-strike on Godzilla by a squadron of F-15J fighters (rendered via CG rather than practical models) adds to the excitement.

Entering the Shinjuku area to confront its opponent, a saucerlike alien villain, Godzilla follows the historic Koshu Kaido road and avoids the giant skyscrapers that would have towered above its head. Reducing Godzilla's size to 180 feet (55 m) and returning the miniatures to traditional ⅕₅ scale led to greater detail even as the miniature sets were smaller overall. Green-screen compositing was employed to situate Godzilla and the miniatures into real-life footage of Tokyo. Rather than looming over buildings, this smaller Godzilla walks through and between the steel canyons, kicking aside cars and making buildings tremble with each step. Because of this, Godzilla becomes part of the city in ways not seen since 1954—one particular shot of the monster walking past a Konica neon sign is particularly striking—even if the effect is not always totally convincing.

The story does not specifically reference events from the Showa or Heisei eras but functions as a sequel nonetheless. Godzilla is essentially a recurrent extreme weather event, like a typhoon. No-nonsense scientist Yuji Shinoda (Heisei series veteran Takehiro Murata) leads a freelance team dedicated to tracking and studying Godzilla and is joined by his precocious young daughter, Io (Mayu Suzuki), and flustered photojournalist Yuki (Naomi Nishida). Shinoda's rival and ex-colleague is Mitsuo Katagiri (Hiroshi Abe), head of the Crisis Control Intelligence Agency, a man hell-bent on killing Godzilla and ending its reign of destruction. Plot points echo earlier films: Shinoda discovers that Godzilla's cells contain a regenerative property—"Organizer G1"—which enables the monster to miraculously heal from mortal wounds. Godzilla is driven to feed not only on reactors but to also attack power plants, symbols of Japan's rampant growth. The appearance of a long-dormant space monster—which hacks into Japan's cyber network to obtain data for its conquest of Earth—shifts the government's focus, and Godzilla, after suffering a beating by the mysterious new threat, now wants payback. "There's only one thing on Godzilla's mind right now: revenge," says Shinoda.

Godzilla 2000: Millennium marks the debut of Godzilla suit actor Tsutomu "Tom" Kitagawa, who would portray the monster in five of the six Millennium series films. "I wanted to express a different color

GODZILLA FACT: This film was the first in the series to receive wide theatrical distribution in the United States since New World's *Godzilla 1985*. TriStar Pictures produced an English-dubbed version and released it in theaters on August 18, 2000, under the shortened title *Godzilla 2000*. The American version featured a number of editorial changes, including the deletion and trimming of scenes, replacement of parts of composer Takayuki Hattori's score, and added comedic dialogue. The producers of this version reached out to director Takao Okawara for input. "It was unusual," Okawara said. "There were consultations with me, including about scene replacements and deletions." The US version nevertheless has a head-scratcher outro, with Yuki wondering, "Why does [Godzilla] keep protecting us?" just as the monster lights Tokyo on fire, set to an inserted Akira Ifukube theme from *Ghidorah, the Three-Headed Monster*. "The ? End" inexplicably appears on-screen—a riff on an old genre trope seen in classic horror movies like *The Blob* (1958).

---

of Godzilla," Kitagawa said. "I didn't want to just copy [Kenpachiro] Satsuma's movements, I wanted to make a completely new creature." This being Kitagawa's rookie turn as Godzilla, he would struggle with the limits of the suit just as his predecessors did, yet SFX director Suzuki praised his performance. The new Godzilla is more expressive—with its bigger eyes and mouth, it exudes anger, confusion, and even fear in its confrontation with the alien. "It was difficult to determine how far we could go" with Godzilla's emotions, said Suzuki. "Godzilla's presence carries the weight of its history, and I felt straying too far from that wouldn't be right. We couldn't risk making the character too lighthearted."

The film earned a respectable ¥1.65 billion, placing sixth at the domestic box office, though well behind the chart-topping *Pokemon the Movie 2000*, which earned more than ¥4.8 billion as "Pokemania" crested. Nevertheless, the rebooted Godzilla series would continue, along with an ongoing influx of new talent and ideas.

BELOW: Another angle of the final face-off between Orga (Makoto Ito) and Godzilla (Tsutomu Kitagawa). The miniature sets for *Godzilla 2000: Millennium* are smaller than those of the Heisei series. SFX director Kenji Suzuki's team created about fifty model structures and rearranged them in different, smaller setups and utilized forced perspective to create a sense of depth and scale, a novel approach pioneered by SFX director Shinji Higuchi on the recent *Gamera* trilogy (1995–99) from Daiei Film. ■ **OPPOSITE TOP:** Seeking to use Godzilla as a genetic host for its conquest of Earth, the alien life-form Orga attempts to swallow Godzilla whole at the climax of the monster battle. Orga begins to assimilate Godzilla, growing to gigantic size and sprouting Godzilla-like dorsal plates on its back. But Godzilla seems to sense the aliens' plan; once inside Orga's maw, Godzilla's body begins to glow with heat and energy, then it releases an explosive blast of its heat ray that blows Orga's head off. ■ **OPPOSITE BOTTOM:** After Godzilla has vanquished Orga and—in an atypical monster-versus-man interaction—done away with its nemesis Katagiri, the movie ends with Godzilla dramatically incinerating entire swaths of Tokyo. "Godzilla is an animal and has a natural desire to break things," said cowriter Hiroshi Kashiwabara.

(GOJIRA TAI MEGAGIRASU: JI SHOMETSU SAKUSEN /
GODZILLA VS. MEGAGUIRUS: G ANNIHILATION STRATEGY)
RELEASED: DECEMBER 16, 2000 (JAPAN)

GODZILLA VS. MEGAGUIRUS

Satellite images detect Godzilla battling an insectoid creature in the Pacific Ocean. Major Kiriko Tsujimori, captain of the G-Grasper anti-Godzilla unit, rushes to the scene with her crew in the Griffon VTOL fighter aircraft. They find a dead Meganula—a giant prehistoric dragonfly—floating there; while they extract tissue samples from the carcass, the sea roils and Godzilla's fins breach the surface, throwing Tsujimori from her raft. Tsujimori climbs onto Godzilla's rugged dorsals, briefly riding the monster like a huge reptilian watercraft . . .

There is a fresh, energetic feeling in *Godzilla vs. Megaguirus*, a one-off reboot set within an alternate timeline—a multiverse of sorts—forsaking continuity with previous films except for the original *Godzilla*. In a break with tradition, the film is largely propelled by the talents of women. Composer Michiru Oshima makes her series debut and delivers the most commanding Godzilla soundtrack in years. For the first time, a female actor from the Showa era returns, as Yuriko Hoshi (of *Mothra vs. Godzilla* and *Ghidorah*) plays a high-ranking scientist, Dr. Yoshino Yoshizawa. Finally, Misato Tanaka stars as Tsujimori, a bona fide action heroine and the first person ever to stand on Godzilla's back. Still, there is a back-to-basics feel; instead of giant robots or make-believe weapons, the effort to stop Godzilla is a science-fiction-style scenario involving misguided technology that unleashes a second monster—with deadly results.

"EVERYONE HAS DEEP AFFECTION FOR GODZILLA, DON'T THEY?
AND COMPARED TO THE AMERICAN GODZILLA, THE JAPANESE
GODZILLA DEFINITELY HAS MORE CHARM. . . . IT'S DIFFERENT
FROM THE GODZILLA OF (THE SHOWA ERA), BUT THAT CUTENESS,
THAT ENDEARING SOMETHING, REMAINS THE SAME. GODZILLA
TRULY IS AN ETERNAL IDOL."

—Yuriko Hoshi (Dr. Yoshino Yoshizawa)

PREVIOUS SPREAD: The film opens with a faux vintage Nichiei News reel that re-creates scenes from the original *Godzilla* using the updated Godzilla suit. ■ ABOVE: A swarm of Godzilla attraction (non-filming) suits head out of Toho Studios' main gate to kick off the "Godzilla Everywhere" publicity campaign. ■ LEFT: Godzilla's appearance is virtually unchanged since *Godzilla 2000: Millennium*, though this story takes place in a different reality. ■ OPPOSITE, CLOCKWISE FROM TOP LEFT: Director Masaaki Tezuka with Misato Tanaka as the captain of the G-Graspers, Major Kiriko Tsujimori. ■ (*left to right*) Free-spirited inventor Hajime Kudo (Shosuke Tanihara), an expert in miniaturization hired by the G-Graspers to help complete the Dimension Tide black hole gun; Dr. Yoshino Yoshizawa (Yuriko Hoshi), a physicist with the Special G Countermeasures science team; and Motohiko Sugiura (Masato Ibu), director of the G-Graspers project. ■ Attaching the Meganula—inspired by ancient dragonflies—to the Godzilla suit. "The dragonflies were handmade pieces, which we stuck to Godzilla's body," said SFX director Kenji Suzuki. "They were very light. You could carry about twenty of them in one hand."

Megaguirus bears the stamp of first-time filmmaker Masaaki Tezuka, who began working as an assistant director in the late 1970s and apprenticed under Kon Ichikawa on numerous films, including *The Makioka Sisters* (1983) and a color remake of *The Burmese Harp* (1985). Tezuka was an assistant on *Godzilla vs. Mothra* and *Godzilla vs. Mechagodzilla II;* known for his creative suggestions, he designed the G-Force uniforms (based on US military garb) for *Mechagodzilla II*. "I felt exhilarated to finally participate in Godzilla films, which I loved since childhood," Tezuka said. "At that time, I was offered a job with Toho. I discussed it with my wife and decided to accept." The female perspective was important to Tezuka—even when offered the opportunity to direct *Godzilla vs. Megaguirus*, he consulted his wife before accepting. And he brought very clear ideas for the film to the studio: "The protagonist had to be a woman, we would [tell the story] without randomly introducing superweapons, and there would be logical reasons for the monsters to appear," he said. "They agreed to [all] my conditions."

Japan's controversial reliance on nuclear energy to power its postwar recovery provides the thematic backdrop. In a unique creative stroke, the film opens with a black-and-white newsreel restaging of Godzilla's first attack on Tokyo, with the updated monster (using the *Godzilla 2000: Millennium* suit) standing in for the original Godzilla via shot-for-shot reenactments and digital compositing into vintage footage. Within the film's historical revisionism, Godzilla did not die in 1954; after disappearing for twelve years, it resur-faces in 1966 to feed on radiation from the Tokai Nuclear Power Plant, Japan's first commercial reactor. Following the ensuing disaster, Japan abandons its nuclear power program to avoid attracting Godzilla, but the demands of economic growth surpass what hydroelectric, solar, and wind power provide, and in 1996, the government announces a plasma fusion energy system generating clean, limitless power. Godzilla suddenly reappears and attacks Osaka, where the project is being developed (though not stated outright, plasma fusion can produce gamma radiation, which lured the monster ashore); as a result of Godzilla's wave of destruction, the plasma project is likewise canceled.

A MONSTER REPRISAL

For Tsujimori, the fight against Godzilla is personal. When the monster attacks Osaka, she is a greenhorn member of a Japanese Self-Defense Forces (JSDF) commando team battling Godzilla. Tsujimori ignores orders to fall back and fires off one last rocket shot against the monster, and her commanding officer is killed by falling debris knocked loose by Godzilla. She blames herself, but blames Godzilla more; swearing revenge, she carries her superior's dog tags with her as a reminder of her purpose. Five years later,

Tsujimori is a fearless fighter with the JSDF's G-Grasper unit, but her drive for payback blinds her to the catastrophic danger of the Dimension Tide, a satellite-mounted weapon that creates a "miniaturized black hole" capable of transporting Godzilla to another realm. When the system is test-fired, it creates a wormhole that a prehistoric insect passes through, leading to the rise of Megaguirus.

"I thought I was too weak a type for this role; I was thin and not muscular, but I started going to the gym to do weight training," said Tanaka, then a twenty-year-old actress and former Toho Cinderella, and star of *Aguri* (1997), a soap opera–like program. The JSDF has long had a gender gap within its ranks (women would not serve on fighters, tanks, and submarines until starting in 2015), and Tanaka hoped to inspire change. "I didn't know anything about Godzilla; those films were more of a boys' thing. . . . I wanted to provide someone for girls to identify with. There weren't many female leaders in [Japanese] society at that time, so for a woman to appear in a leadership role, I thought it could have a positive impact on society."

BRIGHT NOTES
"I was truly moved when I heard the new Godzilla theme," said Tezuka. "I was overwhelmed by the power of the live orchestra. We made the right choice in asking Michiro Oshima to write the music." During early planning, a Toho official had suggested scoring the film using library recordings of Akira Ifukube's

BELOW: Megaguirus is born after the dragonflies siphon Godzilla's energy and return it to their nest. "I imagined that among the many eggs underwater in Shibuya, only one was chosen to become Megaguirus," said SFX director Kenji Suzuki. "The rest serve as worker bees, so to speak, to bring about the emergence of Megaguirus. I felt the egg that becomes Megaguirus is like a queen bee, though it's explained differently in the actual film. But producer [Shogo] Tomiyama felt it wouldn't work if it were female. . . . Basically, to appear stronger, it's more like a king than a queen."

GODZILLA FACT: The scene where Kiriko Tsujimori (Misato Tanaka) swims onto Godzilla's back was partly filmed on location in the ocean. "At first there were boats crowded around me, and everyone was saying it was safe because they were nearby, but when we started shooting, they drifted farther and farther away," said Tanaka. "I thought, *I'm gonna die out here!*" Years later, people still come up to me and say I was the first person who ever touched Godzilla."

themes à la *Godzilla vs. Gigan*. The idea was rejected and a search for a new composer began. After hearing Oshima's theme for the television drama *Shomuni* (*Power Office Girls*, 1998), "I was thrilled," Tezuka recalled. "I said, 'This is the one!'"

An award-winning composer for film, television, and anime, Oshima was surprisingly unfamiliar with the kaiju genre. Nevertheless, her original Godzilla theme is a majestic motif for the King of the Monsters, with large kettle drums representing Godzilla's footsteps and a foreboding, low-register melody. Her music for Megaguirus's various stages (egg, dragonfly nymph, insect, and king) escalates from a repetitive high-pitched pattern representing the cries of the dragonflies (inspired by Bernard Herrmann's score for 1960's *Psycho*) to a heavier, darker theme for the king. In the final battle, Oshima shifts from traditional marches and monster motifs to a rollicking adventure theme with an ethnic flair, driven by drums and horns.

"I wasn't very interested in Godzilla when I was a child," Oshima said. "I wasn't familiar with the music except for the very famous Ifukube 'dun-dun-dun' theme. . . . Director Tezuka said Godzilla was going to be big and scary in this film, more like a bad guy than a hero. He told me how large and heavy Godzilla would be so I could have an idea how to express that. . . . He pretty much just left it all up to me. I had [complete] freedom."

NEW KAIJU VIEWS

Special effects director Kenji Suzuki continues to experiment with new ideas. Views of Godzilla swimming below and above the surface, achieved with both CG and physical suits, surpass all of Toho's prior depictions of Godzilla in the ocean depths. After Megaguirus's eggs clog the storm drain system, scenes of Shibuya underwater evoke the sci-fi classic *Submersion of Japan* (1973) and incorporate CG, models, and live-action sets. Godzilla's confrontation with a swarm of dragonflies on Kiganjima is an inspired, precisely choreographed suite of digital, practical, and suitmation effects; Godzilla (Tsutomu Kitagawa) evinces

ABOVE: Setting up a shot for the final battle. ■ **TOP RIGHT:** Megaguirus prepares to attack Godzilla with its stinger.

"I LIKE WAR MOVIES, AND GODZILLA MOVIES ARE A TYPE OF WAR MOVIE. THE SELF-DEFENSE FORCES ARE THE ONLY THING THAT CAN FIGHT AGAINST GODZILLA IN JAPAN, UNLESS WE WERE TO ASK THE UNITED STATES FOR HELP."

—Hiroshi Kashiwabara, co-screenwriter

GODZILLA FACT: The kaiju Megaguirus, and the scene in which its larva attacks a young couple, are inspired by Meganulon, a prehistoric, man-eating insect featured in *Rodan* (1956). "In *Rodan*, there were tunnels, and it was dark and scary," said cowriter Hiroshi Kashiwabara. "I wanted to use that kind of concept and have the Meganulons kill people. Things were toned down during the Heisei series, but I challenged that and pushed the envelope. Those grotesque things were memorable when I was a kid."

ABOVE: SFX director Kenji Suzuki supervises the modeling staff as they set up the final confrontation between Godzilla and Megaguirus. ■ **LEFT:** For close-ups during its fight against Godzilla, an adult Megaguirus half-suit was created. SFX director Suzuki explains, "It's a flying creature, so only the claws and the face move, but in the clashes with Godzilla, there are actions like punching. I thought it would be difficult without a person inside to give it movement. So we had a suit made."

ABOVE: Godzilla uses its tail to snag Megaguirus. ■ RIGHT: "[SFX director Kenji Suzuki] aimed for unusual or even comical movements by Godzilla in the final battle," said cinematographer Kenichi Eguchi. "I didn't intend to shoot it that way, but [during] editing, I noticed that he had taken quite a bold approach." Added Suzuki, "I wanted the battle to be fast-paced so I tried extreme measures like speeding up and slowing down the action to add contrast. . . . I've been editing with Avid [Media Composer] since last year, and it offers a lot of options for such manipulations." ■ BOTTOM LEFT: "I wanted a human character to directly challenge Godzilla," said co-screenwriter Hiroshi Kashiwabara. "I wrote the scene without holding back, thinking, *Let's see how they bring this to life on set.* It was more interesting that way." Godzilla's dorsal fins were one of the biggest and most expensive props ever created for a Godzilla movie. ■ BOTTOM RIGHT: Godzilla fires its heat ray at the swarm of attacking Meganula.

anger, frustration, and pain as it bites, claws, swipes, and smashes at the impossible foes sucking away the monster's energy. In the final showdown at the Tokyo waterfront, much of the destruction Godzilla causes happens when it fires its heat ray at Megaguirus and misses, hitting buildings instead. Some action sequences are partly executed with a strange frame-removal effect, intermittently rendering the action via a series of weird flipbook-like freeze-frames.

After killing Megaguirus, Godzilla trashes the Bureau of Science and Technology, attracted to a plasma energy lab secretly developed by Motohiko Sugiura (Masato Ibu), the fatherly head of the G-Graspers unit who is revealed to be a corrupt bureaucrat. Infuriated at Sugiura's duplicity, Tsujimori decks him, then risks her life to help the faltering black hole gun make Godzilla disappear. The exciting finish is an uncommon example of a protagonist directly confronting Godzilla. ("What I disliked most was a climax where humans become bystanders," said Tezuka.) She ejects from the Griffon aircraft just before it smashes into Godzilla, but not before placing her fallen commander's dog tags on the control panel, achieving closure for herself and symbolically giving her mentor the honor of delivering the coup de grâce. The anti-Godzilla plan appears to succeed—a rare feat—but in the series' first-ever post-credits scene, Godzilla clearly hasn't gone anywhere.

During a box office season that saw Hayao Miyazaki's *Spirited Away* (2001) gross a then-record ¥31 billion, *Godzilla vs. Megaguirus* underperformed compared to previous entries, earning ¥1.2 billion and ranking thirteenth among domestic films for the year. The Millennium trilogy would continue with yet another hard reset.

(GOJIRA, MOSURA, KINGU GIDORA: DAIKAIJU SOKOGEKI)
aka GMK
RELEASED: DECEMBER 15, 2001 (JAPAN)

GODZILLA, MOTHRA AND KING GHIDORAH: GIANT MONSTERS ALL-OUT ATTACK

For the first time since 1954, Godzilla emerges from the sea to attack Japan, and its destructive fury is devastating. Reanimated by the restless souls of those who died in the Pacific War, Godzilla is a malevolent spirit made flesh, venting its psychic wrath upon present-day Japan for having forsaken the nation's tragic war history. Can the mythical guardian monsters of Yamato—Ghidorah, Mothra, and Baragon—save Japan from devastation?

Godzilla is reimagined as a dark specter bringing destruction and death in *Godzilla, Mothra and King Ghidorah: Giant Monsters All-Out Attack,* a movie commonly referred to as *GMK* for short. Like *Megaguirus,* this one-off story takes place in a different reality imagined by a filmmaker with a unique interpretation of the monster. "It's as if Godzilla is carrying the shadow of the war, and of the atomic bombings," said director Shusuke Kaneko. "A creature that

"I WANTED TO PORTRAY GODZILLA AS THE STRONGEST VILLAIN OF ALL, JUST LIKE KING GHIDORAH WAS PORTRAYED BACK IN THE 1960S. IN MY MIND, THE GODZILLA OF *GMK* IS THE KING GHIDORAH OF *GHIDORAH, THE THREE-HEADED MONSTER*."

—Shusuke Kaneko, director

doesn't die even if it's hit by bullets ultimately resembles a ghost. I wanted to try doing Godzilla as a ghost story, just this once."

Kaneko had long aspired to direct a Godzilla movie. In December 1991, he sent a New Year greeting card to producer Shogo Tomiyama. *Godzilla vs. King Ghidorah* was playing in theaters, and the studio had announced that a new Godzilla movie would follow in 1992. "He was very straight and direct," Tomiyama recalled, "and said, 'Please let me do the next Godzilla.' But [director] Takao Okawara had already been selected." Kaneko was then a rising independent director raised on kaiju, sci-fi, and manga who had cut his creative teeth in a variety of genres. Soon thereafter, Kaneko helmed Daiei Film's reboot of the Gamera franchise, dropping the childish approach of the original giant turtle movies for a more mature storyline incorporating mythology and fantasy. *Gamera: Guardian of the Universe* (1995) was followed by two sequels in 1996 and 1999, and drew critical praise, won awards, and brought new energy to the genre. Kaneko next made the supernatural thriller *Crossfire* (aka *Pyrokinesis,* 2000) for Toho; then, on June 14, 2000, just four days after that film was released, Tomiyama hired Kaneko to direct the third (and presumably final) Godzilla film in the Millennium series. "Ever since I got his New Year card, I wanted to make it happen," said Tomiyama. "It took ten years, but we finally did it."

Most recent Godzilla films had originated with a producer's idea that was spun into a treatment by a writer and then handed off to a director for development. But Kaneko had an unusual degree of control over this production: He developed the script based on his own ideas, selected screenwriters to collaborate with, and oversaw the casting, music, and production team. "I was just there to set up the situation," said Tomiyama. "I left the rest completely up to Kaneko. So from beginning to end—the script, preparation, filming, [and] completion, I was only an observer."

One of Kaneko's early ideas was to pit Godzilla against Kamacuras, the mantis from *Son of Godzilla*—among his son's favorite monsters—"but they'd already done Megaguirus, [which was] an insect monster, and Kamacuras was too obscure," he recalled. He also proposed the story of a Japanese astronaut exposed to radiation in space who transforms into a humanoid kaiju called M and battles Godzilla. This idea was quickly dropped, but one of its main themes—the relationship between a father and daughter—would be carried forward. Kaneko then pivoted to *Godzilla x Varan x Baragon x Anguirus: Giant Monsters All-Out Attack,* an original story with Godzilla challenged by three classic quadrupedal Toho kaiju. In this reimagination, Anguirus was a freezing monster with icicle spikes on its back, Baragon was a geothermal monster, and Varan was described as a "wind monster"; the three would combine their powers and attack in formation. "I thought Varan-Baragon-Anguirus rhymed, and sounded like a great title," Kaneko said. He wrote three drafts, then brought in veteran anime and *tokusatsu* writer Keiichi Hasegawa to flesh out a fourth. A fifth and final draft was attributed to Kaneko, Hasegawa, and Masahiro Yokotani, who had coscripted Kaneko's *Crossfire.* By January 2001, the screenplay was essentially finalized, and the project was ready to move forward when the studio, following underwhelming returns for *Megaguirus,* had second

PREVIOUS SPREAD: As inspiration for creating his first Godzilla, suit maker Fuyuki Shinada said, "I made clay models of all the old Godzillas. But I saw a picture of [Teizo] Toshimitsu's model [from 1954] and thought, *That's the real G.*" Unique among Godzilla suits, Shinada's had moving dorsal fins. "I wanted to make something new. I put that into the suit without being asked. However, you don't see it in the film very much." ■ **BOTTOM LEFT:** (*left to right*) Broadcast journalist Yuri Tachibana (Chiharu Niiyama), writer Mitsuaki Takeda (Masahiro Kobayashi), and BS Digital Q assistant director Jun Maruo (Takashi Nishina) investigate the shrine of the guardian monsters. ■ **BOTTOM RIGHT:** Professor Isayama (Hideyo Amamoto) awakens the thousand-year dragon from its sleep beneath a sheet of ice. "Since the time that I was working on the script, [Amamoto] was exactly the person I had in mind," said director Shusuke Kaneko. "His performance was perfect. He is just like a monster—Godzilla, Baragon, King Ghidorah, Mothra, and Amamoto." ■ **OPPOSITE, TOP & BOTTOM LEFT:** "For the battle between Godzilla and Baragon at the Owakudani volcanic tourist area, I asked SFX art director Toshio Miike to come up with a set plan with as much height difference as possible," said SFX director Makoto Kamiya. "I also made a ridiculous request for the whole background to be hillsides. He built the mountain as high as the ceiling." ■ **OPPOSITE, BOTTOM RIGHT:** "Director Kaneko's original storyboards lacked a bit of the spectacle I wanted in the special effects," said SFX director Kamiya. "So, with his approval, I asked [Shinji] Higuchi to create new storyboards for the fight in Owakudani. The battle was originally depicted mostly on flat ground, but I made changes to utilize the terrain, with Baragon on a cliff [and] jumping down to attack Godzilla below."

thoughts. "Toho wanted to end the Godzilla series right there, but producer Tomiyama spoke up for me and told them that I was already working on the next film," said Kaneko.

At a meeting to discuss the project, Kaneko learned that, for commercial reasons, a major change was required. "The chairman of Toho, Isao Matsuoka, said I would have to use Mothra and King Ghidorah [in order to continue]," Kaneko recalled; he had chosen monsters that were all "on the small side" to showcase the might of Godzilla by comparison. "I wondered whether it was possible to switch Varan, Baragon, and Anguirus with Mothra and King Ghidorah. Mothra comes from Infant Island, and King Ghidorah was a space monster from Venus—how could they be the guardians of Yamato?" he wondered. "After [thinking about it for] fifteen minutes, I made up my mind. If I didn't do it, I would lose this job, and more importantly, all our work would be lost. Fan reaction was a concern, but regardless, I had to come up with a reasonable explanation [for the story]."

A PARALLEL WORLD

The key to that explanation lay in the motivation of the monsters. "Although the [guardian monsters] are somewhat heroic, they are not truly allies of mankind; they protect the country, not the people," said writer Hasegawa. "They vent their anger in retribution upon the Japanese youth, who have become complacent in a time of peace." Those who mock or dishonor the past meet swift ends: A gang of biker thugs and a group of rowdy teenagers desecrate local shrines and then proceed to harass village elders and rob a convenience store, respectively; Baragon rises from the earth and buries the bikers in rubble, and Mothra surfaces in a lake to drown the troublemakers.

Godzilla's vengeance is the most violent and brutal of all. Unlike the original 1954 story, the monster's appearance is unexplainable by science; the first Godzilla died, and it reappears fifty years later as a supernatural revenant, a dead-eyed demon more powerful than the first. It seems to take pleasure as it cruelly stomps, throws, and burns its foes. Its heat ray (reverting to a more traditional blue-white hue) literally blows away tanks and artillery and sends the bodies of soldiers flying. Godzilla's relationship to nuclear weapons is now more than symbolic: annoyed by the screams of a terrified woman, the monster fires its ray, sending a shockwave across the city and raising a mushroom cloud; a schoolteacher miles away mistakes it for an atomic bomb. Disaster shelters teem with the wounded and dying, and tears flow.

ABOVE: "The Godzilla suit was extremely heavy," said SFX director Makoto Kamiya. "And the radio control unit in Godzilla's neck [to open and close its mouth] would break when the suit moved vigorously. We had to protect that part." ■ BELOW, CLOCKWISE FROM TOP LEFT: "I'd never been a suit actor before, so I wondered if I could perform like previous actors," said Rie Ota, the first-ever woman to play a monster in the series. "When Baragon burrows out of the ground, we filmed on an open set on a brutal summer day. The inside of the suit was already hot when I put it on." ■ SFX director Kamiya (right) directs Godzilla suit actor Mizuho Yoshida (left, in shorts). Said Kamiya, "I demonstrated how I wanted the kaiju actors to move. I'd dreamed of being a monster since I was a child, so I wanted to make sure the performances were right." Added Yoshida, "Kamiya explained Godzilla's feelings and movements, and it was hilarious. They should film him as Godzilla." ■ "The battle shows Godzilla's raw power and evil nature, so I tried to make its attack as cruel and nasty as possible," said SFX director Kamiya. "In contrast, Baragon is courageous and even sympathetic. I wanted to make Godzilla look heavy and Baragon to look nimble." ■ "Director Kaneko wanted Baragon to be as small as possible, so suit maker Fuyuki Shinada said Baragon had to be played by a woman," remembered SFX director Kamiya. "Before filming started, we had the monster actors practice the battle with the actual suits on. Rie Ota did a wonderful job."

Q-AND-A: SHUSUKE KANEKO

Q: How did you develop the idea of Godzilla as a spirit-like monster?

A: I was trying to come up with the reason why weapons don't work on Godzilla, and that's the answer I reached: Godzilla is an *onryo* (vengeful spirit). Seeing Roland Emmerich's [version of] Godzilla running from missiles and how it easily dies when it got hit, I thought, *There is no way I can create something immortal in science fiction*. So an *onryo* seemed to be the solution.

Q: This is something of a departure from prior interpretations, when Godzilla was said to specifically represent the atomic bomb. Some critics—particularly in the US—have also interpreted Godzilla as representing America.

A: The image of war is what is embodied in the original Godzilla, as well as the nuclear threat. Japanese people at the time never thought it was a reference to America; they only saw it as representation of the atomic bomb.

Q: *GMK* takes place in an alternate history, where Japan is known as the Japanese Democratic Republic, and it has full military capability.

A: In the real world, there is a security treaty with the US, whereas in the reality of the movie, there is what's called a friendship treaty, [and] Japan is a more autonomous country. There is no limitation on the Self-Defense Forces, since Japan has self-determination. By portraying Japan as an autonomous nation, there is no need to ask for help from the US or others. If Godzilla attacks, this type of fantasy setup is needed to enable the country to fight. But in reality, we would be dependent on America [for help].

Q: *GMK* is unusual in that it depicts death in Godzilla's wake and the suffering and crying of the victims in the aftermath. Why did you choose to show human casualties?

A: I did this to give more expression to the power and fearsomeness of Godzilla. I took care to not show blood; I didn't want to make it a splatter movie or anything like that, but I needed those scenes to show Godzilla's power and to create fear. I thought that the audience could relate to this kind of scene, like when people are sobbing, more than just Godzilla fighting and beating the other monsters, or buildings crumbling.

Q: *GMK* and your previous kaiju films have incorporated mythology- or fantasy-based stories rather than science fiction.

A: I think that the meanings of fantasy and science fiction have been changing over time. I believe that monster movies are actually fantasies; nowadays, [giant] monsters cannot exist in science fiction because science has advanced, and the audience is much more knowledgeable. Back in the 1960s, a 164-foot- (50-m-) tall monster could exist in science fiction; we really did not know whether or not it was possible. But now, if you think in scientific terms, everyone knows a 164-foot- (50-m-) tall monster can't exist. So what we do is—because everyone still wants to see a [giant] monster—we create a fantasy movie that has the atmosphere or mood of a science-fiction movie.

Q: *GMK* realized your dream of directing a Godzilla film. As a filmmaker, what is it about the monster that attracted you?

A: Godzilla is ugly yet beautiful. Godzilla is unthinking and acts without regard for anything else; he just goes his own way and does as he pleases. His violence is ruthless—he has incredible power. He is overwhelming. Other giant beings, like Gamera and Majin, are not like that. They have some kind of motivation to go with their power. Not Godzilla. That is the biggest thing that makes Godzilla so special for me. Godzilla has been imprinted in my blood since childhood.

ABOVE RIGHT: Director Shusuke Kaneko at the press launch for *GMK* in 2001.

(Adapted from interviews conducted by the authors in Tokyo in 2002 and 2023, and via email in 2020; translation by Norman England and Mariko Godziszewski.)

"When I was in middle school, I watched a TV broadcast of [the original] *Godzilla*," Kaneko recalled. "It reminded me of an air raid. Of course, everyone knows it symbolizes the bomb, but I understood Godzilla as a representation of the tragedy and misery of the war. In *GMK*, people have forgotten about Godzilla—just as people had forgotten about the war [in real life]."

The story concerns the unfolding of a prophecy from an ancient text akin to the *Kojiki* or the *Nihongi*. The ghostly Professor Hirotoshi Isayama (Hideyo Amamoto, the old toy inventor in *All Monsters Attack*), warns that Godzilla's return is imminent. Baragon and Mothra appear according to the legend, but to fulfill the prophecy, Isayama must awaken Ghidorah, the mighty thousand-year dragon—even though it has slept for merely a few hundred years and thus is not fully matured.

KANEKO'S VISION

GMK takes place in a parallel postwar world where Japan's military capability has been fully restored and the country, now called the Japan Democratic Republic, is not constitutionally reliant on the US for security (to underscore this point, Japan's forces boast Soviet-style military hardware). Kaneko uses this alternate reality to hammer home the futility of war and the politics that accompany it. The military is hamstrung in its response to Godzilla via indecision at the cabinet level, and the brass continually fret about peacetime cuts to the military budget. The military's status is so tenuous that it has engaged in a fifty-year cover-up, hiding the fact that Godzilla was killed in 1954 not by the army, but by science. The fictional present-day Defense Force's attacks on Godzilla are likewise completely ineffective.

The human story at the center of *GMK* has heart. Yuri Tachibana (Chiharu Niiyama) is a budding broadcaster battling sexism as she attempts to uncover the story of the guardian monsters and cover Godzilla's rampage live from the scene. Her father, Admiral Taizo Tachibana (played by goateed musician Ryudo Uzaki—a successful example of nontraditional casting) lost his parents to Godzilla in 1954 and is determined to defeat the monster. After watching the brass fumble and fail in their efforts, Tachibana enters Godzilla in a submersible research vessel, defeating the monster from within. The warm relationship between the determined reporter and her gruff father is a centerpiece of the movie, and when each bids the other good luck as they bravely embark on their respective missions in the danger zone, it's a rare moment of emotion. "In the end, this was a story about a father and daughter, which had never been done in [a] Godzilla [film]," said producer Tomiyama. "That sets Kaneko apart from other directors."

Among the talents hailing from Kaneko's Gamera trilogy, perhaps no one was more impactful than composer Kow Otani, whose score for *GMK* is centered on a brash, dark Godzilla theme created with digital instrumentation. Otani takes an unusual and effective approach to kaiju scoring; during the final battle, when Godzilla and King Ghidorah tumble from the waterfront to Yokohama Bay, the score serves

"KANEKO'S DIRECTION IS CONSCIOUSLY FOCUSED ON ENTERTAINMENT, BUT IT STILL STANDS AS A LEGITIMATE ANTI-WAR FILM."

—Ryudo Uzaki (Admiral Taizo Tachibana)

Professor Isayama (Hideyo Amamoto) implores the heroes to awaken King Ghidorah so it can join forces with the other guardian monsters and repel Godzilla's attack. The professor is a spirit-like presence, appearing in locations across Japan and then quickly vanishing. As the story concludes, it is revealed that Isayama died nearly fifty years ago. ■ King Ghidorah is smaller than Godzilla, with rounder eyes and features befitting a benevolent monster, and it lacks the classic version's hairy manes. Director Shusuke Kaneko noted, "The monster really isn't a 'king' in this movie; that was difficult to reconcile." Revived with energy from a dying Mothra, the monster awakens as the larger, stronger thousand-year dragon. "Chiharu Niiyama's character says 'King Ghidorah' just once, and that's the only time [the name is] mentioned." ■ Mothra's image is updated to suit the creature's role as a guardian monster rather than the deity of Infant Island. "We wanted adult Mothra to look aggressive, resembling an insect more like a bee than a moth," said SFX director Makoto Kamiya. "It had to be clearly different from previous versions." The *GMK* version of Mothra can fire poisonous stingers. ■ Rather than wires, two of King Ghidorah's three necks were operated by the suit actor. "SFX director Kamiya had worked on *Godzilla vs. King Ghidorah*, so [he] knew it was impossible to manipulate three monsters at the same time if two were done with wires," said Kaneko. "We made King Ghidorah's necks as puppets. It made sense because this was supposed to be a juvenile, so its necks logically would be shorter."

GODZILLA FACT: Godzilla's ray destroys the seventy-three-story Yokohama Landmark Tower. After the September 11 terrorist attacks occurred while the film was in production, special effects director Makoto Kamiya feared the scene would have to be cut, but it was allowed to stay.

TAKASHI NAKAO: A LEGACY OF KAIJU PHOTOGRAPHY

Before Godzilla's special effects were created by men and women in front of computer screens, they were crafted in large, grungy, airplane hangar–like sound stages by crews that often numbered well over a hundred. For decades, Toho's Stage No. 9 was the epicenter of this world—a dimly lit factory where specialized teams formed an assembly line of meticulous organization, bringing impossible scenes of rampaging giant monsters to cinematic life.

In 2001, I was a writer and photographer covering the production of *Godzilla, Mothra and King Ghidorah: Giant Monsters All-Out Attack*, with an open pass to the set—an unprecedented status for a foreign journalist. On my first day on Stage No. 9, I managed to be in someone's way no matter where I set my camera and computer bags down. Eventually, a staffer took pity on me. He was Takashi Nakao, the still photographer for the production.

While other teams had scores of people, still photography was a team of one: Nakao-san. Nestled between the pyrotechnic department and stacks of lumber, his station was an unassuming foldout desk. He pointed to a bench beside it and invited me to keep my bags there. "Free of charge," he said with a sly smile. Nakao-san had a charming, sarcastic wit—a rarity in Japan.

In his early sixties, Nakao-san was older than the rest of the staff, and one of the last remaining members of the Showa crew. He was of the generation that didn't easily share personal information, but I learned that he'd been shooting stills on Godzilla films since *King Kong vs. Godzilla* and had been the series' chief still photographer since *The Return of Godzilla*. Nakao-san began his career as assistant to his mentor, Issei Tanaka; together, the pair photographed the making of numerous productions during Toho's golden age. I was most impressed when Nakao-san revealed that he'd taken many iconic shots of Baragon in *Frankenstein Conquers the World*. As the only *GMK* staff member present during that first production to feature the doglike Baragon, Nakao-san was asked several times by effects director Makoto Kamiya for pointers on how certain moments were created back in 1965.

As a novice to movie-set still photography, I was eager to learn what I could from Nakao-san. On the first day of SFX shooting on *GMK*, I tailed behind him until he found a position he felt would work best. "I take two kinds of photos: those within the world of kaiju and the behind-the-scenes variety," he explained. "Making-of photos are easiest, since I don't have to care about showing the seams of the sets or [any of] the crew. The next shot features a missile blast off of Godzilla, so I've decided to make this one look like it's in the kaiju world."

Squatting beside Nakao-san, I had my camera at the ready. Kamiya yelled for action. *BAM, BAM, BAM!* Godzilla's chest lit up in a blaze of pyrotechnic glory! Following the shot, I looked at my photo. Rattled by the explosion, I must have shaken my camera—the photo was an embarrassing blur.

Nakao laughed. "Don't worry about it. After a few more explosions, you'll get used to it." Sure enough, a couple of days into the shoot, I was taking photos without so much as a flinch as debris flew all around me. When I showed Nakao a rock-solid photo of blasts around Godzilla, a smile spread across his face. "What did I tell you?" he said. "Taken like a pro!"

Near the end of the *GMK* shoot, Nakao-san revealed that this was his last Toho production. He was retiring after more than forty years. I was dumbstruck. Yet, at the same time, grateful to have been the last one to have crawled into the Godzilla trenches with Takashi Nakao—the master of kaiju photography, whose contributions to the legacy of Toho SFX cinema are peerless.

—Norman England

TOP LEFT & RIGHT: Takashi Nakao on the set of *Godzilla, Mothra and King Ghidorah: Giant Monsters All-Out Attack.*
■ **ABOVE:** Norman England (*left*) and Nakao (*right*) on the set of *GMK.*

to punctuate moments of human emotion and danger rather than monster action. The music remains muted for long passages of time; when Godzilla and Ghidorah fight underwater, Otani's score steps aside for the sound effects, then the music swells as Yuri nearly falls to her death—only to be saved by the guardian Ghidorah.

The Millennium series is notable not only for having a revolving director's chair but also for introducing new special effects directors. Makoto Kamiya, an assistant effects director on the Heisei Godzilla and Gamera films, was initially tapped to supervise the special effects photography only, while Kaneko would direct the entire production, but "I changed my mind along the way, and I thought Kamiya should get his due, so I made sure he got credit as special effects director," said Kaneko. The introduction of a new Godzilla suit maker, Fuyuki Shinada, and suit actor, Mizuho Yoshida, lend the film an altogether different look and feel compared to recent entries.

GMK was the first of three consecutive Millennium series films paired on a double bill with an anime feature starring Hamtaro, a popular cartoon hamster with a target audience in the under-twelve crowd. "Godzilla had done well in the nineties, but more recently, small and cute characters like Pokémon were doing better," said Tomiyama. "We thought Hamtaro would bring in moms and daughters and Godzilla would get dads and sons. But a lot of kids who came for Hamtaro cried when they saw Godzilla." The twin bill earned ¥2.71 billion and ranked third at the domestic box office for 2002; Studio Ghibli's *The Cat Returns* was number one at more than ¥6.4 billion.

Godzilla is destroyed, but its living, beating heart rests on the ocean floor, and Akira Ifukube's immortal Godzilla theme provides the coda. In the end, *GMK* was the most successful of the Millennium films, the work of a filmmaker with a unique spin on the monster's origins. Still, Kaneko wondered what might have been. "It was the right decision [to change the monsters to sell] tickets," he said. "As a director, that is my job to think about. But still, in the bottom of my heart, in a very small corner, I still have the feeling that Varan, Baragon, and Anguirus could have been better."

As for the ghostly Godzilla?

"I wondered what producer Tomoyuki Tanaka would have thought," mused Tomiyama. "I knew he probably wouldn't have allowed this. But I wanted to let director Kaneko do what [he] wanted to do. Godzilla is essentially the god of destruction. The idea that Godzilla is also something that transcends natural life is yet another aspect of the character, so I thought it would be an interesting new approach, and we went ahead with it."

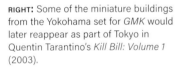

RIGHT: Some of the miniature buildings from the Yokohama set for *GMK* would later reappear as part of Tokyo in Quentin Tarantino's *Kill Bill: Volume 1* (2003).

LEFT: "I really wanted to do a monster version of pro wrestling," said SFX director Makoto Kamiya. "Simple yet intense hand-to-hand combat, like tangling up, pouncing, biting, body-smashing, throwing, stepping on each other, etc. In the end, Anguirus and Varan were replaced with King Ghidorah and Mothra, but I still wanted to keep that hand-to-hand combat style." ■ **BELOW:** "I felt I shouldn't do it the same old way, but not completely differently either," said Godzilla suit actor Mizuho Yoshida. "For [the] fighting style, I referred to Haruo Nakajima's Godzilla from *King Kong vs. Godzilla*, and for regular walking, to Kenpachiro Satsuma's Heisei Godzilla. The common denominator of past Godzillas was that he moved by instinct—he destroys the building because it's in his way. I was always conscious of that kind of thing."

CLOCKWISE FROM TOP LEFT: Admiral Taizo Tachibana (Ryudo Uzaki, *right*) decides to face Godzilla alone in the Satsuma submersible watercraft, a last-ditch effort to defeat the monster by attacking it from within. ■ The ending of *GMK* mirrors the conclusion of the original *Godzilla*. After Godzilla is destroyed on the ocean floor, Yuri Tachibana (Chiharu Niiyama) offers a salute to those who saved Japan: her father, who defeated Godzilla, and the guardian monsters, who sacrificed themselves. ■ Composite shots using aerial footage place the monsters in Yokohama during the final battle, but due to time constraints, the waterfront area was not constructed in detail except for a few locations. "There were many scenes I wanted to film in Yokohama," said SFX director Makoto Kamiya. "For example, kaiju hiding in the city or leaping at Godzilla from the rooftops, but unfortunately, we ran out of time."

GODZILLA FACT: Speaking to a group of military cadets, Admiral Tachibana says a monster recently attacked New York. "That was Godzilla, right?" asks one recruit. "American experts say so, but Japanese scholars disagree," replies another. "That dialogue was taken as a gag," said director Shusuke Kaneko. However, it was not a joke. "The line [was meant] to explain that there are many monsters in this world. It establishes that a kind of monster multiverse exists."

(*GOJIRA X MEKAGOJIRA*)
RELEASED: DECEMBER 14, 2002 (JAPAN)

GODZILLA AGAINST MECHAGODZILLA

Godzilla has faced several facsimiles of itself, but none so powerful as Kiryu ("machine dragon"), an advanced biomechanical robot incorporating DNA from the skeletal remains of the original Godzilla. In keeping with the theme of the Millennium films, *Godzilla Against Mechagodzilla* is the series' fourth consecutive reboot to elide all previous sequels, but—in an interesting twist—it acknowledges that other creatures from the classic Toho universe have terrorized Japan throughout the decades, including Mothra and Gaira, the green humanoid monster from *The War of the Gargantuas* (1966).

The story begins in 1999, when a new Godzilla makes landfall at the Boso Peninsula during a violent typhoon. As in *Godzilla 2000: Millennium* and *Godzilla vs. Megaguirus,* the film opens with a dramatic action sequence, featuring Godzilla trampling a village amid torrential rains and then facing off against the Japan Self-Defense Forces' Anti-Megalosaurus Force (AMF), a special unit created in 1966 to fight monsters. In a forested, mountainous area, tanks and Maser Cannons are deployed against Godzilla—an homage to a similar scene in *The War of the Gargantuas*—but the weapons only provoke the monster's vicious retaliation. A bolt of lightning illuminates the sky, and Godzilla's dorsals crackle as the monster bellows a victory roar while the film's title card appears. "[A]nother Godzilla," says a newscaster. "Forty-five years after the first one, how can we cope with the new one?"

"WHEN I FIRST HEARD PRODUCER TOMIYAMA TALKING ABOUT THE IDEA OF DREDGING UP GODZILLA'S BONES, I SAID, 'WAIT, DIDN'T THEY DISSOLVE IN THE FIRST FILM?' AND HE SAID WITH A LAUGH, 'WELL, THAT WAS THEN.' WE DECIDED FROM THE BEGINNING THAT MECHAGODZILLA WOULD BE BUILT ONTO GODZILLA'S BONES BECAUSE I WANTED THIS MECHAGODZILLA TO BE THE ONE AND ONLY OF ITS KIND. IF IT WERE JUST A REGULAR ROBOT IN THE SHAPE OF GODZILLA, YOU COULD BUILD AS MANY AS YOU WANT. THAT'S NOT AS INTERESTING."

—Masaaki Tezuka, director

The performance of *Godzilla, Mothra and King Ghidorah: Giant Monsters All-Out Attack* dictated that the Millennium arc would continue beyond the originally planned trilogy, but rather than hand the franchise to another new filmmaker, producer Shogo Tomiyama pivoted back to Masaaki Tezuka, who had followed his directorial debut on *Megaguirus* by returning to the assistant director ranks, first with the special effects team under Makoto Kamiya on *GMK* and also on a 2002 episode of the NHK television drama *Tobo* (*Fugitive*) directed by his mentor, Kon Ichikawa. While working on the latter, "I met producer Tomiyama on the street in front of Toho's Stage No. 8 and we had a brief chat," Tezuka recalled. "He told me, 'We're going with Mechagodzilla next.' I replied, 'Mechagodzilla? That sounds cool!' After parting ways, I wondered, *Wait, does that mean I'll be directing it?*"

Godzilla Against Mechagodzilla follows a plot that is broadly similar to *Megaguirus* in that it centers on a tough female action hero; once again, Tezuka links present and past through a Showa-era star, casting Kumi Mizuno in the brief but significant role of Prime Minister Machiko Tsuge. Lieutenant Akane Yashiro (Yumiko Shaku), a Maser Cannon operator, causes an accident that leads to her commanding officers' vehicle being crushed by Godzilla. The story charts Akane's redemption: Demoted to a desk job, she struggles with feelings of guilt, isolation, and worthlessness, even as she trains vigorously in hopes of reinstatement. Three and a half years later, the AMF has developed "a mechanical Godzilla to beat

"KIRYU HAS A LIFE, TOO. WHY MUST IT FIGHT GODZILLA WHEN THEY SHOULD BE FRIENDS?"

—Sara Yuhara (Kana Onodera)

Godzilla," and Akane becomes the lead pilot of the Kiryu Squadron, flying an AC-3 White Heron fighter aircraft that serves as the robot's transport and remote-control unit.

ROGUE ROBOT

When the government unveils the new Mechagodzilla to the public, Godzilla is drawn to its robotic relative, and their first battle occurs near Yokohama. Kiryu's weapons are overpowering, and as Godzilla roars in pain, the deafening sound triggers an instinctual response embedded in the cyborg's genetic coding. Kiryu ceases responding to commands; imbued with the consciousness of the creature whose bones lie beneath its armor, Kiryu's yellow eyes turn red, and it begins to attack Tokyo in Godzilla-like fashion, unleashing deadly firepower and literally walking through buildings until its power supply runs out. "Computers and robots often go rogue, like HAL 9000 in *2001: A Space Odyssey* (1968) or Robby the Robot in *Forbidden Planet* (1956)," said Tezuka, "So I came up with the idea of Kiryu going berserk."

The biological bond between monster and robot is central to the film's themes of grief, loss, and the sanctity of life. Akane is gently courted by the kind but awkward professor Tokumitsu Yuhara (Shin Takuma), a biologist hired to assist the Kiryu project for his expertise in "DNA computers." Yuhara is a widower, and his young daughter, Sara (Kana Onodera), still coping with grief over losing her mother, feels every creature has a right to live—even Kiryu. Sara bonds with Akane and helps the steely heroine emotionally defrost.

"During preproduction, my father passed away," remembered Tezuka. "At that time, I was a bit emotionally unstable. Whenever I was asked about the theme, I said, 'It's about life.'" The terrorist attacks of September 11, 2001, also weighed on the director's mind. "Godzilla is a mirror, reflecting the society of its time," he said. September 11, he added, "[S]hattered the myth of peace and security. . . . It is precisely because of these times that we wanted to create a work that makes people think about peace. Godzilla, born from humanity's nuclear foolishness, causes untold casualties simply due to its natural instincts. In the face of overwhelming devastation, humanity creates the ultimate weapon to defeat Godzilla, fighting destruction with destruction. The foolishness of humanity and the sanctity of life are the themes I want to depict."

In *Godzilla Against Mechagodzilla,* Japan appears—perhaps more so than in any Godzilla movie since 1954—to be primed for combat after decades of monster invasions. For the first time since *Godzilla 2000: Millennium,* Toho received substantial cooperation from the Japan Self-Defense Forces, and ample real-life military hardware, including tanks, Cobra gunship helicopters, truck-mounted anti-ship missiles, destroyer- class warships, and command vehicles, are positioned alongside Toho's mecha. This emphasis on heavy equipment lends Godzilla's final rampage added excitement as the monster surfaces in Shinagawa at night and incinerates attacking jets and fleets of tanks with its powerful heat ray.

PREVIOUS SPREAD, LEFT TO RIGHT: Godzilla advances through the forest during a rainstorm. ■ Kiryu in dry dock. ■ **BELOW:** Kiryu, the third-generation Mechagodzilla, is sleeker and more agile than either the Showa or Heisei robots. "Personally, my preference was more for the Showa Mechagodzilla," said SFX director Yuichi Kikuchi. "I told [artist] Shinji Nishikawa, who was the designer of the character, that my image would be something [sharper], with straight lines and good mobility. What he came up with was incredible."

ABOVE: Kiryu in dry dock, ready for launch. ■ **RIGHT:** Godzilla and Kiryu meet in the city. "This new Godzilla design was more streamlined, and the fins were smaller so I could stand up more easily," said suit actor Tsutomu Kitagawa. "This one's a bit more movable. Mechagodzilla's arms could stretch out more than Godzilla's, so I had a hard time hitting him back when we fought." ■ **BELOW:** Kiryu's numerous powers and weapons include—but are not limited to—the chest-mounted Absolute Zero Cannon, twin Maser Cannons, Maser Blade, multiple interlocking rockets, guided missiles, and the back unit (with dual rocket launchers).

GODZILLA FACT: *Godzilla Against Mechagodzilla* was screened at the Tokyo International Film Festival (TIFF) on November 2, 2002, over one month before its official release date. Compositing work was still being finished, so therefore, the print screened at the festival included incomplete shots. "But there were really just about three or four remaining composite shots left," said director Masaaki Tezuka. "We actually managed to almost complete the film in time for the TIFF. [Producer] Tomiyama said, 'This is the first time something like this has happened,' because with the Heisei Godzilla movies, it was more of a tragic situation [*laughs*], with fifty or a hundred remaining composite shots."

This film is also notable as the first since *The Return of Godzilla* to feature high-ranking politicians as major characters. Prime Minister Hayato Igarashi (series veteran Akira Nakao), having rushed Kiryu into battle with disastrous results the first time, hesitates to dispatch the robot again, agreeing only after being reassured that it has been successfully reprogrammed. Via a combination of practical effects and CG, the White Heron aircraft drop Mechagodzilla into the heart of a flaming Tokyo, where mass evacuations are underway. The robot makes a dramatic entrance just as Godzilla is about to incinerate a nurse (*Megaguirus*'s Misato Tanaka in a cameo) attempting to rescue a child from a hospital. In the ensuing fight, Kiryu appears to knock Godzilla senseless; the robot prepares to shoot its Absolute Zero Cannon, which is capable of atomically freezing Godzilla and collapsing the monster under its own weight. However, Godzilla skillfully fires its heat ray from its prone position, knocking Kiryu back and causing the cyborg's freeze ray to disintegrate several high-rises instead. In the dramatic finish, Kiryu's control system is damaged and its power exhausted; Akane climbs inside to pilot the robot while Tokyo's utility companies divert all their electricity to quickly recharge it (necessitating a region-wide blackout). Akane

CLOCKWISE FROM TOP LEFT: Behind-the-scenes shot of Godzilla's skeleton. When Godzilla's bones are revealed underwater, the model is composited with CG scuba divers swimming alongside it. ■ First-time SFX director Yuichi Kikuchi had previously served as first assistant on *Megaguirus* and *GMK*, as well as numerous *Ultraman* features for Tsuburaya Productions. He augmented the traditional kaiju battle style with nimble movements and evasive maneuvers. "I thought Mechagodzilla should move a lot more than Godzilla," Kikuchi said. "From the start, I decided to do more close combat and martial arts [moves]." As a newcomer, his ideas were met with skepticism from longtime crew members. "Even though I worked on the two previous films, I was still a thirty-two-year-old punk. I needed a certain energy to compete with those big shots. I think I acted really saucy and obnoxious." ■ After running wild and laying waste to much of Tokyo, Kiryu has expended all its energy. The bio-robot powers down as the sun sets on the horizon.

heroically saves a fellow airman whose plane is caught in Godzilla's mouth, then fires the Absolute Zero Cannon point-blank into Godzilla's chest, expelling the monster out to sea and creating a massive ice sculpture akin to Superman's Fortress of Solitude above the surface in Tokyo Bay.

MUSICAL MIGHT

"Creating Mechagodzilla's theme was a challenge, especially because it had to be different from Godzilla's," said composer Michiru Oshima, who returns to the series with powerful music that propels the action. "For Mechagodzilla, I wanted to create a sense of presence, so I made it more like a fanfare. Also, since Godzilla's theme is lower in pitch, I made Mechagodzilla's theme higher." Dueling monster motifs alternate during the final battle, shifting as the tide turns.

Oshima received permission to record the score at the Mosfilm studio in Moscow, using a Russian orchestra. "When we recorded the music for *Godzilla vs. Megaguirus* in Tokyo, it seemed like it had a really big sound at the time, but during the final mix, every time Godzilla roared or when there was some type of sound effect, the music would fade a little bit, and we were unhappy about that," she recalled. "We wanted to have a bigger sound so the music wouldn't lose out to the sound effects. We went to Moscow and [recorded] it with a really large orchestra. In Tokyo, we had maybe fifty musicians, but in Moscow, there were about ninety." Director Tezuka had originally planned to use Akira Ifukube's traditional Godzilla theme in two scenes, and Oshima did not object. "[But] she composed truly fantastic music again, so this time we didn't use Ifukube's theme at all," said Tezuka.

INSIDE GODZILLA

THE CHALLENGES OF MONSTER SUIT ACTING

"In America, films like *The Lost World* and *King Kong* were made with very advanced special effects techniques. In Japan, we couldn't do this; for one thing, there was no one who was experienced in model animation. Our film was a big experiment."
—Eiji Tsuburaya, special effects director

LEFT: Three generations of suit actors demonstrate their individual styles of playing Godzilla: (*left to right*) Tsutomu Kitagawa, Haruo Nakajima, and Kenpachiro Satsuma.

When Eiji Tsuburaya received the go-ahead for his dream of bringing a giant monster to the big screen, he was faced with a tremendous dilemma—how to realize the monster with the meager resources at his disposal. Despite his deep admiration of 1933's *King Kong*, the stop-motion animation method that brought the great ape to life was impractical due to time and financial constraints. By instead creating a gigantic creature and its reign of destruction by filming a man in a monster costume on detailed miniature sets, Tsuburaya devised a simple yet innovative approach: monster suit acting, popularly known as "suitmation." In the beginning, however, there were no guidelines and no prior experience to draw upon, just an idea in the special effects wizard's mind. That idea became the foundation of Godzilla's long and storied history.

THE 1950S

Summer 1954: A typical day at Toho Studios, a sprawling complex located amid the woods and fields of Setagaya on the outskirts of Tokyo. Haruo Nakajima was a twenty-five-year-old actor employed in the studio's "B2" group of performers, the bottom tier of bit players and rugged *keren-shi* (stuntmen) who took on the most dangerous, unwanted roles. The previous year, Nakajima had been a soldier engulfed in flames in a war film; in another movie, he fell off a bridge into a river. He was tough, having joined the Imperial Navy in his teens; after the war, he had joined Toho's acting school not to become a star, but simply to find work in Japan's desperate years following the Second World War.

Waiting for his next job, Nakajima was playing *shogi* (Japanese chess) with other B2 men on the second floor of the acting department, a nondescript, three-story building near the studio's front gate. There was no air-conditioning or electric fans, so the actors cooled themselves with hand fans and kept the windows open in the steaming heat.

Suddenly an office worker appeared in the doorway and called, "Hey, Naka-chan!"

BELOW, LEFT TO RIGHT: Haruo Nakajima
dons the Godzilla suit for his first scene
in 1954's *Godzilla*. ∎ An image of the
Nakajima Godzilla.

A NEW CHALLENGE

"Since B2 actors' pay was so low, I gladly took any stunt job at any time because that would pay better," Nakajima recalled. But he could hardly have imagined what his next job entailed. He was given a script with the title *G Project* on the cover and informed that he would be playing a monster. Taking the script home and reading it, he saw it would be a giant creature that shoots fire and destroys Tokyo. He noted the story's allusions to World War II and the recent *Lucky Dragon* fishing boat incident near Bikini Atoll. "The part where the monster attacks Tokyo reminded me of the air raids," Nakajima recalled. "I understood that this was a [fictional] story, but I didn't understand my character at all." He thought maybe he would be playing something like one of the huge frogs he saw in old silent Japanese ninja movies, where the ninjas used their magic powers to change into the shape of a frog or other animal. "I also thought it might be like two guys playing a horse," he said. *But a job is a job*, he thought. "It doesn't matter. I'll be ready."

The next day, Nakajima went straight to see director Ishiro Honda. But when Nakajima asked about his role and how to play it, Honda had no answers for him. How could the director not know? Calmly, Honda said, "I'm leaving the special effects completely up to Mr. Tsuburaya. Go ask him." Special effects? Nakajima had seen model battleships and airplanes in war movies, but what did that have to do with actors? Making his way up to the second floor of an old building cluttered with film cans and scripts, he met a kindly looking middle-aged gentleman dashingly clad in long sleeves and a tie despite the heat, with round-frame spectacles and a dangling cigarette in his mouth. Tsuburaya spread out some drawings of a giant creature destroying a city. Nakajima still didn't understand where he fit in. "Have you seen *King Kong*?" Tsuburaya asked; Nakajima had not, so Tsuburaya sent him to a projection room to watch it immediately. He instructed the actor to study Kong's movement for inspiration. Kong, however, was an animated model; Tsuburaya estimated it would take seven years to make the movie that way. *G Project* had to be completed in about three months. A different method would be used: an actor in a costume. Nakajima was that actor.

It will be extremely difficult, Tsuburaya told him. "Can you handle it?" Nakajima was not afraid of hard work. He took pride in performing stunts others were afraid to do. And he began to understand the responsibility and honor now bestowed upon him. Most B2 actors never played parts big enough to appear in the credits, much less the title character.

"It will be my pleasure," Nakajima said, bowing.

GETTING IN CHARACTER

Nakajima needed to prepare for the role, but he didn't have much to go on. The script offered no clear description of the monster's physical appearance; storyboard drawings provided Nakajima with his first views of the beast, but it wasn't until the Godzilla suit was finished that he truly saw his character in the rubberized flesh. Now he had to figure out how Godzilla should move and how it should act. "Nobody had ever played a role like Godzilla, so I had no teacher," he said. "But, being an actor, I couldn't say I didn't know how to play the part." Every day for a week, he ate his lunch at the zoo while observing the movements of different animals. Small creatures weren't similar enough, so he studied large animals such as lions and bears. "Godzilla was supposed to have originally been a dinosaur," he reasoned, "so it shouldn't move like a man."

The Godzilla suit was well over 220 pounds (100 kg) of crude, inflexible rubber, thus Nakajima's ability to perform inside it was severely limited. But he saw a silver lining. "I would turn my head, but the suit would not turn with me. In hindsight, I thought the movie was much better because of that. The heavy

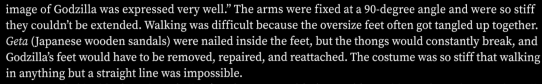

image of Godzilla was expressed very well." The arms were fixed at a 90-degree angle and were so stiff they couldn't be extended. Walking was difficult because the oversize feet often got tangled up together. *Geta* (Japanese wooden sandals) were nailed inside the feet, but the thongs would constantly break, and Godzilla's feet would have to be removed, repaired, and reattached. The costume was so stiff that walking in anything but a straight line was impossible.

Once sealed inside the suit, Nakajima's only contact with the outside world was through several small holes in the monster's neck. Through the holes, the miniature set below looked like a real city—Nakajma truly felt like a giant monster. But during shooting, the solitude inside the suit led to an intense feeling of loneliness. Nakajima could endure the weight of the suit, the sauna-like temperature, and the struggle to breathe. He could tolerate when his sweat would pool at the bottom of the suit and it felt like he was walking through mud. "But all you could hear were muffled sounds through the thick walls of the suit, and it felt as if you were trapped inside once it was sealed up," he said. "I couldn't get used to that so easily, or so I thought."

With the intense heat from studio lights and nonexistent ventilation in the building, Nakajima was limited to working just a few minutes at a time. His routine consisted of an out-of-suit rehearsal, a seven-to ten-minute in-suit rehearsal with the studio lights off, and then a take. Once cameras rolled, Nakajima could barely last three minutes, so every effort was made to shoot the maximum amount of footage in the minimum number of takes. Temperatures reached 140°F (60°C) and higher inside the suit, and Nakajima would be temporarily blinded as perspiration streamed down his forehead. Several times he passed out from heat or lost his balance and fell. He often developed severe muscle cramps, and his skin would get badly blistered from rubbing against the rough cloth of the inner skin. Tea and salt water were constantly on hand for Nakajima to replenish body fluids between takes.

Nakajima shared the role of Godzilla with forty-one-year-old Katsumi Tezuka, a senior performer with high status in the actors' room. Tezuka was selected to perform Godzilla's first scene before the camera: the destruction of the National Diet Building. However, he had difficulty handling the heavy suit and fell onto the miniature set, ruining it. As he was being helped out of the suit, Tezuka lost his temper, saying, "How am I supposed to act in this piece of crap?" He shoved a part-time crew member away and stormed off. Nakajima was taken aback. "I promised myself that I wouldn't make a fuss no matter what," he said. "B2 actors had no luxury to complain; if we did, we'd be told, 'so long, we'll get someone else.' Doing the job was the minimum requirement. If you can't, you're gone."

Suit maker Eizo Kaimai served as chief assistant to Nakajima, helping him in and out of the suit, supervising its maintenance, and relaying directions from Tsuburaya. Because the suit actors were hired only for filming, they did not wear the suit when publicity and advertising stills were shot. Kaimai, being the youngest member of the suit staff, was made to wear the suit for uncompensated after-hours photography sessions. "'Hot' was not even the word for it," Kaimai recalled of the experience. "And the smell! Since

Nakajima drank heavily, the sweat from his hangovers stunk badly. When he drank a lot, the smell of cheap alcohol was embedded in the suit, and you got hit by the overwhelming odor as soon as you opened it."

The aim was for Godzilla to behave naturally, like an animal. Tsuburaya instructed Nakajima not to destroy things randomly or senselessly. When Godzilla destroys the Kachidoki Bridge and heads back out to sea, Tsuburaya directed the actor not to purposely break the bridge but to act as if it were in the way, a nuisance. "[Tsuburaya said], 'Don't act wild, act naturally.' I wasn't allowed to intentionally destroy stuff."

For all his hardships, Nakajima received no screen credit, but it was not a big deal. "I played a character for which no one can even see my face, but I had no complaints," he recalled. "My acting was still very vividly depicted on the screen." Later, sitting in a theater, he watched the audience's reaction. "*Godzilla* was a big success. I whispered, 'thank you' in my heart. It was the first time I'd ever felt that way as an actor. This monster that everyone was looking at was *me*!"

For the second film, a new Godzilla suit was made with lighter and more flexible materials. It was designed specially to fit Nakajima's body and included numerous other improvements. The *geta* sandals were replaced with rudimentary rubber boots attached to a one-inch wooden heel, making it much easier to walk. Nakajima could now perform more robust actions as required by the new scenario. *Godzilla Raids Again* introduced monster-versus-monster action, and with it, Tsuburaya tasked Nakajima with choreographing the fight, a duty he would hold for the remainder of his suit-acting career. Nakajima was both thrilled and intimidated by the challenge.

"He left it all up to me," he recalled. "What a responsibility! It was a bold move to leave the whole thing up to a B2 actor, but it was his way of motivating people." Nakajima understood the logic behind Tsuburaya's decision. "Directors themselves didn't know what was possible with the suit. You had to be inside it and try moving in it in order to decide what to do. Most of the fighting was decided on the day of filming because I had to see the actual set before I could think of anything. . . . Making monster fights interesting was all up to the actors."

For the climactic showdown on Kamiko Island, truckloads of ice were brought to Stage No. 3 and dumped on Godzilla from the top of the set. Nakajima appreciated being buried in ice, a relief from the stifling conditions inside the suit. However, the stunt nearly cost crew member Kaimai his life. Kaimai's job was to hide under the raised floor of the set and control Godzilla's mouth via wires; when the weight of the ice collapsed the floorboards, he was trapped and nearly crushed. His cries for help could not be heard, and at first no one knew the accident had occurred.

THE 1960S

In 1962, *King Kong vs. Godzilla* marked Godzilla's first color and widescreen feature, adding new hardships for the suit actors. Filming in color required significantly more light, and there was no air-conditioning in the studio stages. The set was illuminated by 1,600 kilowatts of light, equivalent to sixteen thousand 100-watt bulbs, making the studio feel hot as midsummer even on the coldest days. From up in the rafters, the lighting staff's sweat dripped down like rain. "In those conditions, when I got out of the Godzilla suit and I squeezed the sweat out of my pants, it was like a waterfall, and it was a struggle just to breathe," Nakajima said.

By now, Nakajima had mastered the basics of Godzilla acting. Tsuburaya had instructed him from the beginning to walk without showing the backs of Godzilla's feet. Godzilla's standing posture was also key. Nakajima would bend a little at the knees to drop the center of gravity and tilt Godzilla's body slightly forward, giving the monster a believable line of sight. "The position of my eyes was much lower than Godzilla's eyes, so if I stood up straight so I could see, Godzilla would not appear to be looking at the set,"

Nakajima said. Because the head of a monster suit sat atop the actor's head, Nakajima raised his arms up high, next to his head, effectively boosting Godzilla's shoulders to a more natural position.

Special effects used high-speed filming to create a sense of scale. When the action was shot at two or three times camera speeds and the footage was then played back at the normal speed of twenty-four frames per second, the monsters' movements would be smooth and exhibit a sense of weight and size. If Nakajima were to act at a normal pace during high-speed filming, his movements would appear unrealistically slow on-screen. Therefore, Nakajima recognized he had to walk and move at a brisk pace in real time to create a believable impression upon playback.

In addition to the physical demands of playing Godzilla, there were other pressures. "Once filming started, I couldn't do anything else for three months. I couldn't afford to be sick, because about a hundred staff members would [then] be forced to sit around doing nothing. My responsibility was that big. I didn't have the luxury of taking a break." Before long, he was in demand not just in Japan. "Hollywood once asked me to come over for a year. I went to talk with [Tsuburaya] about the offer, and he said, 'We can't make a movie without you—no way!' So I didn't go."

To maintain his stamina, Nakajima's daily routine was to eat a good meal in the evening and go to bed early after a relaxing bath and a cold beer. He almost never ate lunch; because he would sweat so much, he only wanted water. Rather than food, what he craved most while working were cigarettes. Emerging from the suit, he would immediately light up. "It was better than after a meal because of the feeling of freedom involved. I always carried cigarettes in the suit. They got damp from sweat. I even smoked inside the suit." The tough nature of his job also complemented his love of alcohol. "Getting in the suit was like being in a sauna, so it cured my hangover at once."

Whether a scene was difficult or dangerous, Nakajima approached things with a professional attitude. "Directors know you are human, so they won't ask you to do something impossible," he said. "We are not supposed to say 'I can't do it.' It's got to be 'Let's do it.' Otherwise, just quit being an actor."

However, by the time of *King Kong vs. Godzilla*, Nakajima had earned a reputation for being nearly indestructible, and he was asked to assume an increasing amount of risk and danger. In *Mothra vs. Godzilla*, a fireball erupted straight into his face. "It was an accident, but it worked out better than if it were planned," he said. "I could feel the fire on my head and neck as the suit burned. It was a direct hit! But I wasn't badly hurt." Afterward, Tsuburaya would tease him: "Hey, Haru-chan, aren't you glad you're still alive?"

Though Nakajima often downplayed the dangers of monster suit acting, there was one near-death experience that he never talked about. In 2018, Jun Arikawa, son of SFX cameraman and director Sadamasa Arikawa, recounted an episode he witnessed in his youth. Nakajima was inside the Godzilla suit for a water tank scene, standing straight up while waiting for his cue. When "Action!" was called, nothing happened—Godzilla did not move. "Everyone dove in and pulled Godzilla out of the water," Arikawa said. "[Nakajima] was electrocuted and unconscious. He regained consciousness soon. It would be a big deal now, but back then, they treated the incident like it was nothing. They should have called an ambulance, but [Nakajima] said he was fine. Then they just continued filming."

Starting around the time of *Mothra vs. Godzilla*, Nakajima would visit the modeling workshop each day to take part in the suit-making process, offering his ideas on how the suits could be made better. "We did a lot of preliminary testing," recalled Nakajima. "I tried it on and would jump around, move harshly, and I always ripped it up. They would constantly patch it up, so by the time it was finished, it would be

BELOW, LEFT TO RIGHT: Katsumi Tezuka (Anguirus) offers Haruo Nakajima a cigarette during the filming of *Godzilla Raids Again*. Between takes, Nakajima would ask anyone within earshot for a smoke while he waited. ▪ Godzilla catches on fire when a pyrotechnic blast erupts in his face in *Mothra vs. Godzilla*.

[broken in], strong and easy to move around in." In those years, only one Godzilla suit was made, so it had to be as strong as possible; repairs during filming were costly in terms of time and money.

Water proved damaging to the costumes and caused a great number of problems for the monster actors. "When I did the water stuff it was usually during the winter," Nakajima said. "I wore a wet suit under the monster suit. During breaks, they built a wood fire to warm us, but it was better not to warm up. I wore scuba gear; when I was underwater, an oxygen tank and mouthpiece were inside the suit with me, but for a scene where I just fell into the water, I didn't wear the apparatus." The environment was uninviting. "The water in the Big Pool was so dirty. Mosquito larvae sprang up, so carp were kept in the pool to eat them."

The title character in *Son of Godzilla* was portrayed by cabaret performer Masao Fukazawa, aka "Machan the Dwarf" or "Little Man Machan." Fukazawa recalled, "At the time, I was a member of a production company doing fantasy comedy shows. I heard about the role of Minilla from Miya-san (Yoshinobu Miyahara, a member of Toho's visual arts division). Around twenty people had been interviewed by both Mr. Tsuburaya and Mr. Arikawa, and they were about to give up. Both directors seemed to like me, and we did a costume fitting that day. I participated in shooting during breaks from my show, so I juggled filming during the day and performing in the show at night." Suit maker Noboyuki Yasumaru recalled that Fukazawa often came to the studio with a female costar from his cabaret act. "He was like a kid. This beautiful dancer addressed [Fukazawa] as sensei (teacher). And when he emerged from the costume, she would offer him a towel."

Nakajima was also often given a bit part in a dramatic scene—a chance to show his face on-screen, albeit briefly. In the first *Godzilla*, he had a small scripted role as a newspaperman; in other films, he frequently had a cameo. "Director Honda was very considerate and invited [the monster actors] to the drama shoot when there was a long wait between special effects scenes. Even though I didn't have any lines, he had me stand in a prominent place."

THE 1970S

Following the death of Tsuburaya in 1970, Nakajima worked for the first time under the direction of Teruyoshi Nakano in *Godzilla vs. Hedorah*. His new boss's penchant for using pyrotechnics didn't faze Nakajima a bit. "Explosives had been used with no regard or hesitation since [Tsuburaya's] time. I didn't see any difference." While fire didn't concern him, Nakajima's professional attitude and willingness to do

what was asked of him were put to the test. "When Godzilla is buried in a pit and has sludge thrown on him, the substance was a kind of glue made from flour," said Koichi Kawakita, assistant SFX director for *Hedorah*. "Nakajima [uncharacteristically] expressed his dissatisfaction, complaining 'This is too much!'"

Nakajima's enthusiasm for the job eventually began to wane. "After Oyaji-san [Tsuburaya] passed away, I still played Godzilla. But I can't lie, I didn't feel the same way without him. The loneliness that I felt when I played the first *Godzilla* was always there in the later films, but I [at least] felt a comfort because Oyaji-san was there. Then he was gone." *Godzilla vs. Gigan* would be Nakajima's last turn as the legendary monster. Looking back on his career, he had no regrets. "There is one thing I can be proud of," he said. "I did not copy anyone else."

THE 1980S AND 1990S

With Godzilla returning to the big screen in 1984, Toho reached out to actor Kenpachiro Satsuma, who had played the monsters Hedorah and Gigan during the previous decade (under his previous stage name, Kengo Nakayama), asking him to recommend a tall performer from his acting troupe for the role of Godzilla, rather than offering him the part. Satsuma had been concentrating on his dramatic acting career and did not miss the anonymity that came with playing a monster. However, the man Satsuma had referred for the job soon complained that it was too demeaning a role for an actor, and backed out while the Godzilla suit was still being fitted. Embarrassed, Satsuma went to apologize to suit maker Nobuyuki Yasumaru. Reluctantly, Satsuma said, "I'll take responsibility and do it." Thus began Satsuma's journey as Godzilla.

Satsuma would suffer because of his offer, laboring in a costume created for a much larger individual and which was rather rigid and heavy. Yasumaru had intentionally made the suit this way because the new Godzilla was bigger than before, as well as to prevent humanlike movement. At 243 pounds (110 kg), the suit was so heavy that Satsuma was barely able to move at all inside it, and his acting was endlessly criticized by SFX director Nakano. He was scarcely able to give much thought to *how* to play the part, and as a result his performance, by his own judgment, was rather stiff. "By the time I had gotten to the point where I could create my own style [as] Godzilla, filming had already completed," he said.

Satsuma would continue to portray the beast through 1995 in six more movies under the leadership of new SFX director Kawakita. Keenly aware that he was walking in the long shadow of Nakajima, Satsuma expressed deep admiration and respect for his predecessor. Nakajima had pioneered the art of suit acting, and now it was Satsuma's turn to create his own Godzilla. Both men were proud and energetic performers, sharing the attitude of toughness and doing whatever it takes. Satsuma would often cite the three qualities required for success: "In order to portray Godzilla, I believe that robust physical strength, sound mental fortitude, and the ability to perform under pressure—three essential qualities—are crucial. With any of them missing, there can't be a good monster-player."

Satsuma's Godzilla would always remain fierce and serious, never imitating the anthropomorphization of the Nakajima Godzilla. "Our approaches to Godzilla differ significantly, and that's what makes it interesting. I strove to create a more biological entity, with animallike qualities, eliminating body movements easily recognized as being human. Some part of Godzilla should always be moving, so I would concentrate

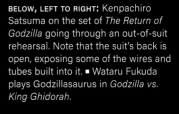

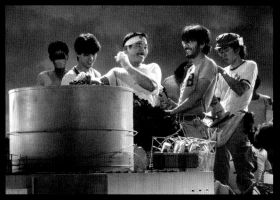

CLOCKWISE FROM TOP LEFT: Kenpachiro Satsuma with his team of "Godzilla handlers" on the nuclear power plant set of *The Return of Godzilla.* ▪ Suit maker Nobuyuki Yasumaru with Satsuma (*inside the Godzilla suit*) during the initial test of the finished costume for *The Return of Godzilla.* ▪ Before entering the suit, Satsuma devises the battle with the Crab Destoroyah puppets in *Godzilla vs. Destoroyah.* ▪ Rehearsing the underwater battle against Battra in *Godzilla vs. Mothra* with the wireworks staff.

on always moving the wrists." Satsuma's Godzilla advanced aggressively, and in contrast to Nakajima, his basic posture was to keep the arms low and close to his sides, his palms facing downward, the arms quickly lashing out when in action.

However, while Satsuma fiercely identified with the character, he never let himself feel bigger than the part. "The star of the Godzilla movies is Godzilla itself, not the actor inside," he said. "I must always recognize that I am not Godzilla, but rather Kenpachiro Satsuma wearing the attire of Godzilla. I must not be complacent and must strive to maintain the three qualities."

Satsuma faced many of the same difficulties as Nakajima—not just physically, but also mentally. "It's pitch-black inside Godzilla. In this sealed environment, I always feel a sense of loneliness and extreme claustrophobia. . . . That feeling gradually intensified. So, to counteract that anxiety, various actions are necessary, even if it's just for my own satisfaction. I scream loudly, hum my favorite song, think of someone I love, or observe the movements of the staff in reverse. Basically, I do silly things to escape [the] claustrophobia. But still, sometimes I feel anxious."

Advances in suit-making techniques resulted in increased comfort as well as new burdens for the suit actors. Beginning in 1984, holes were drilled into the fingertips and toes to allow sweat to exit the suit. "It would start out like a drizzle but later build to a downpour," Satsuma said. "In the old days, we didn't have those [holes], and I would lose my footing in the pools of sweat." The various performance-enhancing mechanics in the 1984 suit were activated by a canister of toxic fluorine gas that was installed in the tail. While rehearsing a scene, Satsuma recalled, "We were testing the mouth. Huh? There's a strange smell. Odd. The voices of the staff around me gradually faded away, and my head started to feel hazy, as if shrouded in fog. I collapsed with a thud. They found that the fluorine tube had come off the cylinder and gas was spraying out. It was a close call—I could have died from gas poisoning." Materials used to make the suits were becoming more robust, and the eyeholes in the neck now provided only minimal ventilation, and Satsuma experienced oxygen deprivation very quickly. "What happens after being inside Godzilla for a while? You gradually start to feel short of breath. Then you can feel your heart pounding violently. Next, your chest feels like it's going to burst. The pain gradually intensifies and throbs in your head, making you feel like you're splitting apart from the top of your head. Then you might start feeling nauseous, and sweat pours down. The more anxious you become, the more sweat pours out. It's agonizing." Without external air being pumped inside, an in-suit session would last no more than ten minutes.

Satsuma felt it important to give ample credit to the large team that supported his Godzilla. In his 1993 book *Inside Godzilla*, Satsuma devoted an entire chapter to the many staff members on the Godzilla team. Lighting crew, miniature makers, scripters, and the women on staff were all recognized. Satsuma also showed his appreciation for the mechanical operators who gave life to Godzilla's tail, and to the radio control operators that expressed Godzilla's emotions on its face; their jobs required them to closely observe and anticipate Satsuma's actions. To achieve this, they would review storyboards together with

Satsuma and make a detailed plan prior to filming. A team of "Godzilla handlers" took care of all matters regarding the suit, assumed responsibility for Satsuma's well-being, and passed directions to him—just as Kaimai had done for Nakajima decades earlier. Satsuma developed his own "Godzilla language," a series of hand signals that he used to communicate with his handlers.

And then there was suit maker Yasumaru, with whom Satsuma had a unique relationship dating back to when Satsuma had played Hedorah and Gigan. Yasumaru was a brilliant model maker and a tough character, famous for saying "The appearance of a kaiju is crucial. The actor inside is secondary." Satsuma's nickname for him was *Oni-Yasu* (Demon Yasu). Unlike the friendly and cooperative relationship between modeler Teizo Toshimitsu and Nakajima, Satsuma constantly clashed with Yasumaru. When making the Gigan suit for *Godzilla vs. Gigan*, Yasumaru constructed the claws as a solid piece of resin, so heavy and unwieldy that they could barely be lifted, much less put to any use. Satsuma's complaints fell on deaf ears until a heated exchange between Yasumaru and SFX director Nakano compelled Yasumaru to hollow out the claws so they could be used. For Godzilla, Yasumaru would tell Satsuma, "I am making Godzilla, not a toy. Professionals should be able to act well even in difficult situations." Satsuma replied, "If you were a professional, you would make it easier to move." And so it went until the inevitable compromise would be made, usually requiring Nakano's intervention.

Back when Nakajima acted with wireworks monsters, he called it a solo performance because he had to not only attack but also react against opponents that offered no physical resistance. In Satsuma's case, many of his opponents—Biollante, Ghidorah, Mothra, Battra, Rodan—were wire-operated and thus required a solo performance, testing his acting skills to the extreme. However, unlike Nakajima, Satsuma did not choreograph the monster battles himself because SFX director Kawakita used detailed storyboards to precisely map out the action.

The old hazards of shooting water scenes in Toho's Big Pool remained, and Satsuma had more than one brush with death. During filming the Uraga Strait battle in *Godzilla vs. Biollante*, an explosion dislodged a metal plate at the bottom of the pool that covered a 13-foot- (4-m-) deep hole. Satsuma was unaware of the hole, but had he stepped into it, he would have surely sunk to the bottom and drowned before the heavy, waterlogged suit could be raised up to save him. Satsuma remarked, "One must not forget that danger is always lurking. A little relaxation or carelessness can be fatal." Also during the *Biollante* shoot, Satsuma suffered intermittent electrical shocks in the pool due to faulty electrical wiring inside the suit.

While filming *Godzilla vs. Mothra*, Satsuma suffered a mysterious series of increasingly severe dizzy spells. A half-body Godzilla suit was created from the remains of the Sea Godzilla suit from *Godzilla vs. Biollante*, and whenever he entered the water in this suit, his symptoms would immediately appear. Eventually, it was discovered that thinner had been mixed into the urethane lining inside the costume—the chemical seeped from the urethane when immersed in water, saturating the inside of the costume. Despite the adverse effects on his health, Satsuma kept going. Drawing on his pride as an actor, Satsuma said, "It wasn't feasible to remake [the suit], so we had to continue as is. But I am the immortal Satsuma Godzilla."

When Godzilla attacked Sapporo in *Godzilla vs. King Ghidorah*, a section of the street was scored so that the monster would appear to fall into an underground shopping center. When the camera rolled, Godzilla broke through the street and the neck of the suit smashed into the rim of the hole, knocking Satsuma nearly senseless. Badly shaken, Satsuma carried on, and when the shot was finished, SFX director Kawakita requested a second take. Having suffered a concussion, Satsuma became angry, especially because no care had been taken to cushion his 3-foot (1-m) fall through the stage. Satsuma insisted mattresses be placed under the hole before reluctantly agreeing to a reshoot. In the end, the first take was used in the final cut.

BELOW, LEFT TO RIGHT: Some of Kenpachiro Satsuma's least favorite scenes involved being shot at by the military while in the water tank. His body parts beneath the thinner portions of the costume (e.g., his hands, arms, and neck) took a beating from the tracer bullets that struck Godzilla. Satsuma likened this experience to having someone throwing rocks at him at high velocity. ▪ Satsuma in the half-body suit, fighting with Battra in *Godzilla vs. Mothra*. This Godzilla suit induced severe dizzy spells due to thinner leaching from the interior when it was submerged in water.

ABOVE, LEFT TO RIGHT: Kenpachiro Satsuma adjusts his breathing apparatus to help him survive noxious CO2 fumes emitted by Burning Godzilla in *Godzilla vs. Destoroyah.* ■ Perhaps the most dangerous stunt Satsuma ever performed—walking blindly through intense fire and smoke in the Mount Fuji eruption scene of *Godzilla vs. Mothra.* One false step or a stumble might have meant serious injury or worse, as no one could have rescued him or moved the heavy suit out of harm's way. ■ Hurricane Ryu as Baby Godzilla on the live-action set of *Godzilla vs. Mechagodzilla II.*
■ BELOW, LEFT TO RIGHT: To combat oxygen deprivation and allow the actor to save the time of taking off the costume between takes, air is pumped into the suit through the eyeholes in this shot from the set of *Godzilla vs. SpaceGodzilla.* ■ SFX director Kenji Suzuki (*left*) and Godzilla actor Tsutomu Kitagawa (*right*) inspect the huge fiberglass fins on the *Godzilla 2000: Millennium* suit. The fins occasionally caused injuries to unsuspecting staff members during filming.

Hurricane Ryu, a storyboard artist as well as an aspiring suit actor, joined Kawakita's staff in 1991. Although he played Godzilla's enemies King Ghidorah and Battra, his dream was to play Godzilla on the big screen. He came close, portraying Baby Godzilla in *Godzilla vs. Mechagodzilla II*, a role that presented unique challenges for a suit actor. Just as Nakajima had done for the first *Godzilla*, Ryu went to the zoo for inspiration. "All baby animals have a special kind of movement. I decided to study peacocks. They say that dinosaurs and birds are related, so I thought I could learn from them." However, because Baby Godzilla interacts with the live-action cast, its scenes were filmed at normal speed rather than the high camera speeds employed for special effects. Ryu essentially had to unlearn the quick and exaggerated movements he'd become accustomed to while playing monsters in the past and learn to move in a more natural and subtle manner. Later, he portrayed Godzilla Junior in *Godzilla vs. Destoroyah.*

Godzilla vs Destoroyah was Godzilla's last hurrah of the 1990s and Satsuma's final film in the role. It ends with Godzilla suffering an agonizing death, and Satsuma nearly suffered the same fate. He recalled, "There was a device installed in the body that emits carbon dioxide gas, but initially, one of the nozzles was pointed [inward] and gas entered the suit directly. As a result, I collapsed from lack of oxygen about three times. It was feared that if this continued, I would die inside, so I started always wearing an Aqua Lung both underwater and on land. I had to bite the mouthpiece with all my strength to keep it from coming off, which made my gums bleed and chipped my teeth."

As Satsuma prepared to film the final, fatal chapter of his Godzilla's story, he waxed nostalgic. "The death of Heisei Godzilla also means the death of Satsuma Godzilla. While I was prepared for my inevitable retirement as a Godzilla actor, I never imagined Godzilla actually dying. Instead of being called an actor, I'd rather be remembered as a Godzilla craftsman. But it's too early for Godzilla to retire."

THE MILLENNIUM SERIES

After Hollywood introduced the first all-CG Godzilla in 1998, Toho responded with a reimagined version of the classic suitmation monster in *Godzilla 2000: Millennium.* For the coveted task of bringing the new Godzilla to life, the surprise pick was Tsutomu (Tom) Kitagawa, who had played many costumed heroes and monsters in series such as *Kamen Rider* and *Super Sentai* (the basis of the Power Rangers franchise) for Toei Studios. "Getting pulled over to Toho was unheard of," Kitagawa said. "Everyone thought, *Who is this guy? Why was he picked?* Godzilla was a much bigger burden I was taking on. I was super nervous." Based on Kitagawa's performance as Grand Ghidorah in *Mothra 3* (1998), SFX director Kenji Suzuki and suit maker Shinichi Wakasa felt he was right for the job.

Climbing into the Godzilla suit for the first time, Kitagawa encountered the same problem all Godzilla actors faced: breathing difficulties. "When I did the camera test, I thought I would die. I couldn't breathe. . . . They would stick an air pipe into the side of the tail and let air into the suit until the camera rolled, then they would remove it for a take. I tried to conserve my air. It didn't last long." Kitagawa was so concerned with breathing that he failed to notice other burdens inherent in the new, more technically sophisticated Godzilla suits. "There was a compressor attached, and lots of other things like dust makers attached to the feet. My limit in the suit was about one minute for actual acting. At first, I didn't realize there were all these extra attachments—did I really have to bear all that extra weight?"

Due to the design of the new Godzilla suit, practical considerations made it impossible for Kitagawa to truly create his own acting style. He had to crouch forward to support the gigantic fins on Godzilla's back, which were made of heavy fiberglass; if he stood up straight, he would fall over backward. The weight of the suit and his forward-leaning posture consequently made it impossible to lift Godzilla's feet up, so even a minor object in Kitagawa's path would cause him to trip and fall.

Special effects director Suzuki praised Kitagawa's performance, understanding his limitations. "Kitagawa is excellent at processing our requests and delivering performances that fit well within his own interpretation," Suzuki said. "With Godzilla, the challenging part is that many actions are done with the body but may not manifest visibly on the surface. He worked diligently to meet those demands, even exaggerating certain aspects to fulfill our requests. We have good communication and understanding between us."

Strong communication and teamwork with suit maker Wakasa influenced Kitagawa's performance. Wakasa explained, "Kitagawa knows that he can create different emotions with the suit because of his own experience in doing *Power Rangers*. Having worn masks previously, he knew that by tilting the head a little, for example, he could create different emotions on the face." Unlike other suit makers, Wakasa himself was always on set to observe and advise the actor. "Kitagawa completely understood what I was trying to do. What to do depended on the angle of the camera placement. I would advise him on things like, 'The camera is over here, so you should angle a certain way.'" By communicating with each other, the two men enhanced and conveyed the emotions and actions of Godzilla.

During the making of *Godzilla vs. Megaguirus*, Kitagawa gained confidence and began to create his own Godzilla acting style. He said, "Last year, I was somewhat conscious of the previous Godzilla, but this year, I wanted to do it my way, a speedy Godzilla. I changed my stride quite a bit." Whereas his crouching posture was once a burden, he now used it to make something new. "I actually wanted to crawl on all fours, almost

ABOVE: Suit maker Shinichi Wakasa advising suit actor Tsutomu Kitagawa on the set of *Godzilla: Tokyo SOS*. ■ **CLOCKWISE FROM TOP LEFT:** Godzilla executes a flying body slam onto Megaguirus in *Godzilla vs. Megaguirus*. Originally, Kitagawa was to perform the stunt in the Godzilla suit, but tests proved far too dangerous, so a mannequin cast from his body was placed in the suit instead. ■ Kitagawa and his support team from Wakasa's creature shop, Monsters Inc. Wakasa (*in blue shirt, arms folded*) stands to the left of Kitagawa. ■ With the extreme weight of Godzilla's head, Mizuho Yoshida had to maintain a more upright posture in the *GMK* Godzilla suit. ■ While he was often frustrated by the limitations of the suit, Kitagawa was given control of the expressive mechanical Godzilla in *Godzilla: Tokyo SOS*.

touching the ground with my hands, but the director told me it was a bit too much." The new, lighter Godzilla suit allowed Kitagawa to be more active, but he still felt frustrated. "I haven't fully gotten where I want to be. What the director describes and what I imagine match, but when I'm in the suit, it doesn't come out. That gap is frustrating."

When director Shusuke Kaneko selected sculptor and modeler Fuyuki Shinada to make monster suits for *Godzilla, Mothra and King Ghidorah: Giant Monsters All-Out Attack,* stunt actor Mizuho Yoshida (who had previously played monsters in Daiei's *Gamera 2: Attack of Legion* as well as Toho's *Rebirth of Mothra* and *Rebirth of Mothra 2*) was chosen to join the ranks of Godzilla suit actors. The new Godzilla suit was the tallest and heaviest ever made, and the tall, muscular Yoshida was ideally fit for the job. While Wakasa's recent Godzilla suits were operated with a forward-leaning crouch out of necessity, the *GMK* Godzilla was purposely designed that way. Still, despite Yoshida's physical prowess, it was impossible to maintain that pose due to the enormous weight of the mechanics in the suit and its raised heels. "It had all sorts of mechanical devices in the chest, head, and back—everywhere, so I could barely keep standing," Yoshida said. But in keeping with the time-honored tradition of can-do suit actors, Yoshida added, "When a suit gets heavier, I'll just work harder. I will never say 'I can't move because my suit is too heavy.' It would ruin [director] Kaneko-san and [SFX director] Kamiya-san's shooting plans." For much of the film, Yoshida was forced to portray Godzilla with an erect posture, much to suit maker Shinada's chagrin.

Following in the footsteps of three veteran Godzillas, Yoshida felt a strong urge to set his portrayal apart. "I felt like I shouldn't do the same old thing. There was a camera test before crank-in [the start of filming], and I tried something new there. But when I saw it on the monitor later, I realized it was definitely not like Godzilla. Ultimately, I decided to learn the basic style from the old films." Like his predecessors, he discovered that subtle movements inside the suit would not translate to the outside, so instead he concentrated on more noticeable nuances for his performance. "The director provides an emotional overview, so we can add details to it," said Yoshida. "If I walk toward something, I can add some hesitation. I wanted to bring little touches like that."

Godzilla x Mechagodzilla saw the return of the Wakasa–Kitagawa team for the final three films of the Millennium series. By now, Kitagawa's concept of Godzilla had emerged. "I'm sorry, but I wanted to change the image of Toho kaiju films," Kitagawa said. "Nakajima's and Satsuma's Godzillas were scarier, but I wanted to make a cool, new type of Godzilla that was like a real creature. My Godzilla doesn't start fighting unless provoked. Godzilla doesn't want to destroy things, but since nuclear energy is what he is after and things are in the way, he destroys. It's really the fault of humans, not Godzilla."

For the fiftieth anniversary production of *Godzilla Final Wars,* Kitagawa was also given the job of "kaiju action advisor," a role not unlike that which Haruo Nakajima had previously served unofficially through-out his monster career. Kitagawa was in charge of coordinating action with a team of novice kaiju suit actors. Kitagawa was also closely involved in the process of creating storyboards, which laid out the action in detail, making him the de facto fight choreographer.

Godzilla Final Wars also saw a fundamental change in the way monster suits were made. Director Ryuhei Kitamura ordered suits that could be used to perform extreme action; the new Godzilla suit was made lighter and form-fitting. Kitagawa was delighted. "It was just like adding another layer of muscle onto my body. I felt, finally, that I could really act and fight. It was such a joy. I had wanted to do this for five years. Compared to the previous four suits, when I was so frustrated with not being able to move, this time I could do what I wanted. I wish I could go back and redo the previous films with this [suit]."

With the success of the CG creatures in *Shin Godzilla* and *Godzilla Minus One,* the era of the Godzilla suit actor effectively came to an end. The extreme physical and mental challenges required to create Godzilla gave way to the painstaking work of digital artists and designers to create a virtual performance. Nevertheless, Godzilla suit actors leave behind a fifty-year legacy of toughness, imagination, courage, and determination upon which the franchise was built.

(GOJIRA X MOSURA X MEKAGOJIRA TOKYO SOS /
GODZILLA × MOTHRA × MECHAGODZILLA: TOKYO SOS)
RELEASED: DECEMBER 13, 2003 (JAPAN)

GODZILLA: TOKYO SOS

T he studio asked me to make a film not about Godzilla wreaking havoc but rather depicting a meticulous, strategically planned battle between Godzilla and the Self-Defense Forces and the anti-Godzilla forces," recalled director Masaaki Tezuka. "With that in mind, I continued in the style of my two previous works, *Godzilla vs. Megaguirus* and *Godzilla Against Mechagodzilla*. It seemed like the studio appreciated that approach."

Tezuka's nostalgic penchant for bridging past and present Toho genre history reaches its apex in *Godzilla: Tokyo SOS*, a direct sequel to the prior film that effectively creates a brief miniseries connecting the only two Millennium films with shared continuity. Seventy-seven-year-old Hiroshi Koizumi reprises his *Mothra* (1961) role as Professor Shinichi Chujo, who led the first expedition to Infant Island four decades earlier. Mothra itself also returns in an authentic-looking re-creation of its original 1960s design—now made more lifelike through a combination of practical and digital effects. There is also a new generation of *shobijin* (Small Beauties), Mothra's tiny muses. Several veteran actors from the Heisei era also play significant supporting roles: Akira Nakao (Prime Minister Hayato Igarashi) makes his fifth series appearance playing a military or government official; familiar character actor Koichi Ueda (Defense Agency director Dobashi) appears in his eleventh consecutive Godzilla film; and Toru

"IN EVERY SINGLE FILM, GODZILLA HAS CHANGED. I HAVE BEEN FOLLOWING THOSE CHANGES FROM (SFX DIRECTOR EIJI) TSUBURAYA'S TIME TO (SFX DIRECTOR TERUYOSHI) NAKANO'S TIME, AND NOW THAT WE ARRIVE AT (SUIT MAKER SHINICHI) WAKASA'S GODZILLA, ITS STYLE IS SO SHARP AND SOPHISTICATED AND COOL. YOU MIGHT EVEN THINK ITS DORSAL FINS ARE SYMMETRICALLY CALCULATED. IT'S A VERY HANDSOME AND FULLY REALIZED GODZILLA."

—Eiichi Asada, special effects director

Minegishi, the heroic Colonel Goro Gondo of *Godzilla vs. Biollante*, has a cameo as a TV commentator. Tezuka is a genre fan at heart, and numerous fan-service moments evoke memories of classic Toho films—especially *Mothra* and *Mothra vs. Godzilla*—and evince the director's affection for lengthy monster battles.

Like Tezuka's previous films, *Tokyo SOS* opens with an exciting action sequence before the main title. Radar monitors at Pearl Harbor detect a UFO heading toward Japan. The Japan Air Self-Defense Force scrambles F-15s to intercept it, and the pilots witness the object, obscured within a bank of clouds, cruising

PREVIOUS SPREAD: Godzilla endures punishing attacks from the military, Mechagodzilla, and Mothra's multiple forms in *Godzilla: Tokyo SOS*. ■ **BELOW:** "To create the National Diet Building, we referred to the design previously used in *Godzilla vs. Mothra,* and it was beautifully detailed," said director Masaaki Tezuka. "We only had one chance to film the scene of Godzilla and Kiryu falling onto it and making it collapse, and the veteran SFX crew handled it splendidly."

CLOCKWISE FROM ABOVE: Radar operators at the US Air Force base at Pearl Harbor detect a UFO headed for Japan. ▪ "Mothra basically doesn't have much room for improvement," said SFX director Eiichi Asada, "so all I changed were things like the way its legs move. We tried to keep the pattern on the wings as close as possible to the original 1961 version." ▪ "I used fishing rods inside Mothra's wings," said creature maker Shinichi Wakasa. "We used the most flexible parts; each wing has probably seven or eight rods inside. Mothra was suspended from wires on an overhead aerial brace [to flap the wings], and we also had wires pulling from below, on the floor. There's also a guy directly behind Mothra—one wire is connected to a pulley that he controls; this was used when Mothra deployed its poison pollen attack." ▪ "We originally intended to have Tokyo Tower destroyed by Godzilla's heat ray in *Godzilla Against Mechagodzilla*," said director Masaaki Tezuka. "But it didn't happen, so this time Godzilla kind of got his revenge. It's surprising that Godzilla had never destroyed Tokyo Tower even once."

at high speed. Warning shots are fired, but the UFO enters Japanese airspace undeterred. Missiles miss their target as the UFO disappears in a cloud of golden fairy dust. A satellite image captures markings on the UFO: the familiar, colorful pattern on the wings of the adult Mothra.

Tezuka sought to meld the look and feel of traditional *tokusatsu* craftsmanship with modern digital effects more effectively. To help achieve this, he sought out Eiichi Asada, an old-school Toho veteran who began his career as a low-ranking assistant special effects director on such films as *Godzilla vs. Megalon*, *Godzilla vs. Mechagodzilla*, *Terror of Mechagodzilla*, and *The War in Space* (1977), and later became first assistant SFX director on *The Return of Godzilla* and other films. Asada came out of retirement to accept the job; though in his early fifties, it was his debut as special effects director. "I had not done anything for Toho for over ten years," Asada said. "This came out of the blue. . . . Before crank-in [the start of filming], I was just excited and didn't feel any pressure. However, I was always worried that the film would get canceled. Once it started, though, I was having the time of my life."

Asada became the fourth SFX director of the Millennium series. His style differs noticeably from those of his predecessors, often emphasizing low camera angles to simulate a human point of view. The interplay between live-action location footage and special effects is nearly seamless as Godzilla—lured back to Japan by its cyborg cousin once again—sets off deadly mines in Tokyo Bay as it approaches. Citizens evacuate amid the chaos, and the military rolls out heavy equipment, with real-life Japan Self-Defense Force tanks and vehicles taking position alongside Maser Cannons more convincingly than ever. Composer Michiru Oshima's pounding Godzilla theme signals the beast's arrival through a rising column

of water. Chujo's grandson cleverly summons Mothra by recreating the iconic Infant Island symbol on a school playground. Mothra confronts Godzilla, and a protracted series of battles transpires, eventually involving Kiryu and a pair of giant caterpillars, the latter beckoned to Tokyo by the twin fairies when the adult Mothra is overpowered. The monster suits, props (including a robotic Godzilla head for close-ups), miniatures, lighting, and overall production values of Asada's effects display a level of polish and detail uncommon to the latter-day films.

SANCTITY OF LIFE

"My main theme," Tezuka said, "is that life is always important. There are people who will fight to protect lives, people who will fight against anything trying to take lives, and people who will watch the fight. 'Life is important' is something I repeat in my films all the time."

Godzilla Against Mechagodzilla was the third consecutive Godzilla movie paired on a double bill with a feature-length *Hamtaro* cartoon to help expand the audience to all ages. *Godzilla Against Mechagodzilla* and *Hamtaro: The Captive Princess* had grossed ¥1.91 billion together, eighth best at the box office among domestic releases in 2003 (for films released just before the new year, tallies are included in Japan's Film Classification and Rating Organization rankings for the following calendar year). This success, along with anticipation for Godzilla's fiftieth birthday in 2004, generated momentum to continue the series, though a sequel to *Godzilla Against Mechagodzilla* was not originally in the offing; other story ideas were proposed.

"Producer Tomiyama's way was to lay out three or four story treatments and have the director pick one," Tezuka said. "For *Godzilla: Tokyo SOS,* they had four stories, but they were all really boring. They all felt somewhat like *Godzilla vs. SpaceGodzilla*. On an island, Godzilla sleeps! And then Mothra arrives! I said, 'I'm sorry, I don't think I can do this.' I was supposed to just pick one. But I asked them to let me think about it. Then I wrote a story overnight and gave it to them."

Tezuka had intended for the heroine Akane to die aboard Kiryu at the end of *Godzilla Against Mechagodzilla*; the idea was for Godzilla and the cyborg to disappear underwater, the Absolute Zero Cannon would detonate,

GODZILLA FACT: The carcass of a giant creature is found on a beach, with slash wounds to its neck, indicating it was likely killed by Godzilla. The creature is Kamoebas, a type of gigantic turtle monster first seen in Toho's *Space Amoeba* (1970). "Originally, I wanted it to be Anguirus," said director Masaaki Tezuka, "but the company was considering Anguirus for a future film, so it wouldn't [have worked]."

the sea would turn to ice and crumble, and the story ends; neither Godzilla nor Kiryu would resurface. He said, "At the time, there were no plans for a sequel, and I thought that would be the end for Mechagodzilla. But I was told, "Toho doesn't want to kill the heroine in their New Year movie." So it ended in a draw as you see in the final film. It would've been a heavy ending if she'd died, but it would've still offered hope."

Tezuka cowrote the *Tokyo SOS* screenplay with Masahiro Yokotani after admiring the screenwriter's work on *GMK*. Tezuka's simple and by-now-familiar theme of the sanctity of life weighs heavily on the hearts and minds of the main characters, from the nominal hero Sergeant Yoshito Chujo (Noboru Kaneko), a Mechagodzilla mechanic and Professor Chujo's nephew; to the prime minister, reluctant to relaunch Kiryu for fear of endangering his son, a pilot; and to the monsters Mothra, Godzilla, and cyborg Mechagodzilla. Mothra's fairies warn that mankind has disturbed the "souls of the dead" in building Kiryu, and Godzilla's bones must be returned to the sea. In a poignant and unexpected ending, Kiryu nearly kills Godzilla by reopening the large chest wound the monster suffered at the end of *Godzilla Against Mechagodzilla*; Godzilla's agonizing cries again trigger the consciousness of the 1954 Godzilla embedded inside Mechagodzilla. The robot gently picks up its severely weakened brethren and plunges deep into the Japan Trench. The two Godzillas are seemingly gone forever, and the souls of the dead are returned to eternal rest.

Godzilla: Tokyo SOS would be the last Godzilla film paired with *Hamtaro* for good luck. The formula had apparently lost its luster, as their latest double bill earned only ¥1.3 billion, a considerable drop-off, and placed just fifteenth at the domestic box office. A post-credits scene—a secret lab where the DNA of Godzilla and other kaiju are stored—hinted at a sequel, but one was not to be. Tezuka would unsuccessfully pitch an idea for the next Godzilla film, but for the monster's fiftieth birthday, the studio would instead opt to make a splash with a disruptive new director and a 180-degree change in tone and style.

OPPOSITE, CLOCKWISE FROM TOP LEFT: The two caterpillars' stealthy and strategic attack succeeds in cocooning Godzilla, much like the final attack of the same creatures in *Mothra vs. Godzilla.* ▪ "Godzilla got covered in that cocoon material," said suit actor Tsutomu Kitagawa. "[SFX assistant director Osamu Kume] was really nervous, telling everyone not to smoke in the studio because the silk was made of gasoline." ▪ The larvae deftly evade Godzilla by maneuvering through the streets. These scenes showcase the film's miniature sets. "For whatever general things I needed, like making monsters or miniatures, the studio provided me with enough budget," said SFX director Eiichi Asada. "We made so many plaster buildings in the Tokyo city set that [SFX art director] Toshio Miike told me, 'I've never destroyed this many buildings in my life!'" ▪ RIGHT: The battle turns when Kiryu stabs Godzilla's chest scar with its Anti-Beast Drilling Device, or "Spiral Claw," a rotating razor-like weapon, then fires its Hyper Maser Beam into the reopened wound, causing Godzilla to collapse in pain. ▪ BELOW: In one of the most exciting moments of the final battle, Godzilla skillfully fires its heat ray through a building and strikes Kiryu, then proceeds to attack the robot.

(GOJIRA FAINARU WOZU)
RELEASED: DECEMBER 4, 2004 (JAPAN)

GODZILLA FINAL WARS

Having defeated every monster on Earth, Godzilla focuses its attack on the Gotengo flying warship, blasting it out of the sky. "Son of a bitch," grunts the Gotengo's sword-wielding captain, Douglas Gordon. "He just won't quit." The ship's survivors—military men, a diplomat, a scientist, and a mutant—now stand face-to-face with Godzilla . . . and certain death. Suddenly, the roly-poly adolescent kaiju Minilla jogs into the scene, intervening between Godzilla and the humans, followed by a little boy and his grandfather arriving in a mini truck. "Hey, Godzilla!" says the old man. "It's over. You must forgive." No response. Grandpa aims his small-caliber rifle—"Damn lizard!" The boy and Minilla now form a human-kaiju shield between the opposing factions; humankind and monster stand down, and Godzilla departs a postapocalyptic Tokyo, bellowing a final victory roar against the majestic, overpowering sun.

"When I was thinking about the ending," said director Ryuhei Kitamura, "I thought, *What if Godzilla does something he has never done before?* When I considered what that could be, I thought about forgiveness. For fifty years, Godzilla has [either] been bullying everyone or he's being beaten up, and in the end, he forgives. I thought, *This is it!*"

Godzilla Final Wars, the fiftieth anniversary Godzilla film, is certainly like nothing before. In the hands of Kitamura, the independent-minded auteur behind a series of mid-budget action-horror cult hits, Godzilla is a one-kaiju

"I WANTED TO CREATE SOMETHING THAT WOULD SURPRISE THOSE WHO WERE PREVIOUSLY NOT INTERESTED IN GODZILLA AND MAKE THEM SAY, 'WOW, GODZILLA IS AMAZING.'"

—Ryuhei Kitamura, director

"IT WAS CONCEIVED AS AN ALL-STAR ACTION FILM. KITAMURA'S NAME CAME UP, AND RIGHT AWAY I SAID, 'THAT'S THE GUY!' SINCE I HAD SEEN HIS FILM *VERSUS* (2000)."

—Shogo Tomiyama, producer

PREVIOUS SPREAD: "I envisioned Godzilla as a 328-foot- (100-m-) tall creature in the ring—headbutting, kicking, throwing [its] opponent," said director Ryuhei Kitamura. "That was my image. When suit actor [Tsutomu] Kitagawa heard this, he said, 'I always wanted to do something like that, but I never had a director who wanted it, [too].'" ▪ FAR LEFT: As the story begins, the Gotengo warship seals Godzilla beneath the ice in Antarctica, a scene not originally in the script. "The higher-ups thought that Godzilla entered the film too late," said screenwriter Isao Kiriyama. "So we added the fight with the Gotengo at the beginning." ▪ LEFT: Godzilla emerges from Area G—the containment zone established by the Earth Defense Force at Antarctica—after being trapped beneath the ice there for an extended period.

army waging worldwide war against a parade of monsters unleashed by the Xiliens, space invaders bent on conquering Earth. The film is unrestrained by genre norms, and yet nostalgia abounds: the plot, monsters, aliens, cast, and character names reflect five decades of Godzilla history. Kitamura recasts it all in a mold of his own making, borrowing tropes and tricks and camera moves from anime (fierce rivalry between superpowered frenemies), *tokusatsu* television (suitmation monsters with human proportions), and Hollywood films like *X-Men*, *Armageddon*, and *Independence Day,* with a soundtrack blending metal, prog rock, and techno—and a dash of Akira Ifukube. *Final Wars* is faster, louder, looser, darker, and crazier than any other Godzilla movie. Even Godzilla itself is over-the-top, an unstoppable dynamo with an über-powerful heat ray that literally blows its foes to bits.

Plans for Godzilla's half-century movie began well in advance—while *Tokyo SOS* was simultaneously in the works. In April 2003, producer Shogo Tomiyama tapped writer Wataru Mimura to develop a story about monsters appearing worldwide under the control of the Xiliens. Mimura wrote a treatment, inserting the Gotengo (originally seen in 1963's *Atragon*) into the center of the action and creating the character of Colonel Douglas Gordon (originally written as a Frenchman in the hopes that Jean Reno would play the role; Kitamura would instead cast MMA [mixed martial arts] fighter Don Frye, whom the director was a fan of) and Earth Defense Force (EDF) commander Reiko Namikawa, written specifically for Kumi Mizuno. The Xiliens and the name "Namikawa" were homages to *Invasion of Astro-Monster*; the paleontologist Hachiro Jingugi, who divines the alien origins of the mummified monster Gigan, was named in honor of producer Tomoyuki Tanaka, who had used that pseudonym years earlier.

"Young people might not understand, but for us Toho actors, Tomoyuki Tanaka is a godlike presence," said veteran star Kenji Sahara, who played the part. "To have my character named after him was a feeling that words like 'happiness' or 'honor' can't adequately express. I was profoundly moved."

After being named director in the fall of 2003, Kitamura brought aboard certain creative personnel who'd worked on his acclaimed female assassin *jidai-geki* actioner *Azumi* (2003); screenwriter Isao Kiriyama reshaped Mimura's outline to suit Kitamura's idiosyncratic style. In early 2004, meetings were held to discuss which monsters would appear. Kitamura, Tomiyama, and the writers sat in a room surrounded by kaiju action figures, debating. "I wanted to [include] as many monsters [as possible], but of course, I couldn't include everything. Everybody has opinions. Even now, people [ask] me why Jet Jaguar is not in the movie [*laughs*]."

Kitamura wasn't interested in following traditions. "When Toho Studios and producer Tomiyama asked me to get on board, I felt [that] Mr. Tomiyama wanted to [disrupt] the franchise and create something new

CLOCKWISE FROM TOP LEFT: Many of the monsters display more agility and quickness in *Godzilla Final Wars* than in their previous incarnations. Notably, Anguirus curls itself into a rolling attack-ball during its fight with Godzilla. ■ The sea serpent Manda (originally from 1963's *Atragon*), was re-created via CG and two models, including a Styrofoam model utilized when Manda is frozen and shatters into dust. ■ After being freed from containment by the Earth Defense Force, Godzilla fights Gigan at the South Pole, then swims to Australia, New Guinea, and finally Japan as it eliminates each monster challenger. ■ (*bottom row*) "Zilla" attacks Sydney. This fully CG monster is quickly tail-whacked into the Sydney Opera House and then incinerated by Godzilla.

for [what would be] the final Godzilla movie for that time," he said. "I'm very straightforward, so in the very first meeting, I told Mr. Tomiyama, 'This is what I love about Godzilla, and this is what I don't love about the recent Godzilla movies.' If he [hadn't wanted] to make changes, he wouldn't have hired me." Kitamura felt the films lacked synergy between the special effects and the human drama. He asked why there wasn't more camera movement, and why monsters often stood far apart and just fired rays at one another. "I told my team, 'I want this Godzilla to be super-fast, to move more like an animal. I don't want slow movement, and I don't want too-bright lighting to make it super obvious that it's a miniature set and a man in a suit.' And they agreed with my vision, so that's how we started to create something very different."

Early on, the director decided to utilize the bleach bypass color processing technique that gave many iconic Hollywood films a darker tint. He wanted to limit CG and focus on "the techniques that Japan has

"THIS FINAL MISSION WILL DECIDE THE FATE OF THE HUMAN RACE. THIS IS OPERATION FINAL WAR."

—Captain Douglas Gordon (Don Frye)

been doing better than anywhere else and present it in a new way." For his part, producer Tomiyama didn't believe Kitamura was completely changing course. "I suggested to Kitamura, since Godzilla movies have rules like 'Godzilla doesn't shed blood in battles,' would you be willing to [adhere to the rules]?" Tomiyama said. "He wanted to make a [new] era of Godzilla films that would surpass Hollywood's. In a sense, he was competing with Hollywood: 'How about you guys make this kind of movie?' That was very interesting for me, but he was still adhering to Godzilla's [established] rules."

BIGGER AND BOLDER

From the opening scenes, *Godzilla Final Wars* is both familiar and radically different. A fast-moving prologue outlines the thin plot in which the world has been besieged by Toho monsters for fifty years, but a period of peace has reigned thanks to the efforts of the EDF and its army of human-mutant soldiers. Kitamura's pledge to create "a rock-style monster movie" is cemented via an opening credits montage by Hollywood title artist Kyle Cooper, which surveys Godzilla history at hyperspeed, and an unusual score by Keith Emerson and other rock artists. Godzilla runs, slides, and performs heretofore impossible stunts. Asada's special effects bear little resemblance to his work on the prior film; some of Wakasa's monsters are wild reinterpretations. But both men were enthusiastic about the new direction. "If I had made the same type of Godzilla [movie] as before," said Asada, "I probably would not have been so adventurous. It may be controversial among fans, but I think Kitamura has given me a lot of inspiration." Added Wakasa, "*Final Wars* had a bigger budget. It wasn't a situation where I had to do ten-plus monster suits on short notice." Whereas he typically had forty-five days to make monster suits, now he had four months.

"It was a huge production," said Kitamura. "Because it was the fiftieth anniversary, we had a lot of money and time to spend, which is very rare in the Japanese film industry. So that was pure fun. I had four different units: my unit, second unit, the man-in-suit monster unit, and the overseas unit. It was a giant production. My first day of shooting that movie was not even in Japan, it was in Sydney."

ABOVE: The Minilla suit was based closely on the 1960s design. The creature is human size at first, an homage to *All Monsters Attack*. "Director Kitamura wanted Minilla to interact with a human child," recalled screenwriter Isao Kiriyama. "I hadn't originally intended to include a child in the story." Both Minilla and Rodan are played by suit actor Naoko Kamio.

■ **BELOW, CLOCKWISE FROM LEFT:** "Keizer Ghidorah resembles Death Ghidorah [from 1996's *Rebirth of Mothra*]," said suit maker Shinichi Wakasa. "Director Kitamura wanted this monster's size to overwhelm Godzilla, so we built it so that two people would be inside." The four-legged monster suit was constructed like a pantomime horse and worn by suit actors Motokuni Nakagawa and Toshihiro Ogura.
■ Monster X (Nakagawa), the last monster dispatched to Earth by the Xiliens, arrives inside the Gorath meteor. When the Xilien mothership is destroyed, Monster X morphs into Keizer Ghidorah, which nearly kills Godzilla before the Gotengo warship comes to the monster's aid. ■ Suit maker Wakasa said, "I made Godzilla's face to be always challenging or fighting. Director Kitamura wanted to make Godzilla do actual battles like pro wrestling. Everything became human-shaped as a result."

RIGHT: (*top & middle rows*) In quick succession, Godzilla faces off against a number of classic foes from the Showa series, including Hedorah, Ebirah, Kamacuras, King Caesar, and Kumonga. Some of these battles last just a few seconds as Godzilla overwhelms its opponent.

■ **BELOW:** The cyborg monster Gigan is unleashed on the world by the Xiliens.

LEFT: Mothra sacrifices itself to defeat Gigan. Originally, the Mothra–Gigan fight had greater significance in the screenplay's logic. "Gigan came to Earth fifty million years ago and exterminated the earthlings," said screenwriter Wataru Mimura. "At that time, Mothra had fought Gigan and lost, and as a result, M-Base [a fictional fifth DNA nucleotide instilling enhanced strength] was scattered on Earth, creating a race of human mutants." This background detail was omitted from the final script, he said. ∎
BELOW: In keeping with director Ryuhei Kitamura's image of monsters engaged in pro-wrestling action, Monster X holds back Godzilla as Gigan prepares to strike with its chain saw claws.

In retrospect, *Godzilla Final Wars* was a far-out experiment that didn't quite click. In Japan, the film ranked No. 20 among domestic releases for the 2005 box office year, at ¥1.26 billion—less than half the return for *GMK*, the current series' high-water mark. Audience tastes had shifted away from kaiju, as the films of Studio Ghibli and other anime productions consistently dominated the box office. Like the previous four Millennium films, *Final Wars* did not attract US theatrical distribution. Still, if Kitamura was indeed issuing a challenge to Hollywood, then that challenge would eventually be met. After a ten-year screen absence, Godzilla would resurface across the Pacific Ocean, reimagined with state-of-the-art technology in a film that would help grow the monster's global audience to an extent once thought unimaginable.

ABOVE, TOP TO BOTTOM: Toho's publicity blitz for *Godzilla Final Wars* included a Hollywood premiere at the world-famous Grauman's Chinese Theatre on November 29, 2004. The director, main stars, and other creative principals were in attendance, along with celebrity guests, and Godzilla walked the red carpet. Earlier that day, Godzilla received a star on the Hollywood Walk of Fame.

■ **RIGHT, TOP & BOTTOM:** The film's most dramatic moment: The Xiliens send the Gorath meteor (a nod to Toho's 1962 film *Gorath*) hurtling toward Earth and promise "the last chapter in the Godzilla saga." Godzilla blasts its heat ray toward the sky. When the smoke clears, the monster stands unharmed in the middle of the impact crater.

"THE COMMON UNDERSTANDING BETWEEN THE DIRECTOR AND ME WAS THAT ACTION IS MORE IMPORTANT THAN EXPOSITION. IF WE NEEDED MORE EXPLANATION, WE JUST ADDED MORE ACTION."

—Isao Kiriyama, screenwriter

TOHO SUPER TECHNOLOGY

A VISUAL GUIDE TO THE IMAGINATIVE WEAPONS, VEHICLES, AIRCRAFT, AND DEVICES OF GODZILLA'S WORLD

TOP ROW: Oxygen Destroyer (*Godzilla*).
■ **LEFT:** High Tension Towers (*King Kong vs. Godzilla*). ■ **BOTTOM LEFT:** Spaceship P-1 (*Invasion of Astro Monster*). ■ **BOTTOM RIGHT:** World Space Authority Radar Telescopes (*Invasion of Astro Monster*).

ABOVE: Artificial Lightning towers (*Mothra vs. Godzilla*). ■ **RIGHT:** A-Cycle Light Ray Cannon (*Invasion of Astro Monster*).

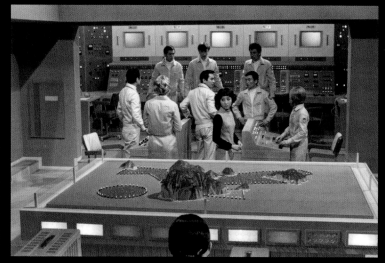

TOP LEFT: Silver Iodide Towers (*Son of Godzilla*). ■ TOP RIGHT: Ogasawara Island Control Center (*Destroy All Monsters*). ■ MIDDLE: Moonlight SY-3 and Exploration Vehicle (*Destroy All Monsters*). ■ LEFT: High Voltage Electrodes (*Godzilla vs. Hedorah*). ■ OPPOSITE: Moonlight SY-3 (*Destroy All Monsters*).

OPPOSITE, CLOCKWISE FROM TOP LEFT:
Maser Canons (*Godzilla vs. Gigan*).
■ High Power Laser Beam Tank
(*The Return of Godzilla*). ■ Super X2
(*Godzilla vs. Biollante*). ■ MB92 Maser
Tank (*Godzilla vs. Biollante, Godzilla
vs. King Ghidorah, Godzilla vs. Mothra,
Godzilla vs. Mechagodzilla II, Godzilla
vs. Destoroyah*). ■ Super X (*The Return
of Godzilla*). ■ ABOVE: Thunder Control
System (*Godzilla vs. Biollante*). ■ RIGHT:
Garuda (*Godzilla vs. Mechagodzilla II*).

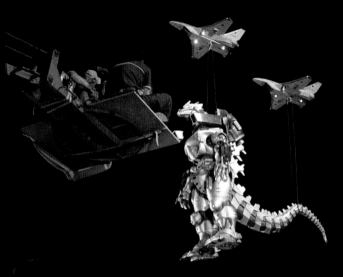

TOP ROW: Super XIII (*Godzilla vs. Destoroyah*). ▪ Freezing Maser Tank (*Godzilla vs. Destoroyah*). ▪ **MIDDLE ROW:** GX-813 Griffon V-TOL aircraft (*Godzilla vs. Megaguirus*). ▪ AC-3 White Heron Kiryu support aircraft (*Godzilla Against Mechagodzilla*). ▪ **LEFT:** Gotengo flying warship (*Godzilla Final Wars*). ▪ **OPPOSITE TOP:** Type 90 Maser Cannon (*Godzilla: Tokyo SOS*). ▪ **OPPOSITE BOTTOM:** Gotengo (*Godzilla Final Wars*).

ANIME:
2017 TO 2021

GODZILLA
怪獣惑星

GODZILLA
決戦機動増殖都市

GODZILLA
星を喰う者

GODZILLA: PLANET OF THE MONSTERS
(GOJIRA: KAIJU WAKUSEI)
RELEASED: NOVEMBER 17, 2017 (JAPAN THEATRICAL RELEASE); JANUARY 17, 2018 (NETFLIX)

GODZILLA: CITY ON THE EDGE OF BATTLE
(GOJIRA: KESSEN KIDO ZOSHOKU TOSHI / GODZILLA: BATTLE MOBILE PROLIFERATION CITY)
RELEASED: MAY 18, 2018 (JAPAN THEATRICAL RELEASE); JULY 18, 2018 (NETFLIX)

GODZILLA: THE PLANET EATER
(GOJIRA: HOSHI O KU MONO)
RELEASED: NOVEMBER 9, 2018 (JAPAN THEATRICAL RELEASE); JANUARY 9, 2019 (NETFLIX)

GODZILLA: THE ANIME TRILOGY

It's something of a mystery as to why Godzilla took so long to enter the world of anime. Ever since the Toei Company founded its animation studio in 1956 with the goal of becoming the "Disney of the East," Japanese animation has grown into a mind-bogglingly diverse entertainment form, encompassing a multitude of subgenres and appealing to international audiences of all ages. The aliens, mecha, robots, youthful heroes, and other tropes of sci-fi anime certainly influenced the Godzilla series; Mechagodzilla is just one example. But—excluding two animated TV shows in the US and a *chibi*-style children's cartoon produced in Japan in the nineties—Godzilla did not cross over from live action.

This changed dramatically with Toho's follow-up to *Shin Godzilla*. In keeping with the recent practice of entrusting Godzilla to independent filmmakers with break-the-mold ideas (e.g., *Final Wars, Shin Godzilla*), the studio's Toho

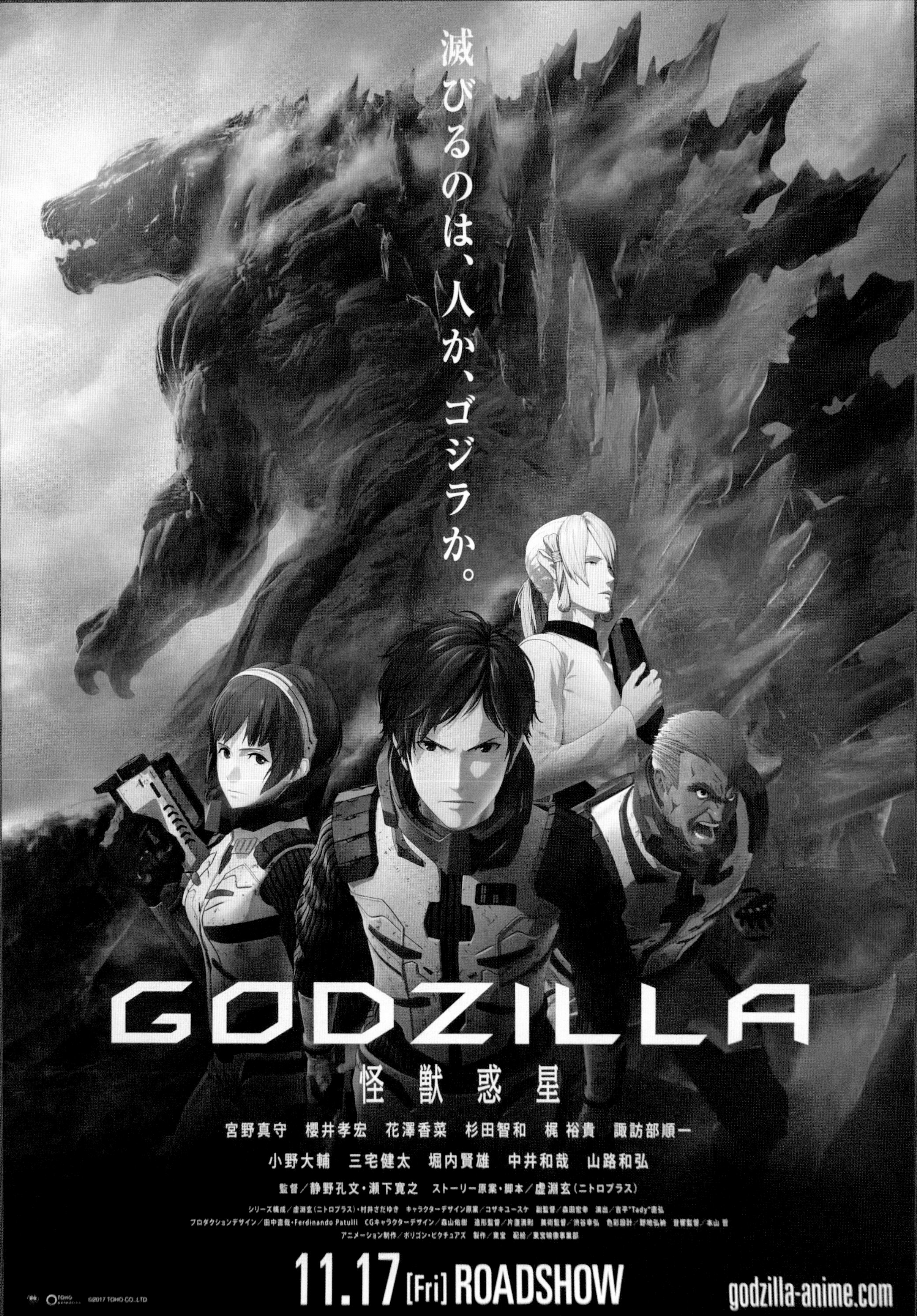

滅びるのは、人か、ゴジラか。
GODZILLA
怪獣惑星
宮野真守　櫻井孝宏　花澤香菜　杉田智和　梶 裕貴　諏訪部順一
小野大輔　三宅健太　堀内賢雄　中井和哉　山路和弘
監督／静野孔文・瀬下寛之　ストーリー原案・脚本／虚淵玄（ニトロプラス）
11.17 [Fri] ROADSHOW
godzilla-anime.com
©2017 TOHO CO.,LTD

> "THE GOAL WAS TO CREATE A GODZILLA FILM THAT HARNESSES THE STRENGTHS OF ANIME. SO WE DECIDED TO GO ALL OUT IN A NEW DIRECTION AND MAKE SOMETHING NOVEL. RIGHT FROM THE START, I EMPHASIZED CREATING A WORK USING AN UNPRECEDENTED WORLDVIEW AND SETTING. HENCE, THE FILM IS SET IN THE DISTANT FUTURE AS A SCIENCE-FICTION PIECE."

—Gen Urobuchi, writer

Animation division entered a collaboration with Japanese 3DCG animation studio Polygon Pictures and Netflix for a trilogy of feature-length anime that would thoroughly reimagine Godzilla in both content and form. Set in a postapocalyptic future, these films present the monster as the most highly evolved life force on Earth, a nature god that has reshaped the planet's ecosystem in its own image. In its ultimate form—Godzilla Earth—the creature stands an astounding 984 feet (300 m) tall and has a muscular, sinewy appearance that is more plantlike than reptilian. "We envisioned Godzilla as a colossal entity resembling a 'world tree' at the heart of this unique environment," said codirector Hiroyuki Seshita. A sober and straightforward hard science-fiction saga, the three-film arc occupies a separate universe from the live-action films. Its digressions into spiritual and existential questions, and its themes of ecological and moral responsibility, steer the Godzilla franchise in ambitious—if divisive—new directions.

A prologue establishes the drama's bleak backdrop. In 1999, Godzilla and other monsters began a worldwide assault, punishing humanity for despoiling Earth with environmental and nuclear pollution, and leaving cities in ruins. Later, after trying and failing to defeat Godzilla for several decades, several thousand surviving humans fled the now-unlivable planet and became refugees aboard the *Aratrum*, an interstellar exploratory ship, searching the galaxies for a habitable world. The humans are accompanied in this voyage by members of two exiled alien races that had joined the fight against Godzilla: the deeply spiritual-philosophical Exif and the technologically focused Bilusaldo. After twenty-two years in space, the refugees' search for a new planet fails; weary of their space-bound existence and short on resources, they return to Earth in the hope that Godzilla has perished and the world is safe for recolonization. But—in shades of the similarly titled *Planet of the Apes* (1968)—due to a space-time warp, they learn

PAGES 366–367: Godzilla Earth unleashes its heat ray. ■ PREVIOUS SPREAD: Japanese theatrical release poster for the first film in the trilogy, *Godzilla: Planet of the Monsters.* ■ LEFT: Humans from the interstellar emigration ship *Aratrum* return to Earth and engage Godzilla in battle, intent on reclaiming the planet as their own.

ABOVE: Godzilla's evolved biology incorporates features of trees and the metallic elements now found throughout Earth's ecosystem. The creature's skin texture and muscle fibers resemble twisted vines. ■ ABOVE RIGHT: During the twenty thousand–plus years since humanity fled Earth in search of a new home, Godzilla has evolved into an animal-plant hybrid. ■ BELOW: Godzilla prepares to fire its heat ray as King Ghidorah (*off-screen*) emerges from an interdimensional portal.

that *twenty-two thousand* years have passed on Earth, and arrive to find a planet where the surface has changed dramatically and Godzilla is now ruler of all living things.

A key distinction between the anime and live-action Godzilla films emerges: humankind is the aggressor, while the kaiju are defending their home. Over the course of the three films, this reversal highlights questions about man's penchant for war, ecological responsibility, the perils of technological arrogance, and what it means to be human—or monster. The protagonist of the trilogy is Captain Haruo Sakaki, an angry young military officer who grew up in space aboard the *Aratrum*. Haruo's parents were killed by Godzilla; he swears revenge and creates a rogue plan that pinpoints Godzilla's mortal vulnerability. In the first chapter, Haruo executes the plan, risking his life and others in the process. Godzilla is killed in a spectacular explosion, but moments later, the even-more-massive and powerful Godzilla Earth—the apex of its species, having grown and evolved for thousands of years—emerges from the ground and attacks the fleeing forces. Victory has turned to defeat and desperation.

The title of the second chapter, *City on the Edge of Battle*, refers to Mechagodzilla City, a military base

GODZILLA FACT: Gen Urobuchi, who penned the Godzilla trilogy, is an acclaimed novelist and screenwriter known for creating and writing several hit anime series, including *Puella Magi Madoka Magica* (2011), *Fate/Zero* (2011-12), and *Psycho-Pass* (2012). Urobuchi acquired the nickname "the Butcher" because of his tendency to kill off main characters in his stories, often in violent ways—as evidenced by the fate of Haruo and others in his Godzilla triptych.

GODZILLA FACT: With its dystopian setting, muted colors, and jumpsuit-wearing heroes, the Godzilla anime trilogy bears the thematic influence of the works of manga creator Tsutomu Nihei. The anime adaptations of Nihei's *Blame!* (2014–15) and *Knights of Sidonia* (2015) were helmed by Godzilla trilogy director Hiroyuki Seshita and were among Netflix's early forays into anime.

constructed from the head of Mechagodzilla, a robot built in an unsuccessful attempt to eradicate Godzilla before Earth was evacuated long ago. The heroes encounter the Houtua people, a peaceful, warpaint-wearing tribe who worship Mothra, an ancient deity. The Houtua warn against fighting Godzilla, but the heroes set a huge trap for the monster. At the crucial moment, however, Haruo aborts the plan to kill Godzilla and instead attempts to rescue his childhood friend Yuko, who was severely injured in the fight. ("What's the point of defeating it if we can't do it with our humanity intact?" he asks.) Haruo's militant attitude begins to change as he accepts the realities of a post-humanity Earth. In the third and final chapter, *Godzilla: The Planet Eater*, Haruo engages in a psychic battle with the archbishop of the cultlike Exif people, and a parallel fight transpires between Godzilla and Ghidorah, a monster summoned from another dimension and appearing here as a trio of disembodied golden snakes. The saga ends with Haruo making the ultimate sacrifice to prevent Ghidorah's return, and Godzilla's reign over the planet continuing unabated. The coda recalls *All Quiet on the Western Front,* with a flower blooming where Haruo perished, a symbol of the tragedy and futility of war.

This description only scratches the surface of the trilogy's dense, dialogue-driven plot, which the *Hollywood Reporter* described as "bonkers." It's notable that Polygon Pictures and codirector Hiroyuki Seshita were experienced not only in film and television productions but had also worked in various capacities on several major video game titles, including the *Final Fantasy, Resident Evil*, and *Street Fighter* series. The influence of *Neon Genesis Evangelion* and other dystopian anime is evident, but with its emphasis

CLOCKWISE FROM TOP LEFT: Promotional art for *Godzilla: Planet of the Monsters* showing the ecology of the future Earth. The difference in size between Godzilla Fillius (*right*), a juvenile Godzilla species, and the enormous Godzilla Earth, apex life-form, is staggering. Winged creatures called Servum swarm the skies. ■ Discovering the remnants of Mechagodzilla. The robot was built to fight Godzilla twenty thousand years earlier, but a mysterious accident destroyed it before it could be deployed. Through the centuries, the Nanometal from Mechagodzilla's carcass continued to grow, creating Mechagodzilla City. ■ Godzilla generates intense electromagnetic waves as it prepares to fire its heat ray.

on detailed planning, philosophical discussions, and interpersonal (and interspecies) conflict, this trilogy at times unfolds more like a role-playing game rather than a movie.

The films are marked by a relative lack of monster action and the tendency to present the kaiju battles in a surreal, transcendental mode. Still, the CG animation and visual design—with imaginative renderings of Earth's diverse surfaces, terraformed in Godzilla's image, and of the monster itself—were praised by critics. "Even skeptics will admit the 3D version of the king of the monsters looks pretty darn cool," wrote Matt Schley in *The Japan Times*. The filmmakers made no secret of their nontraditional approach; codirector Kobun Shizuno had not seen any Godzilla movies beforehand, and Seshita urged him not to do so to "provide a more objective assessment."

"I'm not a Godzilla expert, and so I simply made a film I thought would be enjoyable," Shizuno told the Associated Press. Added Seshita, "We welcome getting bashed by the traditionalists. That proves more than anything we succeeded in creating something different." Seshita would go on to direct the six-episode kaiju anime *Gamera Rebirth* (2023) for Studio ENGI and Netflix.

Though they followed in the wake of *Shin Godzilla*, which placed third at Japan's box office in 2016 (including both imported and domestic films), the three anime films each received a limited theatrical release in Japan. Thus, none would appear in the annual Top 100 for 2017–18, according to Box Office Mojo. The theatrical release of each film was followed within months by its global debut via the digital streaming platform Netflix, a milestone in the distribution of the Godzilla series.

CLOCKWISE FROM ABOVE: Maina and Miana, twin sister priestesses of the humanoid Houtua people who have managed to survive on Earth in the dystopian age of Godzilla. With the telepathic power to communicate with their protector god Mothra, they serve a role similar to the Small Beauties of Infant Island. ▪ Godzilla's heat ray causes unimaginable destruction. ▪ Arriving from a parallel dimension, the ethereal form of Ghidorah attacks Godzilla, making it impossible for the monster to retaliate.

©2017 TOHO CO., LTD.

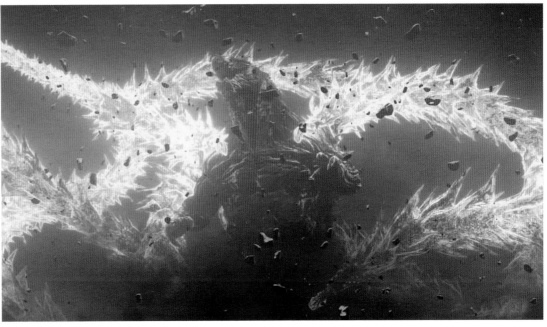

GODZILLA SINGULAR POINT

I'm sure there will be many people who say they can't understand the sci-fi elements, but we've made it so that even if you don't understand, you'll be fine," said Toh EnJoe. "Actually, the characters are smarter than me, so there are plenty of times when the logic they espouse is lost on me."

There is a bit of sly irony in the words of EnJoe, the polymathic writer behind *Godzilla Singular Point*, the first-ever episodic anime starring Godzilla and featuring a handful of imaginatively revived costars from the Toho monster universe. This idiosyncratic series strikes an entertaining balance between kaiju cinema traditions, the conventions of anime, and a science-fiction plotline that veers heavily into theory and formulas and ideas about artificial intelligence. The brainchild of director Atsushi Takahasi—whose mentors include anime titans Hayao Miyazaki and Satoshi Kon—and EnJoe, an Akutagawa Prize–winning novelist, screenwriter, and former physicist, *Godzilla Singular Point* is yet another retelling of Godzilla's origin story—one that leans simultaneously into genre nostalgia and the "science" of science fiction, presenting a unifying pseudo-hypothesis to explain the existence of kaiju.

Set in the year 2030, *Godzilla Singular Point* focuses on the intertwined stories of three archetypal characters within a large ensemble: Mei Kamino, an eccentric genius graduate student interested in cryptids and folklore studies; Yun Arikawa, a brilliant young engineer and troubleshooter employed by the

"I MAINLY THOUGHT ABOUT HOW GODZILLA COULD BE ACTUALIZED AS A LIVING CREATURE. PEOPLE ARE RIGHT WHEN THEY SAY THAT GODZILLA IS SYMBOLIC OF SOME-THING, BUT I WANTED TO TRY REEXAMINING (IT) THROUGH THE PERSPECTIVE OF MODERN BIOLOGY."

—Toh EnJoe, writer

Otaki Factory, an all-purpose, technology-focused small business; and Goro Otaki, the eccentric, elderly owner-operator of the company and inventor of Jet Jaguar, a large fighting robot created to defend humanity. The series follows Mei and Yun's parallel plot lines, which eventually merge as the two protagonists investigate a weird broadcast signal that conjures giant monsters to attack Japan and other nations. The most dangerous of these creatures is the mythical Godzilla, an evolving and growing apex threat that, according to legend, portends the end of the world. Whereas Godzilla's previous foray into anime was bleak, humorless, and centered on militant action heroes and philosophical musings, *Singular Point* is a stylistic and thematic antithesis—it's bright, upbeat, intelligent, and fast-paced, often indulging in rapid, theoretical dialogue. It embraces science geekery and nerd culture and their inherent social awkwardness. Mei and the antisocial Yun work together throughout the series yet never meet face-to-face until the end; they grow closer as they discuss quantum physics and their evolving investigation through texting.

Though the Godzilla of *Singular Point* looks familiar, this is not an irradiated postwar ex-dinosaur but an extra-dimensional entity, a demon-like dragon once worshiped by Japan's feudal peoples as a fearful god. The shape-shifting creature takes on multiple forms—an aquatic form, a quadrupedal terrestrial form, and an upright bipedal monster. In its various stages it can exhale either a highly flammable breath weapon that also freezes objects it reacts with, or energy rings, or a traditional-style heat ray. Godzilla's life force is derived from Archetype, a mysterious, space-time-bending substance that emanates from its body as red dust whenever the monster appears, turning water the color of blood and blanketing the ground with a red snow-like ash. Although Godzilla can be killed, it possesses immortality, having been reincarnated through the ages. The mystery of the monsters is traced to a Godzilla skeleton secretly housed in the bowels of a prewar radio observatory, which is also the source of the signal summoning the apocalyptic monsters. Throughout the series, the drama hinges on Mei, Yun, and Goro's efforts to avert an apocalypse.

These deviations from Godzilla canon were created by EnJoe, who left academia and his studies of physics, linguistics, literary theory, and philosophy to become a science-fiction novelist, and whose writing is known for "scientific lucidity and literary impenetrability," according to the literary journal *Asymptote*.

PREVIOUS SPREAD: Promotional art for *Godzilla Singular Point* featuring main characters Mei Kamino (*left*) and Yun Arikawa (*right*) and Godzilla's silhouette. ■ BELOW: Godzilla Ultima expels its powerful heat ray. The monsters of *Godzilla Singular Point* were designed by Eiji Yamamori of *Howl's Moving Castle* fame. Said director Atsushi Takahashi, "I had worked with him at Studio Ghibli, and I noticed that he had a lot of kaiju figurines lined up on his desk. When this project came up, I needed to consult someone knowledgeable about kaiju."

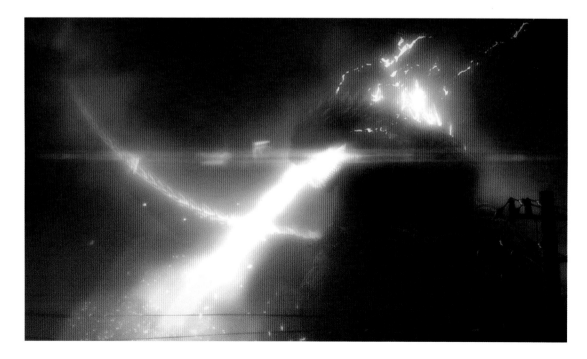

CLOCKWISE FROM TOP LEFT: Godzilla Amphibia is the secondary form of Godzilla, having evolved from the marine creature Godzilla Aquatilis after it comes ashore in Tokyo Bay. After rampaging through the city, the four-legged Godzilla Amphibia encases itself in a crystal cocoon. ▪ The enormous body of Godzilla Ultima, the final form of Godzilla. Created with the original 1954 Godzilla in mind, the lower body is massively wide in an attempt to create a more biologically and physically correct creature. ▪ Godzilla Terrestris is the third evolutionary stage of Godzilla, emerging from the cocoon made by Godzilla Amphibia. While suffering great damage from military bombing, the creature displays the uncanny ability to heal its wounds.

"We brought EnJoe in because there was a movie at the time called *Arrival* (2016), and we wanted to create a sci-fi story as solid as that," said director Takahashi. "EnJoe wanted to create a new theory to replace the existing idea that Godzilla grew big [due to] radiation. That's where the concept of 'Archetype' came in as a new substance that existing physical theories can't explain." Takahashi grappled with EnJoe's dense writing, conscious that it could overwhelm and confuse viewers, but ultimately felt it lent a sense of plausibility. "The amount of information in the script was too much for a typical TV animation, so we had to figure out how to incorporate it into the work," he said. "We decided to pack as much as possible onto the screen, using things like [text] chats or news programs."

Godzilla Singular Point also creatively reinvents Rodan, Anguirus, Manda (the sea serpent from 1963's *Atragon*), Kumonga, and introduces Salunga, a creature somewhat resembling the dream monster Gabara from *All Monsters Attack*. Rodan becomes a flock of dinosaur-size pterosaurs, while Anguirus is a gentle giant with the power to foresee the future. Perhaps the true star of the entire series, however, is Jet Jaguar, which only superficially resembles the grinning robot carrying a child on its shoulders in *Godzilla vs. Megalon*. Over the course of the series, it undergoes numerous structural and software enhancements to grow from a small mecha to a giant AI-powered robot that makes humanity's last stand against Godzilla. In keeping with the series' emphasis on plot machinations, the battles between Jet Jaguar and Godzilla against other monsters are often smaller in scale or shorter in duration than in live-action *tokusatsu*, but the final confrontation in which Jet Jaguar sacrifices itself to save humanity is a beautifully staged clash that ends the saga on a hopeful note.

Godzilla Singular Point was produced by Toho Animation in collaboration with two powerhouse anime studios: Studio Bones (makers of the international hit *My Hero Academia*) produced the dramatic scenes

"WHEN I SAID, 'JET JAGUAR IS COOL, LET'S INCLUDE HIM,' THERE WAS QUITE A BIT OF SILENCE DURING THE MEETING (*LAUGHS*)."

—Atsushi Takahashi, director

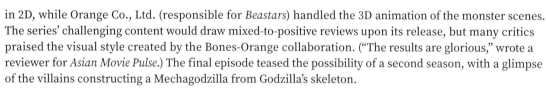

CLOCKWISE FROM TOP LEFT: Jet Jaguar, an invention of the Otaki Factory, battles with Rodan. ■ "Each monster was chosen for different reasons," said director Atsushi Takahashi. "Recent films like *Cloverfield* (2008) used birds flying around [the monster] to convey the massive scale of the kaiju. If something was going to fly around Godzilla, it should be Rodan. We also wanted the first kaiju to appear to have a somewhat recognizable form, on the borderline of something that could actually exist. So we asked designer Eiji Yamamori to emphasize a dinosaur-like design." ■ A harpoon gun is deployed against Anguirus, but the beast easily deflects the attack with its precognitive shield. ■ OPPOSITE TOP: Godzilla Ultima, the monster's final form, is defeated in the end when the giant robot Jet Jaguar explodes. Godzilla disappears, and the red dust and the other monsters are rendered powerless. ■ OPPOSITE BOTTOM: The bones of the original Godzilla, hidden away in the basement of the Misakioku radio observatory, hinting at the possibility that *Godzilla Singular Point* may continue.

in 2D, while Orange Co., Ltd. (responsible for *Beastars*) handled the 3D animation of the monster scenes. The series' challenging content would draw mixed-to-positive reviews upon its release, but many critics praised the visual style created by the Bones-Orange collaboration. ("The results are glorious," wrote a reviewer for *Asian Movie Pulse*.) The final episode teased the possibility of a second season, with a glimpse of the villains constructing a Mechagodzilla from Godzilla's skeleton.

"While we aimed to create it as entertainment, there was concern that the series might appeal to a more selective audience than we had initially planned," Takahashi admitted. "However, [it received] support from a broader audience than I expected, which is a relief. Also, I was surprised by how over-whelmingly positive the reaction to Jet Jaguar has been [*laughs*]."

GODZILLA FACT: The Orthogonal Diagonalizer is a weapon invented by the eccentric scientist Michiyuki Ashihara, who discovered the Archetype element that is key to the monsters' existence. With identical initials ("OD") and a similar design, it is an homage to the monster-killing Oxygen Destroyer from 1954's *Godzilla*. The device is just one of *Singular Point*'s numerous Easter eggs referencing classic Toho kaiju films and *tokusatsu* history that are sprinkled throughout the series.

GODZILLA EVOLUTIONS

THE EVER-CHANGING IMAGE OF A MONSTER ICON

With its reptilian traits, upright stance, dorsal spikes, long arms, thick frame, and fierce gaze, Godzilla is instantly recognizable. The creature's unmistakable appearance is key to its lasting appeal, an imaginative hybrid of prehistoric and living animals grafted onto the shape of the human body. Yet, even as Godzilla's image has remained true to its origins, it has simultaneously evolved and changed—sometimes subtly, sometimes radically—from one production to the next.

From the beginning, the monster's shape and movements were dictated by the limitations of the man-in-suit method. The creative talents of Eiji Tsuburaya's team developed the first Godzilla suits through trial and error, often using crude and untested materials. The very first Godzilla suit was nearly immovable, but as lighter and more flexible materials were discovered, the suits evolved to become more performance-friendly and less uncomfortable for the actor inside. Mechanical devices gave expression to the monster's face. Godzilla's character design evolved with its changing personality: The puppy-dog smile it wears in *Godzilla vs. Megalon* is far removed from the ghostlike harbinger of death of 1954. In addition to suits, analog tools and techniques were developed for filming close-ups and other uses, including robots, hand puppets (called "guignol" per French tradition), prop tails, and even a giant Godzilla foot.

The Godzilla suit served as a traditional foundation of the franchise for the first fifty years, from *Godzilla* to *Godzilla Final Wars*. This tradition has since given way to technological innovation. Hollywood introduced the first computer-generated Godzilla in 1998, and the new era has brought forth even more photorealistic digital versions of the monster. In latter-day productions, Japanese filmmakers have left suitmation behind to create their own live-action CG Godzillas. The monster has likewise made a belated entry into the world of anime.

The following visual history traces the evolution of Toho's Godzilla designs over seventy years, taking note of changes—some small, some big—in the monster's appearance between films and across generations.

GODZILLA 1954

The original *Godzilla* creature modeling by sculptor Teizo Toshimitsu was based upon a traditional (though scientifically outdated) upright-walking dinosaur image with backplates resembling those of the stegosaurus. Its bumpy skin texture symbolized keloid scarring from a the nuclear explosion that created the beast. The arms were thin and so stiff as to be unusable by the suit actor. The hands had a small membrane between the thumb and forefinger. The feet had four toes, making it difficult for the actor to walk without tripping over objects in Godzilla's path. The short and inflexible tail, made with a series of successively smaller segments, was moved by an overhead wire.

Two suits were made. It has been erroneously reported that the first Godzilla suit was so stiff that it failed during a test run and was completely unusable, necessitating construction of a second suit. However, the plan all along was to make two suits to allow for flexibility in filming and to have a spare in case one was under repair. The 1954 suits were finished with a mixture of black and white paint, creating a gray skin tone, not brown as is sometimes misreported.

LEFT TO RIGHT: Sculptor Teizo Toshimtistu and the first 1954 suit, so inflexible that it stood up on its own. This suit was later separated into two pieces. The upper body was used in water scenes, the lower half was worn like pants for close-ups of the feet. ■ The head was large and rounded, with ears. "I heard from Mr. Toshimitsu that the image of Godzilla was inspired by the mushroom cloud of the atomic bomb experiments, especially the face," noted suit maker Noboyuki Yasumaru. The teeth were originally made of wood, but they appeared too pristine, so they were remade with kneaded plastic. The haunting, soulless eyes and the lower jaw were controlled manually by wires accessed outside of the tail. ■ Profile image showing off the massive proportions and signature dorsal fins.

GODZILLA 1955

The suit for *Godzilla Raids Again* prioritized performance and was designed with a slender, muscular shape conforming to the actor's body. The suit's loose-fitting materials would sometimes bunch up, and unnatural folds would become visible, especially on the arms. Godzilla was built first, before Anguirus, so that filming could be done during the end of winter when it was still cold enough to create snowscapes for the film's climax. There were no zippers or fasteners, so whenever the Godzilla actor would be sealed up inside, the suit had to be sewn together.

GODZILLA 1962

The *King Kong vs. Godzilla* suit remains a popular classic design. The fourth toe and ears were eliminated, and the monster has a snakelike face and massive lower body. This is the first suit with radio-controlled mouth movements, devised by Akira Suzuki. Crew members, fascinated by the ability to move Godzilla's jaw, made the monster roar incessantly throughout the film. As this was the first Godzilla filmed in color, the suit was painted charcoal gray, with brownish highlights.

GODZILLA 1964

The iconic suit for *Mothra vs. Godzilla* is Teizo Toshimitsu's masterpiece. For the first time, urethane foam was used to create contoured shapes for the body and legs, adding "meat" and transforming the excessive mass and simpler lines of Godzilla 1962 into a finely sculptured and well-balanced creature. In several scenes, Godzilla's cheeks appear to move, a lifelike effect that was the result of damage to the suit, incurred when Godzilla crashed into Nagoya Castle and when it was hit with napalm bombs. The frame supporting the face was repaired multiple times, but the skin still moved visibly.

LEFT TO RIGHT: The detailed muzzle and malevolent gaze of Godzilla 1964. The nostrils are prominent, and slight wrinkles are added to the cheeks. The striking eyes peer out from under hooded eyebrows that are painted grayish-brown, lending Godzilla an evil-looking visage. ▪ The legs have sufficient bulk to create scale but do not interfere with the actor's ability to walk. Prominent kneecaps are a lifelike touch. Padding in the torso creates mass, and a subtle breastbone runs down the center of the chest. ▪ Sharper teeth, nails, and toes were made with newly discovered FRP (fiberglass-reinforced plastic). Suit actor Haruo Nakajima was so enamored with these nails that he constantly walked on concrete surfaces and clicked his claws together to listen to the sound.

GODZILLA 1964 V2

Until this point, a new Godzilla suit was made for each film, but with *Ghidorah, the Three-Headed Monster* going into production just months after *Mothra vs. Godzilla* and the suit still in good condition, there was no need for a new one. Besides, the suit-making staff had their hands full making King Ghidorah and a new Rodan.

LEFT TO RIGHT: Rubber details on the face have settled and shifted. The eyes undergo modification: the pupils have been moved a bit lower, making them completely visible, and a white center spot is added as an accent. Together, these changes soften Godzilla's villainous image somewhat. ▪ The suit's appearance is virtually unchanged from the previous film, except for some modified facial features.

GODZILLA 1965

For *Invasion of Astro-Monster,* a new Godzilla suit was needed. Despite using the same molds for the head, each new Godzilla would come out differently and show its own personality. The basic look is similar to 1964's, but with simplified features. The legs fit the actor's body more loosely and sometimes look more like pants, showing telltale folds. Later, the head of Godzilla 1965 was combined with the body of Godzilla 1964 to create Jiras, a frill-necked monster that appeared in an episode of the Tsuburaya Productions television show *Ultraman* in August 1966.

LEFT TO RIGHT: The upper body and chest remain much the same, but the tail becomes thicker at the base and tapered at the tip. ▪ Enlarged and widened, the face looks much like Godzilla 1964 V2, with a significant enhancement: lighted and moveable eyes.

GODZILLA 1966

After the Godzilla 1965 suit appeared (in modified form) in *Ultraman*, the original head was reattached to the body, and additional modifications were made for its role in *Ebirah, Horror of the Deep*. Fleshy facial details are added, and the lower jaw is flattened. Water battles took a toll on this suit, and Godzilla's appearance deteriorated visibly and dramatically as shooting proceeded. This Godzilla suit would serve as the monster's seagoing stand-in for the next five years, appearing exclusively in water scenes in *Son of Godzilla*, *Destroy All Monsters*, and *Godzilla vs. Hedorah*.

LEFT TO RIGHT: The neck was slightly elongated compared to Godzilla 1965. The waist area of the body has extra volume, giving Godzilla a more solid appearance. ▪ With so many water scenes in *Ebirah*, the suit quickly deteriorated as filming progressed. Noticeable flaps and folds appeared in the midsection, which was unavoidable as there was not enough time for the suit to fully dry out before the next day's shooting. ▪ The face became visibly deformed due to water damage, with the eyes beginning to bulge, giving Godzilla a dazed expression.

GODZILLA 1967

The monster became an adoptive parent in *Son of Godzilla*, and to draw contrast with the infant (and, in later scenes, toddler) Minilla, this Godzilla suit was the largest created to this point. To make Godzilla appear tall, the proportions are exaggerated in unflattering ways. Atop an elongated neck sits a head with a wide mouth, a pushed-in snout, and a narrow, rounded forehead. The torso is ill-fitting to the actor, as the urethane foam stuffing bunches up at an obvious waistline fold. The elongated neck makes the broad shoulders appear slouched and droopy.

LEFT TO RIGHT: The eyes are large and wide, giving Godzilla a sleepy gaze. The fins originate further down the backside than usual, and the normally straight spiny tips are curved in random directions. ▪ Godzilla's hands have stubby nails and little surface detail. The legs have extra girth, causing Godzilla to often look knock-kneed when standing, and the feet have claws reused from the Godzilla 1964 suit. The chubby tail is attached to the body at a lower point, making for an awkward-looking profile. (With special effects director Sadamasa Arikawa.)

GODZILLA 1968

Although ten monsters appear in *Destroy All Monsters*, only two suits were newly constructed—Godzilla and Anguirus—while all other monster suits and/or props were reused from previous productions. This would be the final suit designed by the original 1954 team of Teizo Toshimitsu and the Yagi brothers (modelers Kanju and Yasuei), and Godzilla reverted to its more traditional proportions. This suit appears slightly smaller than recent ones. It was used, with slight modifications and repairs, on the next three films.

LEFT TO RIGHT: The 1968 suit has detailed muscle definition in the legs, torso, and arms, resulting in a bit more humanlike appearance. The claws are sharp, while the toenails are short and wide. The fins, molded out of latex this time, are visibly thicker, and the spikes have a slight forward curve. ▪ Facial details are rendered with a mixture of latex and oak bark shavings, creating a bristly skin texture. The sharp teeth and fangs are set slightly back from the edge of the mouth. The eyes are large and bold, and when the head is angled downward, the creature has a menacing glare.

GODZILLA 1969

With the scaled-down production of *All Monsters Attack*, and with most of the special effects staff away working on an exhibition for the Japan World Exposition in Osaka, the 1968 suit was reused for the new Godzilla scenes in this film. Because *All Monsters Attack* infamously incorporates stock footage from both *Ebirah* and *Son of Godzilla*, Godzilla's appearance changes drastically from scene to scene.

Although the bristly facial texture has softened, Godzilla's appearance in *All Monsters Attack* is practically identical to the previous film.

GODZILLA 1971

After the passing of Eiji Tsuburaya, budgets available for special effects films declined. As long as the suit was still in one piece, it would be used. Three years out from its initial appearance, the Godzilla 1968 suit shows obvious signs of wear and tear in *Godzilla vs. Hedorah*.

LEFT TO RIGHT: The nicely defined muscles of this suit have begun to give way to latex fatigue, the joint between the neck and the body starts to bulge as its support diminishes, and skin textures easily fray or fall off. The hands have completely lost their skin details. ▪ As Godzilla continues to morph into a hero figure for children, changes in the monster's appearance and its anthropomorphized actions have made the human inside the suit more obvious.

GODZILLA 1972

The 1968 suit underwent some repairs to make it usable one last time in *Godzilla vs. Gigan*. Skin textures were partially reattached, but despite everyone's best efforts, the suit is visibly deteriorating.

LEFT TO RIGHT: In a new modification, the head was cut open in the back and a mechanical device was installed to open and close the monster's eyelids. ▪ Bare patches are visible on the surface of the suit. In certain shots, skin textures can be seen peeling off the body.

GODZILLA 1973

Godzilla vs. Megalon marked Godzilla's full transformation into a hero figure, and the suit created for this film perfectly expresses this new phase. This is the first Godzilla created by suit maker Nobuyuki Yasumaru, and it is considerably thicker and heavier than any since 1954. For scenes of Godzilla in the ocean, an "attraction suit" (made for in-person promotional appearances) was used.

LEFT TO RIGHT: Godzilla's body looks much fuller, but its stocky appearance comes with less flexibility for the actor. The overall impression is more playful than imposing. The puffy fin tips are painted silver. ■ The head appears larger and rounder, with more volume in the rear and a larger and more curved lower jaw. The large eyes, with rust-colored irises and pronounced pupils, are striking. (With special effects director Teruyoshi Nakano.)

GODZILLA 1974

The Godzilla 1973 suit, still in excellent condition, was slightly modified and used again in *Godzilla vs. Mechagodzilla*, pulling double duty as both Godzilla and the impostor Godzilla (i.e., Mechagodzilla in disguise). Wear and tear from previous filming made the suit more flexible, resulting in a more lifelike appearance.

LEFT TO RIGHT: To make Godzilla appear more fierce than friendly, the eyes are smaller, rendered fully in black, and set higher in the eye socket to glare at its opponent. ■ When the real Godzilla and the impostor appear together, the impostor is an attraction suit with an exaggerated face and wide mouth. A second attraction suit appears briefly when Godzilla rises from the ocean for the final battle.

GODZILLA 1975

Godzilla 1973 was reused once again in *Terror of Mechagodzilla*. When Godzilla returns to the sea at the conclusion, another attraction costume with little resemblance to the main suit was used.

LEFT TO RIGHT: The suit begins to show its age as the foam settles and the body loses a bit of its chubby shape. ■ The modified head appears to have been flattened out somewhat. The eye sockets have been narrowed, giving Godzilla an angry expression. When Godzilla topples forward from Mechagodzilla 2's missile strike, the jaw was pushed in and permanently deformed.

GODZILLA 1984

Godzilla's appearance in *The Return of Godzilla* was intended to recapture the terror of the original, and the technology used to create the monster was updated. Two Godzilla suits were built (A and B). Molds were made for the body parts and fins; these molds would be used through 1995, thus there were only subtle differences in these features from one film to the next. Like the 1950s suits, Godzilla 1984 has ears, a fourth toe, and protruding fangs. The dorsals now have much larger rows of secondary fins; this would become a signature characteristic of the Heisei-era Godzilla.

Toho invested ¥105 million (roughly $425,000 in 1984) in a 15.7-foot- (4.8-m-) tall high-tech robot, the Godzilla "Cybot" (i.e., cybernetic robot). Built by a robotics company, this was the first-ever Godzilla ordered to be made outside of the studio. With robotically controlled facial expressions and other movements, the Cybot was designed to portray Godzilla with more lifelike actions than were possible with suits alone. However, the device was plagued by technical problems, and it appears in only a few shots in the finished film. Nevertheless, its public appearances helped promote the film's release.

CLOCKWISE FROM TOP LEFT: Suit A was designated the "water suit," although both A and B were used in land and water scenes. This suit was used in the Mihama nuclear reactor scene, the Tokyo Bay attack, and the climax at Mount Mihara. ▪ Suit B, designated the "land suit," performed most of the Shinjuku attack scenes and shared the Tokyo Bay sequence with Suit A. ▪ In an effort to make Godzilla scary again, the eyes of the 1984 design have an ominous gaze mimicking that of Godzilla 1964. Facial expressions were enhanced via mechanics installed by Akinori Takagi, enabling Godzilla to sneer and open and shut its eyelids. ▪ The Cybot was separated into two halves, and only the upper body appears in the film. The Cybot had great difficulty in performing for the camera. Dust particles contaminated its electrical contacts, causing numerous malfunctions and jittery motion. ▪ The fully assembled Cybot Godzilla was introduced with great fanfare to the press on August 8, 1984.

GODZILLA 1989

Special effects director Koichi Kawakita established the image of his Heisei-era Godzilla in *Godzilla vs. Biollante*. Godzilla's new look emphasizes biological concepts. Two suits were made, each with a head smaller in proportion to the body. In select scenes when Godzilla exhales its heat ray, an alternate set of dorsal fins made of transparent FRP were illuminated with electric lights rather than optical animation in postproduction.

The mechanical Godzilla made for this film was a groundbreaking development. The effects team studied and adopted Western robotic techniques, using twenty-four wires to manipulate the robot and enabling Godzilla to perform unprecedented movements of its head, neck, and mouth. Unlike the Cybot, this robot was built in the same scale and using the same molds as the suits, thus it could be seamlessly integrated with footage of the suits.

LEFT TO RIGHT: The original version of the main suit was newly built using the 1984 molds for the body and fins. It had a protruding chest, a large round head with deep-set eyes, a short neck, wide mouth, and raised hips. Its overall impression was weak and awkward. It was dubbed the NG ("no good") suit. ▪ The NG suit was extensively reworked by slimming it down and replacing the head with a smaller one. The tail was lengthened from seventeen to twenty-four segments. This suit was designated the "land suit." ▪ While the land suit was being reworked, one of the 1984 suits was refitted with a new head and used to film Godzilla's emergence from Mount Mihara, as well as all sea scenes, hence it was dubbed the "sea suit." ▪ The revised head of the sea suit. The whites of the eyes are eliminated, and the teeth are arranged in two rows, much like a shark. The land suit had fuller cheeks.

GODZILLA 1991

With the modeling shop focused on designing and building King Ghidorah, Mecha-King Ghidorah, and Godzillasaurus, both Godzilla 1989 suits were used again, with modifications, in *Godzilla vs. King Ghidorah*. This time there was no distinction in their use between land and sea scenes. The 1989 land suit became the "Shinjuku Battle suit"; the thighs have added bulk, and several areas have been resurfaced with newly cast skin. The 1989 sea suit became the "Hokkaido Battle suit" and was used early in the production despite its poor condition; it was later cut in half, and the upper body was used in close-ups.

LEFT TO RIGHT: The Shinjuku Battle suit: The face was reworked with a flatter snout and the eye color brightened. Compared to its appearance in 1989, the entire suit seems to sag with "latex fatigue." ▪ The Hokkaido Battle suit: The upper body appears to have a new layer of skin, giving it a bulging chest and an odd indentation in the waist, and the head exhibits a pointy silhouette. ▪ With Godzilla fighting airborne opponents, the mechanical Godzilla was once again utilized extensively. The face looks a bit flatter, and the dark eye color was brightened up to increase expressiveness.

GODZILLA 1992

The Shinjuku Battle suit was temporarily stolen from the studio in the spring of 1992, thus the special effects team had no choice but to make a new Godzilla. Since Godzilla would be battling airborne opponents in Mothra and Battra, technician Akinori Takagi devised a radio-controlled device enabling the head to move up and down, giving the suit a new means of expression.

LEFT TO RIGHT: The body and fins were again made from the 1984 molds. The head is bigger compared to Godzilla 1991, and the snout is longer and wider. The torso shows muscular features, and the legs maintain their thick shape throughout filming. ▪ To accommodate the innovative head mechanism, the neck (and consequently the shoulders) is widened a bit, and the skin on the neck took on a thicker, ribbed appearance. The eyes are brightened by the addition of orange coloring.

GODZILLA 1993

Proportions shift toward a smaller upper body, bulkier legs and hips, and more pronounced musculature in *Godzilla vs. Mechagodzilla II*. This new suit was not ready by "crank-in" (a term used in Asian film industries for the start of filming), so Godzilla 1992 was used to film the battle on Adonoa Island with Rodan. An old suit was cut in half, and the leg portion was fitted with suspenders and used for close-ups of the feet, just as in 1954 and 1955.

LEFT TO RIGHT: Due to its longer legs and high waist, the tail attaches to the torso in a noticeably higher position, causing the staff to nickname this suit "High Leg Godzilla." ▪ The clear fold lines on the suit belie the nature of its construction as the limbs are made separately and attached to the torso. The breastbone and large pectoral muscles are more pronounced.

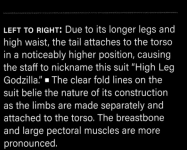 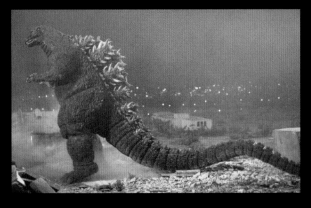 

GODZILLA 1994

The suit for *Godzilla vs. SpaceGodzilla* was the largest made to date. A new device installed in the head gave it the ability to move right and left as well as up and down, eliminating the need for the robot. This enabled the suit to perform actions that previously required multiple camera setups and cutaway edits. The folds in the neck seen on the previous two designs were eliminated.

LEFT TO RIGHT: The addition of internal mechanisms made the neck and head larger and taller. To maintain a balanced image, the overall body size increased. Three sets of skin were cast from the 1984 molds, the heels were elevated, and the tail lengthened, making this the heaviest and tallest Godzilla so far. ▪ This profile view shows how huge the legs of Godzilla 1994 had become.

GODZILLA 1995

In *Godzilla vs. Destoroyah,* the king of the monsters has become so powerful, it's melting away from the inside out, and the suit-modeling team devised special features to create the burning effect. Multiple nozzles were placed around the suit to discharge CO_2 gas, simulating white-hot steam spouting from Godzilla's body. With all the added special devices built into it, this was the heaviest Godzilla suit ever at 280 pounds (127 kg).

LEFT TO RIGHT: Godzilla's translucent fins were made of FRP with internal lighting. ▪ Multiple sections of the skin were cast in translucent red and yellow latex, and over a thousand LEDs were embedded beneath its surface.

GODZILLA 1999

Godzilla 2000: Millennium introduced the first-ever Japanese Godzilla suit made by a company outside of Toho. Shinicihi Wakasa of the creature shop Monsters Inc. was charged with updating Godzilla's image for the new century. Wakasa looked to the designs of Godzilla 1962 and 1964, and a model kit sold by Aurora in the US in the 1960s, for inspiration. For the first time in its history, Godzilla is colored green. Two identical suits were made, plus a highly expressive waist-up robot Godzilla that is indistinguishable from the suit.

LEFT TO RIGHT: The fierce, catlike face with omnidirectional eyes, pointy ears, and a cobra-inspired hooded neck. ▪ The fins were cast in fiberglass resin, making them so heavy that the suit actor had no choice but to assume a forward crouch when performing, lest he lose his balance and fall backward. The inorganic coloring of the fins in silver and metallic red was suggested by special effects director Kenji Suzuki. ▪ Working from a concept by designer Shinji Nishikawa, Wakasa gave Godzilla enormous, spiky fins. The finely chiseled skin textures are a trademark of Wakasa's work.

GODZILLA 2000

For *Godzilla vs. Megaguirus*, two new suits were cast from the previous film's molds. One was for the extensive water scenes ("Sea Godzilla") and the other was the hero suit with performance mechanics built in ("Ground Godzilla"). Their appearance is nearly identical to Godzilla 1999, with minor changes made at the request of director Masaaki Tezuka. One of the suits from *Godzilla 2000: Millennium* was repainted (green once again) and used as well. To portray Godzilla swimming on the ocean surface, a detailed model, sans hands and feet, was cast from the suit molds and attached to an underwater mobile platform.

LEFT TO RIGHT: The catlike face is virtually identical to the design from *Godzilla 2000: Millennium*." ▪ Since Megaguirus is an airborne opponent, lighter materials were used in the neck area to allow the actor to tilt the head toward the sky. The red coloration of the fins was toned down, and the green body color was muted compared to the previous film. ▪ The Sea Godzilla suit in the Big Pool. The long, pointed tail flops around, adding lifelike movement.

GODZILLA 2001

To emphasize Godzilla's overwhelming power compared to its opponents, the suit for *Godzilla, Mothra and King Ghidorah: Giant Monsters All-Out Attack* was the largest ever made. The suit was built to accommodate a tall suit actor (Minoru Yoshida), and the heels were built up several inches for additional height. The face has a fierce expression, protruding fangs, and soulless white eyes. Two suits were made, one with additional performance features for the face and outer rows of fins that splay outward when Godzilla fires its heat ray.

LEFT TO RIGHT: Producer Shogo Tomi-yama was concerned about Godzilla's ghostlike eyes, which were originally completely white. Designer Fuyuki Shinada, working on his first and only Godzilla suit, responded by adding a fine pattern of black blood vessels that form a border around the eyeball. ▪ Godzilla was intended to have a dinosaur-like, forward-leaning posture, but the weight of mechanics in the head made it impossible for the suit actor to maintain that pose. The actor was forced to stand more erectly, which caused Godzilla's stomach to bulge out.

GODZILLA 2002

LEFT TO RIGHT: Director Masaaki Tezuka insisted that Godzilla's color revert to charcoal gray (the previous two suits created by Shinichi Wakasa were green) with grayish-white fins, that the fins be scaled down to a more proportional size, and that Godzilla stand more erect than the crouching pose of Wakasa's prior designs; this was made possible by downsizing the fins and casting them in latex, a lighter material. ▪ More changes compared to Wakasa's previous Godzillas: The hooded neck is deem-phasized, and the eyes revert to white with solid black pupils, eliminating the prior yellowish tint. ▪ The land suit had a mechanism enabling Godzilla to raise its head skyward.

Shinichi Wakasa's suit for *Godzilla Against Mechagodzilla* is based on his previous two Godzilla designs, but with significant differences. In addition to separate suits for land use and sea use, a third suit was made in two halves: a top half for upper body close-ups and a lower half for close-ups of the legs. Wakasa also built a simplified half-suit of Godzilla 1954 that is briefly glimpsed in a flashback reenactment of Godzilla's death by the Oxygen Destroyer.

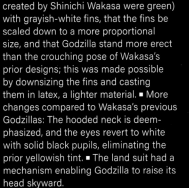   

GODZILLA 2003

Godzilla: Tokyo SOS had five newly made representations of Godzilla: the main suit, action suit, sea upper-body suit, lower-body suit, and a new "Expression" mechanical Godzilla, all meticulously crafted by creature maker Shinichi Wakasa to look identical to their counterparts. The suits from *Godzilla Against Mechagodzilla* were modified and reused to build the 2003 suits.

LEFT TO RIGHT: The Godzilla 2003 main suit. The only major difference from 2002 was a giant scar on Godzilla's chest, the result of a point-blank hit from Kiryu's Absolute Zero Cannon at the conclusion of *Godzilla Against Mechagodzilla*. ▪ The Godzilla 2003 sea suit in the Big Pool. ▪ The "Expression" mechanical Godzilla, without forearms or hands, was manipulated by suit actor Tsutomu Kitagawa (*far left*). Creature maker Shinichi Wakasa preps the robot.

GODZILLA 2004

For *Godzilla Final Wars*, director Ryuhei Kitamura wanted an agile Godzilla that could perform fighting maneuvers. "Back in the seventies, I think that Godzilla had more power and speed. . . . What I wanted to do is to revive that, but not in the same [way]." As with all of Shinichi Wakasa's Godzillas, two identical suits were made, but no robot Godzilla was built.

LEFT TO RIGHT: Godzilla 2004 has decidedly more humanlike proportions, allowing the suit actor excellent mobility and flexibility. The form-fitting arms and legs are reminiscent of Godzilla 1955. This suit has widely spaced and spiky fins, resembling the Godzillas of the 1950s. ▪ The Godzilla 2004 face has strong feline features. Its flattened and elongated snout has a duck-like profile.

GODZILLA 2016

Shin Godzilla was the first Japanese-produced Godzilla movie to feature an entirely CG creature. Godzilla 2016 has a nuclear reactor inside its body; its genes continually combine and divide, causing the creature to evolve quickly. As a result, Godzilla assumes four distinct stages:

First appearance: Godzilla remains submerged in Tokyo Bay. Only its tail rises above the surface.

Stage 2: A four-legged creature stealthily emerges from the shallows of Tokyo Bay. Its slithering form is inspired by the rabuka (frilled shark), with Godzilla's signature dorsal fins growing along the spine. The slits in its neck were originally gills but changed to function as exhaust vents.

Stage 3: This form was not part of the original scenario, but director Hideaki Anno felt the evolution from Stage 2 to Stage 4 was too extreme.

Stage 4: A traditional bipedal dinosaur form. It has a rigid, upright stance as it wanders slowly and aimlessly due to the agonizing pain caused by its mutation, unaware of the people and objects it tramples, creating a scarier, zombified Godzilla. When it exhales its heat ray, the jaw distends, and the mouth expands in three directions. Inspired by Godzilla 1954, the arms and hands are stiff and emaciated, resembling ghost hands in *yurei-zu*, a type of old Japanese painting of supernatural beings.

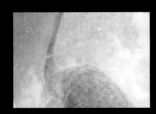 

CLOCKWISE FROM TOP LEFT: In its first appearance, Godzilla is visible only as a tail rising above the waterline in Tokyo Bay. ▪ STAGE 2: With its face at ground level and eyes that "instill fear, since you can't figure out what it is thinking," said director Hideaki Anno, the intent was to make this iteration scary. ▪ STAGE 4: The head sits atop an elongated neck. "I was carried away by the mushroom cloud shape of the head," said designer Mahiro Maeda. The tail is extremely long, with a bony, riblike structure and a bizarre face at the tip. The body glows red beneath skin textures patterned after the weird surface of a gourd that grew in concept artist Takayuki Takeya's office. ▪ STAGE 3: For this intermediate stage, segments of Stage 2 were rearranged into an upright form with larger legs, similar to Stage 4. The skin color changed from tan to reddish brown.

GODZILLA 2017-18 (ANIME)

The Godzilla anime trilogy boldly dispenses with tradition to reimagine the monster for a new medium. This Godzilla is a gigantic, plant-based life-form that has evolved into the most powerful creature on the planet. "Godzilla in this work is the pinnacle of evolutionary life, which led us to the motif of trees," said codirector Hiroyuki Seshita. "Trees can grow the largest and have overwhelmingly long lifespans, spanning thousands of years." Rather than green, Godzilla's body is a monochromatic dark blue. The creature suggests themes of biological evolution and projects a godlike presence.

LEFT TO RIGHT: As can be seen on this 3D Godzilla maquette, the skin texture of the face and torso resembles carved muscle tissue. The lower body is a twisted mass of tree roots. The fins resemble Godzilla's traditional dorsals from a distance, but up close they are revealed to be giant leaves. ▪ Godzilla's body is massive, dwarfing the head and limbs. The lower jaw juts out, but otherwise the face has no defining features. Expressionless blue eyes are set deep in the sockets.

GODZILLA 2021 (ANIME)

Much like *Shin Godzilla*, in *Godzilla Singular Point*, the monster undergoes a four-form evolution: Godzilla Aquatilis, Godzilla Amphibia, Godzilla Terrestris, and Godzilla Ultima. "Godzilla itself is a long series, and the trends of its kaiju designs have changed greatly over time," said director Atsushi Takahashi. "We based this work on the kaiju designs that appear in early Godzilla. The premise behind the designs I asked for was what would happen if you removed the technological restraints of the time."

The emphasis for Godzilla Ultima was to create a biologically correct creature, something that would not resemble a man in a suit, hence the enormous legs necessary to support its weight. The skin is composed of numerous overlapping sheaths that serve as a kind of protective armor. The most distinctive feature of this Godzilla is its gaping alligator-like maw with external fangs, inspired by the skull of a saber tooth tiger, according to designer Eiji Yamamori.

GODZILLA 2023

Godzilla Minus One director Takashi Yamazaki's primary goal was to make Godzilla "a terrifying and grotesque presence, but also somehow alluring, something between a god and an animal." In honor of Godzilla 1954, unconventional features were avoided on this purely CG creation. The head is small compared to the massive body. The rough skin is covered with many irregular rocklike textures, and while the basic color is black, parts of the body that have suffered damage have a different, lighter color to emphasize the imperfect nature of its regeneration. The most dramatic feature of this Godzilla is its oversize dorsal fins, which are accented with long, exaggerated spikes.

CLOCKWISE FROM LEFT: To express Godzilla's overwhelming power, the body is massive and muscular, with clearly defined shoulders, a broad chest, and humanlike arms, as seen in this 3D model. The legs and feet are enormous, with four toes—another homage to Godzilla 1954. ▪ Modeler Kosuke Taguchi defied director Takashi Yamazaki's repeated orders to copy the "half-moon" eyes of Godzilla 1964, and designed beady, humanlike eyes instead. ▪ The fierce gaze of Godzilla. Numerous rocklike bumps protrude from the neck.

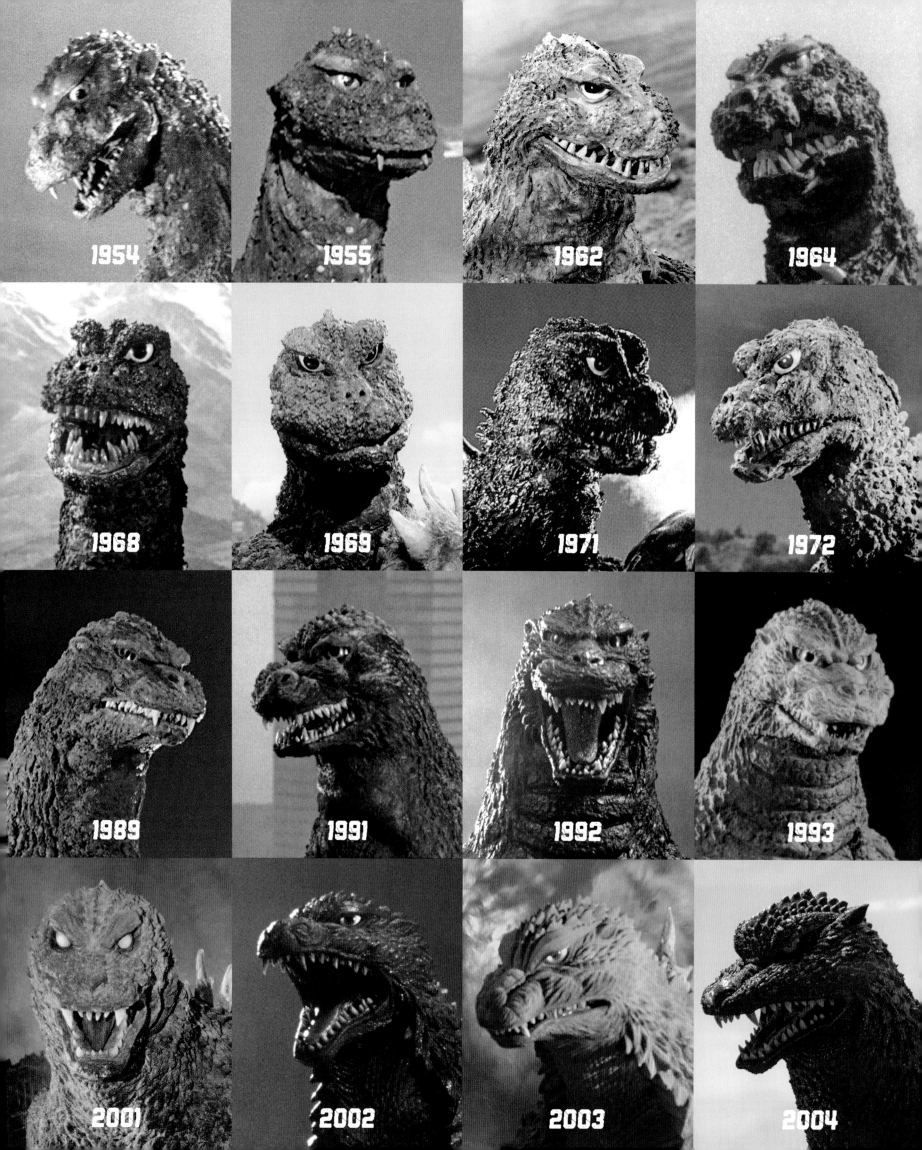

1954

1955

1962

1964

1968

1969

1971

1972

1989

1991

1992

1993

2001

2002

2003

2004

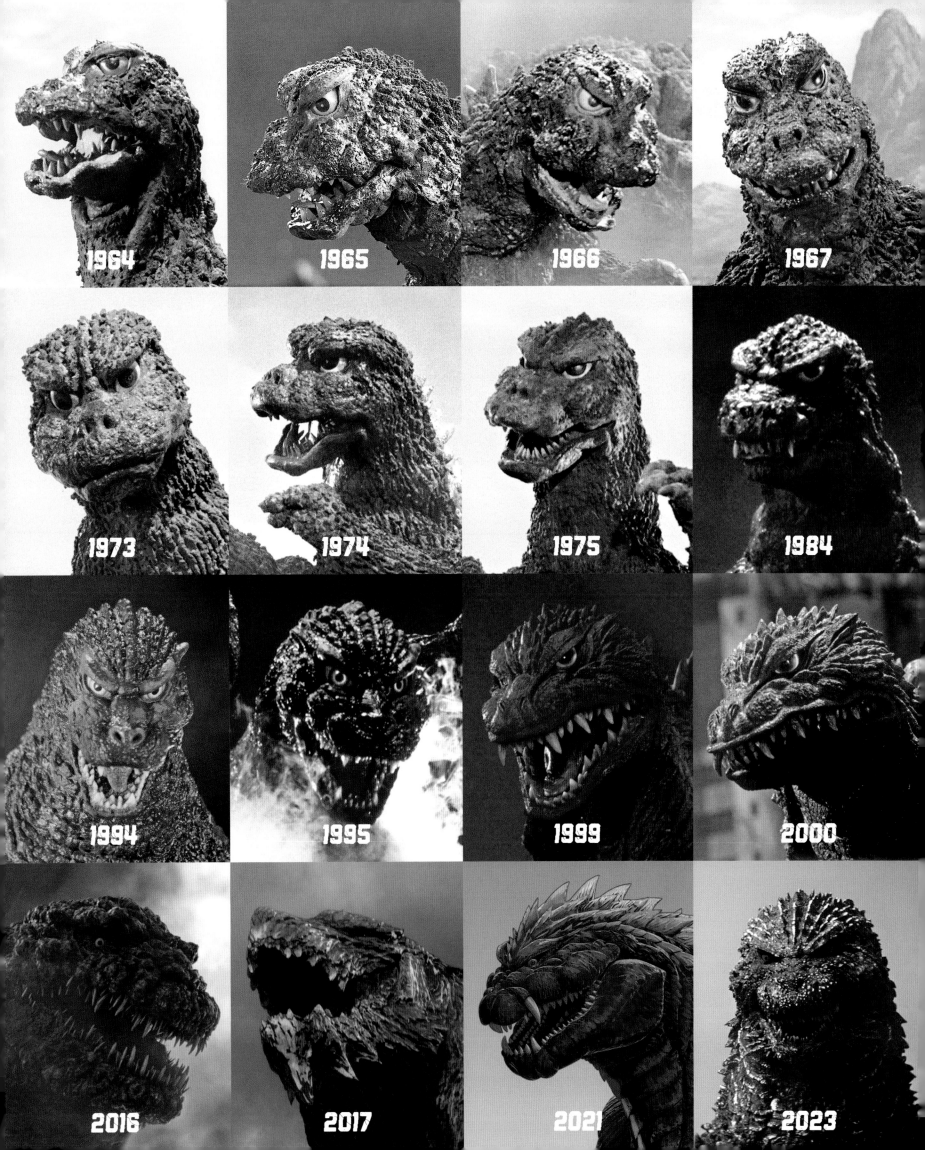

FIVE

MUTATIONS:
2016 TO 2024

SHIN GODZILLA

"I give my word that the new Godzilla film is indeed new," codirector Shinji Higuchi said prior to the release of *Shin Godzilla*. Higuchi kept his promise—the twenty-ninth Japanese Godzilla movie stands apart in both style and substance. This is not a sequel but a completely new origin story in which Godzilla functions less as a living creature and more like a walking natural catastrophe of world-ending scale. There are many analogies to Japan's triple disaster that began on March 11, 2011—often referred to simply as the 3/11 events—when a magnitude 9.1 earthquake, a tsunami, and a nuclear power plant meltdown led to widespread death, chaos, and fear. Made five years later, *Shin Godzilla* leverages the kaiju movie format to satirize the national leadership's response to the real-life crisis. The fast-paced, docudrama scenario unfolds largely within a high-level bureaucratic bubble and challenges long-held assumptions about Japan's political and social hierarchy and national security. A significant step forward in terms of both content and technical achievement, the film was a major commercial and critical success.

Shin Godzilla reflects the vision of Hideaki Anno, the enigmatic creator of *Neon Genesis Evangelion*, perhaps the most influential anime ever made. Anno began his professional career on Hayao Miyazaki's *Nausicaä of the Valley of the Wind* (1984) and then formed his own company, Studio Gainax, with Higuchi—then a teen just starting his cinematic journey—and a core creative team. *Evangelion* was launched in 1995 and achieved worldwide popularity with its idiosyncratic mix of giant monsters, robots, teen angst, philosophical

"IF I COULD MAKE THE NEW GODZILLA IN A REALISTIC WAY, WITH POLITICAL SUSPENSE (SET) IN MODERN JAPAN, THAT WOULD BE THE ONLY NEW GODZILLA (FILM) THAT MIGHT COMPETE WITH THE ORIGINAL *GODZILLA* FROM A DIFFERENT ANGLE. THAT WOULD BE A WORTHWHILE CHALLENGE FOR ME. THAT WAS MY TRUE STARTING POINT."

—Hideaki Anno, codirector

and spiritual themes, and romance. Anno, who has publicly battled mental health issues, described the material as personal and cathartic.

A lifelong fan of *tokusatsu*, in 2012, Anno curated a historical exhibition of monster suits, miniatures, and props that drew more than two hundred thousand visitors over four months at the Museum of Contemporary Art Tokyo. Soon thereafter, in January 2013, Toho invited Anno to direct a new Godzilla movie, but he declined because he was feeling "mentally unstable" and struggling with what would eventually become the film *Evangelion: 3.0+1.0 Thrice Upon a Time* (2021). "But I was swayed by Toho's sincerity and the enthusiasm of my good friend, director Shinji Higuchi," Anno said. "By that March, I'd accepted [because of] my desire to see fantastic science fiction revived, and because of all the love I'd poured into the special effects museum project. I wanted to repay the creative pioneers who gave life to their dreams." Anno also felt that "if I didn't take on a new job, something that wasn't *Evangelion,* I couldn't move forward."

RIGHT: After American B2 stealth bombers drop their payload on the monster as it tramples Tokyo, Godzilla launches a massive, devastating counterattack. ■ BELOW, CLOCKWISE FROM TOP LEFT: In some past Godzilla movies, Self-Defense Force tanks, artillery, and other equipment were actual military hardware photographed with permission. In *Shin Godzilla*, many armored vehicles and aircraft were digitally created via CG. "The SDF cooperated extensively," said VFX supervisor Atsuki Sato. "They gave us the information we needed on various types of machinery and equipment." ■ Godzilla's third form has small forearms and rumpled, brownish-red skin. ■ "[Concept artist] Takayuki Takeya made the tail of the model longer because it was easier to shorten it than to lengthen it later," said director Hideaki Anno. "[We] all immediately agreed that it would not be realistic for a tail to be that long for a [man in suit]. This film was designed to be CG, so that length was OK." ■ "The third form was not in our original plan," said Anno. "We had planned to transform the quadrupedal form into a bipedal form [once it reached] Kitashinagawa. However, when the model of the second form was completed, I felt that it was too much to ask [the VFX team] for a metamorphosis between this form and the fourth form, so I asked, 'Can we add an intermediate form?'"

FEAR AND ANXIETY

"After *Godzilla Final Wars*, it was a bad time for Godzilla movies," said producer Akihiro Yamauchi. "Ten years passed, and we realized there would be an entire generation that was unfamiliar with Godzilla, so we decided to go for it." The 2011 disaster created a renewed sense of "fear and anxiety," and it was important to "use Godzilla as a symbol to depict that fear and anxiety," Yamauchi said. He admittedly was "a bit worried" about entrusting the franchise to the mercurial director; however, "Godzilla is one of our most precious assets . . . but on the other hand, there's no point or profit in doing the same thing over and over."

While Anno began working on the screenplay, his curiosity about the *Kasumigaseki*—a euphemism for Japan's tangled official bureaucracies, named for that area of Tokyo where their offices are clustered—was piqued. Anno was also interested in the official response to the triple disaster. In May and July of 2013, he visited the areas around the Fukushima Daiichi Nuclear Power Plant to view the aftermath of the event. "I wondered what happened to [the] people who were directly affected, and their reaction to the government and [nuclear power plant operator Tokyo Electric Power Company] personnel who handled the matter," Anno said. His enthusiasm for the Godzilla project grew as he envisioned a story focusing on government officials rather than stock characters like scientists or military heroes. He would abandon certain established tropes: There would be no opponent monster, no children, and the word "kaiju" would not be spoken. "I wanted to create an impact like the first *Godzilla* had on people. The only way to do that was for Godzilla to show up for the very first time in modern Japan—a complete reset, as if all the other films never happened."

Shin Godzilla represents further steps in the transition from practical special effects to computer-generated visual effects. Although a robotic upper-body puppet of Godzilla with moveable hands and facial

"(HIDEAKI) ANNO'S SCRIPT WAS SO STRONG, (AND) THE AMOUNT OF TALKING WAS MASSIVE. THE SPEED OF THE DIALOGUE WAS SO FAST. WHEN THE ACTORS REHEARSED, I SAID, 'IT WILL BE LIKE NO OTHER FILM YOU'VE WORKED ON.' DURING FILMING, THEY WERE SAYING THEIR LINES FASTER AND FASTER. IT WAS SO INTENSE."

—Shinji Higuchi, codirector

features would be created and filmed against a green screen, none of that footage made the final cut. For the first time in a full-length, Japanese-made feature film, Godzilla would be strictly portrayed via CG. Miniatures were utilized in a few shots, including in the climax sequence in which Godzilla is immobilized, but otherwise, all effects were digital. "The world of this film is generally [realistic]," Anno said, "The handmade warmth of miniatures and the pseudo-loose atmosphere—in a positive sense—did not fit." Still, Anno attempted to retain the feel of classic *tokusatsu* to some extent. "The film must maintain the entertainment value of a monster movie," he said. "The difficult thing is to find the right balance. I wanted to incorporate a suitmation feel to the CG depiction of Godzilla and give the images of destruction a moderately miniature look."

A DISASTER MONSTER

The 3/11 events cascaded like dominoes. The most powerful earthquake in Japan's history struck off the Tohoku Pacific Coast, triggering a tsunami that washed away coastal towns within minutes. Giant waves flooded the Fukushima nuclear reactor, causing explosions and meltdowns that released radioactive material into the atmosphere and ocean. Nearly twenty thousand people died, and nearly a half million

CLOCKWISE FROM TOP LEFT: Despite the filmmakers' intention to differentiate this Godzilla from previous versions of the monster, Akira Ifukube's classic Godzilla theme is heard when Godzilla comes ashore, as well as during other scenes, lending a sense of familiarity and continuity. ■ The skin of Godzilla's fourth form is rough and scarred, with heat and blood coursing just beneath the surface. Godzilla's eyes are small and recessed; the monster has no eyelids, but instead has "anti-flash defensive membranes" to shield its eyes from harm. The mouth has no tongue, and the large teeth are crooked and irregular, some jutting out the sides of its mouth. ■ In the first moments of Godzilla's Stage 3 evolution, its body pulsates with energy.

CLOCKWISE FROM TOP LEFT: Digital VFX enable the filmmakers to present heretofore unseen views of Godzilla's size in relation to skyscrapers, houses, people on the ground, and the city as a whole. ■ In many shots, Godzilla is portrayed via motion capture by Mansai Nomura, a *kyogen* (a traditional form of Japanese drama) theater actor; this marks the first use of mo-cap in Toho's Godzilla series. ■ The monster appears completely impervious to conventional weaponry. Hundreds of shells explode on impact with no effect other than a metallic clang. ■ Godzilla is bombarded by numerous JSDF weapons, including Type 10 tanks, Howitzer guns, missile and rocket systems, Apache and Cobra helicopters, and F-2 fighter jets, as well as the USAF B-2 Spirit stealth bomber.

survivors were displaced as a result of the quake and tsunami. The imagery of *Shin Godzilla* strongly resembles the disaster—the monster's evolving state mirroring an earthquake, tsunami, and meltdown. Its arrival is mistaken for seismic or volcanic activity in Tokyo Bay as tremors damage the Aqua-Line underwater highway and raise a plume of red fluid on the sea's surface. Only the tail of Godzilla's first form is seen, revealing that the crisis is caused not by a natural disaster but a giant creature. When it swims up the Nomi River, Godzilla's fishlike second form pushes boats up the channel and floods the streets of Ota Ward. Then, walking on all fours, Godzilla causes mass panic as it topples buildings and tosses cars and trains about. Godzilla writhes in pain and secretes bloodlike fluid from its gills; it collapses in the street, then morphs into an upright-walking, salamander-like third form and bellows the familiar Godzilla roar of 1954. After much debate over constitutional military protocols, the prime minister sends Apache helicopters to the scene. Godzilla appears vulnerable in this transitional stage, but the choppers must hold their fire due to the presence of civilians, and the creature flees back to the sea.

Godzilla's roar, and the insertion of Akira Ifukube's classic motifs into Shiro Sagisu's modern soundtrack, are reminders that this is a Godzilla movie even if the monster is almost unrecognizable. When Godzilla's fourth form lumbers into Tokyo, its movements are glacial and its expression blank. Its red-blackened skin appears hideously scarred. Godzilla's purpose is not to feed on radiation or—despite one character's description of "a god incarnate"—to deliver otherworldly judgment. Godzilla, it is learned, is a highly evolved mutation of prehistoric sea organisms exposed to nuclear waste illegally dumped in the Pacific by the US sixty years earlier, and capable of rapid propagation that may wipe out humankind. As it plods forward, Godzilla seeks only self-preservation. Its destruction is incidental rather than intentional—only when attacked does Godzilla lash out with incredible power, emitting a heat ray from its maw and a multitude of dorsal beams that illuminate the sky and eliminate incoming bombs and aircraft. Unprecedented military might is deployed by the Japan Self-Defense Forces (JSDF) and the US Air Force, which sends B2 stealth bombers to Tokyo. Godzilla's retaliation turns the city into a flaming holocaust.

CRISIS AND CHAOS

The government's response to the 3/11 crisis was described by Harvard historian Theodore Bestor as "bumbling, inept, and paralyzed." A report by a citizen commission, appointed by the National Diet to investigate the disasters, described chaos and confusion within the upper echelons of government as the prime minister and senior cabinet members held endless meetings, watching events unfold on TV and struggling to formulate both a response and coherent messaging. The fiction of *Shin Godzilla* is a satirical facsimile of these events, and of the multilayered hierarchy of seniority, rank, and decorum that hampered decision-making. The film's protagonist, Rando Yaguchi (Hiroki Hasegawa), is a young deputy chief cabinet secretary whose suggestions that a giant creature might be causing the disturbances are initially dismissed by the old guard. Yaguchi is admonished not to "stir things up," but social media videos (a key source of information in the 3/11 disaster) soon prove him right. Anno's rapid-fire dialogue, quick-cut

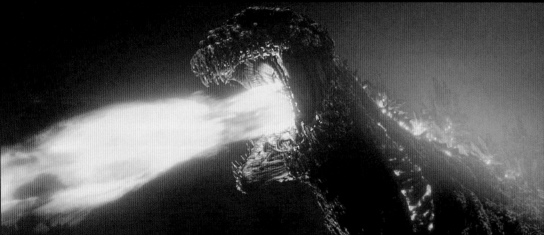

THIS PAGE: Godzilla's breath weapon starts out like a traditional heat ray and changes into a narrow, purplish energy stream that cuts through row upon row of buildings like a razor and travels a great distance. Godzilla's dorsal fins are surrounded by a purple-colored glow when its heat ray is emitted. "In previous films, Godzilla used its ray in anger," said artist Mahiro Maeda. "For this film, I felt Godzilla was shooting its ray as if it were vomiting because it's in pain."

"PRINCE HAS ALWAYS HAD AN INFLUENCE ON MY WORK. WHAT HE SINGS ABOUT IS ACTUALLY VERY SERIOUS. THE SONG 'PURPLE RAIN' IS ACTUALLY ABOUT EMOTIONAL TURMOIL. THIS HAS BEEN A RECURRING THEME THROUGHOUT MY WORK. GODZILLA IS EMOTIONAL TURMOIL FOR JAPAN. GODZILLA IS THE PURPLE RAIN."

—Hideaki Anno, director

GODZILLA FACT: An early concept for *Shin Godzilla* by directors Hideaki Anno and Shinji Higuchi would have seen Godzilla evolve from its traditional form into something entirely different. "We wanted to do a movie where Godzilla transforms . . . and it was rejected," Higuchi said at the G-Fest Godzilla convention in Chicago in 2017. Director Anno also unsuccessfully proposed a sequel, *Shin Godzilla Strikes Back*, which was to be directed by Higuchi. Anno created a rough outline of a story in the style of the Toho Champion Matsuri–era movies, and "aimed at people who weren't fans of Shin Godzilla," he said.

editing, and pronounced camera angles turn scenes of long, talky meetings (cleverly truncated for the audience) set in huge, symmetrical conference rooms into a commentary on high-level paralysis by analysis—the innumerable government and military officials (identified via screen titles) are not characters but cogs in a dysfunctional machine.

An ad-hoc group of esteemed scientists (played by several acclaimed film directors making cameos) is convened to investigate the creature, but these establishment types are likewise too concerned about stature and reputation to be of help. As Godzilla's destruction thins out the upper government ranks, Yaguchi and his colleagues gain more authority by attrition. The story pivots to a meditation on Japan's dependence on the US for security and a tribute to the emergency responders who risked their lives in the 3/11 crisis by working to stabilize the crippled nuclear plant. Kayoko Anne Patterson (Satomi Ishihara), a Japanese American special envoy, at first seems a pushy, privileged American official pressuring the

RIGHT: At approximately 387 feet (118 m) tall, the fourth form of Shin Godzilla became Toho's tallest iteration of the monster to date. ▪ BELOW: Godzilla fires multiple rays from between its dorsal fins, striking targets in the air and at ground level.

Japanese government to divulge information about Godzilla, but when she learns of a US-led plan to kill the monster with a nuclear explosion in Tokyo, she recalls that her grandmother survived Hiroshima and pledges to help prevent another such tragedy. Yaguchi assembles a team of genius science nerds who succeed where the government and academics could not. Poring over impenetrable data left behind by a disgraced biologist who predicted the monster's rise, these misfit geeks crack the code of Godzilla's radioactive makeup and develop a plan to freeze it with a blood coagulant, racing to head off America's nuclear strike. Yaguchi, Kayoko, and Hiromi Ogashira (Mikako Ichikawa)—a brainy scientist who rarely looks up from her laptop—are Anno's trio of anime-style young archetypes; rebels who buck the rules for good reason yet are ambitious and not wholly altruistic, either.

ONE VISION, TWO DIRECTORS

Shinji Higuchi made his mark as the innovative SFX wizard of Daiei's Heisei Gamera trilogy before becoming a full-fledged director of such films as *Sinking of Japan* (2006) and *Attack on Titan* (2015), both released by Toho. Anno's original plan was to delegate the on-set duties to Higuchi ("A friend in whom he could trust to reflect his own intentions," observed VFX supervisor Atsuki Sato), but those plans evolved. "I was the one who took the lead most of the time, only because I'm more accustomed to working on that kind of movie, whereas Anno is more accustomed to working on anime," said Higuchi. "What Anno was good at, with his experience directing anime, were the camera angles. Usually that's the work of a

THIS PAGE: As part of Operation Yashiori—the plan to freeze Godzilla—Japan Railways trains loaded with explosives are rammed into Godzilla's legs. Buildings are blown up, crashing down on Godzilla and forcing the monster to the ground, where trucks pump freezing coagulant into its mouth. At one point, Godzilla bites the tubes and attempts to rise again, but the operation ultimately proves successful. The plan is named after Yashiori sake, which the storm god Susano used to intoxicate and kill Yamata no Orochi, the fearsome eight-headed serpent of Japanese mythology.

GODZILLA FACT: *Shin Godzilla* won the most awards (seven) and received the most nominations (eleven) at the 40th Japan Academy Film Prize ceremonies honoring domestic films released in 2016. The film was honored with Picture of the Year, Director of the Year (Hideaki Anno and Shinji Higuchi), and Outstanding Achievement in the following categories: Cinematography (Kousuke Yamada), Art Direction (Yuji Hayashida and Eri Sakushima), Lighting Direction (Takayuki Kawabe), Sound Recording (Jun Nakamura and Haru Yamada), and Editing (Hideaki Anno and Atsuki Sato). Additionally, it received nominations for Outstanding Performance by an Actor in a Leading Role (Hiroki Hasegawa) and Actress in a Supporting Role (Satomi Ishihara, Mikako Ichikawa), and Outstanding Achievement in Music (Shirou Sagisu). It was also honored by the prestigious *Kinema Junpo* Awards, the Mainichi Film Awards, and the Seiun Awards for Japanese speculative fiction.

THIS PAGE: With Operation Yashiori concluded, Godzilla stands frozen like a statue in the middle of Tokyo. The disaster has been avoided for now, but the threat remains as the US pledges to resume plans for a nuclear strike if the creature ever becomes active again. As the film ends, the camera focuses on the monster's tail, revealing what appear to be skeletons of nascent Godzilla-human hybrids. "It is the same concept as the worldview of Eva (aka *Evangelion*), that if we evolve on this planet, we will end up in a humanoid form," director Hideaki Anno said. "If that is the case, Godzilla's final form would also be humanoid."

director of photography, but in our case, Anno handled it. Anno was meticulous; sometimes he wanted to move the camera just one millimeter."

Anno ended up spending considerable time on set. "I had no choice but to be there as much as possible," he said, "I felt I had to change the mindset of the workplace." He was concerned that the crew regarded *Shin Godzilla* as a normal job. "It is difficult to create anything interesting or new from routine work," he said, "so I decided to [disrupt] the routine. I wanted to create a paradigm shift among the staff." He admitted being "always angry" on-set but felt that his unchecked emotions did not negatively affect the production and helped elevate the quality of work overall.

Shin Godzilla earned ¥8.25 billion and ranked second at the 2016 domestic box office, far exceeding all previous Japanese-made Godzilla movies in sheer earnings; it sold 5.7 million tickets and was the most-attended Godzilla movie since 1964's *Mothra vs. Godzilla*. Its positive reception among critics and awards ceremonies was mirrored in the US, where the film received a limited theatrical release. Anno's ambitious vision and the film's urgent subject matter had elevated the conversation about Godzilla—*The New Yorker* and other US publications parsed the film's politics. Japan's Godzilla was relevant again.

The effort to neutralize Godzilla, with hazmat-suited workers entering the irradiated zone on a high-risk mission ("Japan's future we place in your hands," Yaguchi says in a rousing, patriotic speech), is successful. The frozen monster remains standing in the middle of Tokyo, a disaster monument analogous to the decaying remains of the Fukushima reactor. Godzilla, it is said, will eventually thaw, leaving the door ajar for a sequel—but Anno would return to his *Evangelion* project, and *Shin Godzilla* remains a singular, unique entry in the franchise.

RELEASED: NOVEMBER 3, 2023 (JAPAN)

GODZILLA MINUS ONE

*D*o you want to live? Come on!"

Noriko, paralyzed with fear, is knocked to the ground amid a wave of fleeing citizens. Miraculously, Shikishima is suddenly there. He lifts Noriko to her feet, and together they run. Close behind, people are crushed beneath Godzilla's feet, and buildings are instantly turned to clouds of rubble by a slash of its tail. Then it happens: Tanks bombard Godzilla with artillery shells and the creature responds by exhaling a powerful heat ray, igniting an explosion with the force of a mass-destruction event. In that panicked moment, Noriko shoves Shikishima into a safe space just before the shockwave comes. Moments later, the city is a silent, burning hull. There are no bodies, living or dead. Noriko is gone. A mushroom cloud looms above. Godzilla roars to the sky and black rain begins to fall like tears. His heart broken and soul crushed, Shikishima wails in overwhelming grief and terror.

No one might have predicted the underdog success story of *Godzilla Minus One*, the only film in the monster's nearly seventy-year history to be nominated for—and to win—an Academy Award. Though it was made on a miniscule budget, with a tiny team of thirty-five digital artists creating 610 complex CG shots, the film was honored with the Oscar for Best Visual Effects over Hollywood productions costing nearly twenty times as much and employing hundreds of digital artists around the globe. At the box office, *Minus One* set an all-time record for the Godzilla franchise by earning more than $116 million (as of July 2024) internationally. Just as significantly, director Takashi Yamazaki's

GODZILLA FACT: With *Godzilla Minus One*, Takashi Yamazaki became the first director to be nominated for an Academy Award for visual effects since Stanley Kubrick, who won the award for *2001: A Space Odyssey* (1968).

unique rewriting of Godzilla's origin story received critical acclaim worldwide and changed the conversation about what a Godzilla film could be, technically and dramatically. Old clichés about men in suits and low budgets gave way to praise for a living, breathing, terrifying Godzilla. A distinctly Japanese character-driven story about trauma, loss, and redemption, rooted in the tragic history of the Second World War, somehow resonated with audiences worldwide.

"Given our limited resources, we knew we had to maximize what we could do to put the best possible interpretation of Godzilla on [the] screen," Yamazaki said. "From a VFX perspective, [we had to take] inventory of what the team was capable of. Having said that, I never let that distract me from writing a good story, which is the most fundamental component in making a good film."

Godzilla Minus One personalizes Godzilla's symbolic representation of war and death to achieve an emotional link between the protagonist and monster that no other film has attempted. In the waning days of the war, Imperial Navy *tokko* (kamikaze) pilot Koichi Shikishima (Ryunosuke Kamiki) feigns a mechanical problem with his plane to avoid his suicide mission. He takes refuge at a tiny airfield on fictional Odo Island, a remote Japanese outpost in the South Pacific, but the specter of war soon follows in the form of Godzilla—a legendary sea creature of the island's folklore, which comes ashore and attacks the base by night. Terror-stricken, Shikishima fails to fire on Godzilla in defense of his comrades. The monster savagely kills the entire ground crew, sparing only Shikishima and the mechanic Sosaku Tachibana (Munetaka Aoki), who now despises Shikishima for failing to stop the massacre. Fast-forwarding to the months immediately after the war, the story finds Shikishima returning to his home in a burned-out Tokyo decimated by American fire raids. Shikishima's parents are dead, his neighborhood is in ruins, and the people live in famine and dire poverty. Godzilla haunts Shikishima's dreams. The monster is an avatar of the shame, guilt, and blame experienced by the military men who returned to a defeated Japan—Godzilla is the demon of Shikishima's personal hell.

NEW DIRECTIONS

A filmmaker and visual effects supervisor, Yamazaki came to the Godzilla franchise with a reputation as one of Japan's most prolific, versatile, and commercially successful directors. Inspired by a love of *Star Wars* (1977) and *Close Encounters of the Third Kind* (1977), he graduated from Asagaya College of Art and Design and then joined Shirogumi Inc., an animation and visual effects studio, in 1986, where he honed his craft by creating effects for commercials and feature films. Yamazaki would maintain a close association with Shirogumi throughout his career, and the company would serve as the VFX house on *Godzilla Minus One*.

After launching his directorial career with a pair of modest science-fiction films, Yamazaki broke through with the nostalgic period dramedy *Always: Sunset on Third Street* (2005), which used VFX to re-create Tokyo in the late 1950s. The film won twelve Japan Academy Film Prize awards, including Best Picture and Best Director. From there, Yamazaki genre-hopped between live action and anime. Among his films' numerous accolades, the war drama *The Eternal Zero* (2013) and the anime *Stand by Me Doraemon* (2014) won the Japan Academy Film Prize for Best Picture and Best Animation Film, respectively.

PREVIOUS SPREAD: US theatrical release poster for *Godzilla Minus One*. ▪ **BELOW LEFT:** When Godzilla attacks the Odo Island air base, pilot Koichi Shikishima (Ryunosuke Kamiki) freezes in fear, unable to fire his gun. "It was about creating a sense of proximity between the people [and] Godzilla himself . . . bringing them as close as possible," said director Takashi Yamazaki. The director was inspired by his work on *Godzilla the Ride* for the Seibuen amusement park. "When I saw Godzilla up close, it was a frightening presence." The Odo Island attack also helped establish what Godzilla looked like before being exposed to atomic fallout. "It was very different in size and movement," Yamazaki said. "I also think it's more terrifying sometimes when the creature you're facing is smaller and you can put it in the same shot as everything else. It creates a sense of reality. You can imagine this creature is attacking you." ▪ **BELOW RIGHT:** Shikishima grapples with guilt and shame after deserting a suicide mission under false pretenses.

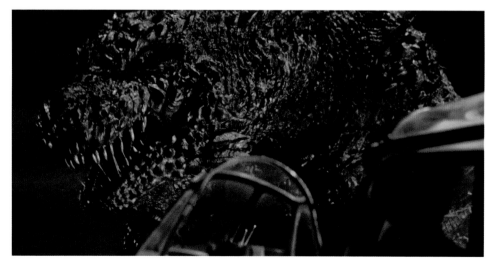

ABOVE: "When Godzilla acts like a beast, its hands are pointed down," said director Takashi Yamazaki. "When it is more like a god, its hands are turned upward." ■ **TOP RIGHT:** "Godzilla's heat ray might have looked more powerful and scary than ever in this film," said Yamazaki. "I felt that people had forgotten that Godzilla was originally a metaphor for war and the fear of the nuclear age. I wanted to re-create that fear." ■ **RIGHT:** Godzilla's brownish skin color and bumpy texture are created via a complex pattern of polygons (the basic building block of 3D computer graphics). The head required two hundred million polygons and the chest area required one hundred million polygons. "We were concerned about whether we would be able to render [Godzilla] on the screen because of the sheer amount of data that needed to be computed," said Yamazaki. "Luckily, we [lightened] some of the polygons and ensure Godzilla was renderable."

Yamazaki first received an offer to direct a Godzilla film around the time of *Always: Sunset on Third Street* but declined because he felt it would be impossible to make a fully CG kaiju film with Japan's then-available technology. Two years later, Yamazaki gave Godzilla a cameo in *Always: Sunset on Third Street 2* (2007), fueling speculation that the director was next in line for the series, but sixteen years would pass before *Godzilla Minus One*. "The plan for a live-action Godzilla film by Yamazaki had been on hold within Toho, not as a question of if but when to do it," said *Minus One* producer Kazuaki Kishida. Following *Shin Godzilla*, the studio had passed on several proposals for a follow up. "[To] meet the expectations of fans who watched [*Shin Godzilla*], we needed an entirely new and unprecedented concept," Kishida said.

In February 2022, Toho and Robot Communications, an independent production company closely associated with Yamazaki's filmography, announced a casting call for extras to appear in a new kaiju feature tentatively titled *Blockbuster Monster Movie*. The story was said to take place roughly in the years 1945–47; filming was scheduled from mid-March to June 2022 in Tokyo, Yokohama, and other locations. Yamazaki had recently directed the five-minute film *Godzilla the Ride: Giant Monsters Ultimate Battle*, part of an attraction at Seibuen amusement park in Saitama. This fueled online speculation that "this seemingly original monster film could secretly be the next installment in the Godzilla franchise," said the Tokusatsu Network website. The rumors were confirmed on Godzilla Day, November 3, 2022, Toho's annual celebration marking the anniversary of the original film's release. The official Godzilla Twitter account announced Yamazaki's attachment to write and direct the still-untitled next Godzilla production, scheduled for release exactly one year later.

GODZILLA FACT: Acknowledging the work of his VFX team, who often put in long hours because they believed *Minus One* had the potential to reach international audiences, director Takashi Yamazaki also acknowledged that the film's small budget was possible in part due to lower wages for such artists in Japan compared to their counterparts in Hollywood. "Hopefully, in due time, VFX budget increases will allow [us to] pay creatives more," he told *Vulture*.

Yamazaki greatly admired *Shin Godzilla* but was determined not to follow in its giant footsteps. "We were trying to do everything counter to *Shin Godzilla*," he told one interviewer. "Be it the story elements or the design, this was our response to the success of that film and taking a different approach." Yamazaki has long had a nostalgic interest in subject matter related to the Second World War and its aftermath, as evidenced by his *Always* movies and other films set during those times. "If I were to make a Godzilla film," he told another interviewer, "I always had the desire to set it in an era with the lingering scent of war—right after the end of World War II in Japan. [That's how] we arrived at the idea of portraying the shift from one era, when people were required to risk their lives in battle, to another era, when everyday citizens are actively fighting to survive."

GODZILLA FACT: The *Godzilla Minus One* score, composed by frequent Takashi Yamazaki collaborator Naoki Sato, features several reworkings of Akira Ifukube's kaiju themes. "While the instrumentation is slightly different, I tried to remake his music as faithfully as possible," Sato said. "I intended for Ifukube's compositions to create a firm axis, and [my original] pieces to permeate into the body unconsciously, creating music that is felt rather than heard."

LEFT: Noriko (Minami Hamabe) and young Akiko (Sae Nagatani), along with Shikishima, form a makeshift family in the ruins of postwar Tokyo. ■ **BELOW:** Godzilla bites down on a commuter train in which Noriko (Hamabe) is riding. This scene offers a visual homage to an iconic moment in the original *Godzilla*.

"MY WAR ISN'T OVER YET."

—Koichi Shikishima (Ryunosuke Kamiki)

TOP TO BOTTOM: In response to an artillery attack, Godzilla unleashes its heat ray, obliterating the National Diet Building and creating an enormous shockwave that levels the surrounding area. ■ In the wake of Godzilla's heat ray blast, a mushroom cloud rises above the city. ■ Although Godzilla's powerful heat ray leaves the monster with self-inflicted burns, Godzilla is capable of immediately regenerating and healing serious wounds.

Q AND A: TAKASHI YAMAZAKI

Q: *Godzilla Minus One* is the series' first-ever period piece. How did you decide to set your story in the years immediately after the Second World War?

A: That was a time when the Japanese people were emotionally devastated and beaten down. Among the people were those who persevered; they raised Japan back up to where the country is today. By making a film about the people back then, I felt I might inspire or give hope to today's generation. I have made films like *The Great War of Archimedes* (2019) and *Always: Sunset on Third Street* (2005), and the perseverance of the Japanese people [as well as] the war are major themes of mine that appeared in them.

The [returning] soldiers felt bad that they couldn't save the country. Their friends, and everyone they had fought alongside, had died; those left behind had survivor's guilt. I believe this theme applies not just to Japan but to anyone or any country, even America. When we premiered the film in the US, I saw that the subject of PTSD [post-traumatic stress disorder] is taken much more seriously in America than in Japan. Before bringing the film overseas, I worried that because this is such a domestic story about Japan right after the war, I wasn't sure how foreign people would take it, or if they would understand the situation. But after the screening, I realized that it was more than [just] a domestic issue.

For the Japanese people, the war was a long time ago. People today don't know much about it, so I thought it was my mission to remind the current generation.

Q: Do you view Godzilla as an animal? A monster? A god?

A: I see Godzilla as a *tatarigami*, a curse god. This is a very Japanese concept. It is the idea of someone who was abused or hurt in the past [who] then returns in a completely different form to exact revenge. The people then try to calm that god down, to settle the situation. In Japan, Godzilla is something like this. After making this film, I felt it was just like a ritual for calming this kind of god down. I believe that's one of the reasons why Godzilla films have been made all this time—for that ritual.

Q: Why does Godzilla attack Japan?

A: This is sort of like what [author and philosopher] Yoro Takeshi says. His writings inspired me. In a Noh play, there might be a ghost, and it shows up and tells [the audience] why it is in such pain. The people listen, and when they finally understand, the ghost goes away. I think Godzilla is similar to that, but Godzilla's way of telling his story is through violence. He shows up, tells his story by destroying things, and when he's done, he moves on. When I started thinking this way, everything fell into place.

Q: *Godzilla Minus One* visibly connects Godzilla to the atomic bomb in an unprecedented way. We actually see the monster being affected by the tests at Bikini Atoll in 1946.

A: The first *Godzilla* was made right after the *Lucky Dragon* incident, so that's how Godzilla and nuclear weapons were connected. But after so many movies, the fact that Godzilla is a metaphor for the bomb wasn't clear any longer. Maybe it's because I value the first film so much that I felt this was one of the most important points. I needed to make it clear again.

Q: Godzilla is now created exclusively via CGI.

A: Traditionally, we used miniatures and monster suits. People knew that it didn't look real, but they viewed it through a filter. But when we use digital VFX, there is no filter needed. I wanted to make a more fearful image, a picture that is more realistic and believable—something you don't need to see through a filter. That can only be done with VFX. Yes, the traditional monster suit Godzilla was a wonderful thing, but technology has advanced, and now we have something better. To make a believable Godzilla—something that looked real—was my ultimate goal.

Q: In the last scene, Noriko survives, but a mark in the shape of one of Godzilla's fins appears on her neck. Is this an ominous sign?

A: I really wanted Shikishima to reunite with Noriko at the end, [but] under normal circumstances, she would have been dead. Therefore, I didn't want to make the ending seem like, "Hurray, she's alive, and they lived happily ever after." Godzilla is a metaphor for war and human misfortune, so a Godzilla movie shouldn't have a simple, happy ending. I didn't want a pathetically sad ending either, just something a little

ABOVE: Takashi Yamazaki at Toho's offices, November 2023.

happier. So I wanted to leave some type of wound somewhere—that's what shows up at the end. It's also a subtle clue [as to] why she didn't just die. A few people did understand, but most did not. That's OK.

Q: Godzilla causes a great amount of visible death and destruction. Traditionally, the carnage mostly occurred off-screen.

A: I don't feel I broke that tradition. In the past, Godzilla killed a lot of people, but because of the visual techniques, they couldn't show much. But now [that the] visual quality and technology have gotten so much better, we can create a more [realistic] picture. Before *Shin Godzilla*, Godzilla was made to be more of a good guy. People had often forgotten that Godzilla was a metaphor for fear. I wanted to make a film where people are killed without any holding back. From there, the interesting part would be how these powerless humans would fight back against adversity, even though they had nothing.

Q: Were you able to fully achieve your vision of Godzilla?

A: I think I did. One thing that I didn't do was to have Godzilla face off against another monster, [as] then Godzilla would have been separated from the human story. In this film, the human drama was of the utmost importance. So I am really satisfied with how the character drama and Godzilla were completely merged. That was the best thing about the original *Godzilla*.

Q: What message do you want the audience to take from this film?

A: My generation may be the last one connected to the people who experienced the war. My main message is anti-war; that was very important to me. But still, it's entertainment, so more than stating my message, I wanted the audience to enjoy the film.

(Adapted from interviews conducted by the authors in Los Angeles and Tokyo, November 2023.)

GODZILLA FACT: To make Godzilla's iconic original roar louder than ever, the *Godzilla Minus One* team rented ZOZO Marine Stadium, home field of the Chiba Lotte Marines baseball team, and captured the sound as it played over the public address speakers. "[We] created this sense of a massive creature roaring in a vast, open environment," said director Takashi Yamazaki. "We got a lot of complaints afterward from the neighbors who lived near the baseball stadium."

SECOND CHANCES

Life, death, love, and hope are among the interwoven themes of *Godzilla Minus One*. Shikishima is haunted by traumatic memories of his cowardice in the face of battle, yet he tries nonetheless to move on and gradually finds a semblance of connection and community even as Tokyo itself slowly rises from the war's ashes. In the chaotic, decimated streets, he meets Noriko Oishi (Minami Hamabe), a homeless young woman stealing food to survive. She becomes his (uninvited at first) live-in companion, and together they raise Akiko (Sae Nagatani), a baby orphaned in the air raids. To support his makeshift family, Shikishima takes a risky job manning the gun aboard a boat tasked with finding and destroying wartime mines along Japan's coastline. The boat's motley crew of mostly ex-military men becomes a tight-knit group of friends bonding over shared wartime memories. Time passes. Japan and its people regroup, but those dark memories soon become flesh when Godzilla—exposed to an atomic bomb test and transformed from the 50-foot- (15-m-) tall, dinosaur-like creature of Odo Island into a 165-foot- (50-m-) tall leviathan—surfaces in the waters off Japan and soon makes landfall in Tokyo. The creature appears to be invulnerable, capable of immediately regenerating and healing when wounded. Godzilla lays utter waste to the resurgent Ginza district, a symbol of the nation's peaceful postwar renewal.

While the story takes place during the US-led postwar occupation of Japan, there is no evidence of the thousands of American military and civilian personnel who lived and worked there. Yamazaki creates this fictional reality to pay tribute to the war generation—the people compelled to fight for the Japanese empire, whose lives were deemed expendable. "When I made films about the Second World War, I conducted research and became acutely aware of how Japan had devalued human life during the war," Yamazaki said. Though these individuals are ex-military, Yamazaki notes that they are now ordinary citizens, acting as volunteers rather than soldiers, who rise together to save their country—essentially unassisted—in a time when the nation's military had been disbanded and its government was subjected to a constitutional

LEFT: Shikishima and Noriko struggle to survive in the harsh reality of postwar Japan, where they contend with food shortages, poverty, and meager living conditions. ■ **BELOW:** Godzilla tramples through the Ginza district of postwar Tokyo. "The first *Godzilla* movie is still my favorite," said director Takashi Yamazaki. "I really wanted to give the audience the same fear that I experienced when I saw the first *Godzilla*. But twenty-first century audiences are very discerning, thanks to advances in VFX. Still, we didn't want to run away from the challenge of creating a realistic postwar Ginza scene in broad daylight."

overhaul. "It was very intentional that there is no [visible] Japanese government, there is no US military, and the civilians are on their own. They obviously would have needed permission from the US government [in reality]. But I really wanted to focus on these civilian heroes."

The plan to kill Godzilla by subjecting it to massive oceanic pressure involves two decommissioned destroyers stripped of weapons, several rickety tugboats, and an experimental anti-bomber plane that was mothballed after the war. The plan fails, but Shikishima reclaims his courage and flies the plane, which is loaded with explosives, directly into Godzilla's mouth at a pivotal moment, blowing the monster's head off. At the last second, Shikishima ejects from the cockpit—a repudiation of war and an affirmation of the value of his own life and the lives of his fellow civilian fighters. The film makes numerous callbacks to the original *Godzilla*—the monster's rampage fells the Ginza clock tower and Nichigeki Theater, and Geiger counters click madly in the aftermath, to cite just a few—but none are so poignant as the volunteers saluting Godzilla as it sinks to its death, a tribute to a fallen adversary and an acknowledgment of the monster's godlike import. "[They] didn't necessarily defeat this massive evil creature as much as quell the anger of this divine being," said Yamazaki. "It was almost this offering to restore balance between God and mankind." Via the final battle, Yamazaki allows the heroes to cast off the ignominy of war and live again. Shikishima is reunited with Noriko, who somehow survived the Ginza explosion. His story ends with hints of love and hope—but nothing is certain, for Godzilla's undying flesh has begun to regenerate on the ocean floor.

A GLOBAL MONSTER

On July 11, 2023, Toho revealed *Godzilla Minus One* as the title of its secretive Godzilla project, and in the months preceding the film's November 3 release date, the studio employed an aggressive advance marketing campaign via traditional and social media. A red-carpet theatrical premiere was held at the Toho Cinemas in Shinjuku, and the film closed out the 36th Tokyo International Film Festival on November 1. An aggressive domestic and international distribution strategy followed. Toho released the film to more than five hundred cinemas in Japan; it earned ¥5.6 billion during its theatrical run, placing fifth at the 2023 domestic box office. In an unprecedented move, Toho immediately followed the Japanese release with a US premiere at the Director's Guild of America in Hollywood on November 10, 2023, with Yamazaki and lead actor Kamiki walking the red carpet and taking part in a post-screening Q and A. Through Toho International, its new international distribution arm, the company subsequently distributed the film across more than two thousand, five hundred screens in the US, and it remained in theaters until February 2024. *Godzilla Minus One* quickly became the all-time top-grossing live-action Japanese film and the third-highest- grossing foreign-language film ever released in North America, according to *Forbes.* To simulate the atmosphere of the original *Godzilla,* Yamazaki created an alternate, black-and-white version, *Godzilla Minus One/Minus Color,* which premiered in January 2024.

Praise in the West was widespread, with critics often citing the film's themes as well as its visual achievements. "I wasn't expecting to cry as much as I did," wrote a *New York Times* film critic. "This is a

RIGHT: Newscasters gathered on a Ginza rooftop get much too close a look at Godzilla's reign of terror. ■ **BELOW:** Shikishima is forced to confront his darkest fears after Godzilla's devastating Ginza attack appears to have wiped out everyone in sight, including Noriko.

story about finding community in the wake of destruction and learning to value yourself in a society that deems you worthless." Britain's *The Guardian* judged it "[u]nabashedly nationalistic and sentimental in approach . . . [but] it's a testament to the quality of writing, and to the action direction, that this never feels as corny or as crass as you might expect."

Propelled largely by word of mouth, enthusiasm for *Godzilla Minus One* culminated in the announcement on January 23, 2024, that the film was nominated for the Academy Award for Best Visual Effects alongside 2023 Hollywood movies costing exponentially more, including *Guardians of the Galaxy Vol. 3* (budget: $250 million) and *Mission: Impossible—Dead Reckoning Part One* (budget: $291 million). A charming video clip of Yamazaki and the Shirogumi Inc. VFX team celebrating as they learned of their nomination generated thousands of online views. Rather than a dark horse candidate, some critics viewed *Godzilla Minus One* as the favorite. Many noted the symmetry between *Minus One* and Christopher Nolan's *Oppenheimer* (2023), a biopic of the father of the atomic bomb which would win seven Oscars, including Best Picture and Best Director.

Onstage at the Academy Awards, actors Arnold Schwarzenegger and Danny DeVito read the nominees in the Best Visual Effects category, and Schwarzenegger announced the winner with a single word: "Godzilla." In a heartfelt acceptance speech, Yamazaki paid tribute to producer Shuji Abe, an instrumental figure in his career and in the making of *Godzilla Minus One*, who died shortly after the film's release. Yamazaki recalled his youthful inspiration from the films of George Lucas and Steven Spielberg and called the David-and-Goliath nature of the film's Oscar triumph "a miracle."

"This award," he said, "is proof that everyone has a chance."

LEFT: Godzilla's dorsal fins realign and emit blue light as the monster charges up its devastating heat ray. "We wanted to go back to the original reason for Godzilla's existence," director Takashi Yamazaki said. "The creature is a metaphor for nuclear weapons, so we mimicked the way a weapon would work inside of [its] body. Each element would come together and create an implosion, and that's when the blue rays would come out." ■ **BOTTOM LEFT:** Shikishima (Ryunosuke Kamiki, *far right*) meets the crew of the minesweeper boat: (*left to right*) Shiro Mizushima aka "the kid" (Yuki Yamada), Kenji Noda (Hidetaka Yoshioka), and Kuranosuke Sasaki (Yoji Akitsu). ■ **OPPOSITE TOP:** Godzilla chases the minesweeper boat. "We had a very young compositor [Tatsuji Nojima], who loved VFX," said Yamazaki. "He did some water simulations at home and brought them to the office one day. We said, 'Oh wow, this is some pretty high-quality water simulation!' That allowed me to write more scenes that took place on the ocean." ■ **OPPOSITE MIDDLE:** "I could have shot in the studio and used digital compositing for the boat, but I deliberately chose to film at sea because I wanted a documentary-like, realistic atmosphere," said Yamazaki. "It turned out to be even more challenging than expected. We used drones to capture various shots by flying them alongside the boat." ■ **OPPOSITE BOTTOM:** Godzilla chases after the experimental Shinden aircraft, piloted by Shikishima, which lures the monster from the mainland out to sea, where a deadly trap has been set.

AFTERWORD

BY SHOGO TOMIYAMA

⎯⎯⎯⎯⎯⎯⎯⎯⎯⎯⎯⎯⎯⎯⎯

I couldn't help but smile when I learned that the title of this book would be *Godzilla: The First 70 Years*. Many years from now, at the end of the twenty-first century, future researchers will likely write a book called *Godzilla: The Second 70 Years*. Between 1954 and 2024, a total of thirty live-action Godzilla films have been made in Japan and five in the United States. Godzilla has been around for more than half the roughly 130-year history of cinema. But although Godzilla's own history now spans more than three generations, it seems as if this history is only just beginning.

I think of Godzilla's mysterious appeal as "More Than Human"—to borrow the title of a classic science-fiction novel by Theodore Sturgeon. Godzilla was born as a consequence of nuclear testing, a trade-off of humanity's scientific advancement. Our science created this living being, yet our science cannot defeat it. In this way, Godzilla is beyond our comprehension, or more than human.

Some may point out that Godzilla was defeated in 1954 by the Oxygen Destroyer. Indeed, that's true—Godzilla did die at the end of the first film. However, audiences watching in the theater felt affection for Godzilla as it perished and wished for the monster's return. And with Dr. Serizawa, the Oxygen Destroyer disappeared as well. Thus, Godzilla was resurrected the following year in *Godzilla Raids Again*. Seven years later, Godzilla was revived as a movie star in a widescreen color film, sinking a nuclear submarine and facing off against the American film industry's biggest star in *King Kong vs. Godzilla*.

Since those beginnings, and over the course of thirty-five films, Godzilla's existence has reflected adaptations and shifts in line with the times, and this legacy has been carried on to the present day.

Producer Tomoyuki Tanaka, the creator of Godzilla, often described Godzilla's appeal as "scary but lovable." His words perfectly encapsulate the duality that makes Godzilla such a compelling character. The fear of the destruction Godzilla brings and the audience's emotional connection to the creature are the essence of this duality. Scary yet beloved—that is Godzilla.

RECENT GODZILLA FILMS

With all of this in mind, how have filmmakers interpreted Godzilla in the last decade?

In *Shin Godzilla*, the unpredictably evolving Godzilla is a truly unknowable and more-than-human entity. The film focused on humanity's struggle against this unknown, massive creature. In *Godzilla Minus One*, Godzilla is depicted as a fear that must be overcome. The human characters are forced into life-and-death conflicts like those faced in wartime. Both films share common themes via an ensemble drama and strategic battle narratives. Meanwhile, the Hollywood films show humanity responding to newly surfaced giant creatures. Here, humans are observers, watching the battles between colossal species.

In Japan, Godzilla is currently portrayed as a singular entity, while in the American context, Godzilla is one of many giant monsters. This contrast between Japanese and American Godzillas is striking, but it also mirrors the content of the original 1954 *Godzilla* and the subsequent series. The present-day versions of Godzilla in both Japan and the US are part of the ongoing history of Godzilla, which has experienced continuing changes and evolutions over time.

THE FUTURE OF GODZILLA

What developments can we expect for Godzilla in the future—perhaps the next seventy years?

As an action movie franchise, the Hollywood productions will likely continue to showcase battles with new monsters. With classic star monsters such as Mothra, Rodan, and King Ghidorah having made appearances, the next step might involve bio-robots surpassing Mechagodzilla, space monsters, or interdimensional creatures. Meanwhile, the Japanese Godzilla, a solitary figure, will continue to explore narratives centered around the conflict between Godzilla and humanity.

My dream is to create a family-friendly monster series apart from the storylines of *Shin* and *Minus One* that would be released annually in theaters around the new year. This would be a fun series centered on monster battles, combining traditional miniature models and suitmation techniques with modern visual

effects for a unique look. Maybe Godzilla wouldn't be the main character. So how about Mothra? King Ghidorah? My recommendation is Mechagodzilla. Imagine Mechagodzilla battling a new monster every year. Wouldn't it be wonderful to celebrate Christmas and New Year with such films in theaters each year?

GODZILLA AND THE WORLD

Today, Godzilla has surpassed the James Bond series in terms of years and number of films and now stands as the longest-running film series in the world. In my view, the only sci-fi film series that rivals Godzilla globally is the *Alien* franchise, which also continues to produce new installments intermittently. What the xenomorph and Godzilla share is a terrifying combat ability and vitality that defy the laws of nature, along with an infernal, captivating form that is unmatched by other creatures of cinema.

Recently, I've come to feel that a new rival to Godzilla has emerged: the Joker. The Joker, like Godzilla and the xenomorph, is more than human, possessing both demonic qualities and an undeniable charm. The world yearns for icons, and the screen has produced many through the efforts and imaginations of filmmakers.

In the twenty-first century, we must acknowledge our vulnerabilities and the mistakes we make rather than be consumed by self-righteousness and convinced of our own strength. This is a great challenge faced by the younger generation. Looking at the world today, many people tend to believe only what they want to believe and see only what they want to see. As a powerful counterpoint to such closed-mindedness, Godzilla forces us to confront the things we dislike or wish to avoid.

Destruction can only be prevented if we understand its terrifying consequences. When faced with a being greater than humanity, we recognize our powerlessness and learn humility. This humility fosters mutual understanding among people. I hope that by using Godzilla as a mirror, we can protect our world from destruction.

I wish to continue watching new Godzilla films, revisiting the old ones, and engaging in discussions with people worldwide, deepening our understanding of each other's perspectives. Connecting with people around the globe through Godzilla—I strongly believe this book serves as an excellent guide for that purpose.

FILMOGRAPHY: JAPANESE PRODUCTIONS (AS OF 2024)

GODZILLA
(*Gojira*)
Director: Ishiro Honda
Producer: Tomoyuki Tanaka
SFX: Eiji Tsuburaya
Writers: Shigeru Kayama (story); Takeo Murata and Ishiro Honda (screenplay)
Composer: Akira Ifukube
Distributor: Toho
Release date: November 3, 1954 (Japan)

GODZILLA, KING OF THE MONSTERS!
(Reedited version of *Godzilla*)
Distributor: Trans World Releasing Corp.
Release date: April 27, 1956 (USA)

GODZILLA RAIDS AGAIN
(*Gojira no Gyakushu*)
Director: Motoyoshi Oda
Producer: Tomoyuki Tanaka
SFX: Eiji Tsuburaya
Writers: Shigeru Kayama (story); Shigeaki Hidaka and Takeo Murata (screenplay)
Composer: Masaru Sato
Distributor: Toho
Release date: April 24, 1955 (Japan)

GIGANTIS, THE FIRE MONSTER
(Reedited version of *Godzilla Raids Again*)
Distributor: Warner Bros.
Release date: May 21, 1959 (USA)

KING KONG VS. GODZILLA
(*Kingu Kongu tai Gojira*)
Director: Ishiro Honda
Producer: Tomoyuki Tanaka
SFX: Eiji Tsuburaya
Writer: Shinichi Sekizawa
Composer: Akira Ifukube
Distributor: Toho
Release date: August 11, 1962 (Japan)

MOTHRA VS. GODZILLA
(*Mosura tai Gojira*)
Director: Ishiro Honda
Producers: Tomoyuki Tanaka and Sanezumi Fujimoto
SFX: Eiji Tsuburaya
Writer: Shinichi Sekizawa
Composer: Akira Ifukube
Distributor: Toho
Release date: April 29, 1964 (Japan)

GHIDORAH, THE THREE-HEADED MONSTER
(*Sandai Kaiju Chikyu Saidai no Kessen*)
Director: Ishiro Honda
Producer: Tomoyuki Tanaka
SFX: Eiji Tsuburaya

Writer: Shinichi Sekizawa
Composer: Akira Ifukube
Distributor: Toho
Release date: December 20, 1964 (Japan)

INVASION OF ASTRO-MONSTER
(*Kaiju Daisenso*)
Director: Ishiro Honda
Producers: Tomoyuki Tanaka, Henry G. Saperstein, and Reuben Bercovitch
SFX: Eiji Tsuburaya
Writer: Shinichi Sekizawa
Composer: Akira Ifukube
Distributor: Toho
Release date: December 19, 1965 (Japan)

EBIRAH, HORROR OF THE DEEP
(*Gojira Ebira Mosura: Nankai no Daiketto*)
Director: Jun Fukuda
Producer: Tomoyuki Tanaka
SFX: Eiji Tsuburaya
Writer: Shinichi Sekizawa
Composer: Masaru Sato
Distributor: Toho
Release date: December 17, 1966 (Japan)

SON OF GODZILLA
(*Kaijuto no Kessen: Gojira no Musuko*)
Director: Jun Fukuda
Producer: Tomoyuki Tanaka
SFX: Eiji Tsuburaya and Sadamasa Arikawa
Writers: Shinichi Sekizawa and Kazue Shiba
Composer: Masaru Sato
Distributor: Toho
Release date: December 16, 1967 (Japan)

DESTROY ALL MONSTERS
(*Kaiju Soshingeki*)
Director: Ishiro Honda
Producer: Tomoyuki Tanaka
SFX: Sadamasa Arikawa
Writers: Ishiro Honda and Kaoru Mabuchi
Composer: Akira Ifukube
Distributor: Toho
Release date: August 1, 1968 (Japan)

ALL MONSTERS ATTACK
(*Oru Kaiju Daishingeki*)
Director: Ishiro Honda
Producer: Tomoyuki Tanaka
SFX: Ishiro Honda and Teruyoshi Nakano
Writer: Shinichi Sekizawa
Composer: Kunio Miyauchi
Distributor: Toho
Release date: December 20, 1969 (Japan)

GODZILLA VS. HEDORAH
(*Gojira tai Hedora*)
Director: Yoshimitsu Banno
Producer: Tomoyuki Tanaka
SFX: Teruyoshi Nakano
Writers: Yoshimitsu Banno and Kaoru Mabuchi
Composer: Riichiro Manabe
Distributor: Toho
Release date: July 24, 1971 (Japan)

GODZILLA VS. GIGAN
(*Chikyu Kogeki Meirei: Gojira tai Gaigan*)
Director: Jun Fukuda
Producer: Tomoyuki Tanaka
SFX: Teruyoshi Nakano
Writer: Shinichi Sekizawa
Composer: Akira Ifukube
Distributor: Toho
Release date: March 12, 1972 (Japan)

GODZILLA VS. MEGALON
(*Gojira tai Megaro*)
Director: Jun Fukuda
Producer: Tomoyuki Tanaka
SFX: Teruyoshi Nakano
Writers: Shinichi Sekizawa (story); Jun Fukuda (screenplay)
Composer: Riichiro Manabe
Distributor: Toho
Release date: March 17, 1973 (Japan)

GODZILLA VS. MECHAGODZILLA
(*Gojira tai Mekagojira*)
Director: Jun Fukuda
Producer: Tomoyuki Tanaka
SFX: Teruyoshi Nakano
Writers: Shinichi Sekizawa and Masami Fukushima (story); Hiroyasu Yamaura and Jun Fukuda (screenplay)
Composer: Masaru Sato
Distributor: Toho
Release date: March 21, 1974 (Japan)

TERROR OF MECHAGODZILLA
(*Mekagojira no Gyakushu*)
Director: Ishiro Honda
Producer: Tomoyuki Tanaka
SFX: Teruyoshi Nakano
Writer: Yukiko Takayama
Composer: Akira Ifukube
Distributor: Toho
Release date: March 15, 1975 (Japan)

THE RETURN OF GODZILLA
(*Gojira*)
Director: Koji Hashimoto
Producer: Tomoyuki Tanaka

SFX: Teruyoshi Nakano
Writers: Tomoyuki Tanaka (story); Hideichi Nagahara
   (screenplay)
Composer: Reijiro Koroku
Distributor: Toho
Release date: December 15, 1984 (Japan)

GODZILLA 1985

(Reedited version of *The Return of Godzilla.*)
Distributor: New World Pictures
Release date: August 23, 1985 (USA)

GODZILLA VS. BIOLLANTE

(*Gojira tai Biorante*)
Director: Kazuki Omori
Producer: Tomoyuki Tanaka
SFX: Koichi Kawakita
Writers: Shinichiro Kobayashi (story); Kazuki Omori
   (screenplay)
Composer: Koichi Sugiyama
Distributor: Toho
Release date: December 16, 1989 (Japan)

GODZILLA VS. KING GHIDORAH

(*Gojira tai Kingu Gidora*)
Director: Kazuki Omori
Producers: Tomoyuki Tanaka and Shogo Tomiyama
SFX: Koichi Kawakita
Writer: Kazuki Omori
Composer: Akira Ifukube
Distributor: Toho
Release date: December 14, 1991

GODZILLA VS. MOTHRA

(*Gojira tai Mosura*)
Director: Takao Okawara
Producers: Tomoyuki Tanaka and Shogo Tomiyama
SFX: Koichi Kawakita
Writer: Kazuki Omori
Composer: Akira Ifukube
Distributor: Toho
Release date: December 12, 1992 (Japan)

GODZILLA VS. MECHAGODZILLA II

(*Gojira tai Mekagojira*)
Director: Takao Okawara
Producers: Tomoyuki Tanaka and Shogo Tomiyama
SFX: Koichi Kawakita
Writer: Wataru Mimura
Composer: Akira Ifukube
Distributor: Toho
Release date: December 11, 1993 (Japan)

GODZILLA VS. SPACEGODZILLA

(*Gojira tai Supesugojira*)
Director: Kensho Yamashita
Producers: Tomoyuki Tanaka and Shogo Tomiyama
SFX: Koichi Kawakita
Writer: Hiroshi Kashiwabara
Composer: Takayuki Hattori
Distributor: Toho
Release date: December 10, 1994 (Japan)

GODZILLA VS. DESTOROYAH

(*Gojira tai Desutoroia*)
Director: Takao Okawara
Producers: Tomoyuki Tanaka and Shogo Tomiyama
SFX: Koichi Kawakita
Writer: Kazuki Omori
Composer: Akira Ifukube
Distributor: Toho
Release date: December 9, 1995 (Japan)

GODZILLA 2000: MILLENNIUM

(*Gojira Nisen: Mireniamu*)
Director: Takao Okawara
Producer: Shogo Tomiyama
SFX: Kenji Suzuki
Writers: Hiroshi Kashiwabara and Wataru Mimura
Composer: Takayuki Hattori
Distributor: Toho
Release date: December 11, 1999 (Japan)

GODZILLA VS. MEGAGUIRUS

(*Gojira tai Megagirasu: Ji Shometsu Sakusen*)
Director: Masaaki Tezuka
Producer: Shogo Tomiyama
SFX: Kenji Suzuki
Writers: Hiroshi Kashiwabara and Wataru Mimura
Composer: Michiru Oshima
Distributor: Toho
Release date: December 16, 2000 (Japan)

GODZILLA, MOTHRA AND KING GHIDORAH:
GIANT MONSTERS ALL-OUT ATTACK

(*Gojira, Mosura, Kingu Gidora: Daikaiju Sokogeki*)
Director: Shusuke Kaneko
Producer: Shogo Tomiyama
SFX: Makoto Kamiya
Writers: Keiichi Hasegawa, Masahiro Yokotani, and
   Shusuke Kaneko
Composer: Kow Otani
Distributor: Toho
Release date: December 15, 2001 (Japan)

GODZILLA AGAINST MECHAGODZILLA

(*Gojira tai Mekagojira*)
Director: Masaaki Tezuka
Producers: Shogo Tomiyama and Takahide Morichi
SFX: Yuichi Kikuchi
Writer: Wataru Mimura
Composer: Michiru Oshima
Distributor: Toho
Release date: December 14, 2002 (Japan)

GODZILLA: TOKYO SOS

(*Gojira x Mosura x Mekagojira Tokyo SOS*)
Director: Masaaki Tezuka
Producer: Shogo Tomiyama
SFX: Eiichi Asada
Writers: Masaaki Tezuka and Masahiro Yokotani
Composer: Michiru Oshima
Distributor: Toho
Release date: December 13, 2003 (Japan)

GODZILLA FINAL WARS

(*Gojira Fainaru Wozu*)
Director: Ryuhei Kitamura
Producer: Shogo Tomiyama
SFX: Eiichi Asada
Writers: Wataru Mimura and Isao Kiriyama
Composer: Keith Emerson
Distributor: Toho
December 4, 2004 (Japan)

SHIN GODZILLA

(*Shin Gojira*)
Directors: Hideaki Anno and Shinji Higuchi
Producer: Minami Ichikawa
Writer: Hideaki Anno
VFX: Atsuki Sato
SFX: Shinji Higuchi and Katsuro Onoue
Composer: Shiro Sagisu
Distributor: Toho
Release date: July 29, 2016 (Japan)

GODZILLA: PLANET OF THE MONSTERS

(*Gojira: Kaiju Wakusei*)
Directors: Kobun Shizuno and Hiroyuki Seshita
Producer: Keiji Ota
Writer: Gen Urobuchi
Composer: Takayuki Hattori
Distributor: Toho Visual Entertainment/Netflix
Release date: November 17, 2017 (Japan); January 17,
   2018 (worldwide streaming)

GODZILLA: CITY ON THE EDGE OF BATTLE

(*Gojira: Kessen Kido Zoshoku Toshi*)
Directors: Kobun Shizuno and Hiroyuki Seshita
Producer: Keiji Ota
Writers: Gen Urobuchi (story); Sadayuki Murai,
   Tetsuya Yamada, and Gen Urobuchi (screenplay)
Composer: Takayuki Hattori
Distributor: Toho Visual Entertainment/Netflix
Release date: May 18, 2018 (Japan); July 18, 2018
   (worldwide streaming)

GODZILLA: THE PLANET EATER

(*Gojira: Hoshi o Ku Mono*)
Directors: Kobun Shizuno and Hiroyuki Seshita
Producer: Keiji Ota
Writer: Gen Urobuchi
Composer: Takayuki Hattori
Distributor: Toho Visual Entertainment/Netflix
Release date: November 9, 2018 (Japan); January 9,
   2019 (worldwide streaming)

GODZILLA MINUS ONE

(*Gojira -1.0*)
Director: Takashi Yamazaki
Producer: Minami Ichikawa
VFX: Takashi Yamazaki and Kiyoko Shibuya
Writer: Takashi Yamazaki
Composer: Naoki Sato
Distributor: Toho
Release date: November 3, 2023 (Japan)

BIBLIOGRAPHY

BOOKS AND PERIODICALS

Anno, Hideaki (editor). *The Art of Shin Godzilla.* Color Co. Ltd., 2016.

Arikawa, Sadamasa. *Sadamasa Arikawa, the Son of Godzilla and Eiji Tsuburaya.* Yosensha Publishing Co. Ltd., 2018.

Bessatsu Eiga Hiho Editing Team. *Always Together with Godzilla: Toho Special Effects VIP Interview Collection.* Yosensha Publishing Co. Ltd., 2016.

Galbraith, Stuart IV. *Monsters Are Attacking Tokyo! The Incredible World of Japanese Fantasy Films.* Feral House, 1997.

Galbraith, Stuart IV. *The Toho Studios Story: A History and Complete Filmography.* McFarland & Company, 2008.

Godziszewski, Ed. "Making of Godzilla (1984)." *Japanese Giants* No. 7, December 1985.

Godziszewski, Ed. "Making of Godzilla vs. Biollante." *Japanese Giants* No. 8, April 1994.

Godziszewski, Ed. "Making of Godzilla, Mothra and King Ghidorah: Giant Monsters All-Out Attack." *Japanese Giants* No. 9, June 2002.

Godziszewski, Ed. "The Making of Godzilla." *Japanese Giants* No. 10, September 2004.

Hikawa, Ryusuke; others. T*echniques of Japanese Tokusatsu Films: Film Making, History, Film Criticism, Behind the Scenes.* Gakken, 2016.

Hobby Japan Editorial Department. *Ghidorah, the Three-Headed Monster Completion.* Hobby Japan, 2023.

Hobby Japan Editorial Department. *Godzilla 1984 Completion.* Hobby Japan, 2019.

Hobby Japan Editorial Department. *Godzilla, Mothra and King Ghidorah: Giant Monsters All-Out Attack Completion.* Hobby Japan, 2022.

Hobby Japan Editorial Department. *Godzilla vs. Biollante Completion.* Hobby Japan, 2015.

Hobby Japan Editorial Department. *Godzilla vs. Destoroyah Completion.* Hobby Japan, 2017.

Hobby Japan Editorial Department. *Godzilla vs. SpaceGodzilla Completion.* Hobby Japan, 2021.

Hobby Japan Editorial Department. *Godzilla x Mechagodzilla Completion.* Hobby Japan, 2016.

Hobby Japan Editorial Department. *King Kong vs. Godzilla Completion.* Hobby Japan, 2021.

Hobby Japan Editorial Department. *Mothra vs. Godzilla Completion.* Hobby Japan, 2023.

Hobby Japan magazine (various).

Honda, Ishiro. *Godzilla and My Movie Life.* Jitsugyo no Nihonsha, 1994.

Igarashi, Yoshikuni. *Bodies of Memory: Narratives of War in Postwar Japanese Culture, 1945–1970.* Princeton University Press, 2012.

Kalat, David. *A Critical History and Filmography of Toho's Godzilla Series.* McFarland & Company, 1997.

Kawakita, Koichi. *Heisei Godzilla Chronicle.* Kinema Junpo, 2009.

Kawakita, Koichi. *Heisei Godzilla Perfection* (Dengeki Hobby Books). Kadokawa, 2012.

Kawakita, Koichi. *The Art of Godzilla.* Wani Books, 1991.

Kawakita, Koichi. *The Art of Godzilla vs. Mothra.* Wani Books, 1992.

Kawakita, Koichi. *Tokusatsu Spirit: The Epic Chronicle of Toho's Special Effects Battles.* Yosensha Publishing Co. Ltd., 2010.

Kawakita, Koichi and Kabuki, Shinichi. *Why Don't You Try to Create Godzilla Too–Koichi Kawakita Special Effects World.* Tokuma Orion, 1993.

Kayama, Shigeru. *Godzilla and Godzilla Raids Again* [translated and with an afterword by Jeffrey Angles]. University of Minnesota Press, 2023.

Kodansha Editorial Dept. *Godzilla & Toho Special Effects Official Mook Vol. 1: Godzilla.* Kodansha, 2023.

Kodansha Editorial Dept. *Godzilla & Toho Special Effects Official Mook Vol. 2: Mothra vs. Godzilla.* Kodansha, 2023.

Kodansha Editorial Dept. *Godzilla & Toho Special Effects Official Mook Vol. 3: King Kong vs. Godzilla.* Kodansha, 2023.

Kodansha Editorial Dept. *Godzilla & Toho Special Effects Official Mook Vol. 5: Godzilla vs. Biollante.* Kodansha, 2023.

Kodansha Editorial Dept. *Godzilla & Toho Special Effects Official Mook Vol. 6: Ghidorah, the Three-Headed Monster.* Kodansha, 2023.

Kodansha Editorial Dept. *Godzilla & Toho Special Effects Official Mook Vol. 7: Godzilla, Mothra and King Ghidorah: Giant Monsters All Out Attack.* Kodansha, 2023.

Kodansha Editorial Dept. *Godzilla & Toho Special Effects Official Mook Vol. 9: Godzilla vs. Destoroyah/Godzilla vs. SpaceGodzilla.* Kodansha, 2023.

Kodansha Editorial Dept. *Godzilla & Toho Special Effects Official Mook Vol. 10: Godzilla Final Wars.* Kodansha, 2023.

Kodansha Editorial Dept. *Godzilla & Toho Special Effects Official Mook Vol. 11: Godzilla vs. King Ghidorah/Godzilla vs. Mothra.* Kodansha, 2023.

Kodansha Editorial Dept. *Godzilla & Toho Special Effects Official Mook Vol. 12: Destroy All Monsters.* Kodansha, 2023.

Kodansha Editorial Dept. *Godzilla & Toho Special Effects Official Mook Vol. 15: Godzilla vs. Mechagodzilla II.* Kodansha, 2023.

Kodansha Editorial Dept. *Godzilla & Toho Special Effects Official Mook Vol. 16: Meteor Man Zone.* Kodansha, 2024.

Kodansha Editorial Dept. *Godzilla & Toho Special Effects Official Mook Vol. 18: Godzilla vs. Hedorah.* Kodansha, 2024.

Kodansha Editorial Dept. *Godzilla & Toho Special Effects Official Mook Vol. 21: Godzilla x Mechagodzilla/Godzilla x Mothra x Mechagodzilla.* Tokyo SOS. Kodansha, 2024.

Makino, Mamoru; others. *Godzilla Days: A Forty Year History of Godzilla Movies.* Shueisha Publishing, 1993.

Makino, Mamoru and Endo, Sekkei. *Toho Special Effects Movie Series Vol. 1: Godzilla.* Toho Publishing, 1985.

Makino, Mamoru and Endo, Sekkei. *Toho SF Special Effects Movie Series Vol. 2: Mothra vs. Godzilla.* Toho Publishing, 1985.

Makino, Mamoru and Endo, Sekkei. *Toho SF Special Effects Movie Series Vol. 3: Godzilla, Godzilla Raids Again, Giant Monster Varan.* Toho Publishing, 1985.

Makino, Mamoru and Endo, Sekkei. *Toho SF Special Effects Movie Series Vol. 4: Atragon, Gorath, Space Monster Dogora.* Toho Publishing, 1985.

Makino, Mamoru and Endo, Sekkei. T*oho SF Special Effects Movie Series Vol. 5: King Kong vs. Godzilla, The Mysterians.* Toho Publishing, 1986.

Matsumoto, Hajime and Iizuka, Sadao. *The Man Who Was Always Drawing Rays: Legend of Iizuka Sadao.* Yosensha Publishing Co. Ltd., 2016.

Miike, Toshio; Moriyama, Tomoe; Masuta, Tatsuya. *The Art of Special Effects Production Designer Yasuyuki "Taiko" Inoue.* Kinema Junpo, 2022.

Mizuno, Kumi and Higuchi, Naobumi. *Actress Kumi Mizuno: Monster/Action/Melodrama.* Yosensha Publishing Co. Ltd., 2012.

Motoyama, Sho; Matsunomoto, Kazuhiro; Asai, Kazuyasu; Suzuki, Yoshitaka; Kato, Masashi. *Toho Special Effects Movie Complete Works.* Village Books, 2012.

Nakajima, Haruo. *Monster Life: Original Godzilla Actor Haruo Nakajima.* Yosensha Publishing Co. Ltd., 2010.

Nishikawa, Shinji. *Shinji Nishikawa Design Works.* Genkosha, 2019.

Ragone, August. *Eiji Tsuburaya: Master of Monsters; Defending the Earth with Ultraman, Godzilla, and Friends in the Golden Age of Japanese Science-Fiction Film.* Chronicle Books, 2007.

Ryfle, Steve. *Japan's Favorite Mon-Star: The Unauthorized Biography of 'The Big G.'* ECW Press, 1998.

Ryfle, Steve and Godziszewski, Ed. I*shiro Honda: A Life in Film, from Godzilla to Kurosawa.* Wesleyan University Press, 2017.

Sahara, Kenji. *A Wonderful Tokusatsu Life.* Shogakukan, 2005.

Satsuma, Kenpachiro. *Inside Godzilla.* Chikuma Shobo, 1993.

SCREEN Editorial Dept. *SCREENα (Alpha) Movie "Godzilla-1.0" Special Issue Wonderful Godzilla Movie and VFX.* Kindaieigasha, 2023.

Shimakura, Fuchimu. *The Sky of Special Effects.* Hobby Japan Publishing, 2021.

Shimizu, Toshifumi; Nakamura, Satoshi; Kihara, Hirokatsu. *Godzilla Toho SFX Unreleased Documents Archive.* Kadokawa Shoten, 2010.

Shiraishi, Masahiko and Tomyama, Shogo. Heisei *Godzilla Encyclopedia: 1984–1995.* Futabasha, 2003.

Someya, Katsuji and Nakano, Teruyoshi. *Special Effects Director Teruyoshi Nakano.* Wides Publishing, 2014.

Takeuchi, Hiroshi. *Complete Works of Ishiro Honda.* Asahi Sonorama, 2000.

Takeuchi, Hiroshi and Murata, Hideki. *Godzilla 1954 ("Panel Discussion of the Godzilla Era").* Jitsugyo no Nihonsha, 1999.

Toho Godzilla Association. *Tokusatsu Tsuburaya Group: Godzilla and the Youth Devoted to Toho Special Effects.* Yosensha Publishing Co. Ltd., 2010.

Uchusen Magazine, Vol. 51, Winter 1990.

Uncredited author(s). *Battle of King Ghidorah.* Tokyo: Futabasha, 2020.

Uncredited author(s). *Eiji Tsuburaya Museum Special Movie— Godzilla Appears in Sukagawa.* Hobby Japan, 2019.

Uncredited author(s). *Godzilla 1954 Research Masterpiece.* Hobby Japan, 2023.

Uncredited author(s). *Godzilla's Roar.* NTT Mediascope Inc., 1993.

Uncredited author(s). *Godzilla Singular Point Fan Book.* Futabasha, 2021.

Uncredited author(s). *Godzilla vs. King Ghidorah Encyclopedia.* Gakken, 1991.

Uncredited author(s). *Mothra Movie Encyclopedia.* Yosensha Publishing Co. Ltd., 2011.

Uncredited author(s). *Shin Godzilla eMook.* Takarajimasha, 2016.

Uncredited author(s). *Shin Godzilla Walker: A New Legend of the King of Monsters.* Kadokawa, 2016.

Uncredited author(s). *Toho SFX Actress Encyclopedia.* Yosensha Publishing Co. Ltd., 2011.

Uncredited author(s). *Toho SF Special Effects Movie Series Special Edition: Godzilla 2000 Millennium with CD-Rom.* Toho Publishing Co., 1999).

Uncredited author(s). *Toho SF Special Effects Movie Series Special Edition: Godzilla Final Wars with CD-Rom.* Toho Publishing Co., 2004.

Uncredited author(s). *Toho SF Special Effects Movie Series Special Edition: Godzilla vs. Megaguirus with CD-Rom.* Toho Publishing Co., 2000.

Uncredited author(s). *Toho SF Special Effects Movie Series Special Edition: Godzilla x Mechagodzilla 2003 with CD-Rom.* Toho Publishing Co., 2002.

Uncredited author(s). *Toho SF Special Effects Movie Series Special Edition: Godzilla x Mothra x Mechagodzilla Tokyo SOS with CD-Rom.* Toho Publishing Co., 2003.

Uncredited author(s). *Toho SF Special Effects Movie Series Special Edition: Godzilla, Mothra and King Ghidorah: Giant Monsters All-Out Attack with CD-Rom.* Toho Publishing, 2001.

Uncredited author(s). *Toho SF Special Effects Movie Series Vol. 6: Godzilla vs. King Ghidorah.* Toho Publishing, 1992.

Uncredited author(s). *Toho SF Special Effects Movie Series Vol. 7: Godzilla vs. Mothra.* Toho Publishing, 1993.

Uncredited author(s). *Toho SF Special Effects Movie Series Vol. 8: Godzilla vs. MechaGodzilla.* Toho Publishing, 1994.

Uncredited author(s). *Tokusatsu Hiho Vol. 8.* Yosensha Publishing Co., Ltd., 2018.

Uncredited author(s). *Uncovering the Missing Films of Godzilla (1954).* Tokusatsu-DNA Partners, 2019.

Yamada, Masami; Nishimura, Yuji (supervised by). *Big Pictorial Book of Godzilla.* Hobby Japan, 1995.

Yoshimi, Shunya. *Atoms for Dream.* Chikuma Shobo, 2012.

OTHER SOURCES

Ghidorah, the Three-Headed Monster. CD liner notes. Toho Music Corp., 2004.

Godzilla (Blu-Ray). The Criterion Collection, 2012.

Godzilla 1984. CD liner notes. Toho Music Corp., 2006.

Godzilla Final Wars (Perfect Collection 6). CD liner notes. Toho Music Corp., 2010.

Godzilla on Monster Island. CD liner notes. Toho Music Corp., 2005.

Godzilla Raids Again. CD liner notes. Toho Music Corp., 2004.

Godzilla vs. Biollante. CD liner notes. Toho Music Corp., 2006.

Godzilla vs. Destroyer. CD liner notes. Toho Music Corp., 2008.

Godzilla vs. Hedorah (Perfect Collection 3). CD liner notes. Toho Music Corp., 2005.

Godzilla vs. King Ghidorah (Perfect Collection 4). CD liner notes. Toho Music Corp., 2006.

Godzilla vs. Megalon (Perfect Collection 3). CD liner notes. Toho Music Corp., 2005.

Godzilla vs. The Bionic Monster. CD liner notes. Toho Music Corp., 2005.

Godzilla vs. The Sea Monster. CD liner notes. Toho Music Corp., 2004. *Godzilla vs. The Thing.* CD liner notes. Toho Music Corp., 2004.

Godzilla, Mothra and King Ghidorah: Giant Monsters All-Out Attack. CD liner notes. Toho Music Corp., 2001.

Godzilla's History: Zone, The Human Meteor (Perfect Collection 4). CD liner notes. Toho Music Corp., 2006.

Godzilla's Revenge. CD liner notes. Toho Music Corp., 2004.

Sound Effect of Godzilla. CD liner notes. Toshiba-EMI, 1995.

Toho SFX Champion Festival. CD liner notes. VAP Inc. Records, 2001.

Toho theater pamphlets (various, 1956–2023)

ONLINE SOURCES

Aframe.oscars.org: "How the 'Godzilla Minus One' VFX Team Took the Titan to Terrifying New Heights (Exclusive)," uncredited, March 2024.

Asiablooming.com: "Quelling God's Anger: A Conversation with Director Yamazaki and Producer Yamada of Godzilla Minus One," by Kalai Chik, March 2024.

Businessinsider.com: "Why 'Godzilla' Cut A Cameo of The Star from The Original 1954 Movie," by Kirsten Acuna, May 2014.

Cercle.co.jp: "Interview with Akira Tsuburaya, third son of Eiji Tsuburaya (1997)," March 2002.

Cyprus-mail.com: "Godzilla Minus One," by Jason Jones and Beatrice Trefalt, February 2024.

Evangelion.jp: "Hideaki Anno's comments on 'Shin Evangelion Theatrical Version' and the new Godzilla movie," April 2015.

Godzilla.store: "1st Mr. Shogo Toyama, former Toho Pictures President and Producer," March 2014.

Godzilla.store: "2nd Special Skills Director Koichi Kawakita (Part 1)," December 2014.

Godzilla.store: "3rd Special Skills Director Teruyoshi Nakano (Part 1)," May 2015.

Godzilla.store: "Part 4: Godzilla actor Haruo Nakajima (Part 2)," November 2015.

Godzilla.store: "6th Director: Mr. Takao Okawara (Part 1)," February 2018.

Hivemind.modlangs.gatech.edu: "Kaiju x Kami: The Origins of Japanese Monster Films," by Sofi Sanders, October 2021.

Ign.com: "Godzilla Minus One Director on the Genesis of Godzilla Minus One Color and Those Oscar-Nominated VFX," by Tara Bennett, March 2024.

International.ucla.edu: "Ryuhei Kitamura: Revitalizing Godzilla," by Carl Wakamoto, transcription by Chi Tung and Brian Yang, December 2004.

Japantimes.co.jp: "'Godzilla Minus One' fought the odds and won big at the Oscars," by Mark Schilling, March 2024.

Latimes.com: "How VFX updates take Godzilla back to its nuclear roots," by Bob Strauss, February 2024.

Otakuusamagazine.com: "Shin Godzilla Producer Talks Hideaki Anno, Future of Franchise at Film Festival," by Matt Schley, October 2016.

Riken.jp: "The RIKEN Story," undated.

Theguardian.com: "Godzilla Minus One review—a thunderously entertaining prequel," by Wendy Ide, December 2023.

Tohokingdom.com: "Kaneko's Ambition: Godzilla x Varan, Baragon and Anguirus Story Translation," by Joshua Sudomerski, May 2022.

Vantagepointinterviews.com: "Untold Tales of Godzilla! Roger Holden on His Unmade Godzilla Projects and Working with Director Yoshimitsu Banno!" by Brett Homenick, undated.

Youtube.com: "Godzilla vs. Megalon (1973) Audio Commentary by Steve Ryfle & Stuart Galbraith IV,"

by GORIZARD, March 2018.Youtube.com: "Godzilla Redacted (LIVE At G-Fest 2023 with Steve Ryfle and Kyle Byrd)," by Kaiju Masterclass, August 2023.

Youtube.com: "History of Godzilla Singular Point | Development to Release," by Monstrosities, April 2021.

Youtube.com: "Interview: Bear McCreary," by Kaiju Masterclass, October 2020.

Youtube.com: "Interview: Kazuki Omori," by Kaiju Masterclass, November 2021.

Youtube.com: "Interview: Michiru Oshima," by Kaiju Masterclass, October 2020.

Youtube.com: "Interview: Reijiro Koroku," by Kaiju Masterclass, November 2021.

Youtube.com: "Interview: Ryuhei Kitamura," by Kaiju Masterclass, November 2021.

Youtube.com: "Interview: Shinji Higuchi," by Kaiju Masterclass, October 2020.

Youtube.com: "Interview: Shusuke Kaneko," by Kaiju Masterclass, October 2020.

Youtube.com: "Mothra (1961) Audio Commentary by Steve Ryfle & Ed Godziszewski," by GORIZARD, March 2018.

Youtube.com: "Mothra vs. Godzilla (1964) Audio Commentary by Steve Ryfle & Ed Godziszewski," by GORIZARD, March 2018.

Youtube.com: "Smog Monster Director Extra," by CHO Japan, September 2014.

Youtube.com: "The Lost & Unmade History of Godzilla Singular Point," by MONSTROSITIES, January 2022.

Youtube.com: "Ryuhei Kitamura—Godzilla Final Wars, Versus, Vessel—Comikaze 2015," by DNwriter, November 2015.

Youtube.com: "Tokyo SOS Director EXTRA," by CHO Japan, September 2014.

INTERVIEWS BY THE AUTHORS

Sadamasa Arikawa	Toshio Miike
Toshiro Aoki	Kumi Mizuno
Yoshimitsu Banno	Keizo Murase
Tomoo Haraguchi	Haruo Nakajima
Shinji Higuchi	Teruyoshi Nakano
Shinji Hiruma	Megumi Odaka
Tomomi Higuchi	Takao Okawara
Kimi Honda	Kazuki Omori
Ryuji Honda	Kenji Sahara
James Hong	Kenpachiro Satsuma
Akira Ifukube	Fuyuki Shinada
Yasuyuki Inoue	Jiro Shirasaki
Koji Kajita	Akira Takarada
Ryunosuke Kamiki	Misato Tanaka
Shusuke Kaneko	Seiji Tani
Hiroshi Kashiwabara	Shogo Tomiyama
Koichi Kawakita	Mutsumi Toyoshima
Richard Kay	Yoshio Tsuchiya
Tsutomu "Tom" Kitagawa	Takashi Yamazaki
Ryuhei Kitamura	Akihiro Ugajin
Jared Krichevsky	Shinichi Wakasa

OVERLEAF: An observation helicopter gets too close to Godzilla as the monster's first battle with Kong looms (*King Kong vs. Godzilla*).

AUTHOR + CONTRIBUTOR BIOS

STEVE RYFLE is coauthor, with Ed Godzisze-wski, of *Ishiro Honda: A Life in Film, from Godzilla to Kurosawa*. His writing has been published in *Cineaste*, *Criterion Current*, *The Los Angeles Times*, the *Virginia Quarterly Review*, *Zyzzyva*, and other publications, and he has contributed audio commentaries, essays, and other material to numerous home-video releases. He is cowriter, with Joal Ryan, of the documentary feature film *Miracle on 42nd Street*, which won the 2020 New York Emmy Award for Best Documentary. He is also coproducer and cowriter, with Ed Godziszewski, of the documentary feature film *Bringing Godzilla Down to Size*.

ED GODZISZEWSKI is coauthor, with Steve Ryfle, of *Ishiro Honda: A Life in Film, from Godzilla to Kurosawa*. He is the longtime editor in chief and publisher of the independent genre magazine *Japanese Giants* and was an original contributor to *Fangoria* magazine. He has contributed audio commentaries and other materials to numerous home-video releases, and is coproducer and cowriter, with Steve Ryfle, of the documentary feature film *Bringing Godzilla Down to Size*.

JOHN CARPENTER has brought to the screen some of the most popular and influential films in history, beginning with his 1978 breakthrough *Halloween*. He directed such horror classics as *The Thing*, *The Fog*, *Christine*, and *In the Mouth of Madness*, as well as *Assault on Precinct 13*, *Escape from New York*, and *Escape from L.A.*, the Oscar-nominated *Starman*, *Big Trouble in Little China*, *Village of the Damned*, *Vampires*, *Memoirs of an Invisible Man*, *Ghosts of Mars*, and *The Ward*. Carpenter is the recipient of dozens of awards and honors, including the Le Carrosse D'Or (Golden Coach) from the French Directors Guild during the 2019 Cannes Film Festival, and lifetime achievement honors from the Bram Stoker Awards, the Online Film Critics Society, and the Saturn Awards (George Pal Memorial Award).

MEGUMI ODAKA portrayed psychic Miki Saegusa in six consecutive films, from 1989's *Godzilla vs. Biollante* through 1995's *Godzilla vs. Destoroyah*. As Miki, Ms. Odaka has made the most appearances and had the greatest longevity of any character in the Godzilla film series. A former idol, singer, and actress, Ms. Odaka won the Japan Academy Film Prize for Newcomer of the Year for her debut in *Princess from the Moon* (1987) opposite Toshiro Mifune. She retired from acting in 2000.

SHOGO TOMIYAMA originally joined Toho in the film promotion department, eventually assuming the role of film producer. Tomiyama assisted Tomoyuki Tanaka on the Godzilla series starting with *Godzilla vs. Biollante* in 1989 and eventually succeeded Tanaka as executive producer for all of Toho's science-fiction and monster films through 2004's *Godzilla Final Wars*. He also served as president of Toho Pictures from 2004–10.

ACKNOWLEDGMENTS

Godzilla: The First 70 Years is, in many respects, the culmination of several decades spent collectively by the authors in pursuit of Godzilla's somewhat elusive history. Jointly and independently, we have made numerous trips to Japan, conducted innumerable meetings and interviews, and pored over countless books, articles, documents, archival materials, and other sources. To the best of our abilities, and with the limited resources available, we have navigated the challenges of conducting research that is largely dependent on information in a language other than our native tongue.

This process of discovery would never have been possible without the enthusiastic support of family, friends, and colleagues, and the generous assistance of many individuals who were first-hand participants in the making of films in Japan and even the remaking of those same films in the US. We have been fortunate to be able to contribute to the growing body of work on Godzilla's history by writing books, articles, producing a documentary feature film, speaking at film screenings and other events, and creating supplemental content for many home video releases. We have learned a great deal and enjoyed sharing what we've learned. Simply put, we could not have done it alone.

And so, this book is not only a capstone project of sorts, but more importantly, it represents a collaborative effort by the authors and those who have lent their support in the form of research assistance, translation and interpreting, interviews, access to materials, editorial feedback, and more. We wish to thank the following persons and organizations for their contributions to this work, and we respectfully apologize if anyone's name has been inadvertently omitted.

Keith Aiken
Matt Burkett
Kyle Byrd
Cristopher Cerasi
Amanda Derendorf
Kevin Derendorf
John Desentis
Aria Devlin
Norman England
Hisakazu Fujiwara

Kevin Fukuhara
Stuart Galbraith IV
Patrick Galvan
Kyle Gilmore
Mariko Godziszewski
Aaron John Gregory
Bill Gudmundson
Tomoo Haraguchi
Shinji Higuchi
Tomomi Higuchi

Erik Homenick
Maaserhit Honda
Jan Hughes
Suzi Hutsell
Kaiju Masterclass
Ryunosuke Kamiki
Shususke Kaneko
Hiroshi Kashiwabara
Tsutomo "Tom" Kitagawa
Eric Klopfer

Jared Krichevsky
Connor Leonard
Sean Linkenback
Toshio Miike
Oki Miyano
Iain R. Morris
Joko Mizukami
Christopher Mowry
Keizo Murase
Michi Nishimura

Yuji Nishimura
Megumi Odaka
Takao Okawara
Matt Parmley
Richard Pusateri
Joal Ryan
Stefano Ryan-Ryfle
Pat Saperstein
Fuyuki Shinada
Jiro Shirasaki

Misato Tanaka
Toyomi Togo
Toho Co., Ltd.
Shogo Tomiyama
William Tsutsui
Takashi Yamazaki
Akihiro Ugajin
Kohei Umino
Kyle Yount
Shinichi Wakasa

INDEX

Ito, Hisaya, 89, 91
Ito, Makoto, 292, 296
Iwanabe, Amy, 37
Iwanaga, Frank, 36

J

Jissoji, Akio, 249
J. O. Studio, 19
Jurassic Park (1993), 245, 282

K

Kagemusha (1980), 247
Kaida, Yuji, 202
Kaimai, Eizo, 22, 52, 75, 94, 98, 236–38, 242, 330, 331, 333, 336, 339
Kajita, Koji, 21, 236
Kakeshita, Keikichi, 30
Kamiki, Ryunosuke, 408, 411, 415, 416
Kamio, Naoko, 354
Kamiya, Makoto, 248, 250, 310, 313–17, 320, 339
Kaneda, Ryunosuke, 219, 225
Kaneko, Noboru, 347
Kaneko, Shusuke, 241, 250, 307–8, 310–13, 315, 317, 339
Kano, Gendai, 150
Kashiwabara, Hiroshi, 269–71, 275, 292, 296, 303–5
Kato, Shigeo, 35
Kawabe, Takayuki, 405
Kawai, Toru, 183, 197, 200
Kawakita, Koichi, 58, 71, 85, 94, 169, 183, 186, 189, 202, 203, 215, 220–25, 227, 228, 233, 239, 241, 245–48, 256–59, 264, 270, 272–76, 278, 280, 282, 283, 292, 293, 295, 327, 334, 336, 337, 386
Kawamoto, Saburo, 18
Kawase, Hiroyuki, 157, 158, 176
Kay, Richard, 37
Kayama, Shigeru, 20–21, 25, 29, 41, 49
Kemmerling, Warren, 216
Kikuchi, Yuichi, 321, 324, 326
Kill Bill: Volume I (2003), 315
Kimura, Takeshi. *See* Mabuchi, Kaoru
King Kong (1933), 19–21, 31, 46, 56, 58, 328, 329
King Kong (1976), 178
King Kong Escapes (1967), 119, 125–26, 134, 170, 239, 259
The King Kong Show (1966), 110
King Kong vs. Godzilla (1962), 7, 10, 52, 55–67, 70, 75, 76, 81, 84, 99, 202, 235, 239, 257, 314, 316, 331, 332, 358, 381, 418, 425
King Kong vs. Godzilla 2 (unmade), 70
Kiriyama, Isao, 352, 354, 357
Kishida, Kazuaki, 409
Kishida, Kuichiro, 22
Kishida, Shin, 189, 192

Kitagawa, Tsutomu, 292, 295–96, 303, 325, 328, 337–39, 349, 352, 390
Kitamura, Ryuhei, 339, 351–54, 356, 357, 390
Kizer, R. J., 216
Kobayashi, Akiji, 248, 249
Kobayashi, Akira, 150
Kobayashi, Hideyuki, 266
Kobayashi, Ichizo, 19, 35
Kobayashi, Keiju, 207, 211, 217
Kobayashi, Masahiro, 308
Kobayashi, Satomi, 248
Kobayashi, Shinichiro, 220–21
Kobayashi, Tomoki, 98, 239, 241
Kobayashi, Yukiko, 134, 137
Kochi, Momoko, 21, 27, 29, 31–33, 278, 280, 381
Kodo, Kokuten, 31
Koizumi, Hiroshi, 41–43, 70, 71, 84, 89, 189, 192, 211, 343, 346
Komada, Tsugutoshi, 182
Kon, Satoshi, 375
Koroku, Reijiro, 215, 216
Koseki, Yuji, 76, 249
Kubo, Akira, 103, 108, 122, 126, 140
Kubrick, Stanley, 408
Kume, Osame, 250, 349
Kurobe, Susumu, 91, 137
Kurosawa, Akira, 18–20, 25, 31, 36, 37, 43, 45, 89, 94, 118, 158, 182, 200, 247, 249

L

Latitude Zero (1969), 126
Levine, Joseph E., 37
Lin, Beru-Bera, 187, 189
The Lost World (1925), 21, 328
Lourié, Eugène, 19
Lucas, George, 416
Luke, Keye, 53

M

Mabuchi, Kaoru (Takeshi Kimura), 132, 134, 135, 157, 166, 177
Maeda, Bibari, 122, 124
Maeda, Mahiro, 390, 402
The Makioka Sisters (1983), 300
Manabe, Riichiro, 159, 162, 182
Mari, Keiko, 156, 158
Maron, Mel, 178
Matango (1963), 333
Matsumoto, Koji, 222
Matsumoto, Seicho, 257
Matsumoto, Somesho, 65
Matsuoka, Isao, 310
Matsushita, Tadashi, 25
Melchior, Ib, 52
Meteor Man. See Zone Fighter (TV show)
Mifune, Toshiro, 8
Mighty Joe Young (1949), 20, 39
The Mighty Peking Man (1977), 278

Miike, Toshio, 214, 308, 327, 349
Mimura, Wataru, 256–59, 269, 292, 352, 356
Minawa, Ichiro, 172–73
Minegishi, Toru, 223, 225, 343–44
Miner, Steve, 203
Minus One. See Godzilla Minus One (2023)
Mishima, Yukio, 35, 85
Mitamura, Kunihiko, 223–25
Mitani, Koki, 265
Miyahara, Yoshinobu, 333
Miyauchi, Kunio, 150, 170
Miyazaki, Hayao, 305, 375, 396
Miyazaki, Hideaki, 80
Mizuki, Takayoshi, 166
Mizuno, Kumi, 89, 103, 104, 108, 118, 320, 352
Monster Planet Godzilla (ride), 265
Monsters Inc., 241, 270, 338, 388
Monster Zero. See Invasion of Astro-Monster (1965)
Mori, Iwao, 19, 20
Mori, Kazunari, 188, 200
Morse, Terry, 37
Mothra (1961), 7, 43, 55–56, 101, 179, 228, 248–50, 343, 344
Mothra 3 (1998), 337
Mothra vs. Godzilla (1964), 10, 46, 69–81, 85, 89, 95, 96, 98, 102, 113, 242, 248, 259, 263, 299, 332, 339, 344, 346, 349, 359, 382, 405
Mukoyama, Hiroshi, 95
Murakami, Katsushi, 256
Murao, Akira, 202, 210
Murase, Keizo, 93, 98, 99, 238–39
Murata, Takehiro, 248, 293, 295, 320
Murata, Takeo, 21, 25, 35, 41
Musashi Miyamoto (1954), 19, 35
Mutsumi, Goro, 189, 192
The Mysterians (1957), 7, 55, 71, 88, 101, 102, 275

N

Nagahara, Hideichi, 208, 210–11
Nagasawa, Masami, 346
Nagatani, Sae, 410, 413
Nakagawa, Anna, 229, 232
Nakagawa, Kazuhiro, 265–67
Nakagawa, Motokuni, 354
Nakajima, Haruo, 20, 22, 23, 25, 28, 34, 41, 46, 48, 56, 58, 62, 65–67, 73, 75, 80, 84, 88, 91, 98, 99, 105, 108, 112, 113, 118, 119, 122, 124–26, 137, 140, 148, 159, 169, 171, 179, 236, 238, 242, 250, 316, 328–34, 336, 339
Nakamura, Jun, 405
Nakanishi, Ryuzo, 202, 210
Nakano, Teruyoshi, 62, 81, 94, 95, 105, 113, 148, 152, 156, 157, 159, 166, 168, 171, 176, 177, 179, 182, 183, 186, 187, 192–94, 200, 207–8, 214–15, 239, 333, 334, 336, 385
Nakao, Akira, 326, 343, 346
Nakao, Takashi, 95, 314

OPPOSITE: Godzilla and Minilla prepare for hibernation as Solgel Island is inundated with snow (*Son of Godzilla*).

Editors: **Jan Hughes** & **Connor Leonard**
Creative Director: **Iain R. Morris**
Designer: **Suzi Hutsell**
Managing Editor: **Jan Hughes**
Production Manager: **Kathleen Gaffney**

Kristin Parcell: Executive Officer, TOHO International
Alexander C. Lee: Head of Licensing and Brand
Partnerships, TOHO International
Kohei Umino: Brand Manager, TOHO Global Inc.
Yutaro Nanakuri: Brand Manager, TOHO Global Inc.
Aaron John Gregory: Godzilla Product Development
Manager, TOHO International
Kevin Fukuhara: Licensing and Brand Partnerships
Manager, TOHO International
Sayumi Hasegawa: Business Operations Manager
Todd Whitford: Head of Legal Affairs

Library of Congress Control Number: 2024948589
ISBN: 978-1-4197-6211-6
e-ISBN: 979-8-88707-672-0

Additional photography credits: Courtesy Norman
England: 241, 288–289, 306–307, 308 (bottom right), 309
(II), 310 (top right, bottom left), 311, 313 (bottom left, top
right, bottom right), 312 (all), 314 (all), 315, 316 (all), 317
(top right, bottom), 321, 322, 323, 324, 325 (bottom), 326
(top right), 338 (middle right), 339 (left), 392 (bottom left)
■ Courtesy Ed Godziszewski: 13 (bottom), 19, 30 (right),
31 (far left), 92 (bottom), 95 (top), 95 (top right), 97 (top),
99 (bottom left), 178 (bottom), 240, 247, 250 (top), 251 (all),
252–253, 266 (middle left), 310 (top left), 328, 389 (middle
left), 391 (bottom left), 412, 419 ■ Courtesy Keizo Murase:
93 (top) ■ Courtesy Megumi Odaka: 9 (right) ■ Courtesy
Steve Ryfle: 357 (top left) ■ Courtesy Pat Saperstein: 75
(top left) ■ Courtesy Fuyuki Shinada: 229 (bottom right)

Printed and bound in China
10 9 8 7 6 5 4 3 2 1

Abrams books are available at special discounts when
purchased in quantity for premiums and promotions as
well as fundraising or educational use. Special editions
can also be created to specification. For details, contact
specialsales@abramsbooks.com or see address to the right.

All efforts have been made to locate the contributors and
to credit them with the appropriate copyright information.
Requests for changes will be considered by the publisher,
and any necessary corrections or revisions will be amended
in future reprints.

Abrams® is a registered trademark of Harry N. Abrams

ABRAMS The Art of Books
195 Broadway, New York, NY 10007
abramsbooks.com

TOHO   TOHO INTERNATIONAL

TM & © TOHO CO., LTD.

PAGE 1: After defeating Mothra and escaping the military's
artificial lightning trap, the malevolent Godzilla heads for
Iwa Island (from *Mothra vs. Godzilla*).

PAGES 2–3: Godzilla goes on the offensive against King
Ghidorah (from *Ghidorah, the Three-Headed Monster*).

BELOW: Farewell, Godzilla: The King of the Monsters
departs toward the horizon at the end of *Godzilla vs.
SpaceGodzilla*.